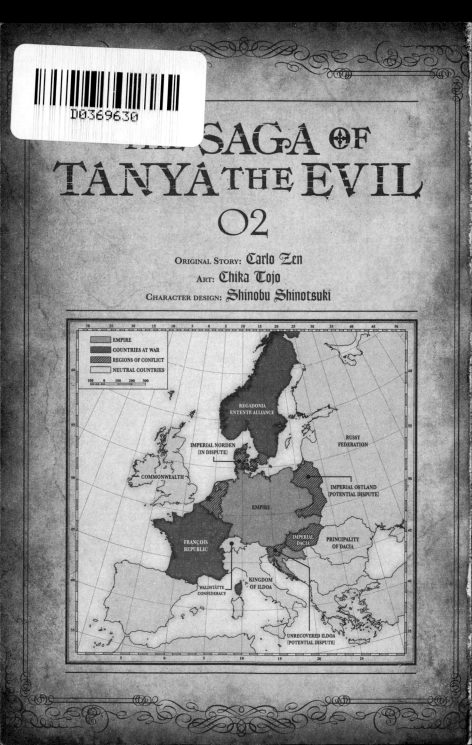

THE SAGA OF TANYA THE EVIL

O2

ORIGINAL STORY: Carlo Zen

ART: Chika Tojo

CHARACTER DESIGN: Shinobu Shinotsuki

D0369630

EMPIRE
COUNTRIES AT WAR
REGIONS OF CONFLICT
NEUTRAL COUNTRIES

REGADONIA
ENTENTE ALLIANCE

RUSSY
FEDERATION

IMPERIAL NORDEN
(IN DISPUTE)

COMMONWEALTH

IMPERIAL OSTLAND
(POTENTIAL DISPUTE)

EMPIRE

IMPERIAL
DACIA

PRINCIPALITY
OF DACIA

FRANÇOIS
REPUBLIC

KINGDOM
OF ILDOA

WALDSTÄTTE
CONFEDERACY

UNRECOVERED ILDOA
(POTENTIAL DISPUTE)

The Saga of Tanya the Evil

02

Original Story: Carlo Zen   Art: Chika Tojo
Character Design: Shinobu Shinotsuki

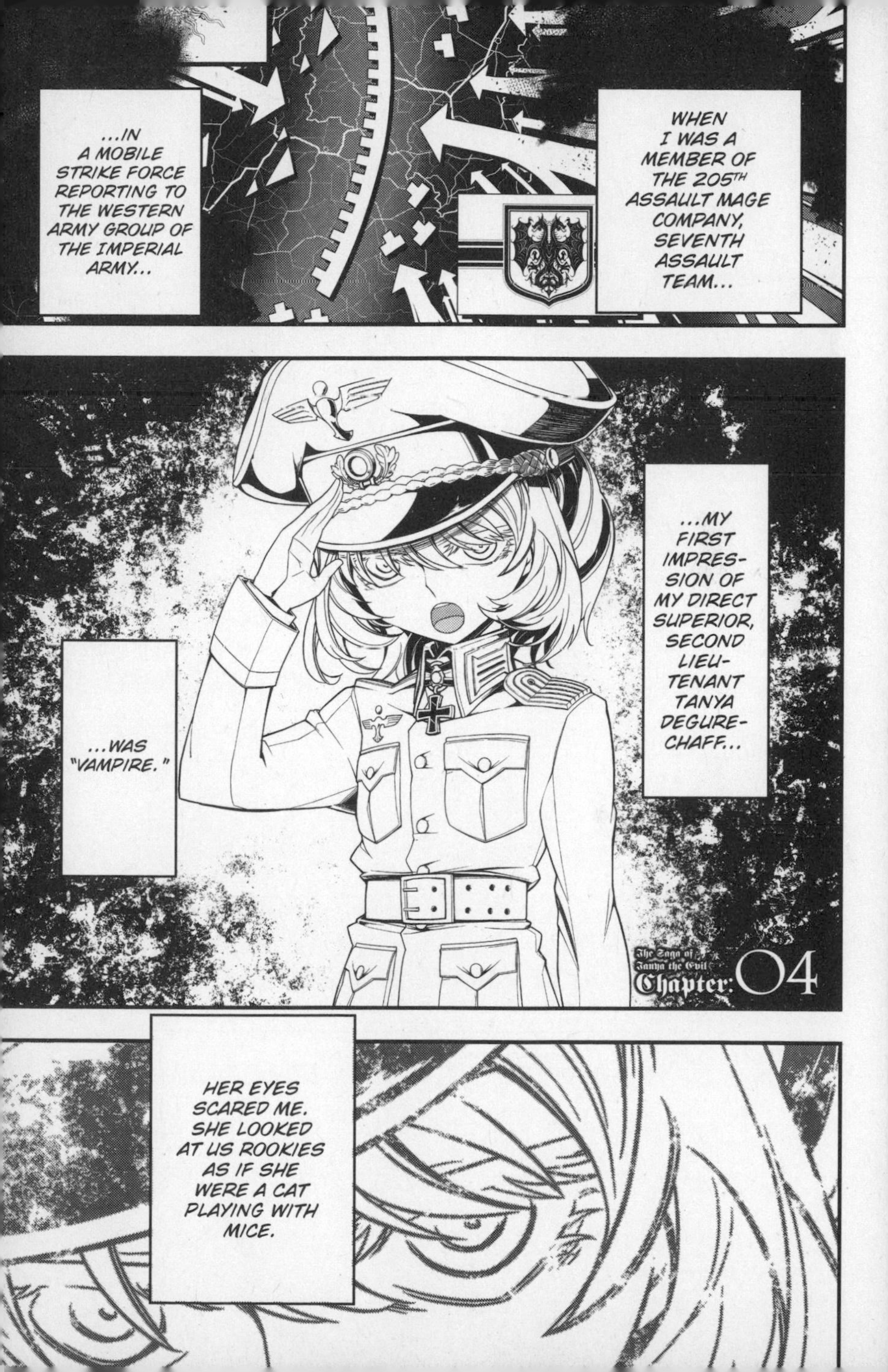
WHEN I WAS A MEMBER OF THE 205TH ASSAULT MAGE COMPANY, SEVENTH ASSAULT TEAM...
...IN A MOBILE STRIKE FORCE REPORTING TO THE WESTERN ARMY GROUP OF THE IMPERIAL ARMY...
...MY FIRST IMPRESSION OF MY DIRECT SUPERIOR, SECOND LIEUTENANT TANYA DEGURECHAFF...
...WAS "VAMPIRE."
The Saga of Tanya the Evil
Chapter: 04
HER EYES SCARED ME. SHE LOOKED AT US ROOKIES AS IF SHE WERE A CAT PLAYING WITH MICE.

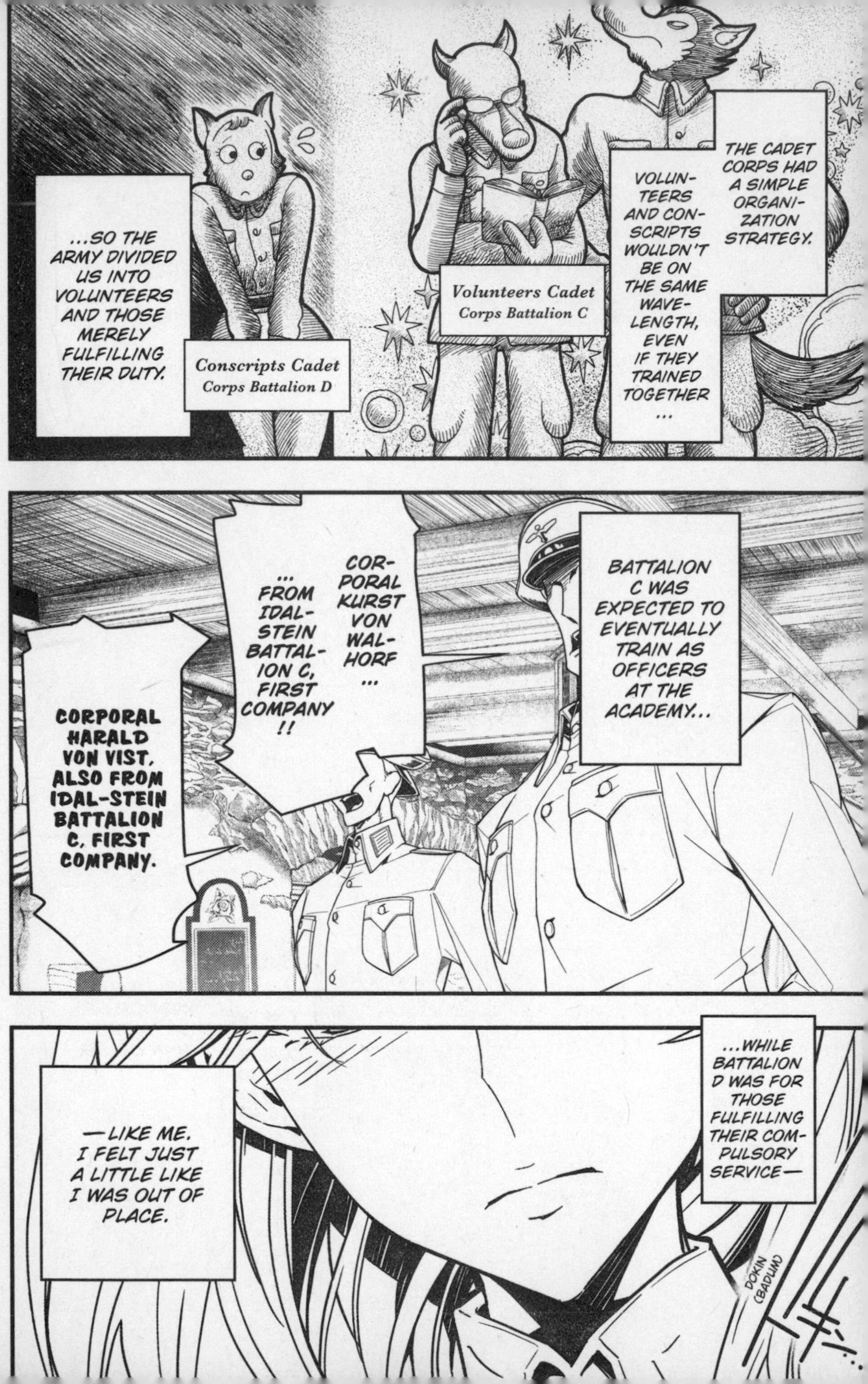
THE CADET CORPS HAD A SIMPLE ORGANIZATION STRATEGY.
VOLUNTEERS AND CONSCRIPTS WOULDN'T BE ON THE SAME WAVELENGTH, EVEN IF THEY TRAINED TOGETHER...
Volunteers Cadet Corps Battalion C
...SO THE ARMY DIVIDED US INTO VOLUNTEERS AND THOSE MERELY FULFILLING THEIR DUTY.
Conscripts Cadet Corps Battalion D
BATTALION C WAS EXPECTED TO EVENTUALLY TRAIN AS OFFICERS AT THE ACADEMY...
CORPORAL KURST VON WALHORF...
...FROM IDALSTEIN BATTALION C, FIRST COMPANY!!
CORPORAL HARALD VON VIST. ALSO FROM IDAL-STEIN BATTALION C, FIRST COMPANY.
...WHILE BATTALION D WAS FOR THOSE FULFILLING THEIR COMPULSORY SERVICE—
—LIKE ME. I FELT JUST A LITTLE LIKE I WAS OUT OF PLACE.
DOKIN (BADUM)

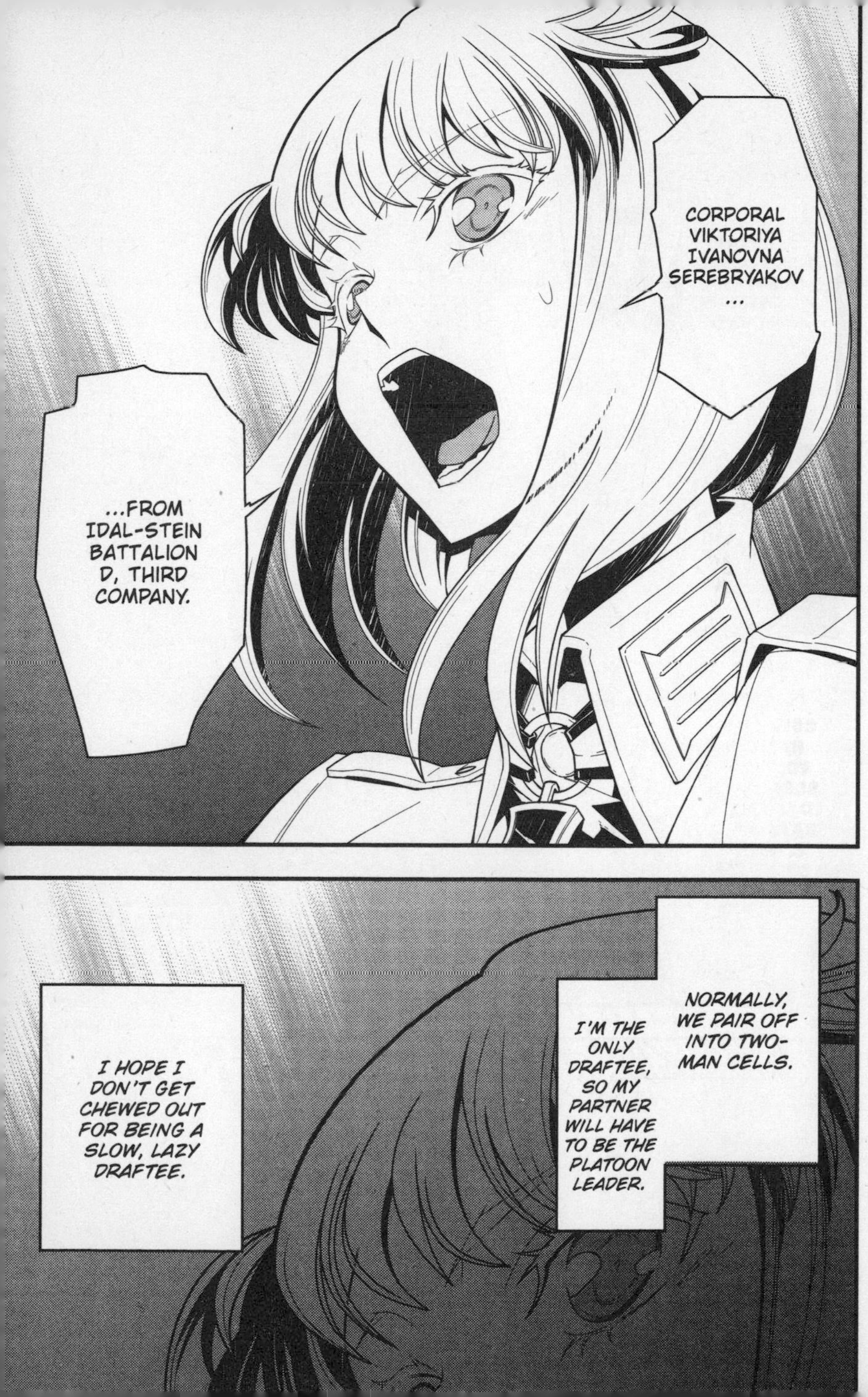
CORPORAL VIKTORIYA IVANOVNA SEREBRYAKOV ...
...FROM IDAL-STEIN BATTALION D, THIRD COMPANY.
NORMALLY, WE PAIR OFF INTO TWO-MAN CELLS.
I'M THE ONLY DRAFTEE, SO MY PARTNER WILL HAVE TO BE THE PLATOON LEADER.
I HOPE I DON'T GET CHEWED OUT FOR BEING A SLOW, LAZY DRAFTEE.

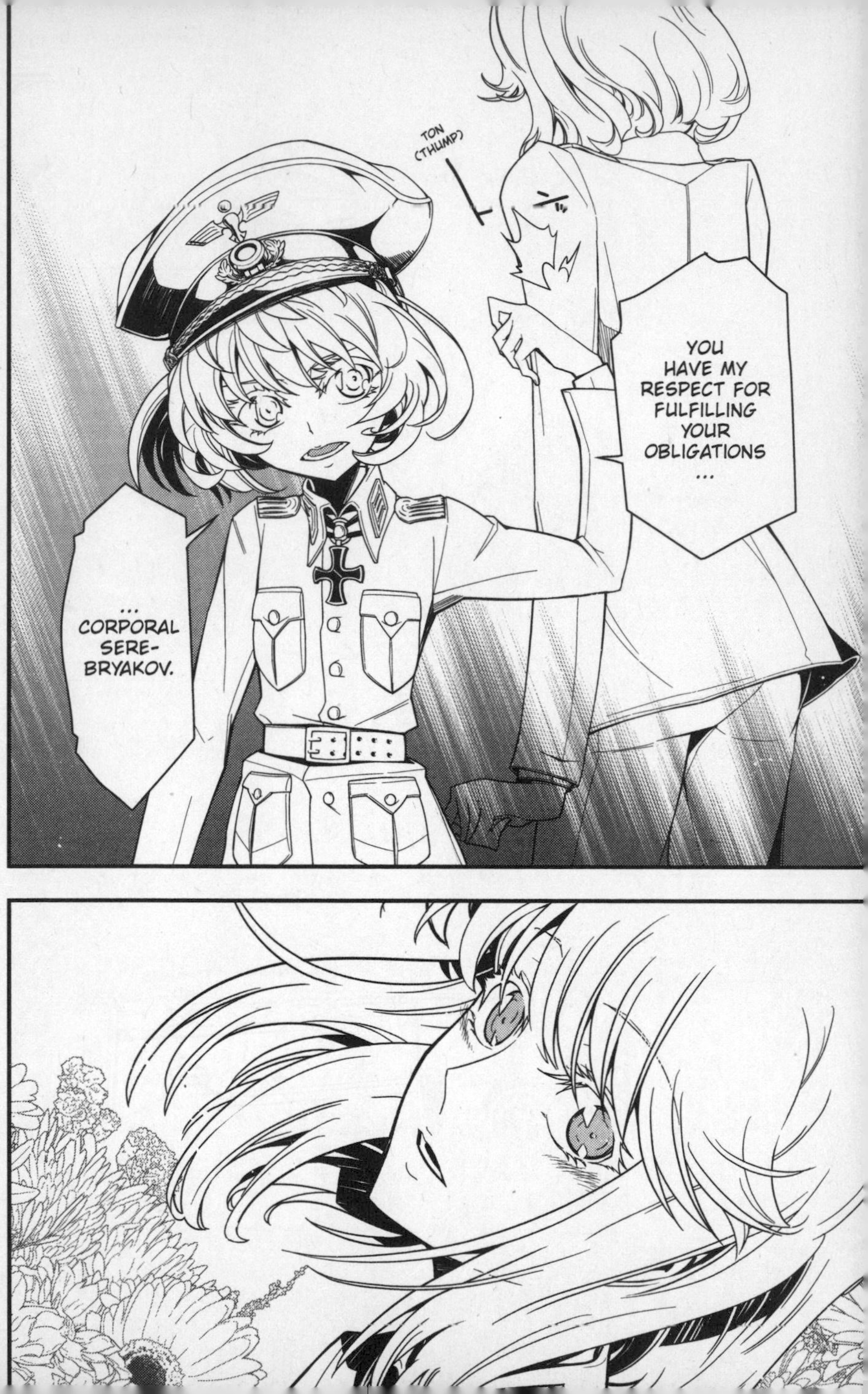
TON (THUMP)
YOU HAVE MY RESPECT FOR FULFILLING YOUR OBLIGATIONS ...
... CORPORAL SERE-BRYAKOV.

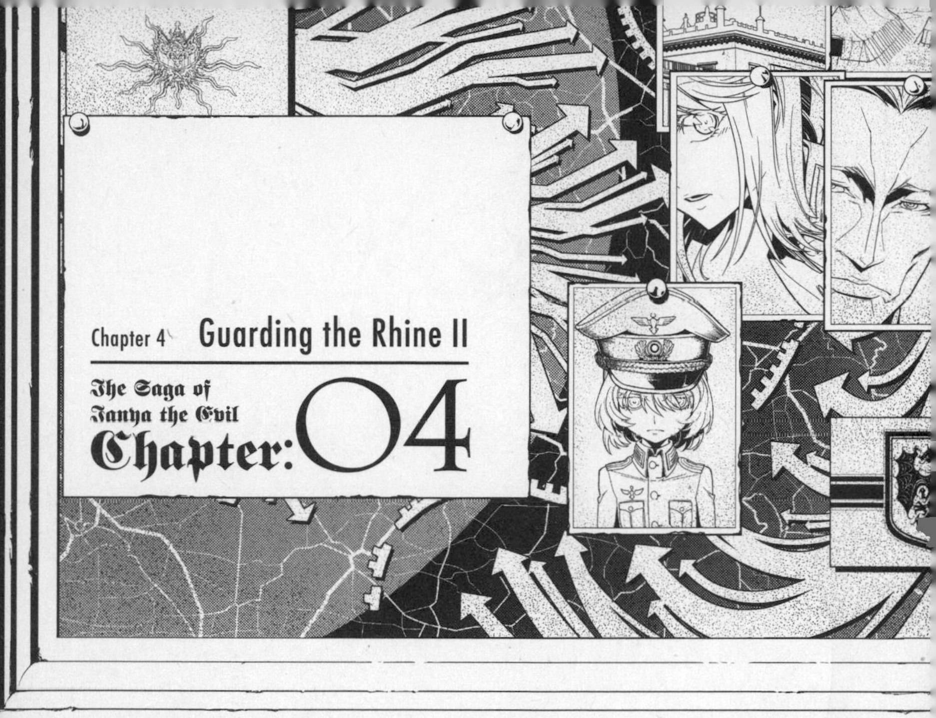
Chapter 4 Guarding the Rhine II
The Saga of Tanya the Evil
Chapter: 04

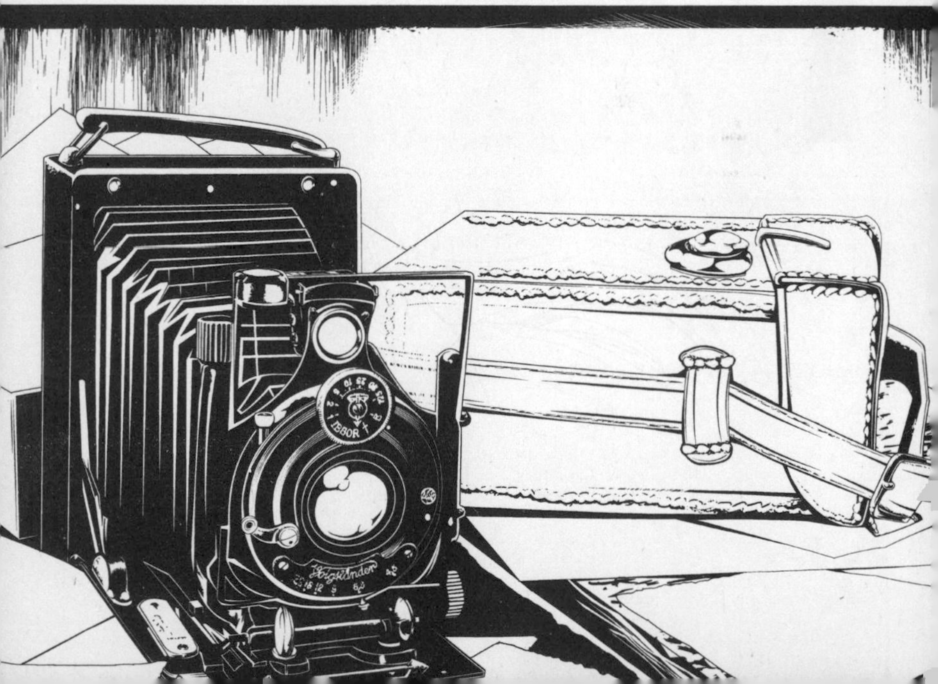

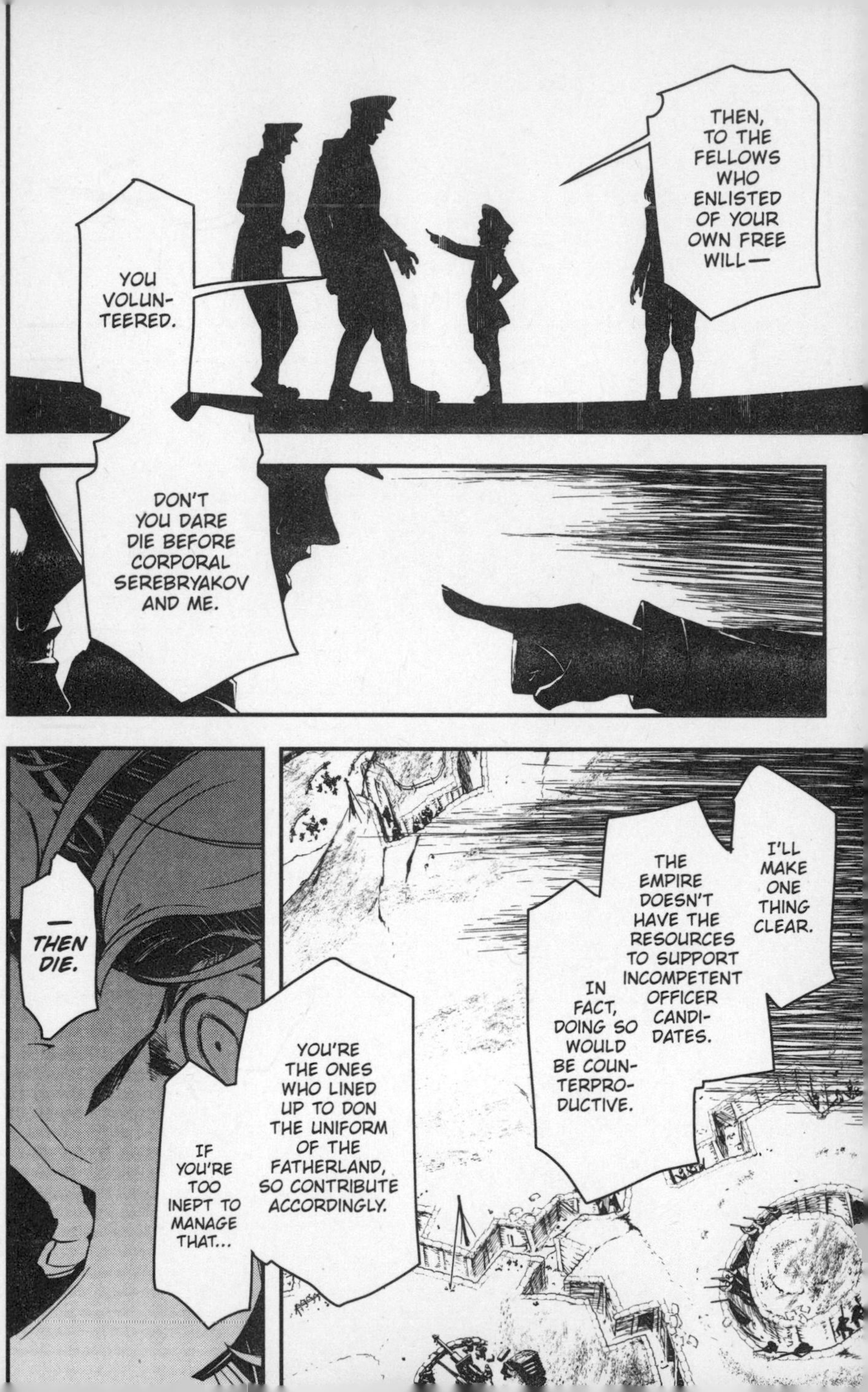
THEN, TO THE FELLOWS WHO ENLISTED OF YOUR OWN FREE WILL—
YOU VOLUNTEERED.
DON'T YOU DARE DIE BEFORE CORPORAL SEREBRYAKOV AND ME.
I'LL MAKE ONE THING CLEAR.
THE EMPIRE DOESN'T HAVE THE RESOURCES TO SUPPORT INCOMPETENT OFFICER CANDIDATES.
IN FACT, DOING SO WOULD BE COUNTERPRODUCTIVE.
YOU'RE THE ONES WHO LINED UP TO DON THE UNIFORM OF THE FATHERLAND, SO CONTRIBUTE ACCORDINGLY.
IF YOU'RE TOO INEPT TO MANAGE THAT...
—THEN DIE.

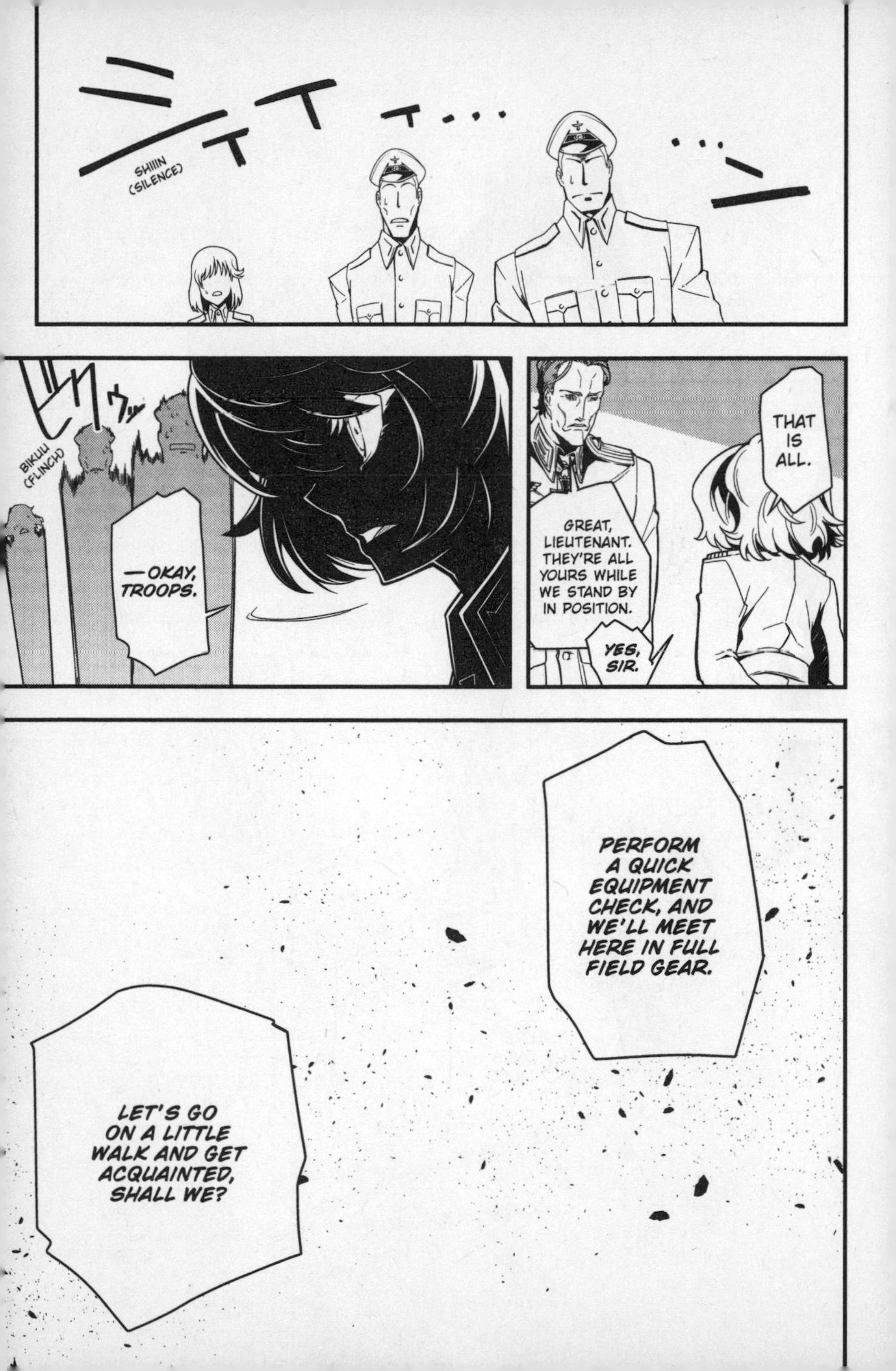

SHIIIN (SILENCE)
THAT IS ALL.
GREAT, LIEUTENANT. THEY'RE ALL YOURS WHILE WE STAND BY IN POSITION.
YES, SIR.
BIKUU (FLINCH)
—OKAY, TROOPS.
PERFORM A QUICK EQUIPMENT CHECK, AND WE'LL MEET HERE IN FULL FIELD GEAR.
LET'S GO ON A LITTLE WALK AND GET ACQUAINTED, SHALL WE?

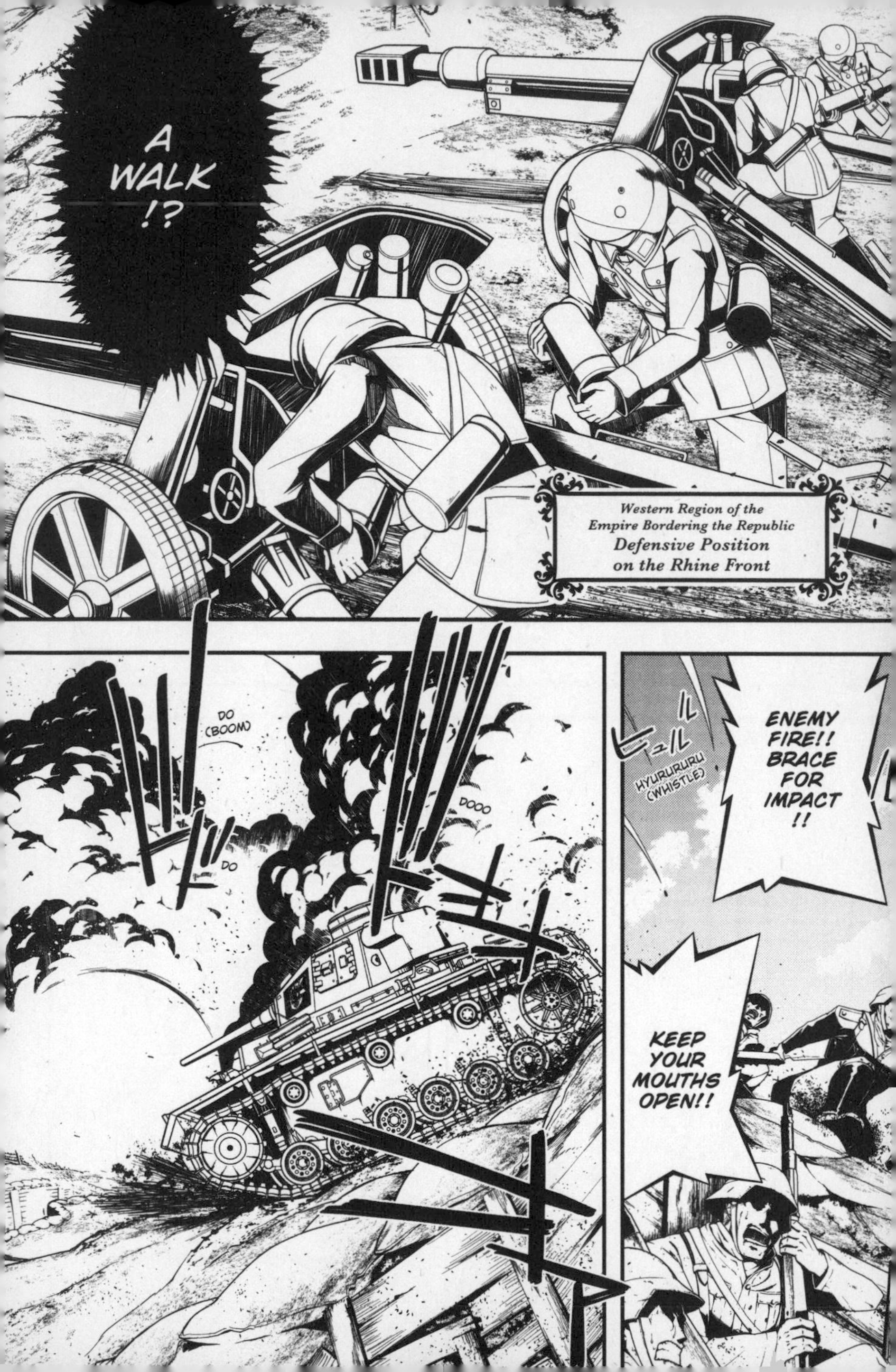
A WALK!?
Western Region of the Empire Bordering the Republic
Defensive Position on the Rhine Front
ヒュルル
HYURURURU (WHISTLE)
ENEMY FIRE!! BRACE FOR IMPACT!!
KEEP YOUR MOUTHS OPEN!!
DO (BOOM)
DOOO
DO

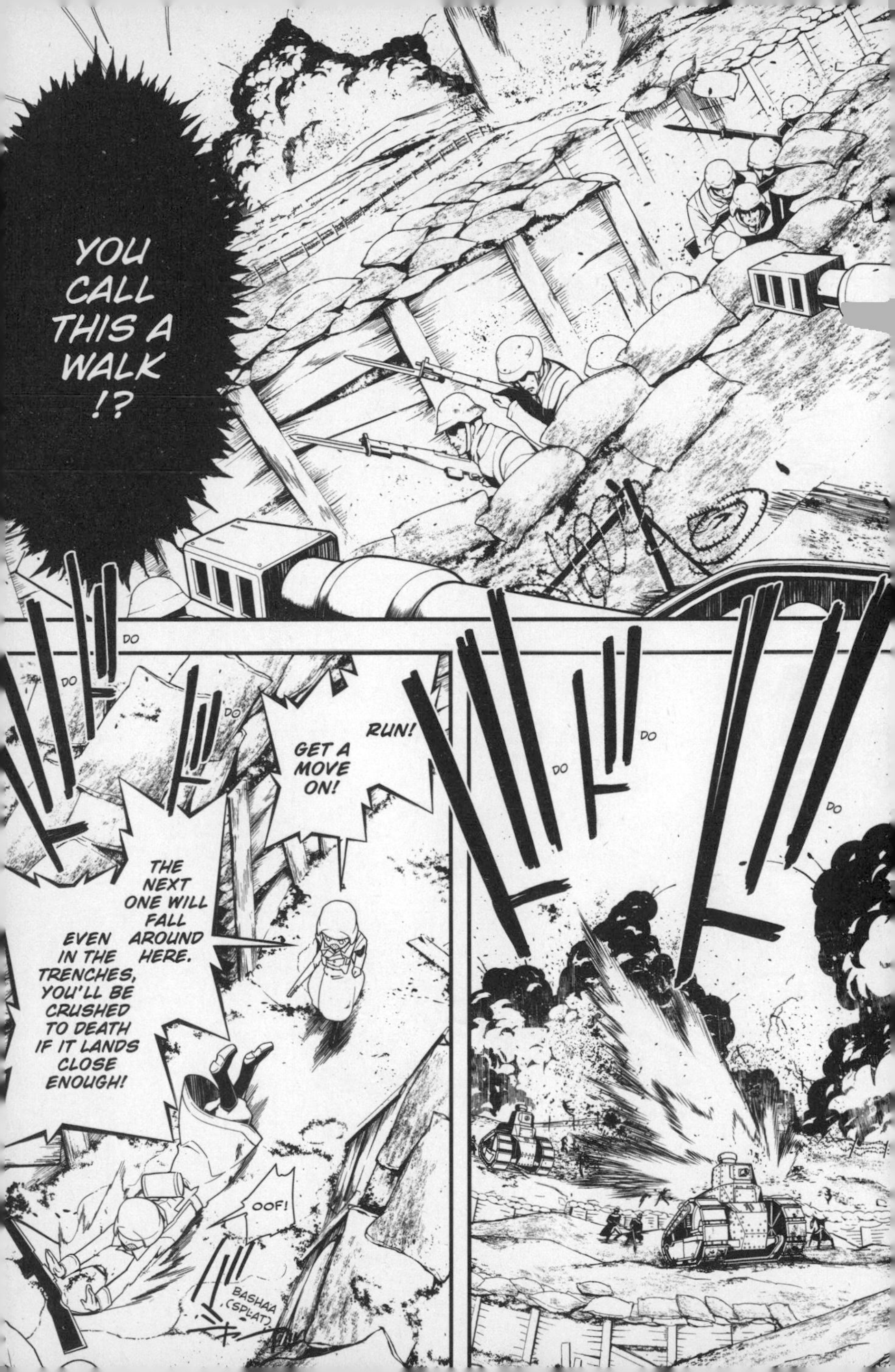

YOU CALL THIS A WALK!?
DO
DO
DO
DO
DO
DO
RUN!
GET A MOVE ON!
THE NEXT ONE WILL FALL AROUND HERE.
EVEN IN THE TRENCHES, YOU'LL BE CRUSHED TO DEATH IF IT LANDS CLOSE ENOUGH!
OOF!
BASHAA (SPLAT)

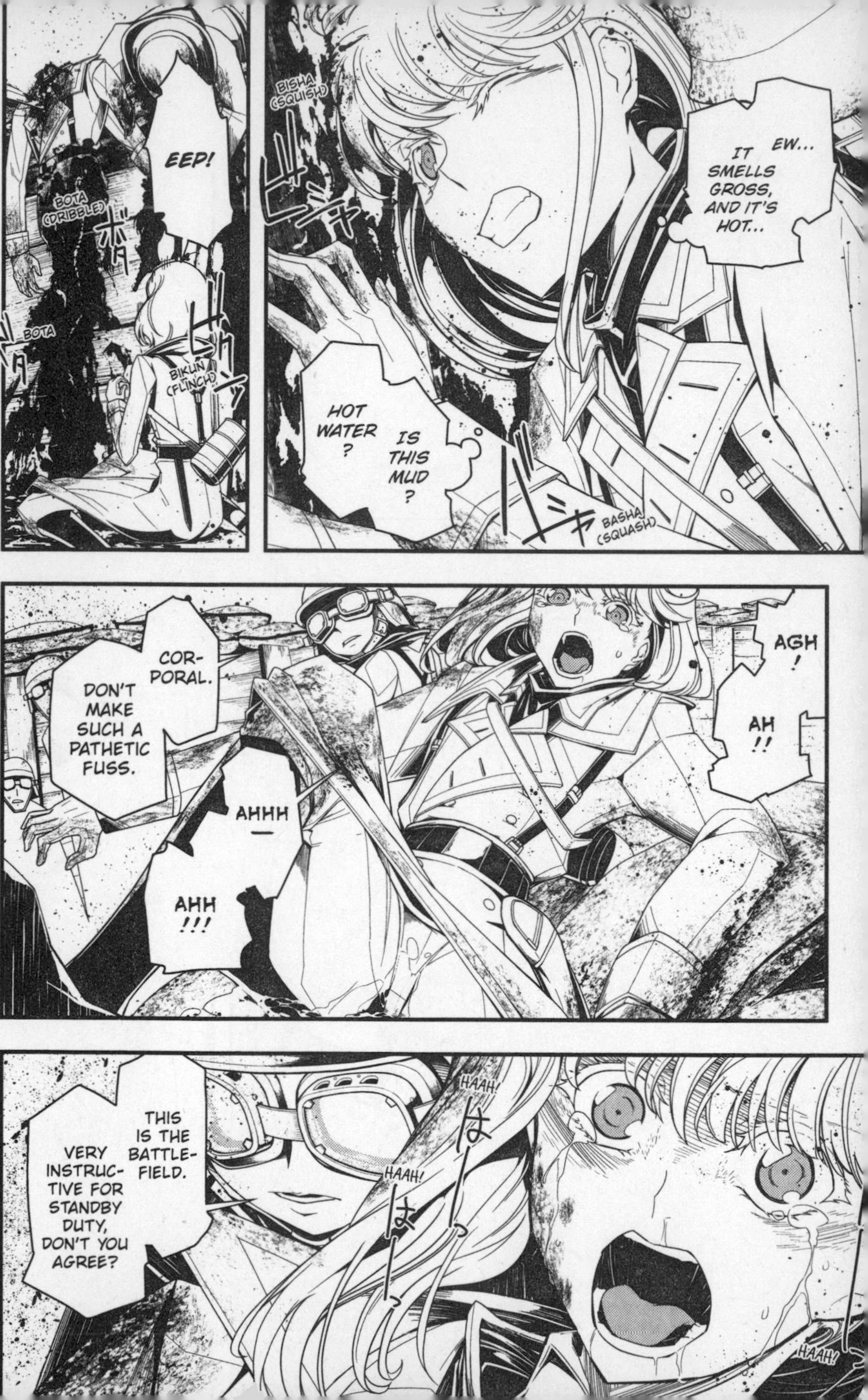

EW... IT SMELLS GROSS, AND IT'S HOT...
BISHA (SQUISH)
IS THIS MUD?
HOT WATER?
BASHA (SQUASH)
EEP!
BOTA (DRIBBLE)
BIKUN (FLINCH)
BOTA
AGH! AH!!
AHHH—
AHH!!!
CORPORAL. DON'T MAKE SUCH A PATHETIC FUSS.
HAAH!
HAAH!
HAAH!
THIS IS THE BATTLEFIELD.
VERY INSTRUCTIVE FOR STANDBY DUTY, DON'T YOU AGREE?

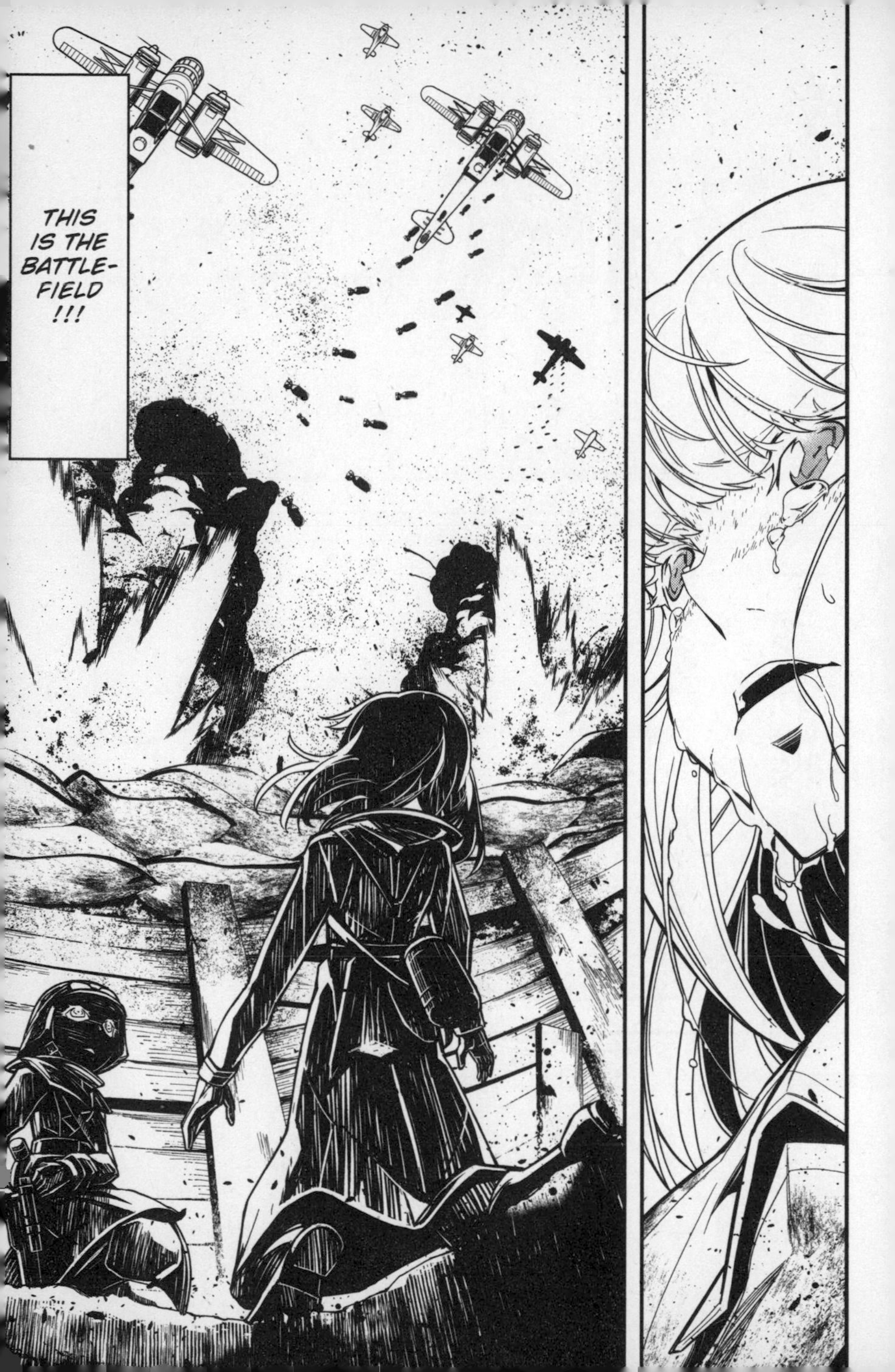
THIS IS THE BATTLE-FIELD !!!

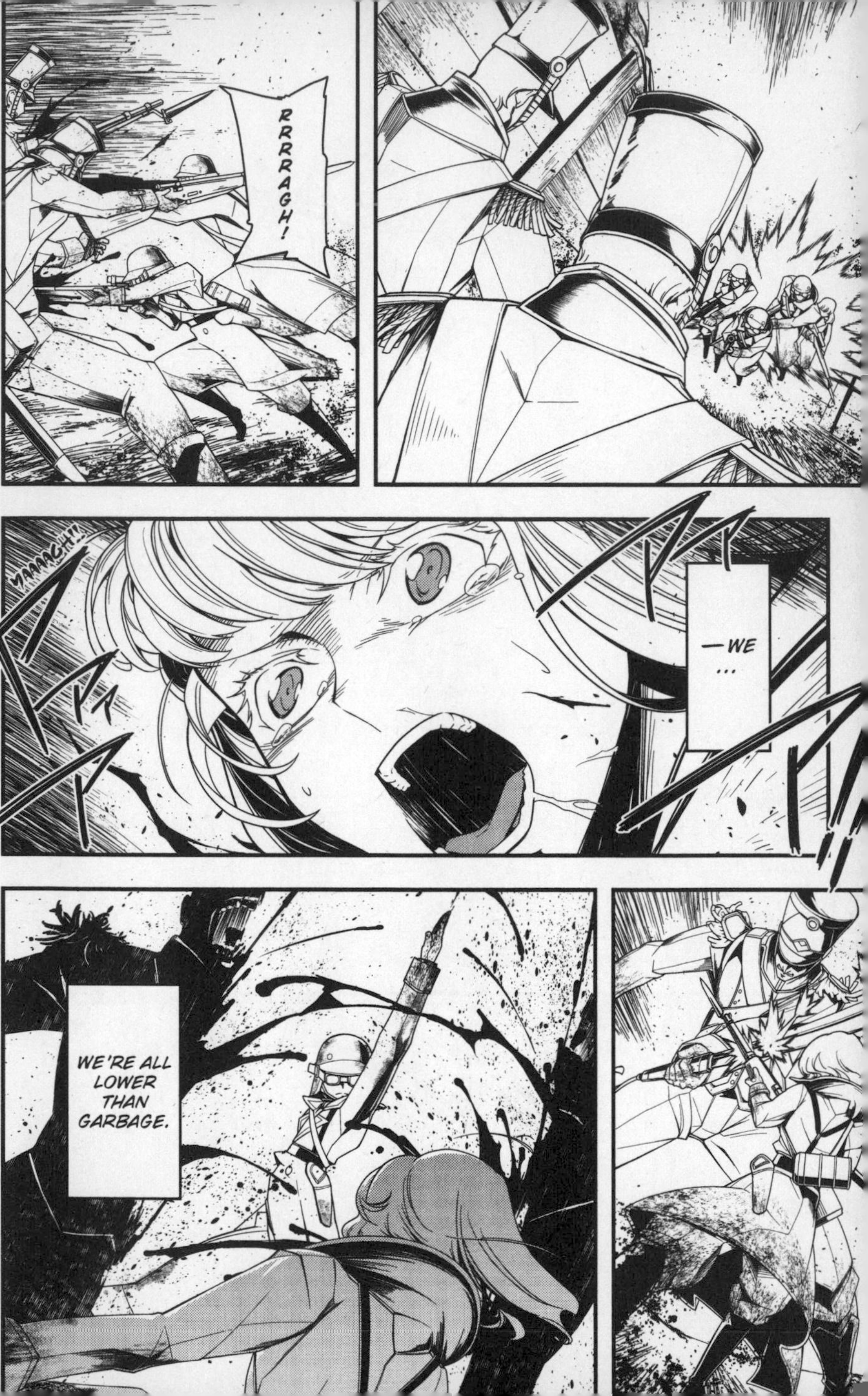
RRRRAGH!
—WE ...
YAAAAGH!!
WE'RE ALL LOWER THAN GARBAGE.

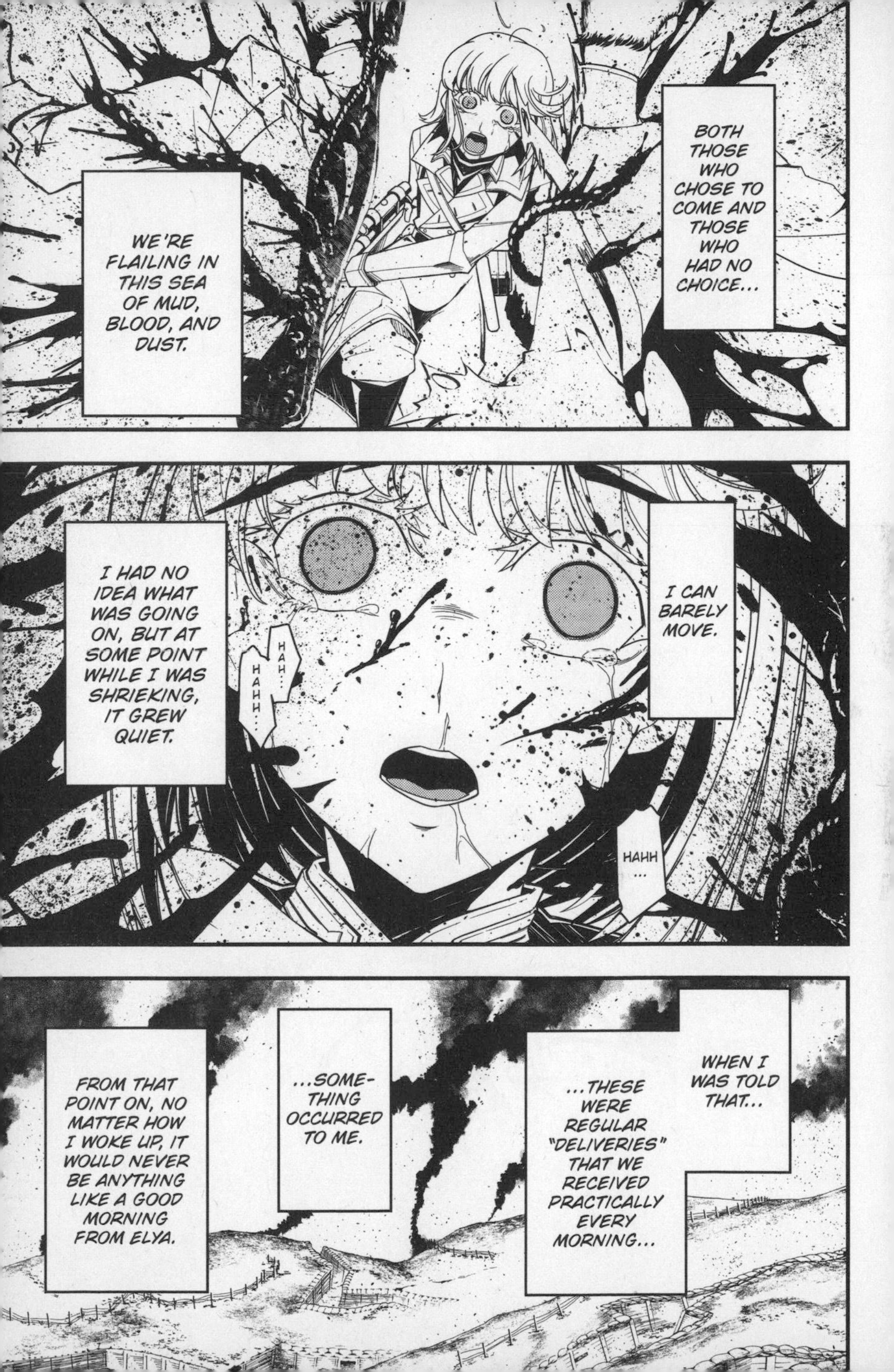
BOTH THOSE WHO CHOSE TO COME AND THOSE WHO HAD NO CHOICE…
WE'RE FLAILING IN THIS SEA OF MUD, BLOOD, AND DUST.
I CAN BARELY MOVE.
HAHH…
I HAD NO IDEA WHAT WAS GOING ON, BUT AT SOME POINT WHILE I WAS SHRIEKING, IT GREW QUIET.
HAH… HAHH…
WHEN I WAS TOLD THAT…
…THESE WERE REGULAR "DELIVERIES" THAT WE RECEIVED PRACTICALLY EVERY MORNING…
…SOME-THING OCCURRED TO ME.
FROM THAT POINT ON, NO MATTER HOW I WOKE UP, IT WOULD NEVER BE ANYTHING LIKE A GOOD MORNING FROM ELYA.

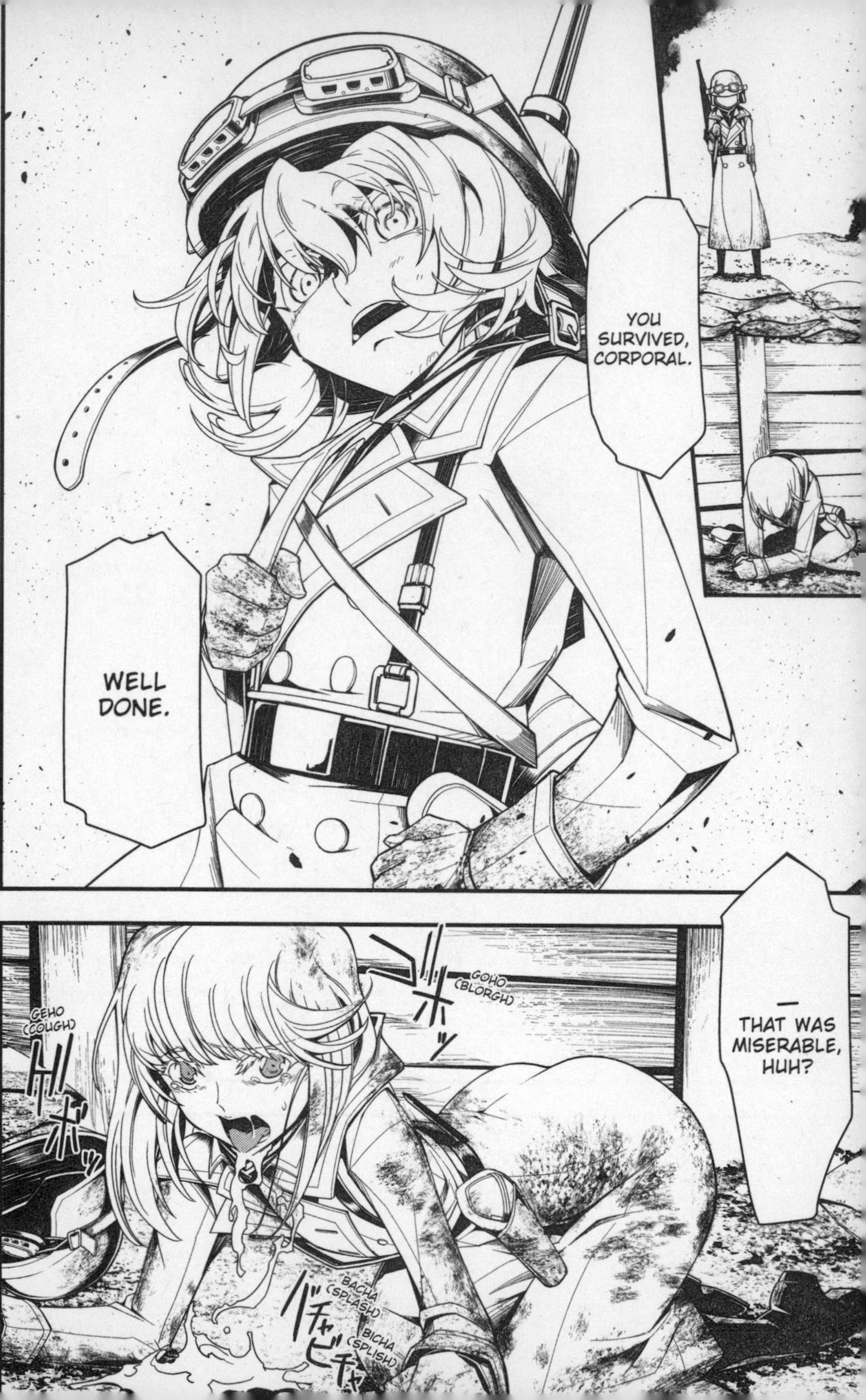
YOU SURVIVED, CORPORAL.
WELL DONE.
—THAT WAS MISERABLE, HUH?
GOHO (BLORGH)
GEHO (COUGH)
BACHA (SPLASH)
BICHA (SPLASH)

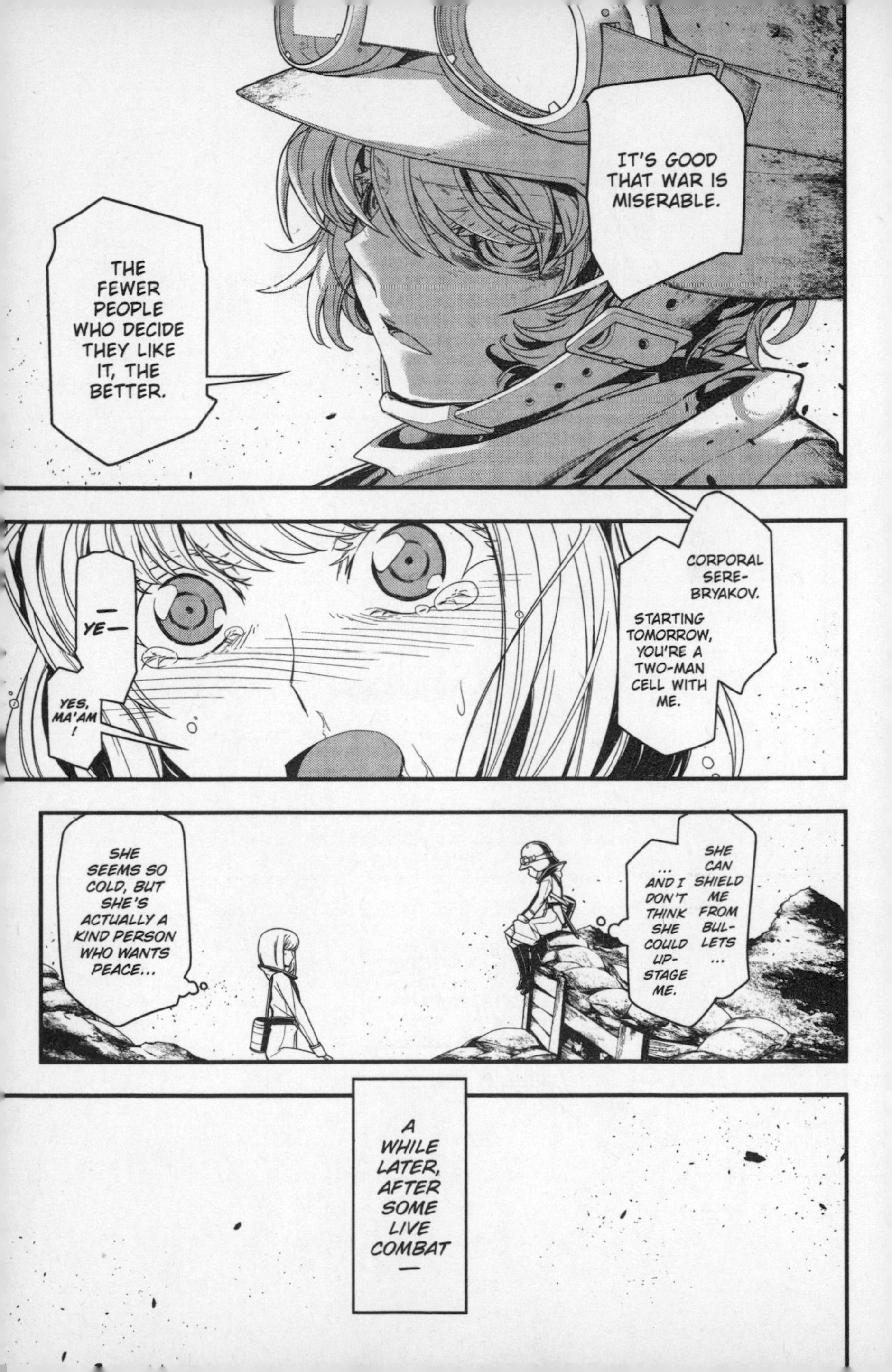
IT'S GOOD THAT WAR IS MISERABLE.
THE FEWER PEOPLE WHO DECIDE THEY LIKE IT, THE BETTER.
CORPORAL SEREBRYAKOV.
STARTING TOMORROW, YOU'RE A TWO-MAN CELL WITH ME.
—YE—
YES, MA'AM!
SHE CAN SHIELD ME FROM BULLETS...
...AND I DON'T THINK SHE COULD UPSTAGE ME.
SHE SEEMS SO COLD, BUT SHE'S ACTUALLY A KIND PERSON WHO WANTS PEACE...
A WHILE LATER, AFTER SOME LIVE COMBAT—

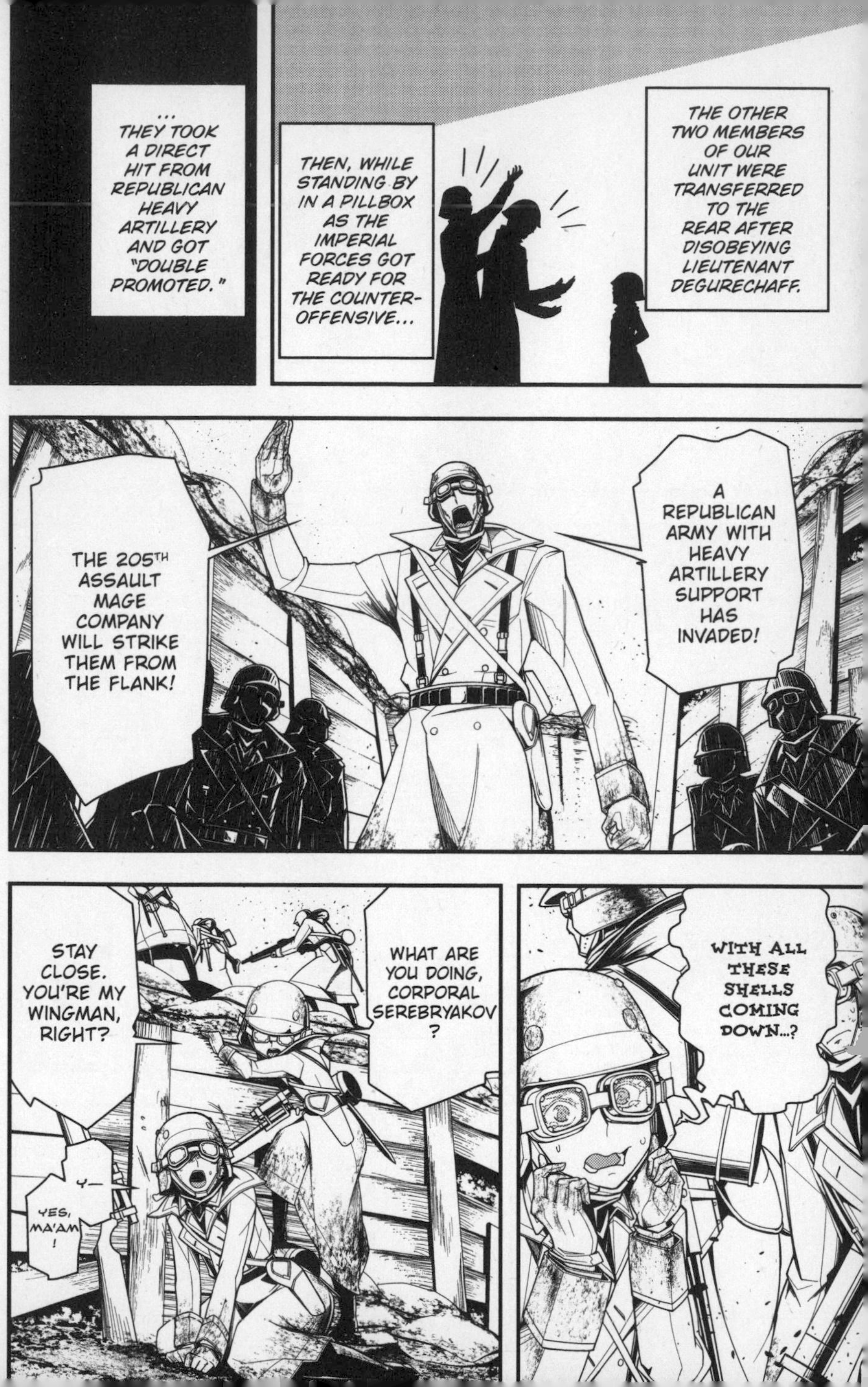
THE OTHER TWO MEMBERS OF OUR UNIT WERE TRANSFERRED TO THE REAR AFTER DISOBEYING LIEUTENANT DEGURECHAFF.
THEN, WHILE STANDING BY IN A PILLBOX AS THE IMPERIAL FORCES GOT READY FOR THE COUNTER-OFFENSIVE...
... THEY TOOK A DIRECT HIT FROM REPUBLICAN HEAVY ARTILLERY AND GOT "DOUBLE PROMOTED."
A REPUBLICAN ARMY WITH HEAVY ARTILLERY SUPPORT HAS INVADED!
THE 205TH ASSAULT MAGE COMPANY WILL STRIKE THEM FROM THE FLANK!
WITH ALL THESE SHELLS COMING DOWN...?
WHAT ARE YOU DOING, CORPORAL SEREBRYAKOV?
STAY CLOSE. YOU'RE MY WINGMAN, RIGHT?
Y— YES, MA'AM!

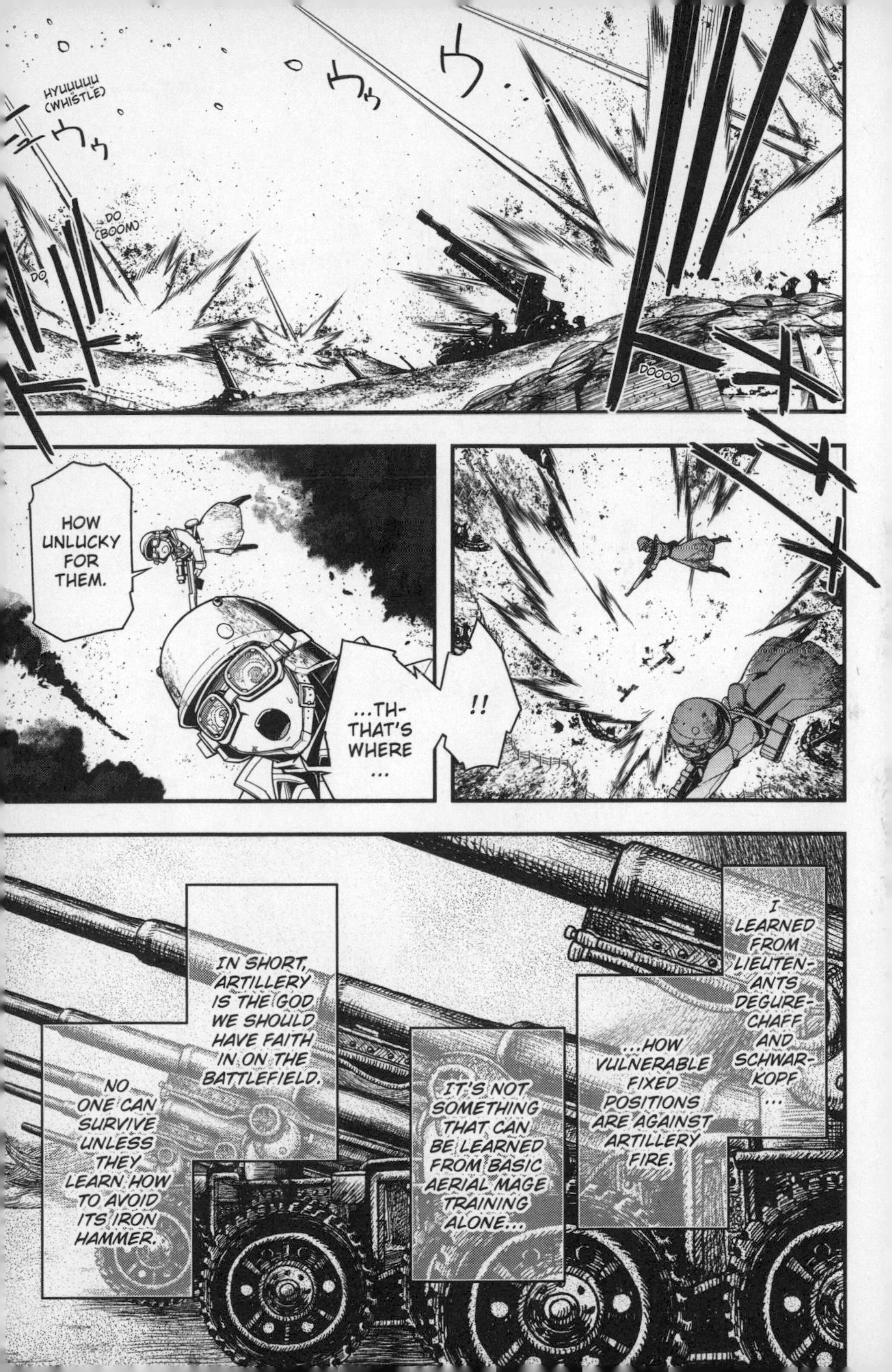
HYUUUUU (WHISTLE)
DO (BOOM)
DO
DOOOO
HOW UNLUCKY FOR THEM.
!!
...TH-THAT'S WHERE...
I LEARNED FROM LIEUTENANTS DEGURECHAFF AND SCHWARKOPF...
...HOW VULNERABLE FIXED POSITIONS ARE AGAINST ARTILLERY FIRE.
IT'S NOT SOMETHING THAT CAN BE LEARNED FROM BASIC AERIAL MAGE TRAINING ALONE...
IN SHORT, ARTILLERY IS THE GOD WE SHOULD HAVE FAITH IN ON THE BATTLEFIELD.
NO ONE CAN SURVIVE UNLESS THEY LEARN HOW TO AVOID ITS IRON HAMMER.

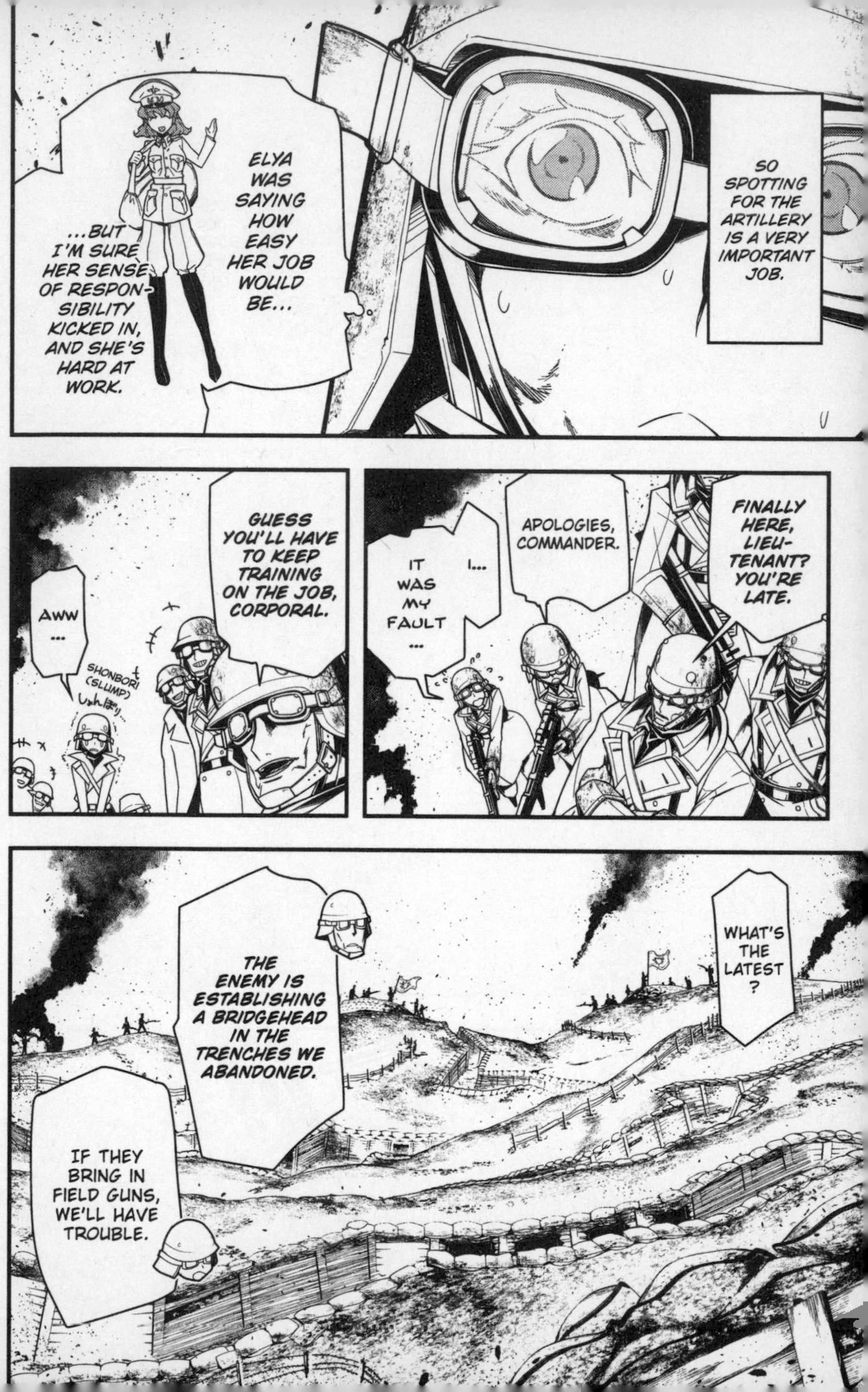
SO SPOTTING FOR THE ARTILLERY IS A VERY IMPORTANT JOB.
ELYA WAS SAYING HOW EASY HER JOB WOULD BE...
...BUT I'M SURE HER SENSE OF RESPON-SIBILITY KICKED IN, AND SHE'S HARD AT WORK.
FINALLY HERE, LIEU-TENANT? YOU'RE LATE.
APOLOGIES, COMMANDER.
I...
IT WAS MY FAULT ...
GUESS YOU'LL HAVE TO KEEP TRAINING ON THE JOB, CORPORAL.
AWW ...
SHONBORI (SLUMP)
しょんぼり
WHAT'S THE LATEST?
THE ENEMY IS ESTABLISHING A BRIDGEHEAD IN THE TRENCHES WE ABANDONED.
IF THEY BRING IN FIELD GUNS, WE'LL HAVE TROUBLE.

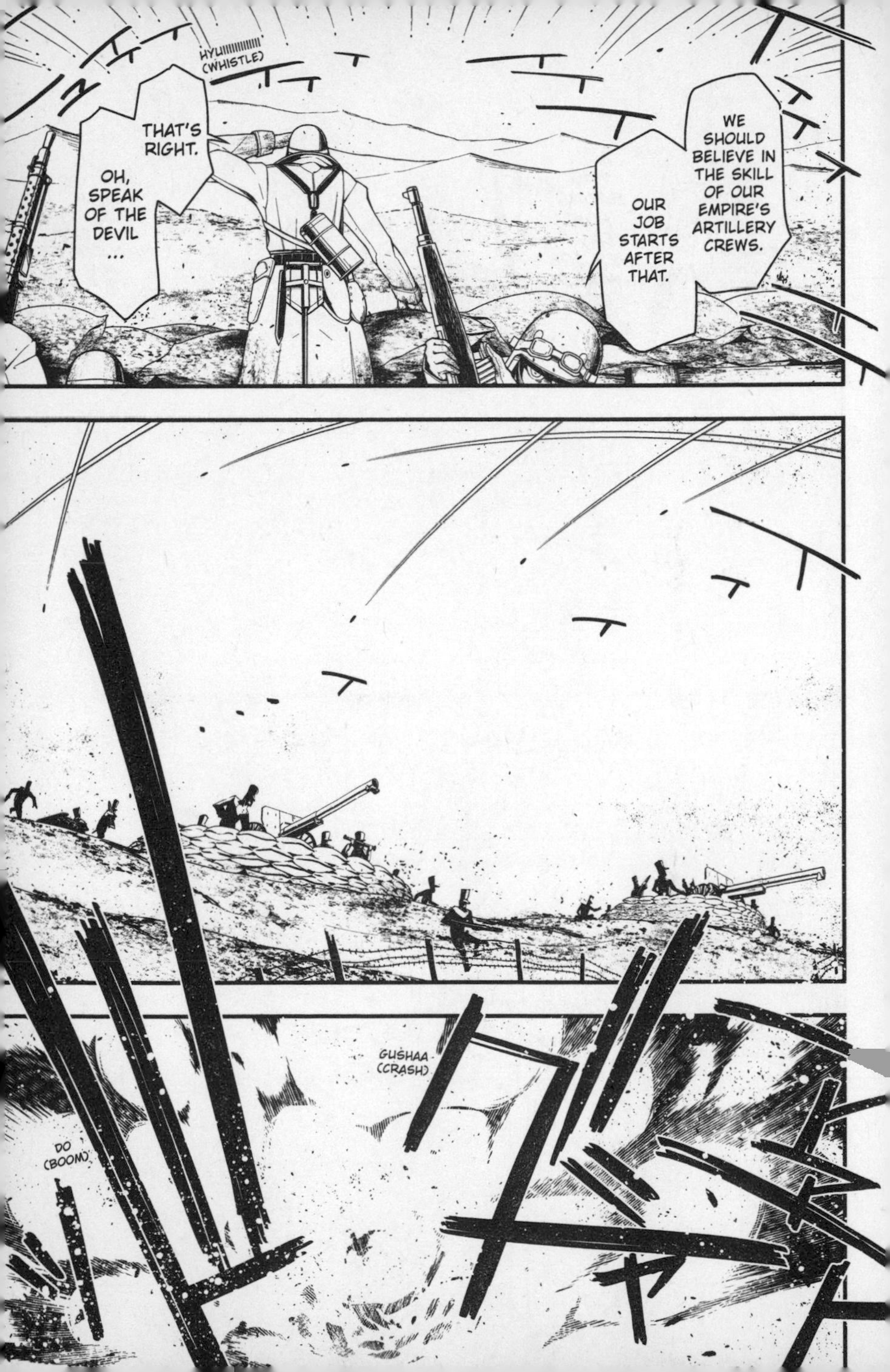
WE SHOULD BELIEVE IN THE SKILL OF OUR EMPIRE'S ARTILLERY CREWS.
OUR JOB STARTS AFTER THAT.
HYUIIIIIIIIIII (WHISTLE)
THAT'S RIGHT.
OH, SPEAK OF THE DEVIL ...
GUSHAA (CRASH)
DO (BOOM)

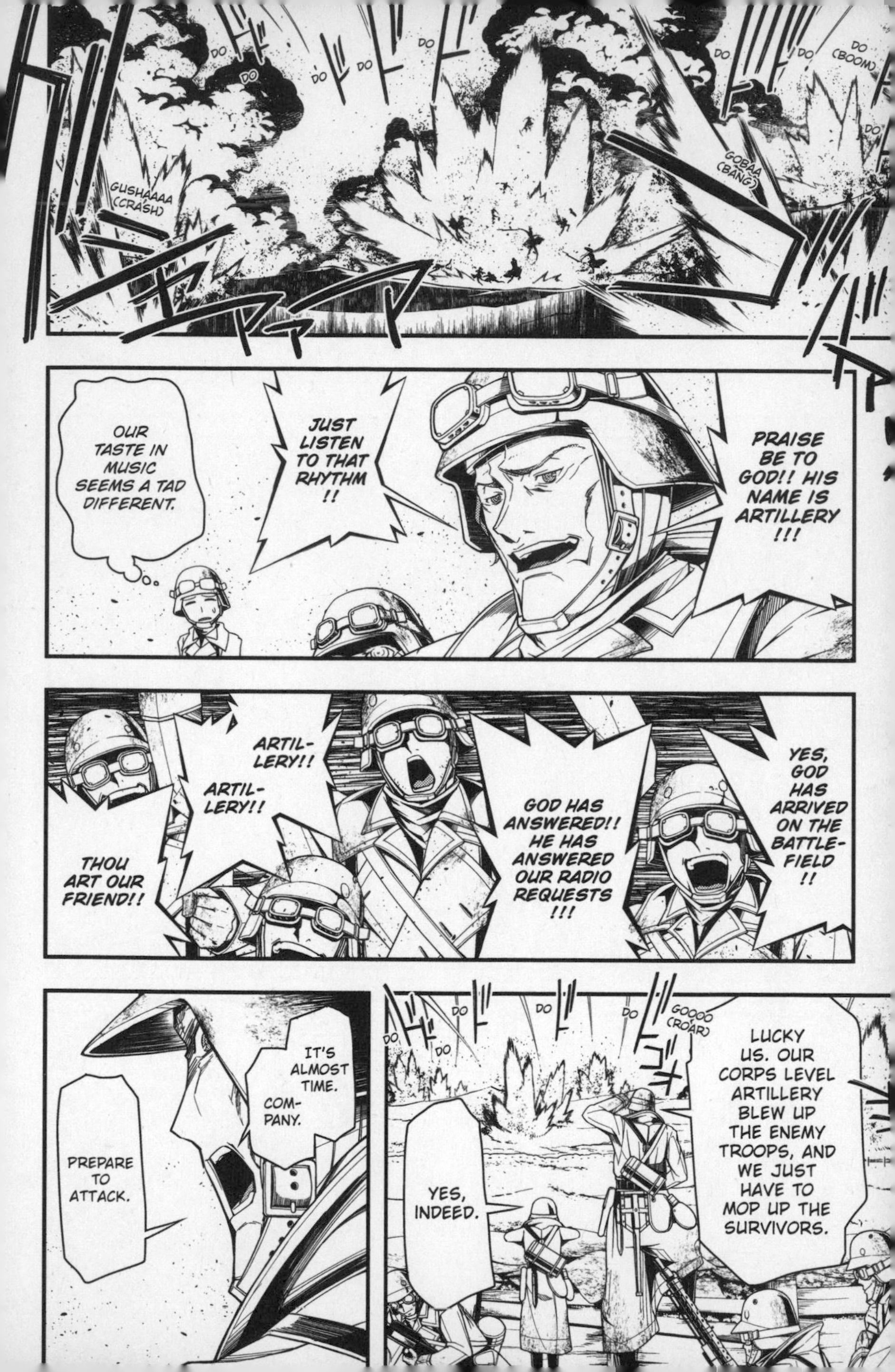
DO (BOOM)
DO
DO
GOBAA (BANG)
DO
DO
DO
DO
DO
GUSHAAAA (CRASH)
PRAISE BE TO GOD!! HIS NAME IS ARTILLERY!!!
JUST LISTEN TO THAT RHYTHM!!
OUR TASTE IN MUSIC SEEMS A TAD DIFFERENT.
YES, GOD HAS ARRIVED ON THE BATTLE-FIELD!!
GOD HAS ANSWERED!! HE HAS ANSWERED OUR RADIO REQUESTS!!!
ARTIL-LERY!!
ARTIL-LERY!!
THOU ART OUR FRIEND!!
GOOOO (ROAR)
DO
DO
DO
DO
DO
LUCKY US. OUR CORPS LEVEL ARTILLERY BLEW UP THE ENEMY TROOPS, AND WE JUST HAVE TO MOP UP THE SURVIVORS.
YES, INDEED.
IT'S ALMOST TIME. COM-PANY.
PREPARE TO ATTACK.

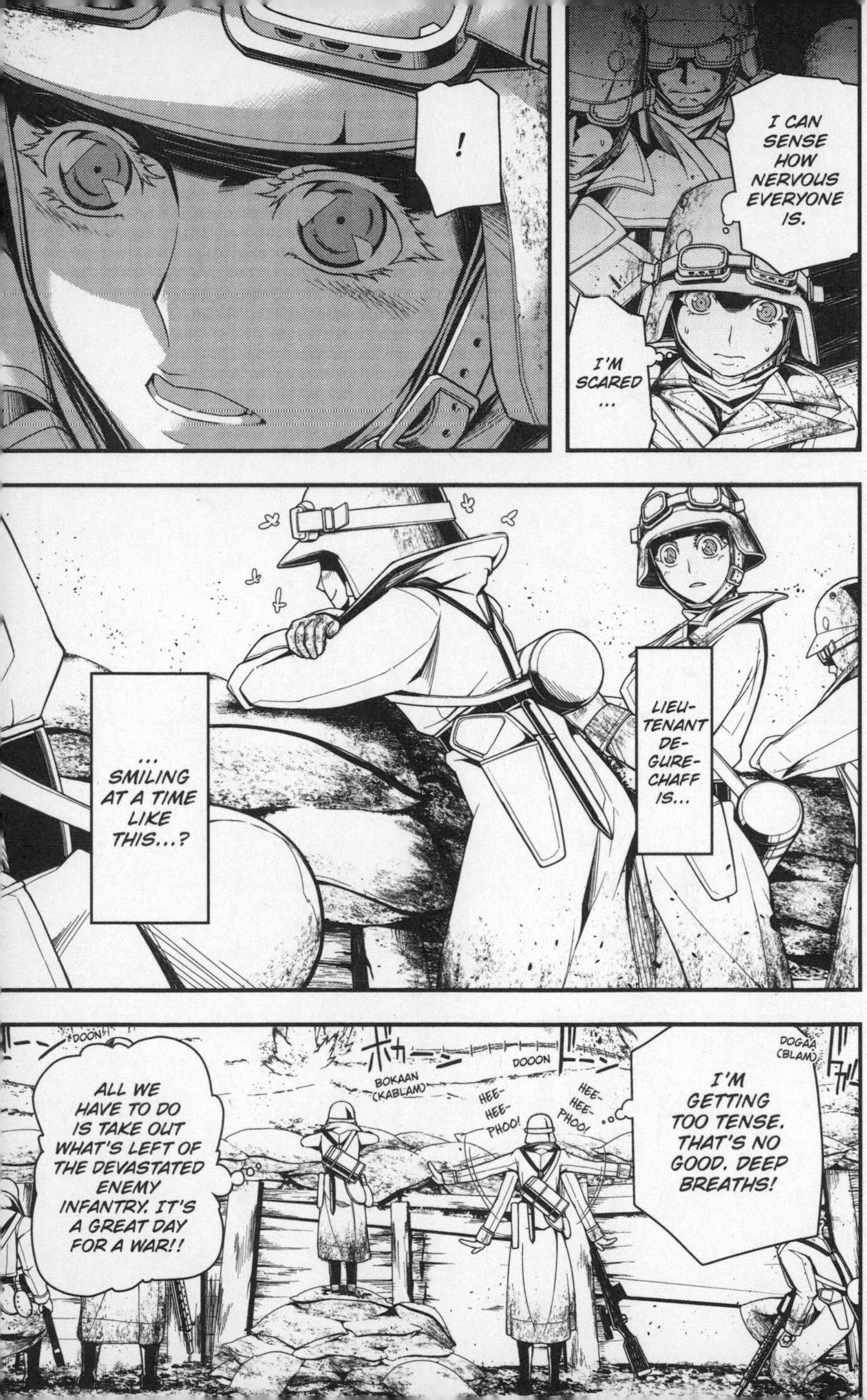
I CAN SENSE HOW NERVOUS EVERYONE IS.
I'M SCARED...
!
LIEUTENANT DEGURECHAFF IS...
...SMILING AT A TIME LIKE THIS...?
DOGAA (BLAM)
I'M GETTING TOO TENSE. THAT'S NO GOOD. DEEP BREATHS!
HEE-HEE-PHOO!
HEE-HEE-PHOO!
DOOON
BOKAAN (KABLAM)
DOON!!
ALL WE HAVE TO DO IS TAKE OUT WHAT'S LEFT OF THE DEVASTATED ENEMY INFANTRY. IT'S A GREAT DAY FOR A WAR!!

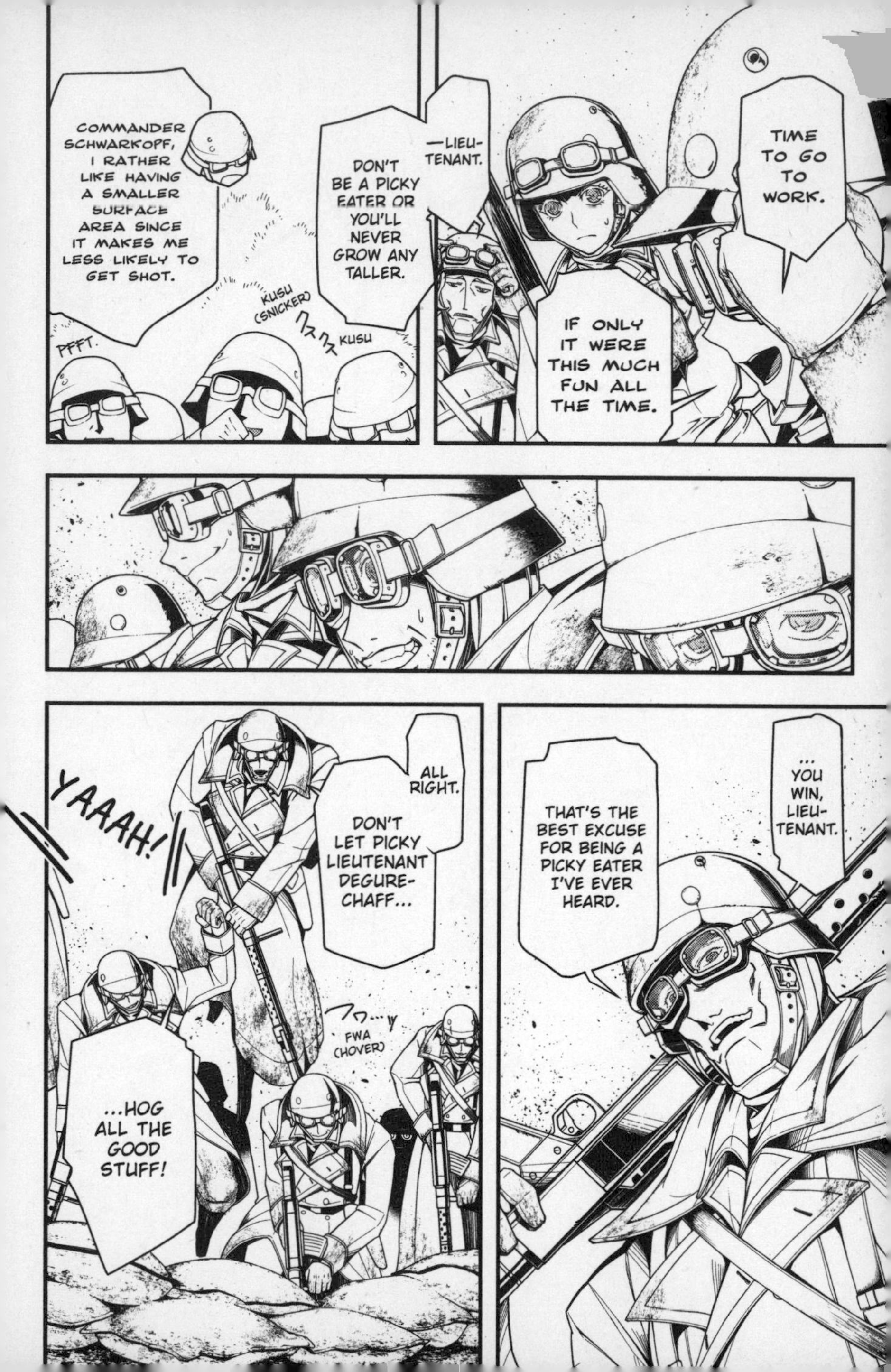
TIME TO GO TO WORK.
—LIEU-TENANT.
IF ONLY IT WERE THIS MUCH FUN ALL THE TIME.
DON'T BE A PICKY EATER OR YOU'LL NEVER GROW ANY TALLER.
COMMANDER SCHWARKOPF, I RATHER LIKE HAVING A SMALLER SURFACE AREA SINCE IT MAKES ME LESS LIKELY TO GET SHOT.
KUSU (SNICKER)
KUSU
PFFT.
... YOU WIN, LIEU-TENANT.
THAT'S THE BEST EXCUSE FOR BEING A PICKY EATER I'VE EVER HEARD.
ALL RIGHT.
DON'T LET PICKY LIEUTENANT DEGURE-CHAFF...
YAAAH!
FWA (HOVER)
...HOG ALL THE GOOD STUFF!

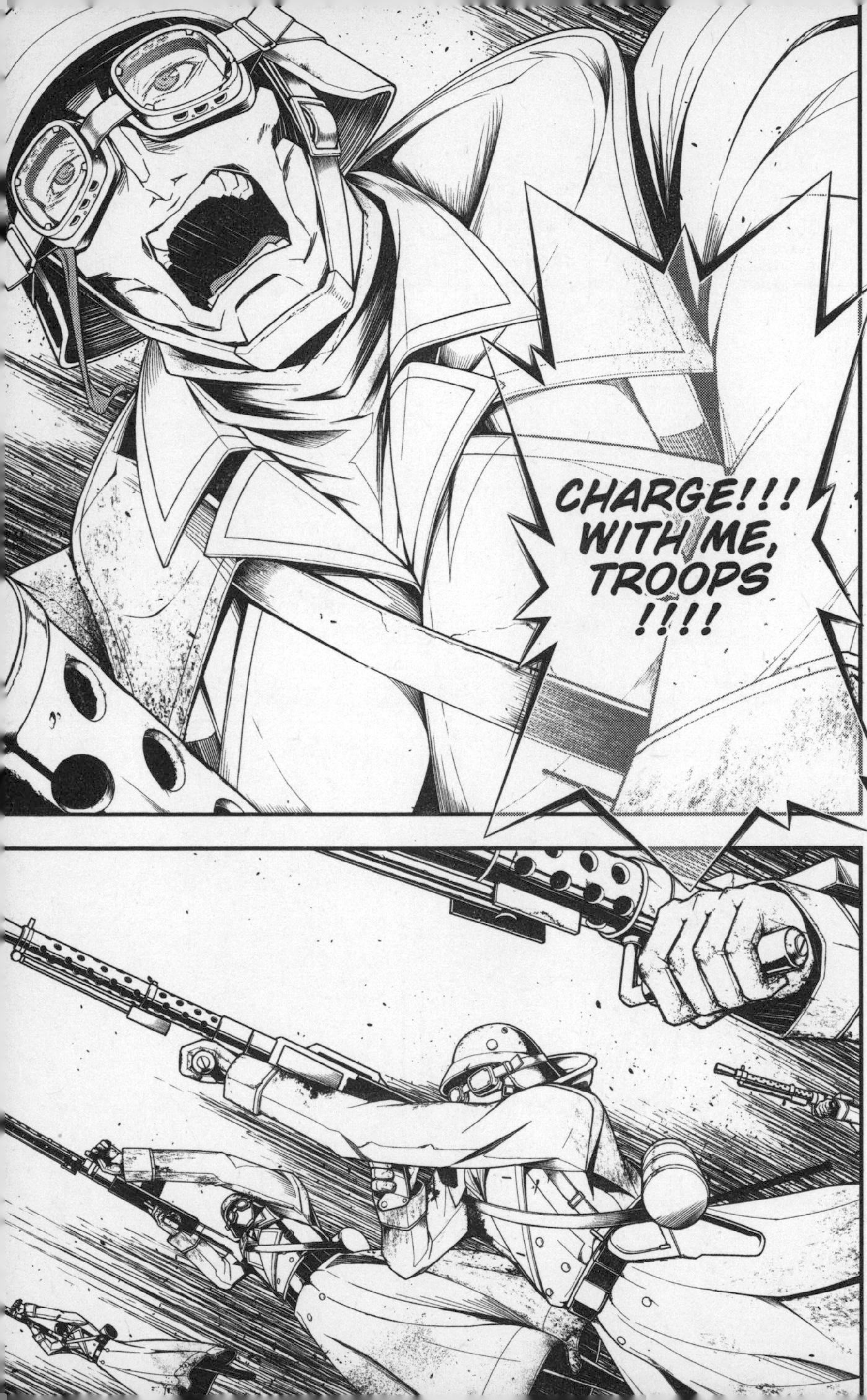
CHARGE!!! WITH ME, TROOPS !!!!

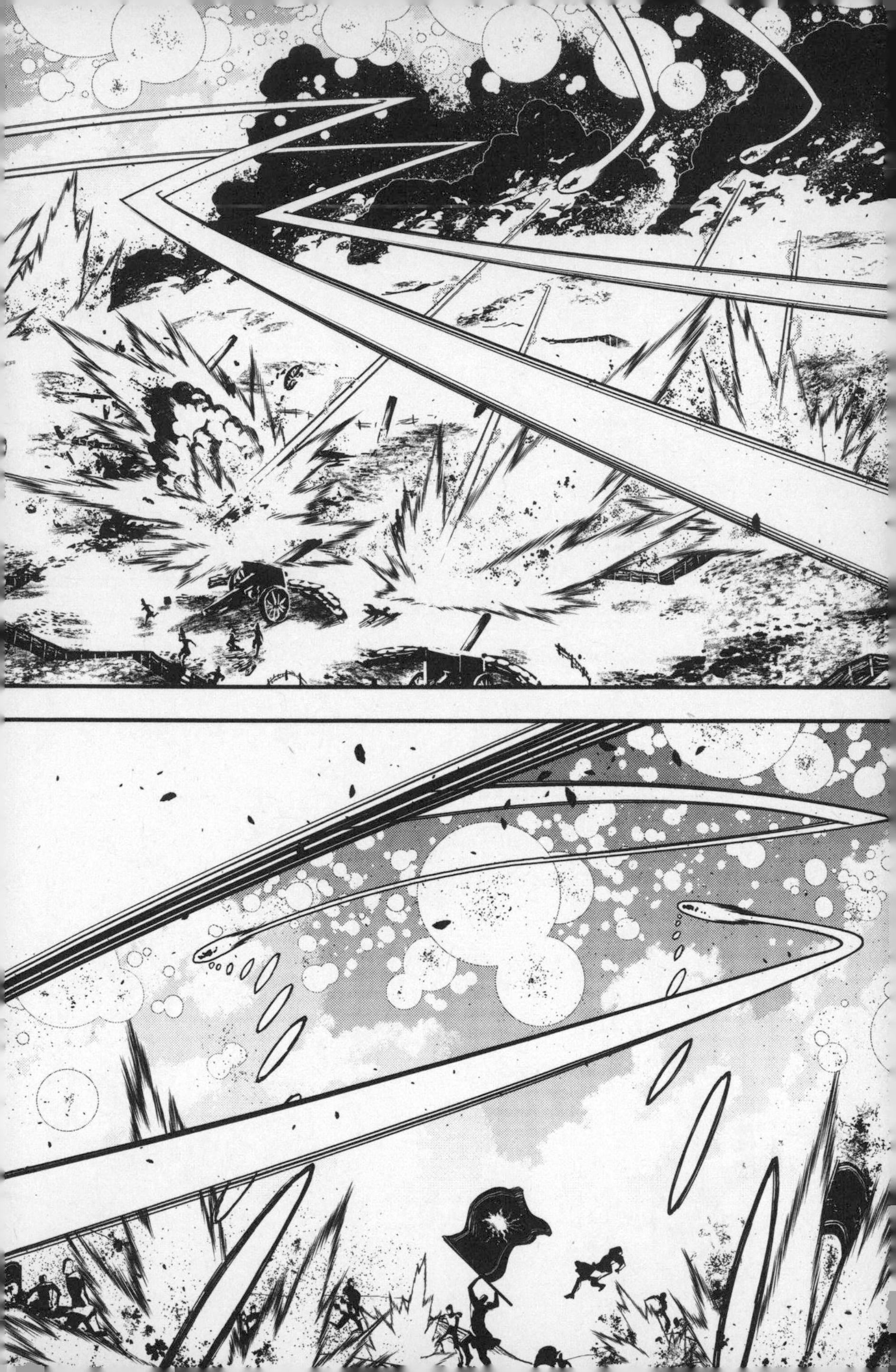

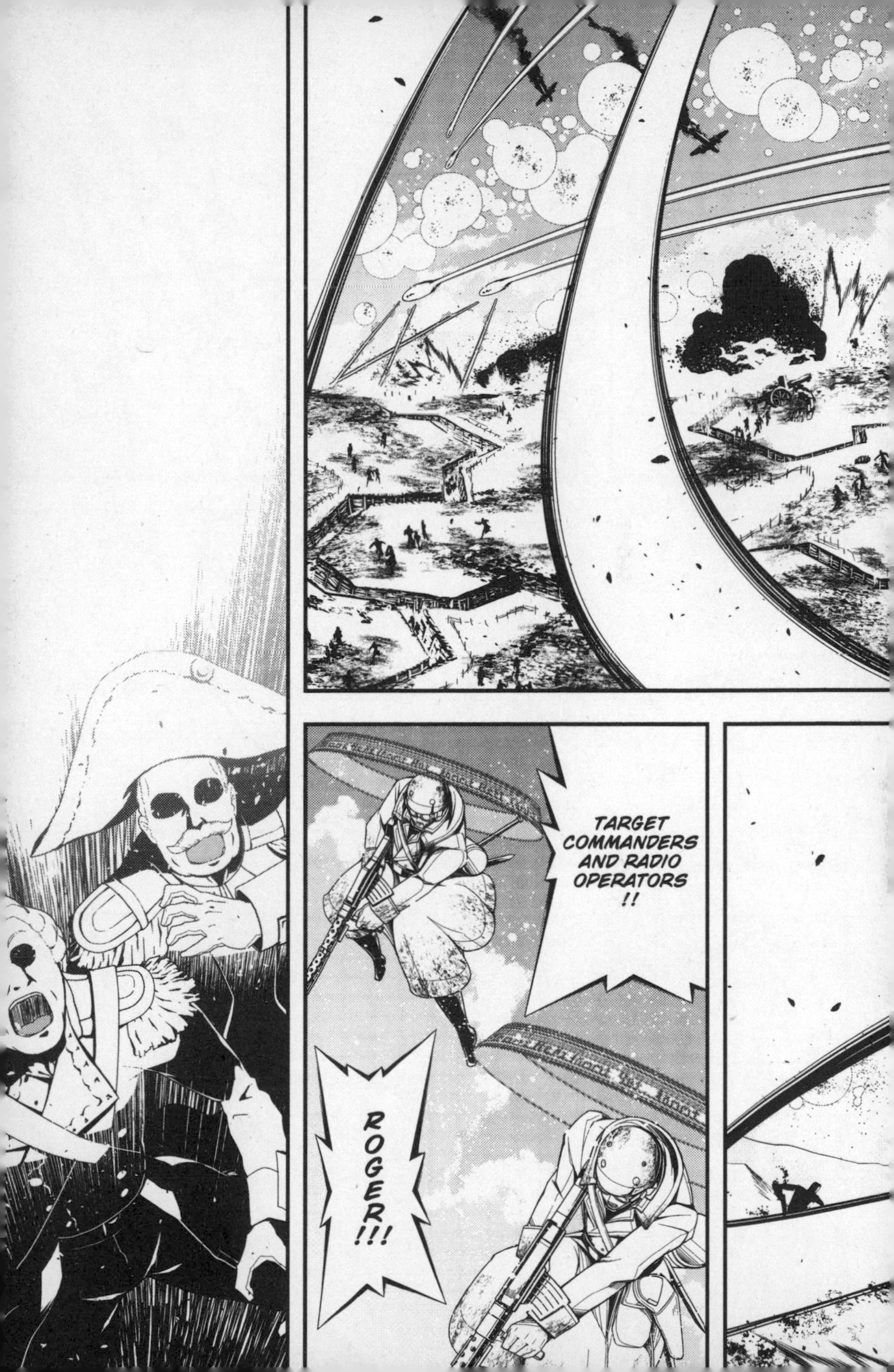
TARGET COMMANDERS AND RADIO OPERATORS !!
ROGER!!!

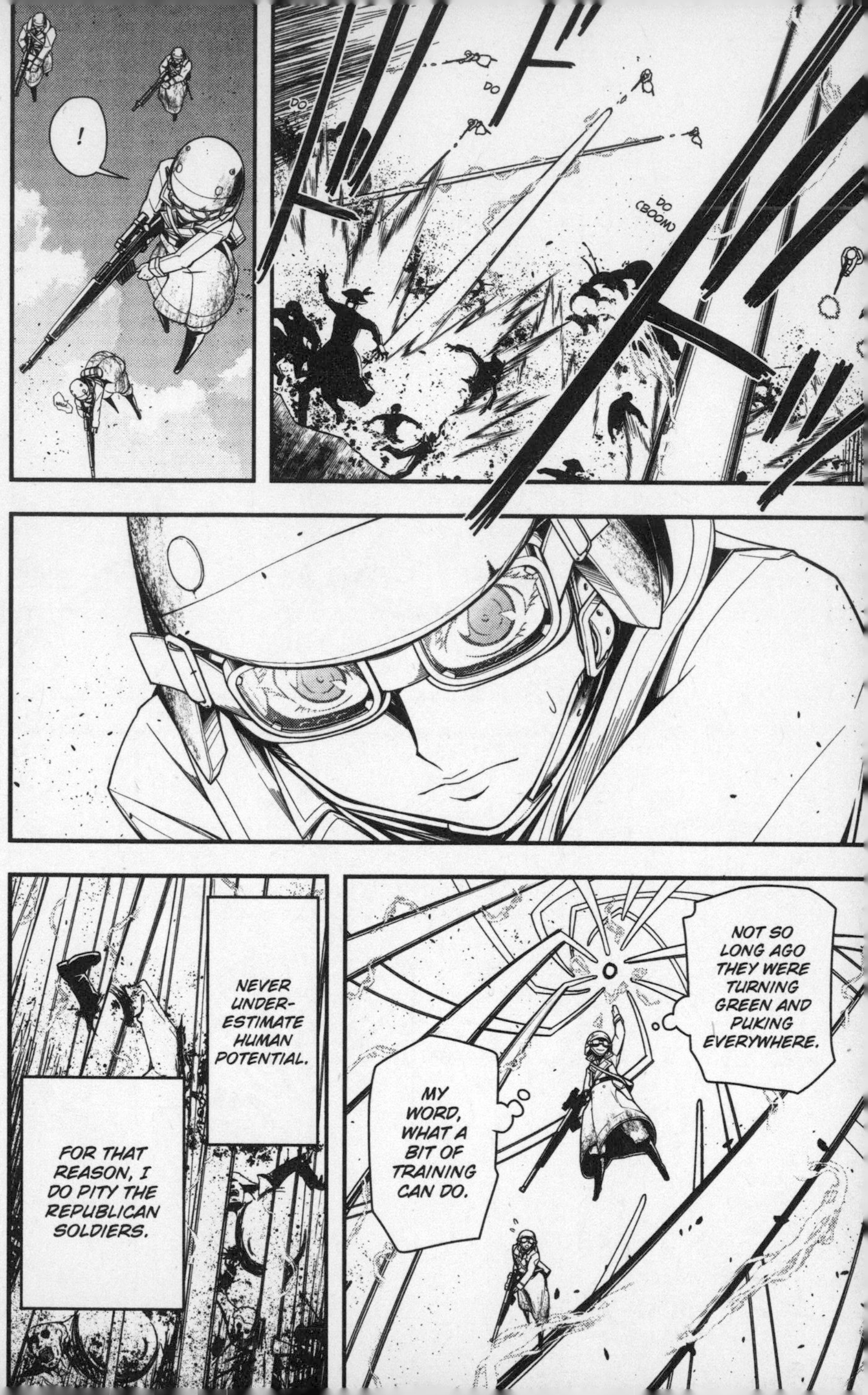

DO
DO
DO (BOOM)
!
NOT SO LONG AGO THEY WERE TURNING GREEN AND PUKING EVERYWHERE.
MY WORD, WHAT A BIT OF TRAINING CAN DO.
NEVER UNDER-ESTIMATE HUMAN POTENTIAL.
FOR THAT REASON, I DO PITY THE REPUBLICAN SOLDIERS.

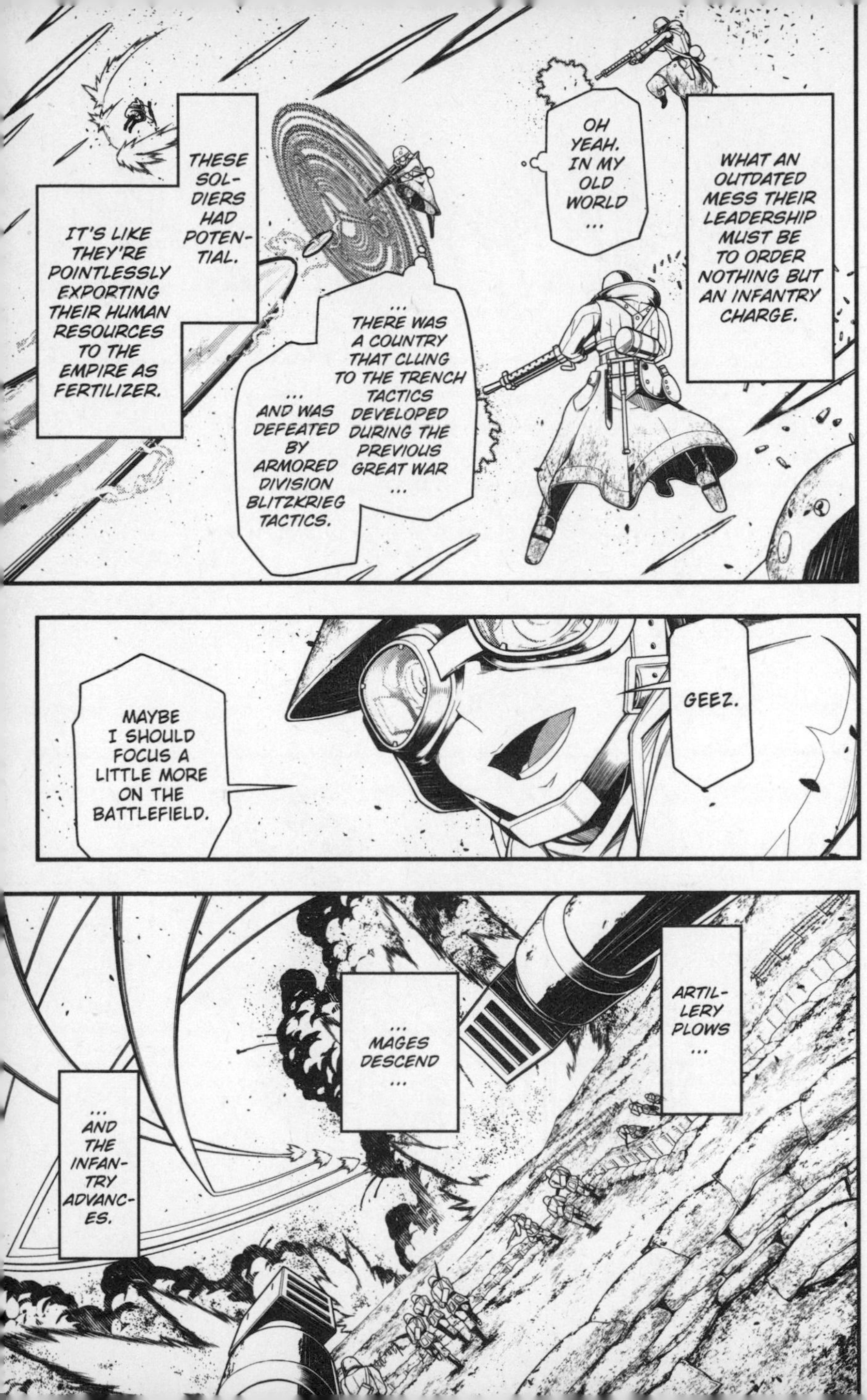
WHAT AN OUTDATED MESS THEIR LEADERSHIP MUST BE TO ORDER NOTHING BUT AN INFANTRY CHARGE.
THESE SOL-DIERS HAD POTEN-TIAL.
IT'S LIKE THEY'RE POINTLESSLY EXPORTING THEIR HUMAN RESOURCES TO THE EMPIRE AS FERTILIZER.
OH YEAH. IN MY OLD WORLD ...
... THERE WAS A COUNTRY THAT CLUNG TO THE TRENCH TACTICS DEVELOPED DURING THE PREVIOUS GREAT WAR ...
... AND WAS DEFEATED BY ARMORED DIVISION BLITZKRIEG TACTICS.
GEEZ.
MAYBE I SHOULD FOCUS A LITTLE MORE ON THE BATTLEFIELD.
ARTIL-LERY PLOWS ...
... MAGES DESCEND ...
... AND THE INFAN-TRY ADVANC-ES.

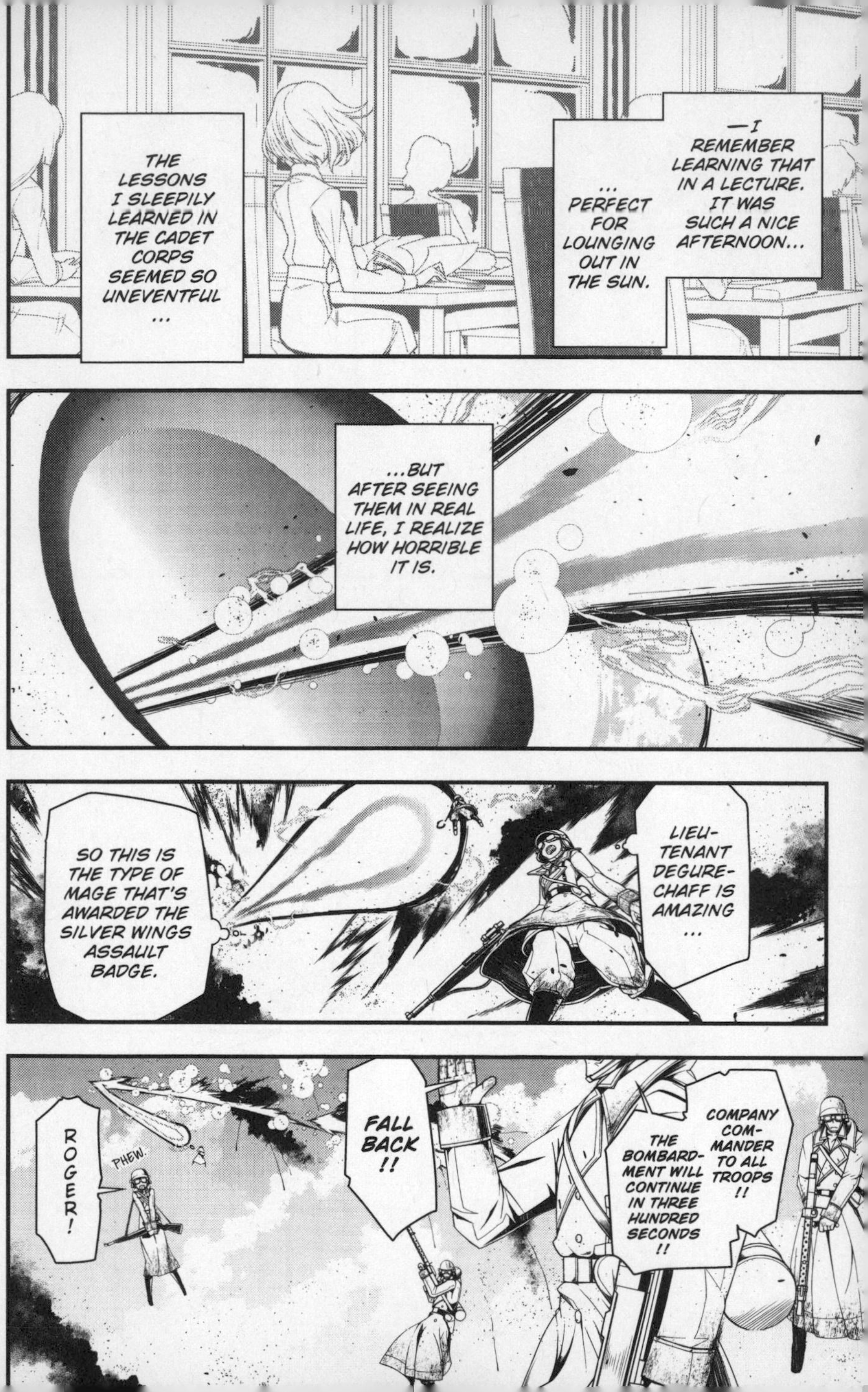
—I REMEMBER LEARNING THAT IN A LECTURE. IT WAS SUCH A NICE AFTERNOON…
…PERFECT FOR LOUNGING OUT IN THE SUN.
THE LESSONS I SLEEPILY LEARNED IN THE CADET CORPS SEEMED SO UNEVENTFUL…
…BUT AFTER SEEING THEM IN REAL LIFE, I REALIZE HOW HORRIBLE IT IS.
LIEUTENANT DEGURECHAFF IS AMAZING…
SO THIS IS THE TYPE OF MAGE THAT'S AWARDED THE SILVER WINGS ASSAULT BADGE.
COMPANY COMMANDER TO ALL TROOPS!!
THE BOMBARDMENT WILL CONTINUE IN THREE HUNDRED SECONDS!!
FALL BACK!!
PHEW.
ROGER!

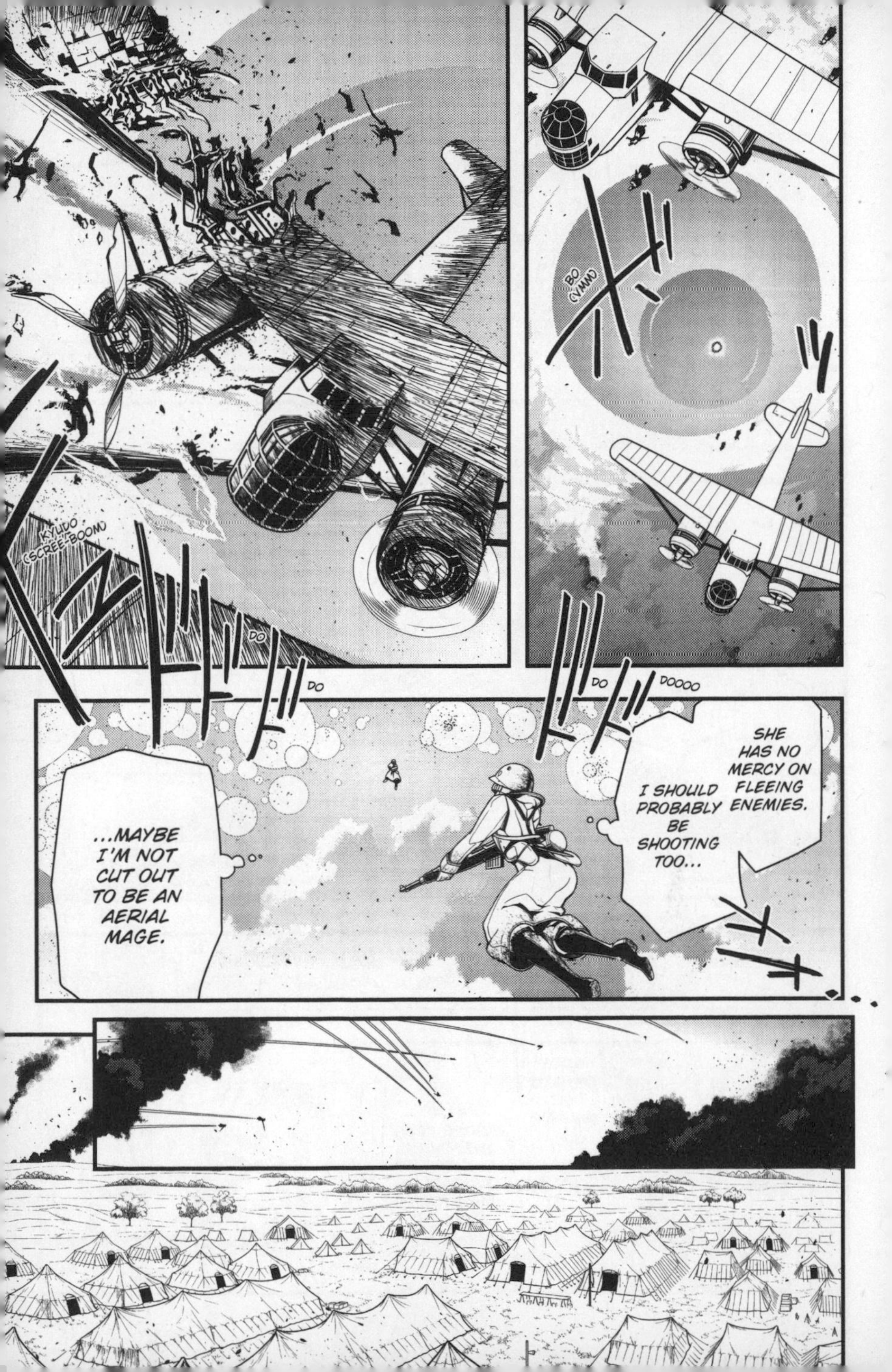
BO (VMM)
KYUDO (SCREE-BOOM)
DO
DOOOO
DO
DO
SHE HAS NO MERCY ON FLEEING ENEMIES.
I SHOULD PROBABLY BE SHOOTING TOO...
...MAYBE I'M NOT CUT OUT TO BE AN AERIAL MAGE.

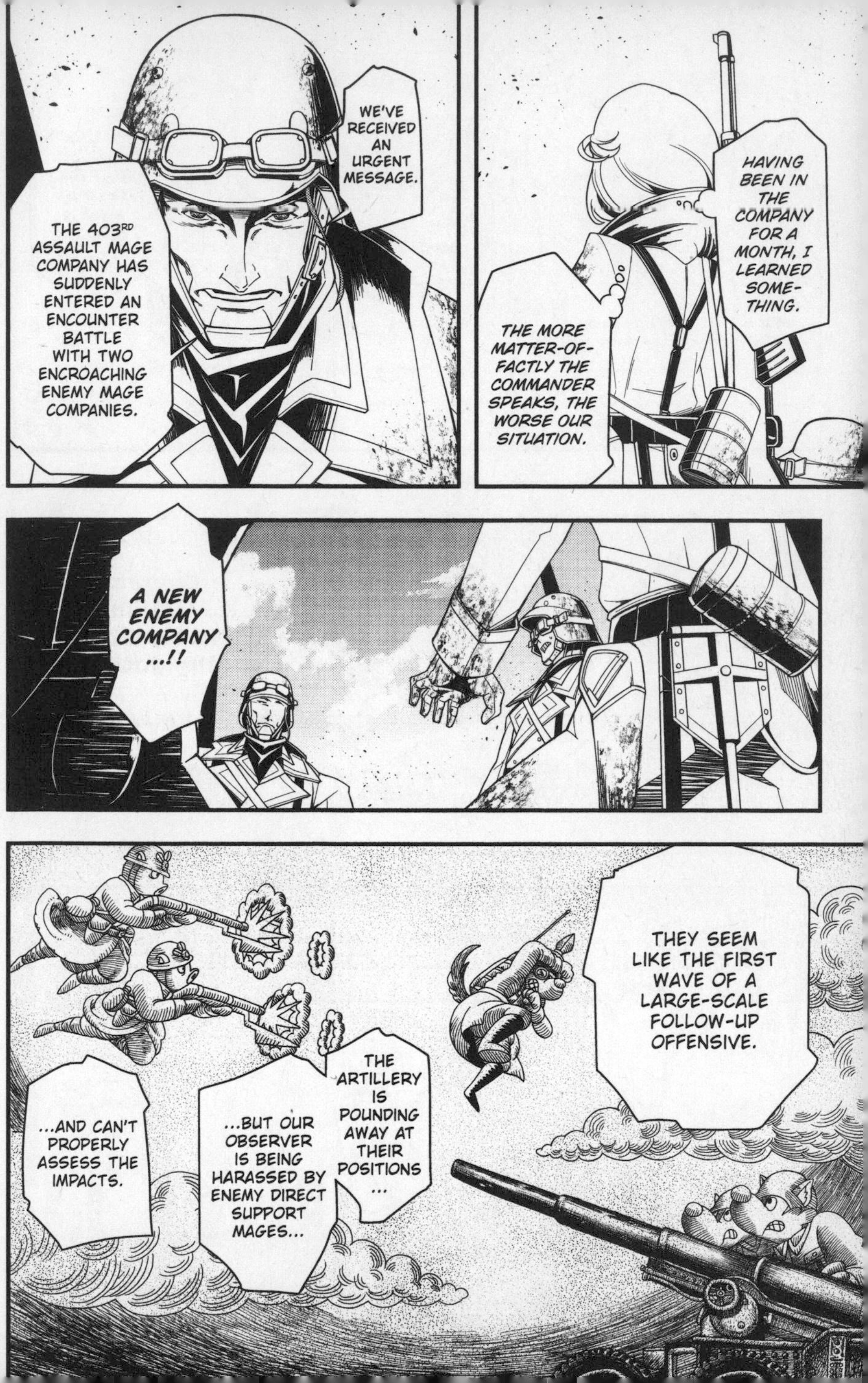
HAVING BEEN IN THE COMPANY FOR A MONTH, I LEARNED SOME-THING.
THE MORE MATTER-OF-FACTLY THE COMMANDER SPEAKS, THE WORSE OUR SITUATION.
WE'VE RECEIVED AN URGENT MESSAGE.
THE 403RD ASSAULT MAGE COMPANY HAS SUDDENLY ENTERED AN ENCOUNTER BATTLE WITH TWO ENCROACHING ENEMY MAGE COMPANIES.
A NEW ENEMY COMPANY ...!!
THEY SEEM LIKE THE FIRST WAVE OF A LARGE-SCALE FOLLOW-UP OFFENSIVE.
THE ARTILLERY IS POUNDING AWAY AT THEIR POSITIONS ...
...BUT OUR OBSERVER IS BEING HARASSED BY ENEMY DIRECT SUPPORT MAGES...
...AND CAN'T PROPERLY ASSESS THE IMPACTS.

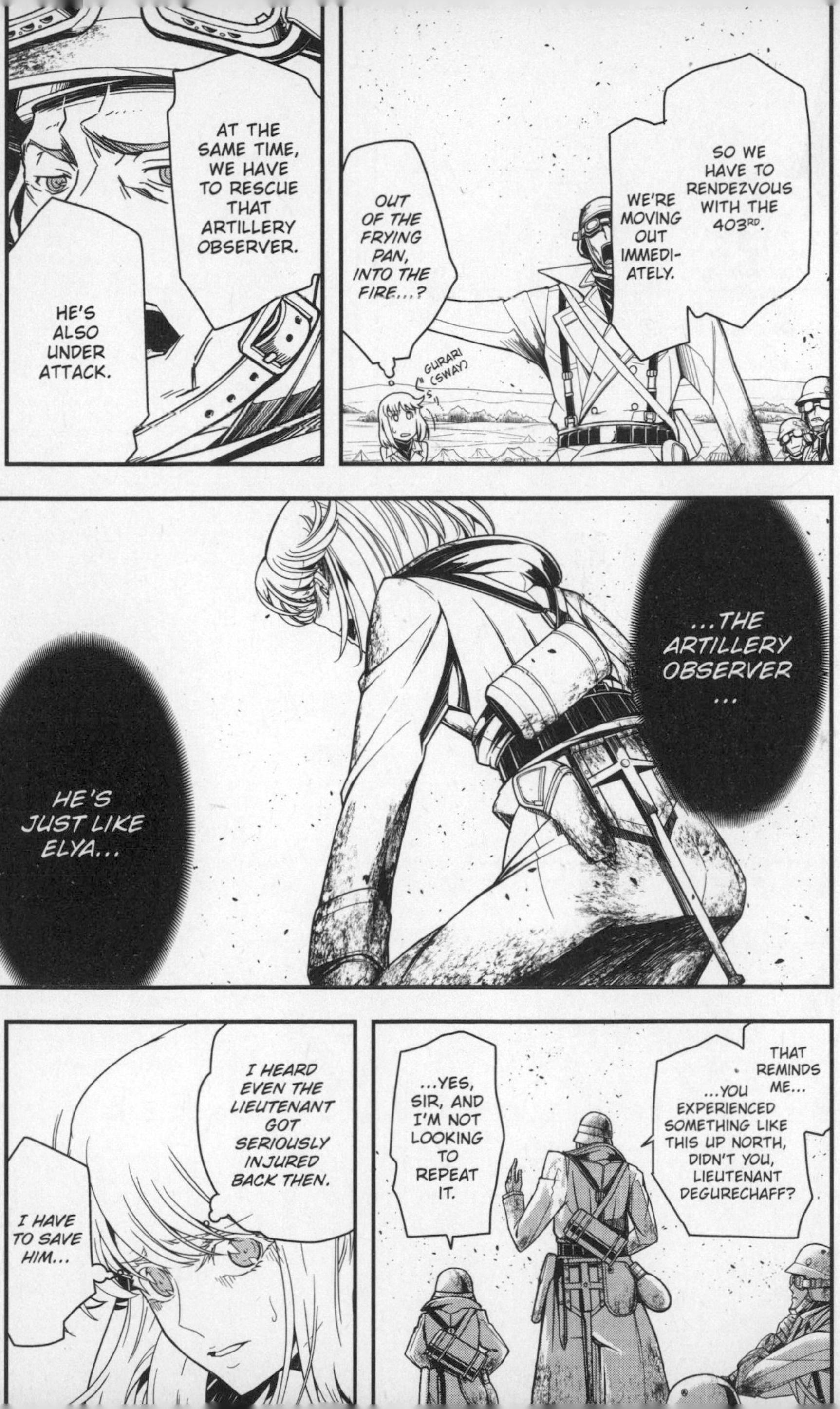
SO WE HAVE TO RENDEZVOUS WITH THE 403RD.
WE'RE MOVING OUT IMMEDIATELY.
OUT OF THE FRYING PAN, INTO THE FIRE...?
GURARI (SWAY)
AT THE SAME TIME, WE HAVE TO RESCUE THAT ARTILLERY OBSERVER.
HE'S ALSO UNDER ATTACK.
...THE ARTILLERY OBSERVER...
HE'S JUST LIKE ELYA...
THAT REMINDS ME...
...YOU EXPERIENCED SOMETHING LIKE THIS UP NORTH, DIDN'T YOU, LIEUTENANT DEGURECHAFF?
...YES, SIR, AND I'M NOT LOOKING TO REPEAT IT.
I HEARD EVEN THE LIEUTENANT GOT SERIOUSLY INJURED BACK THEN.
I HAVE TO SAVE HIM...

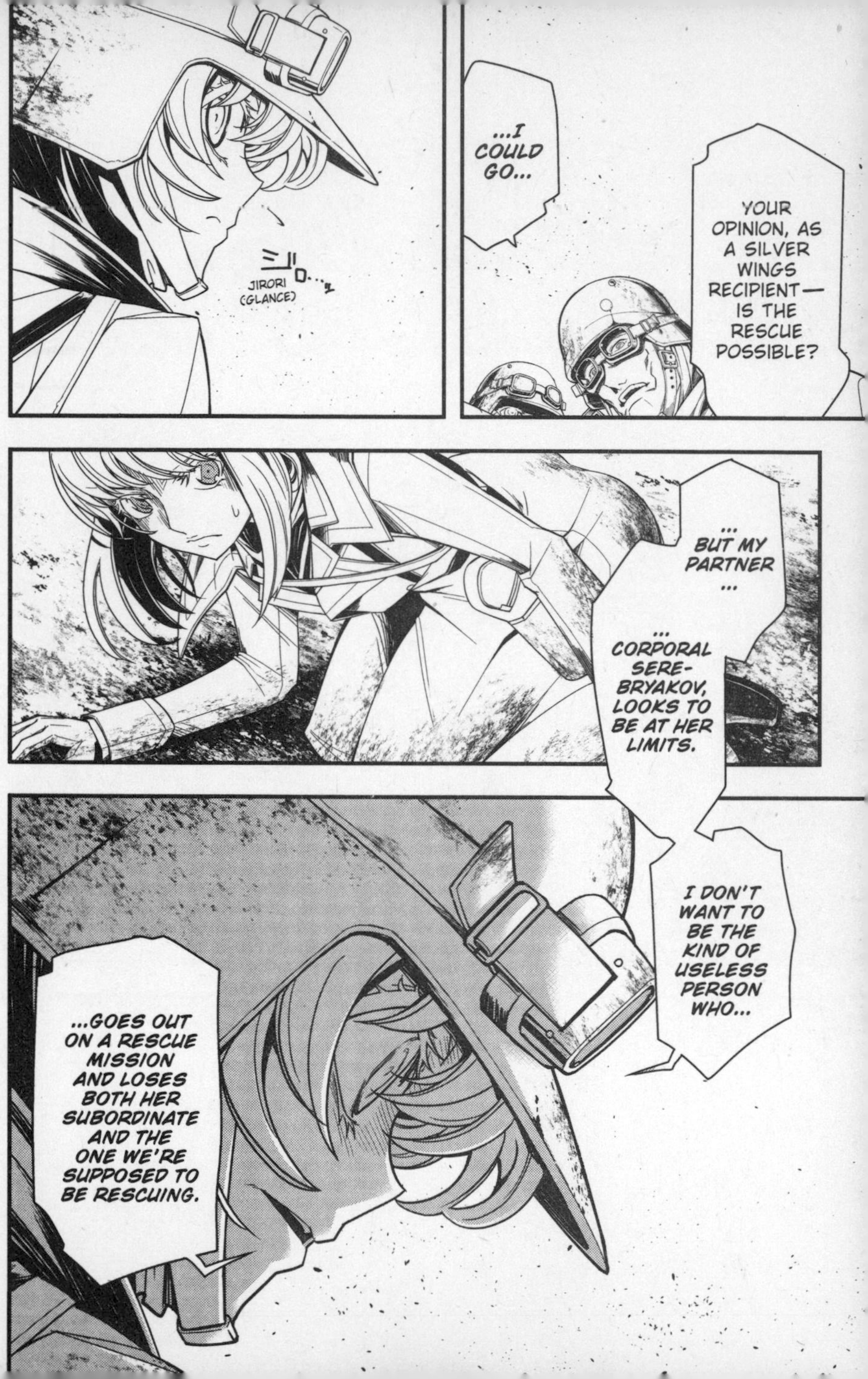
YOUR OPINION, AS A SILVER WINGS RECIPIENT—IS THE RESCUE POSSIBLE?
...I COULD GO...
ジロ...
JIRORI (GLANCE)
...BUT MY PARTNER...
...CORPORAL SERE-BRYAKOV, LOOKS TO BE AT HER LIMITS.
I DON'T WANT TO BE THE KIND OF USELESS PERSON WHO...
...GOES OUT ON A RESCUE MISSION AND LOSES BOTH HER SUBORDINATE AND THE ONE WE'RE SUPPOSED TO BE RESCUING.

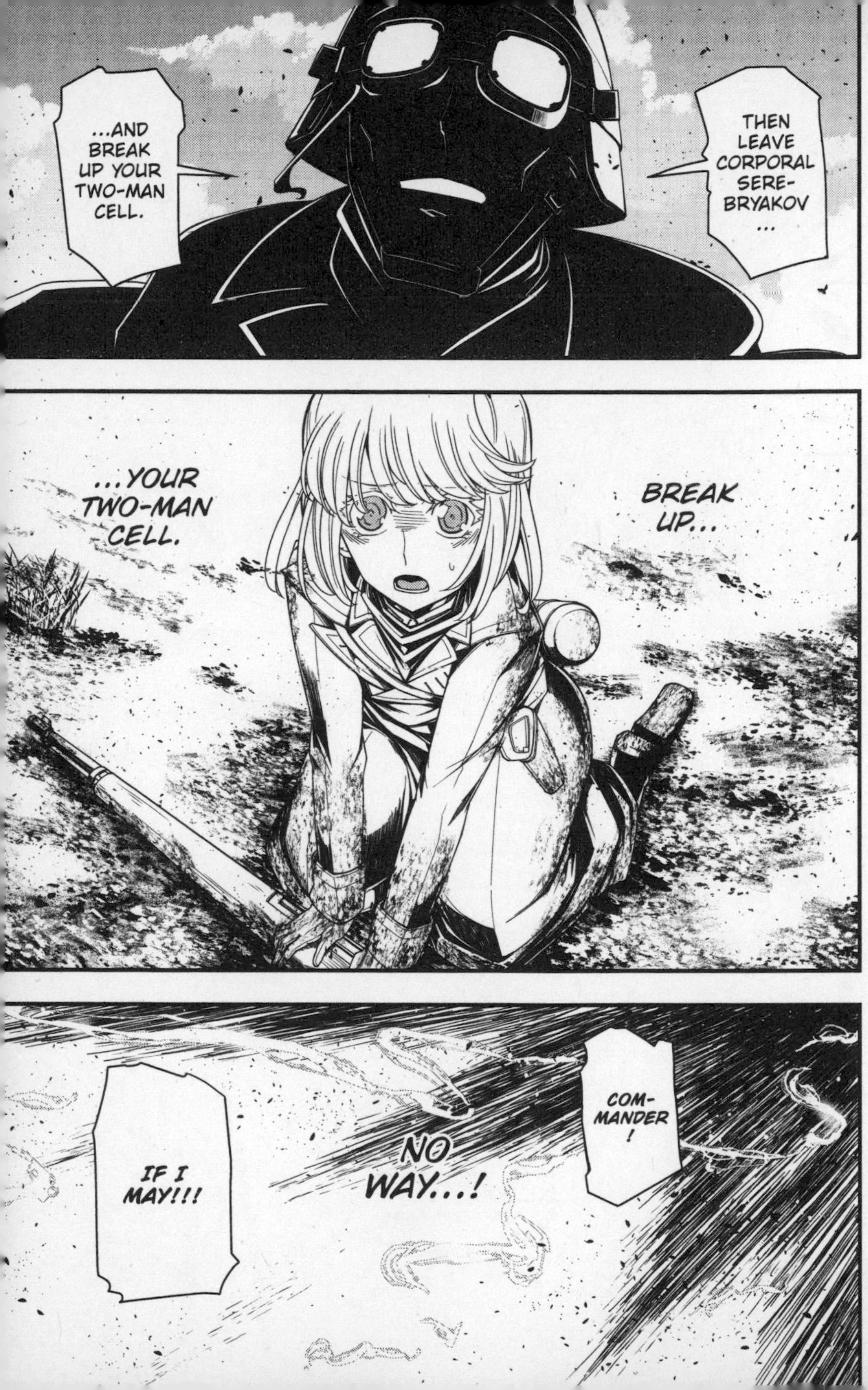
THEN LEAVE CORPORAL SERE-BRYAKOV ...
...AND BREAK UP YOUR TWO-MAN CELL.
BREAK UP...
...YOUR TWO-MAN CELL.
COM-MANDER!
NO WAY...!
IF I MAY!!!

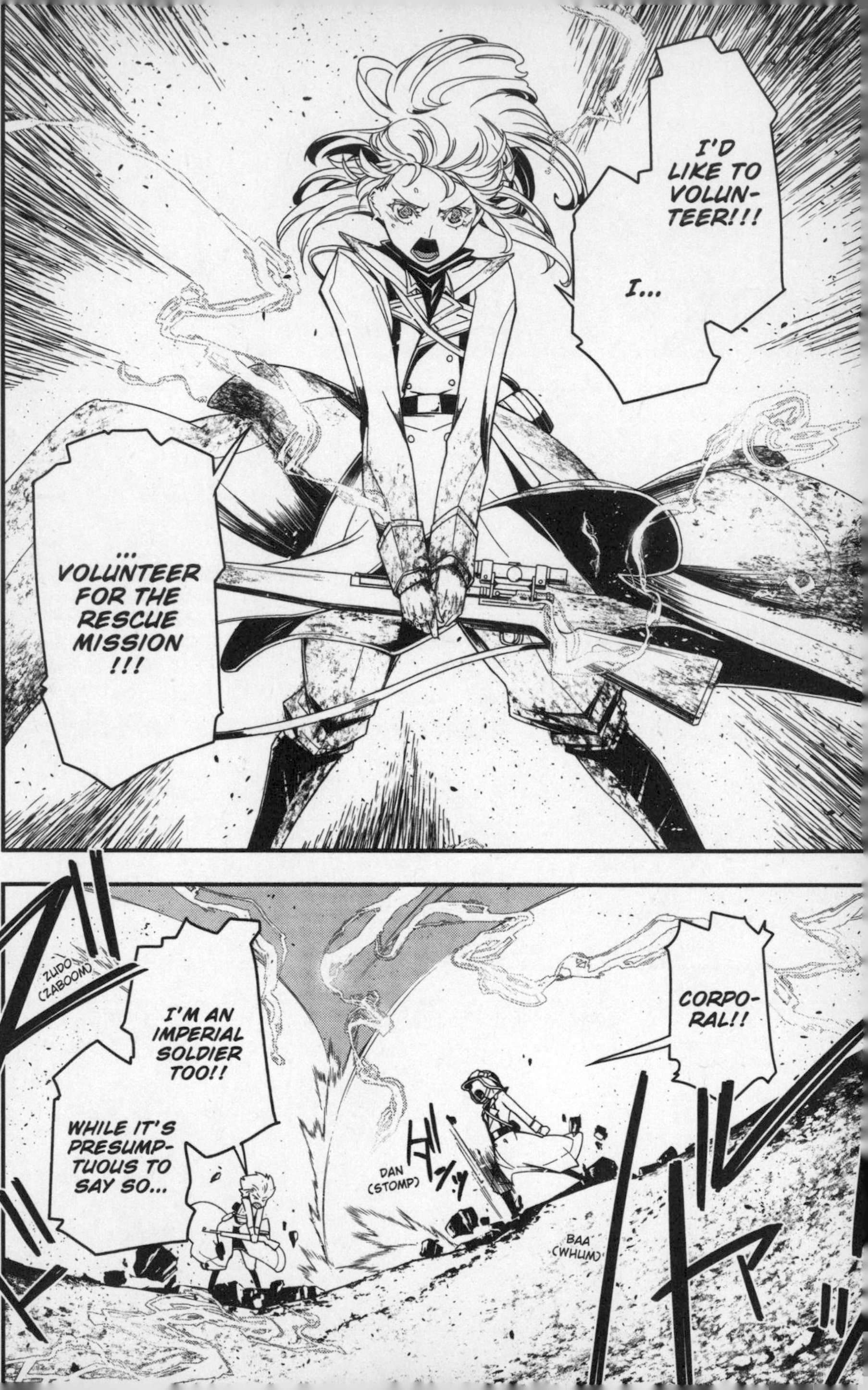
I'D LIKE TO VOLUN-TEER!!!
I...
...VOLUNTEER FOR THE RESCUE MISSION!!!
CORPO-RAL!!
BAA (WHUM)
DAN (STOMP)
I'M AN IMPERIAL SOLDIER TOO!!
WHILE IT'S PRESUMP-TUOUS TO SAY SO...
ZUDO (ZABOOM)

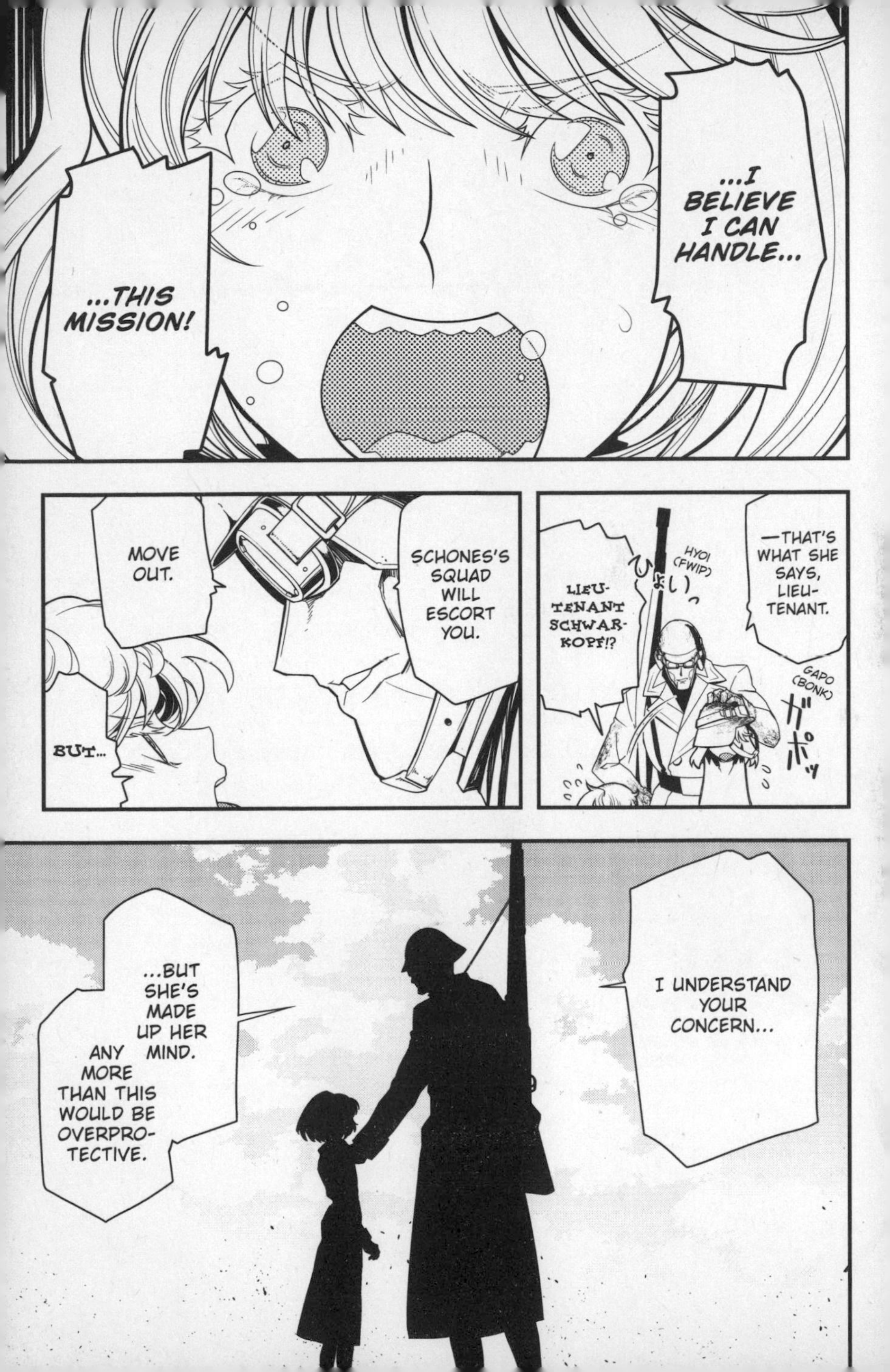
...I BELIEVE I CAN HANDLE...
...THIS MISSION!
—THAT'S WHAT SHE SAYS, LIEU-TENANT.
ひょい HYOI (FWIP)
LIEU-TENANT SCHWAR-KOPF!?
ガポッ GAPO (BONK)
SCHONES'S SQUAD WILL ESCORT YOU.
MOVE OUT.
BUT...
I UNDERSTAND YOUR CONCERN...
...BUT SHE'S MADE UP HER MIND.
ANY MORE THAN THIS WOULD BE OVERPRO-TECTIVE.

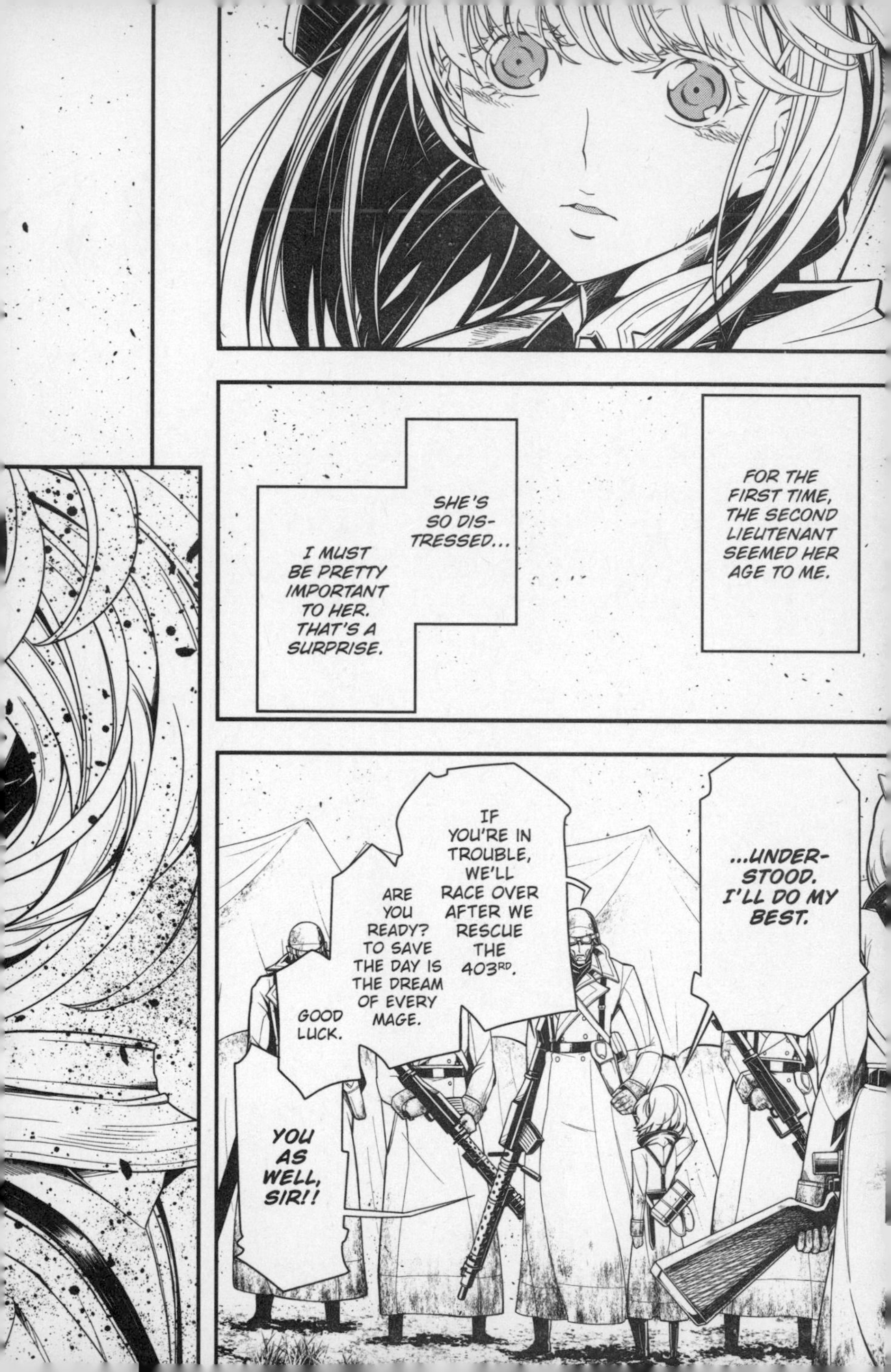
FOR THE FIRST TIME, THE SECOND LIEUTENANT SEEMED HER AGE TO ME.
SHE'S SO DIS-TRESSED...
I MUST BE PRETTY IMPORTANT TO HER. THAT'S A SURPRISE.
...UNDER-STOOD. I'LL DO MY BEST.
IF YOU'RE IN TROUBLE, WE'LL RACE OVER AFTER WE RESCUE THE 403RD.
ARE YOU READY? TO SAVE THE DAY IS THE DREAM OF EVERY MAGE.
GOOD LUCK.
YOU AS WELL, SIR!!

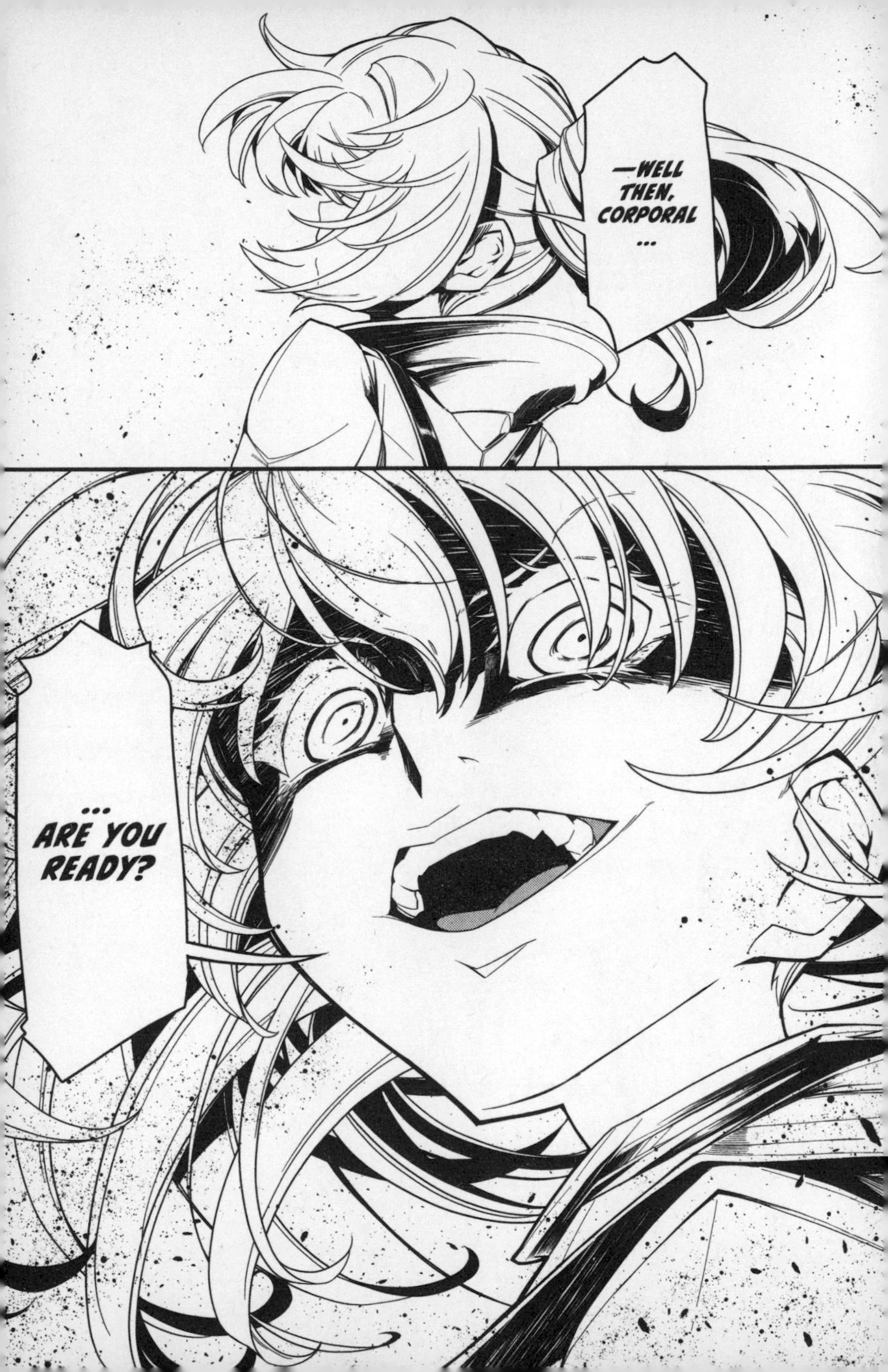
—WELL THEN, CORPORAL ...
... ARE YOU READY?

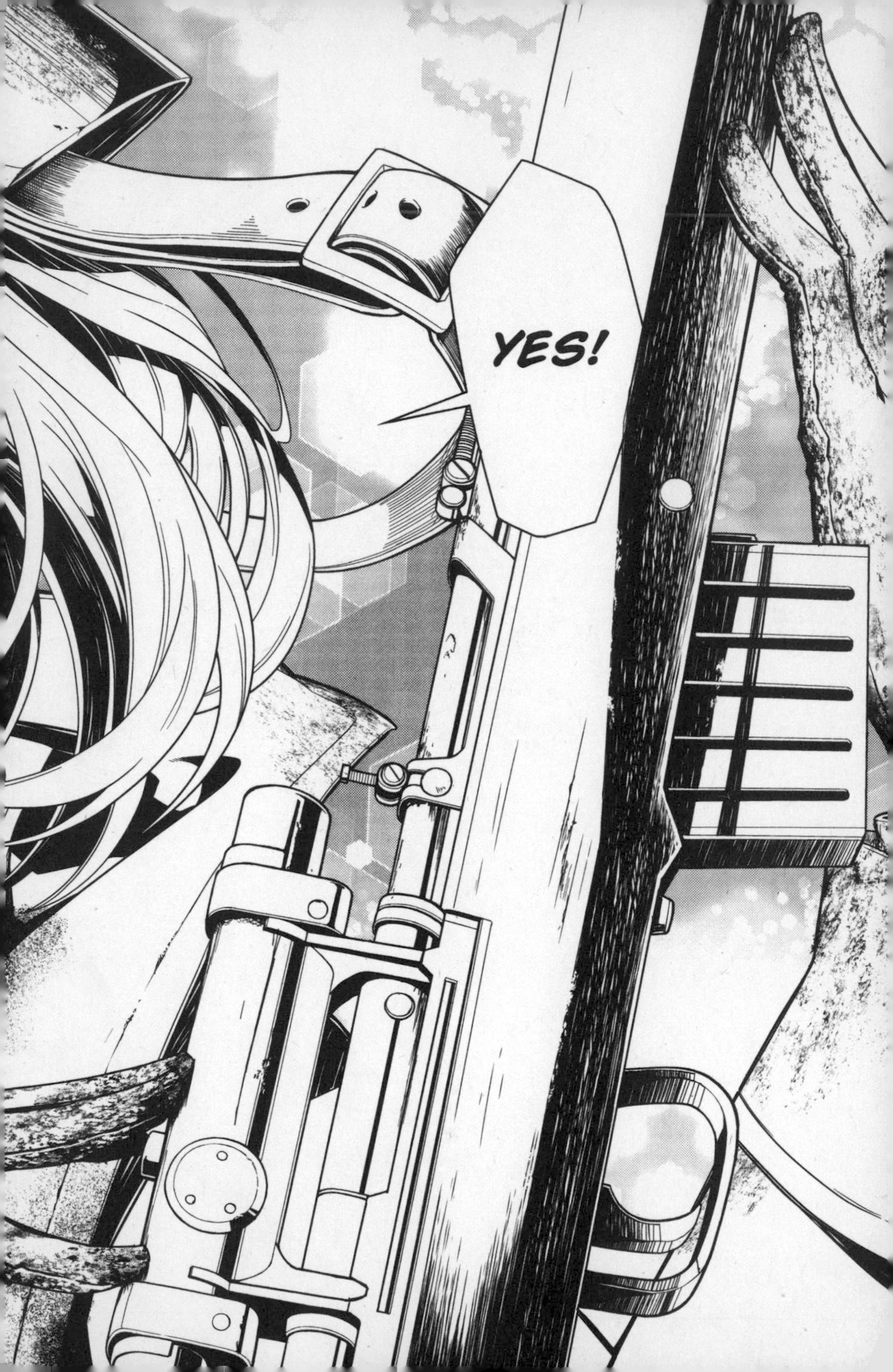
YES!

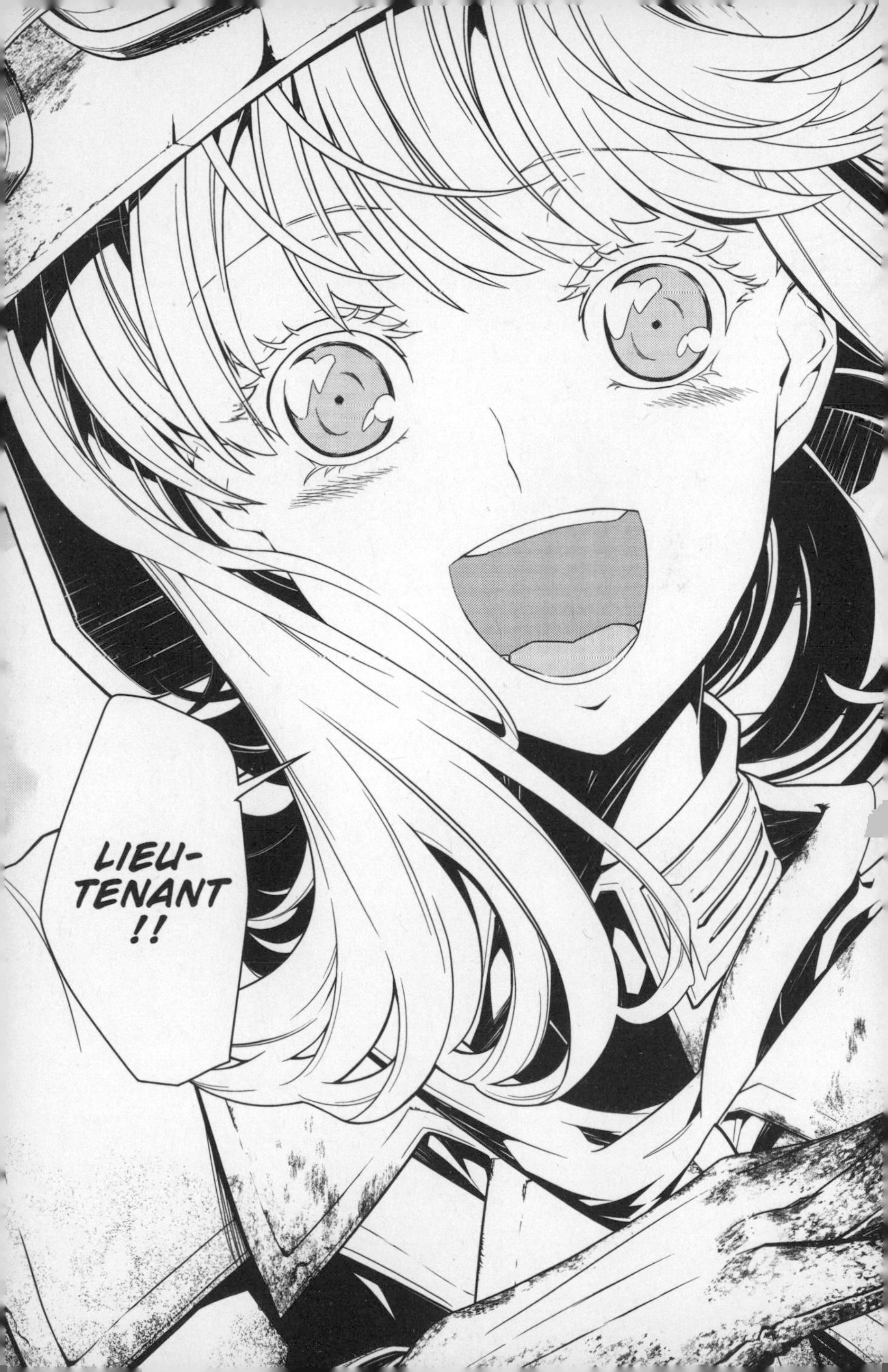
LIEU-
TENANT
!!

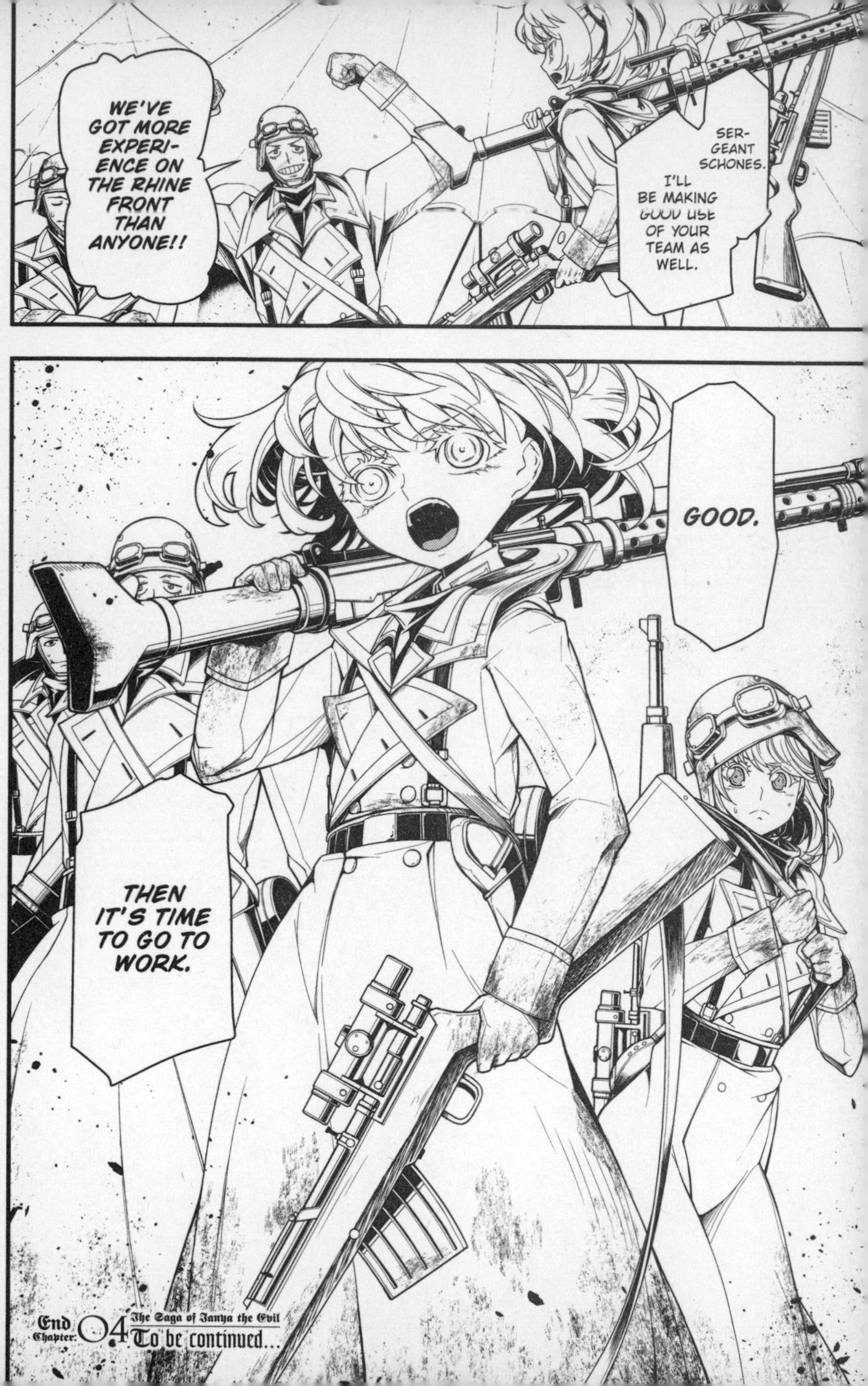
SERGEANT SCHONES.
I'LL BE MAKING GOOD USE OF YOUR TEAM AS WELL.
WE'VE GOT MORE EXPERIENCE ON THE RHINE FRONT THAN ANYONE!!
GOOD.
THEN IT'S TIME TO GO TO WORK.
End Chapter: 04 The Saga of Tanya the Evil To be continued...

Glossary Chapter 01

Bogey

A slang term for an aircraft whose affiliation is unknown and could be an enemy. Also sometimes called an "unknown" or "UFO" (unidentified flying object). If it doesn't reply to transponder interrogation to distinguish itself as friend or foe, a pilot in the vicinity needs to ascertain its affiliation. Once a bogey has been identified as an enemy, it's called a "bandit" in order to distinguish it.

ROE (Rules of Engagement)

The rules for what weapons can be used in what circumstances by military forces, police, and so on. If horribly oversimplified, it's basically "fighting etiquette." Even on a battlefield, soldiers can't decide on their own how to engage; they have to act according to the authorized ROE. Soldiers who violate the ROE are punished.

While the ROE limit the soldiers' actions, they also protect their status. If there were no ROE and soldiers' actions were left up to their own judgment, a soldier who used a weapon could be suspected of excessive self-defense or murder afterward. As long as a soldier is properly following the ROE, it's considered that their actions are undertaken on military orders.

Mayday

An international distress signal used in emergencies by ships, planes, trains, and so on. It comes from the French phrase Venez m'aider, which means, "Come help me."

Once a Mayday call is sent, all communication on that frequency must pertain to the rescue, so it is prohibited to signal Mayday unless you are in imminent danger. Sending a false Mayday signal is generally treated as a crime.

Decorations

Badges and medals given by a country or head of state to an individual for remarkable achievements in a specific field. In the military, it's one of the systems that exist to boost morale. Awards are given to soldiers who achieve splendid results.

Some are pinned to the chest, while others are worn as cords on the shoulder, but since displaying them could mean losing them, there aren't very many occasions to wear them. Instead most people wear service ribbons to indicate their awards.

Another reason decorations aren't worn very much is that anyone wearing one on the battlefield would be identified as an officer and end up a prime target.

Glossary Chapter 02

Altitude 12,000

This is about 3,600 meters. It's said that increasing altitude by a hundred meters drops the temperature by 0.6 degrees Celsius. So at 3,600 meters, it's 21.6 degrees lower than the surface, and oxygen concentration is only 63 percent of what would normally be found at sea level. Above 3,000 meters, symptoms of altitude sickness such as dizziness, headache, and nausea begin to appear, and in the worst cases, accumulated fluid in the brain or lungs can cause death.

Lieutenant Degurechaff acclimated at 6,600 before ascending to 12,000, but even with insulated clothing and an oxygen tank, it's too harsh an environment for an unprotected human to stay in for very long.

Dr. von Schugel's Elinium Type 95 can theoretically ascend to 18,000, which in meters is about 5,400.

Mobile Defense

Older defense tactics involved concentrating fighting power on the front lines, but when using this doctrine, if the attackers broke through, any further attempts at defense were weak, and the rear was exposed, which could lead to general collapse. This danger became most pronounced when the lines grew long, so armies devised the tactic of stationing static infantry troops on the front lines and positioning a mobile defense unit behind them to strike once the attackers broke through.

Lieutenant Degurechaff seemed to think she belonged to a mobile defense unit that would sortie from a fortified position in the rear against long-range enemy artillery and beat back the enemy that broke through the line, but actually, the defense had become so desperate that her unit had to go over the top, moving into no-man's-land to repulse enemy attackers that the infantry had been holding off.

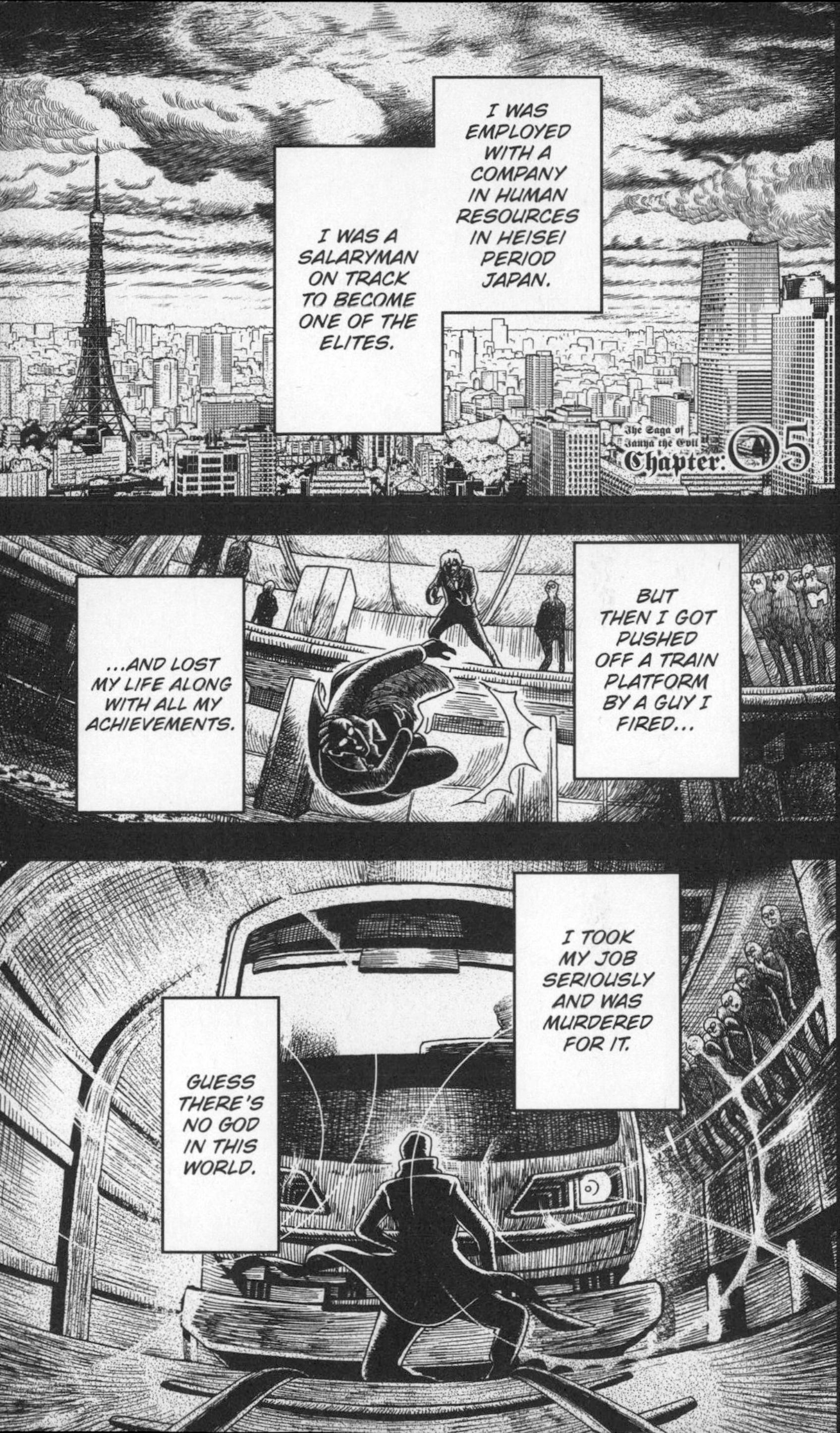

I WAS EMPLOYED WITH A COMPANY IN HUMAN RESOURCES IN HEISEI PERIOD JAPAN.
I WAS A SALARYMAN ON TRACK TO BECOME ONE OF THE ELITES.
The Saga of Tanya the Evil
Chapter: 05
BUT THEN I GOT PUSHED OFF A TRAIN PLATFORM BY A GUY I FIRED...
...AND LOST MY LIFE ALONG WITH ALL MY ACHIEVEMENTS.
I TOOK MY JOB SERIOUSLY AND WAS MURDERED FOR IT.
GUESS THERE'S NO GOD IN THIS WORLD.

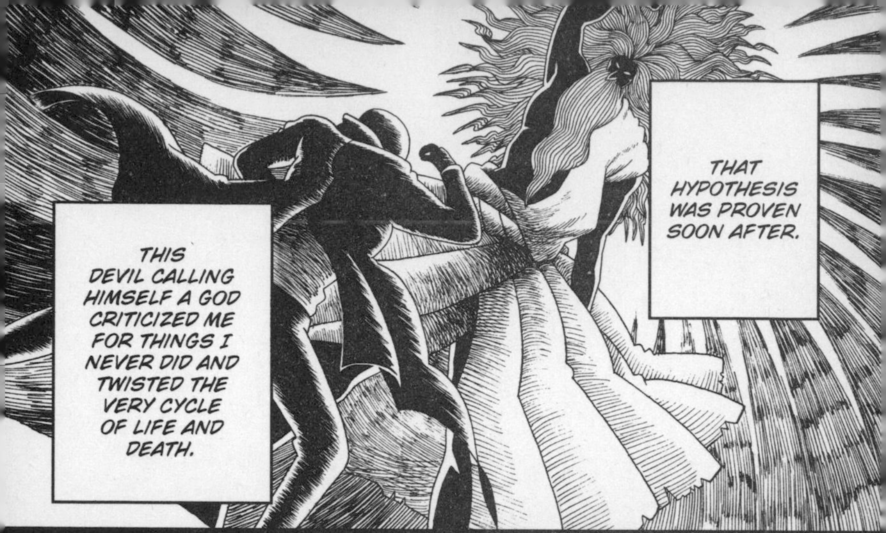
THAT HYPOTHESIS WAS PROVEN SOON AFTER.
THIS DEVIL CALLING HIMSELF A GOD CRITICIZED ME FOR THINGS I NEVER DID AND TWISTED THE VERY CYCLE OF LIFE AND DEATH.

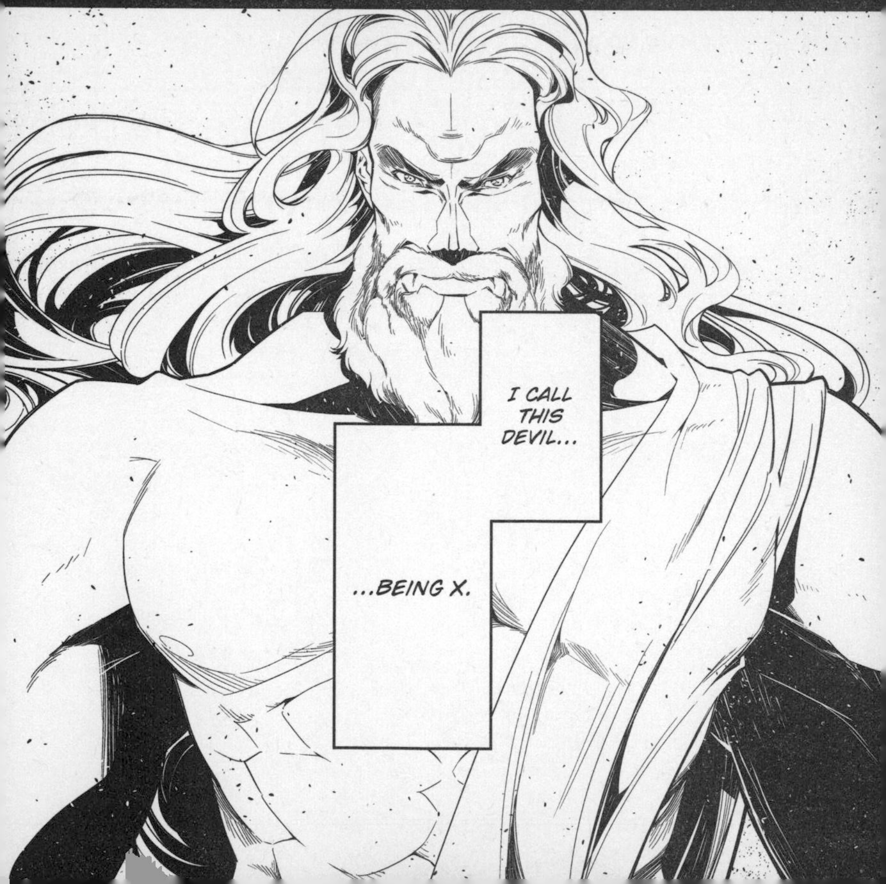
I CALL THIS DEVIL...
...BEING X.

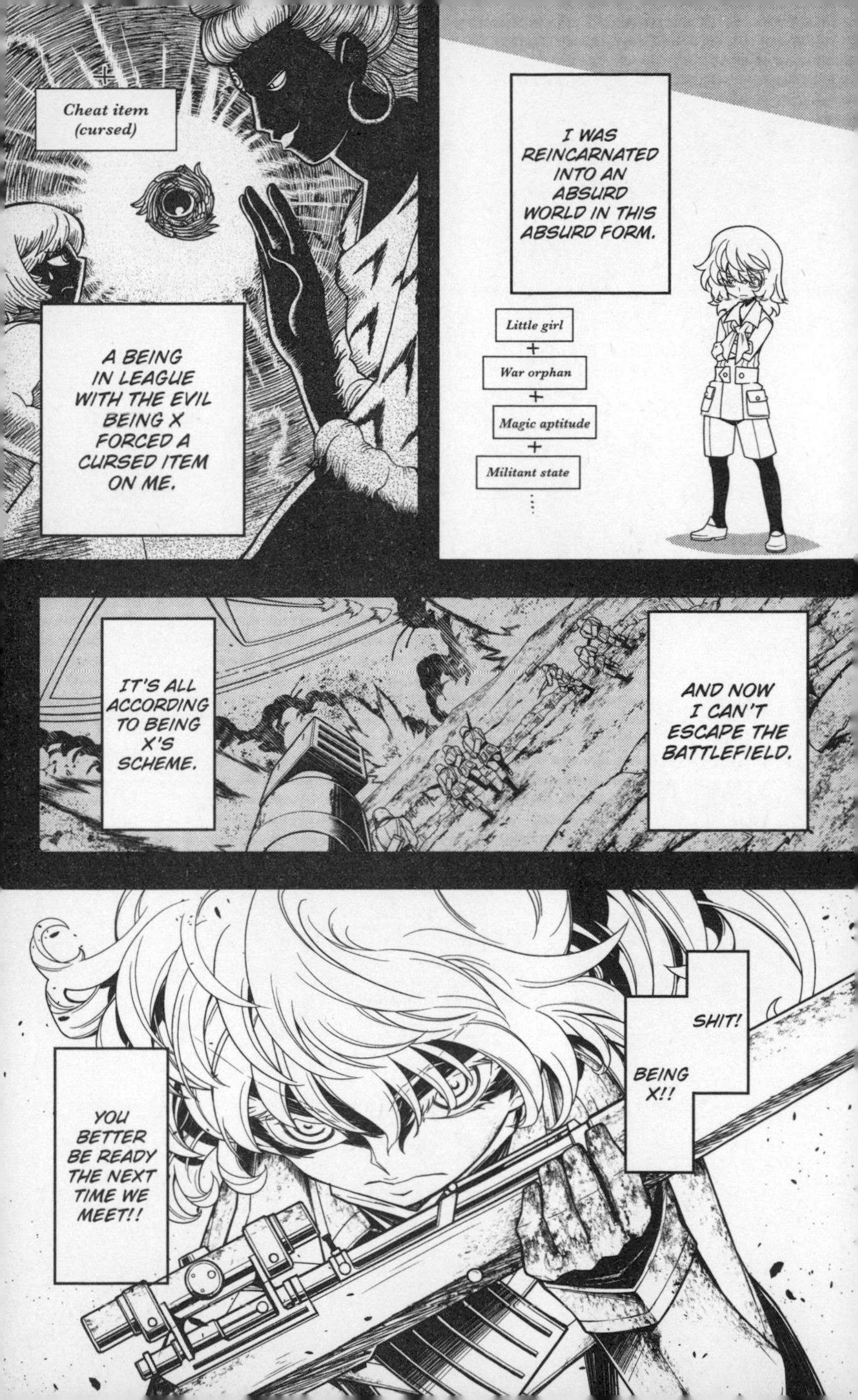
I WAS REINCARNATED INTO AN ABSURD WORLD IN THIS ABSURD FORM.
Little girl
+
War orphan
+
Magic aptitude
+
Militant state
...
Cheat item (cursed)
A BEING IN LEAGUE WITH THE EVIL BEING X FORCED A CURSED ITEM ON ME.
AND NOW I CAN'T ESCAPE THE BATTLEFIELD.
IT'S ALL ACCORDING TO BEING X'S SCHEME.
SHIT!
BEING X!!
YOU BETTER BE READY THE NEXT TIME WE MEET!!

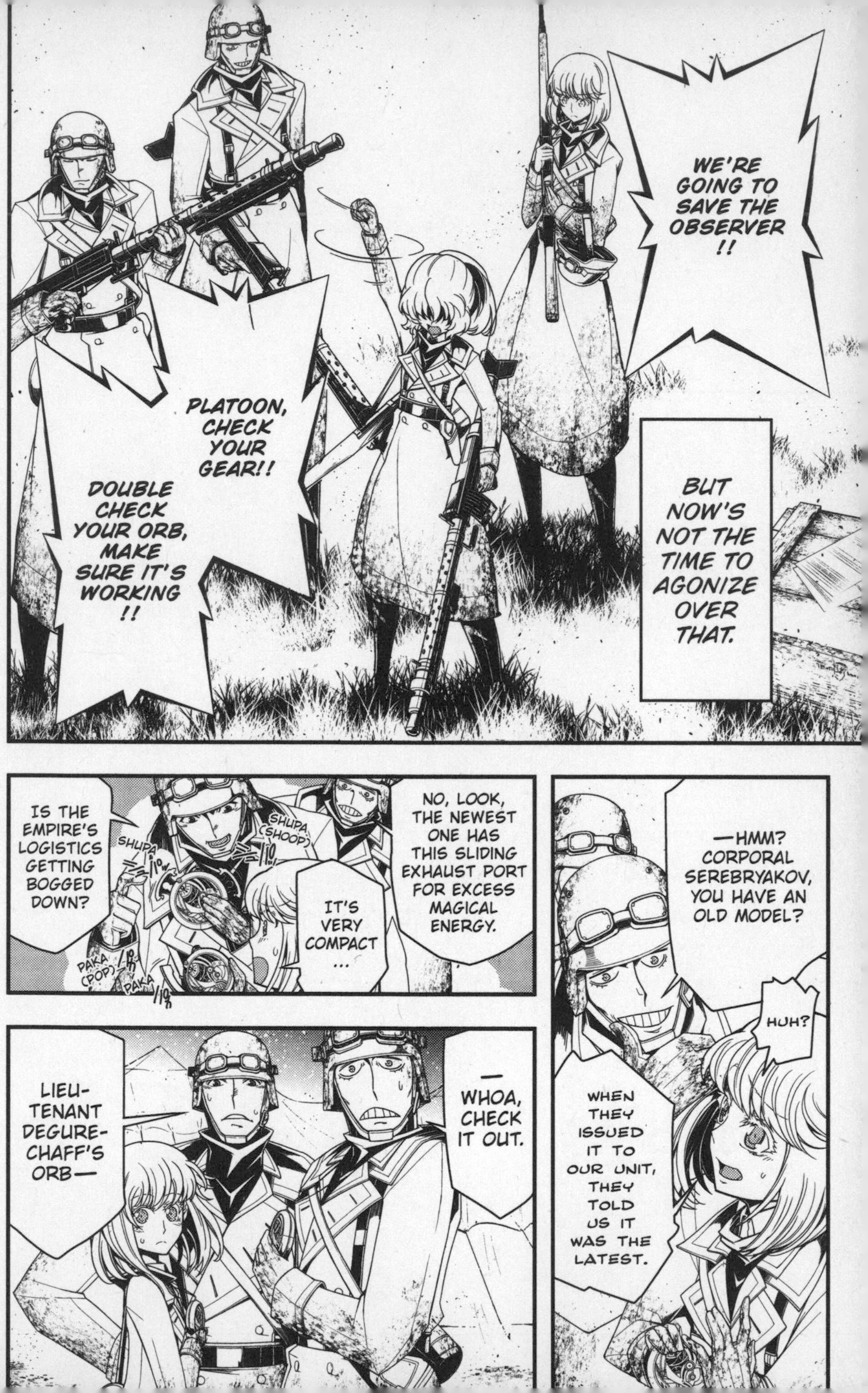
WE'RE GOING TO SAVE THE OBSERVER!!
BUT NOW'S NOT THE TIME TO AGONIZE OVER THAT.
PLATOON, CHECK YOUR GEAR!!
DOUBLE CHECK YOUR ORB, MAKE SURE IT'S WORKING!!
—HMM? CORPORAL SEREBRYAKOV, YOU HAVE AN OLD MODEL?
HUH?
WHEN THEY ISSUED IT TO OUR UNIT, THEY TOLD US IT WAS THE LATEST.
NO, LOOK, THE NEWEST ONE HAS THIS SLIDING EXHAUST PORT FOR EXCESS MAGICAL ENERGY.
SHUPA (SHOOP)
IT'S VERY COMPACT...
IS THE EMPIRE'S LOGISTICS GETTING BOGGED DOWN?
SHUPA
PAKA (POP)
PAKA
—WHOA, CHECK IT OUT.
LIEUTENANT DEGURECHAFF'S ORB—

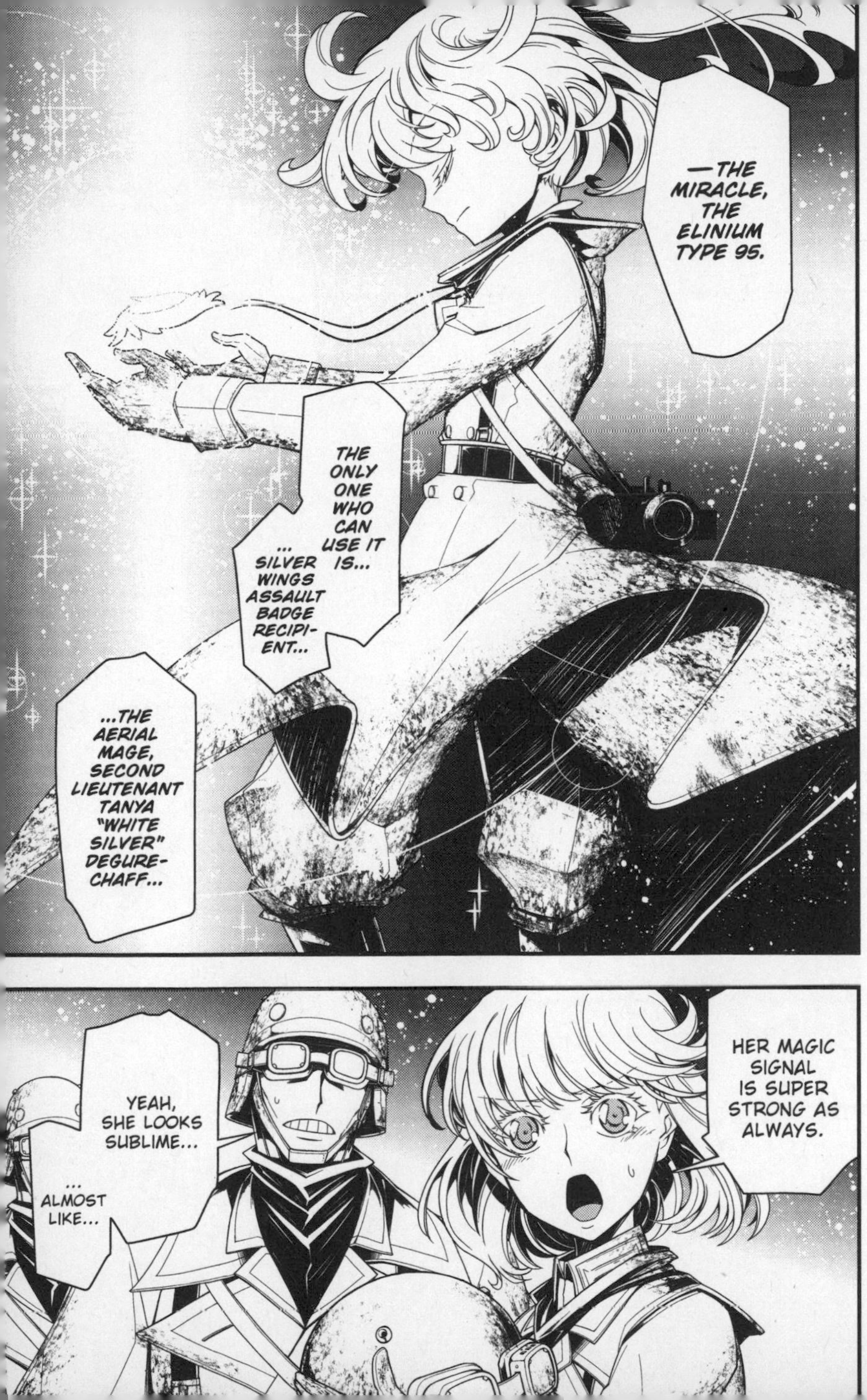
—THE MIRACLE, THE ELINIUM TYPE 95.
THE ONLY ONE WHO CAN USE IT IS...
...SILVER WINGS ASSAULT BADGE RECIPIENT...
...THE AERIAL MAGE, SECOND LIEUTENANT TANYA "WHITE SILVER" DEGURECHAFF...
HER MAGIC SIGNAL IS SUPER STRONG AS ALWAYS.
YEAH, SHE LOOKS SUBLIME...
...ALMOST LIKE...

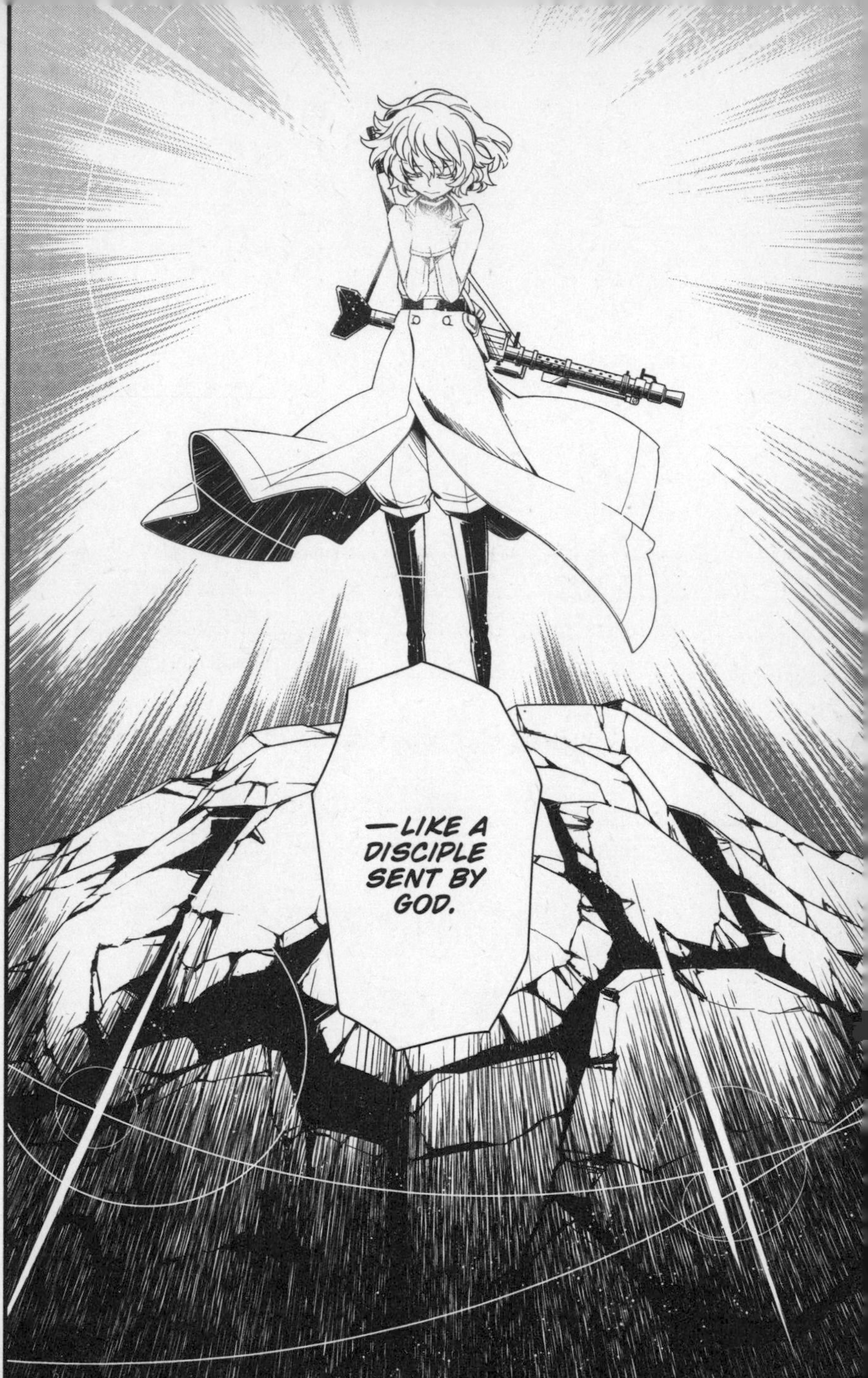
—LIKE A DISCIPLE SENT BY GOD.

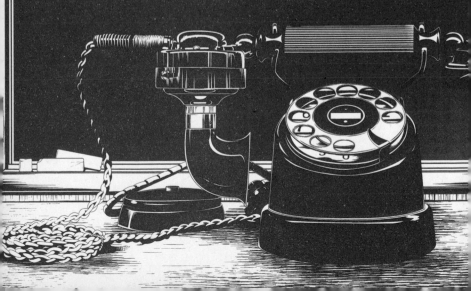

Chapter 5 Guarding the Rhine III

The Saga of Tanya the Evil

Chapter: 05

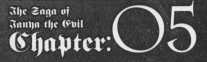

[redacted]th, Unified Year 1923: Magic Second Lieutenant Tanya Degurechaff is released from her duty of assisting with the development of a new orb and transferred to the 205th Mage Company in the west.

[redacted]h: Becomes leader of the Third Platoon. Works to train her platoon members in the thick of it. Achieves much on the western front. Forty enemies downed to date (not counting unconfirmed victories).

Today, [redacted]h: She takes her platoon on a detached mission.

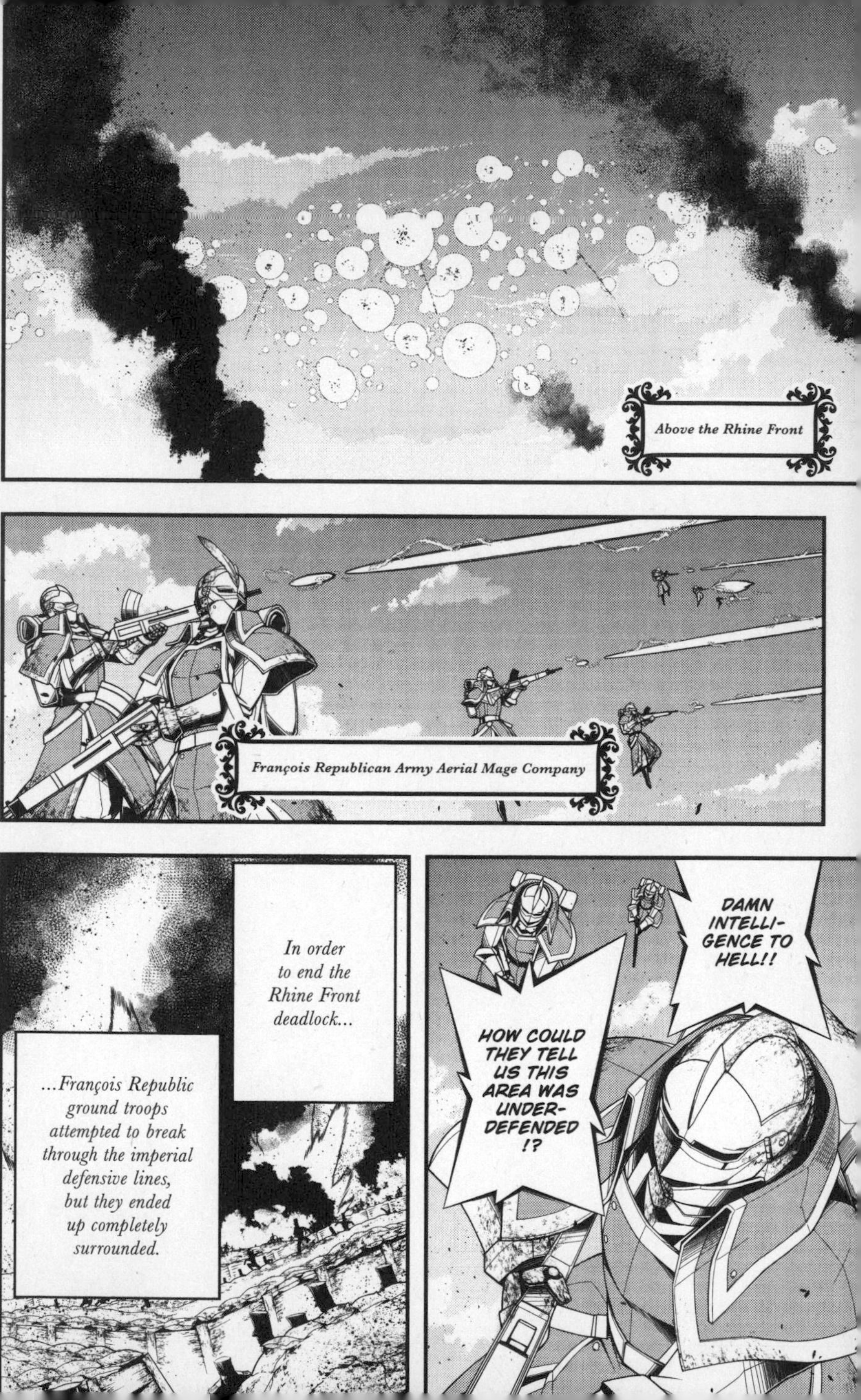
Above the Rhine Front
François Republican Army Aerial Mage Company
DAMN INTELLI-GENCE TO HELL!!
HOW COULD THEY TELL US THIS AREA WAS UNDER-DEFENDED!?
In order to end the Rhine Front deadlock...
...François Republic ground troops attempted to break through the imperial defensive lines, but they ended up completely surrounded.

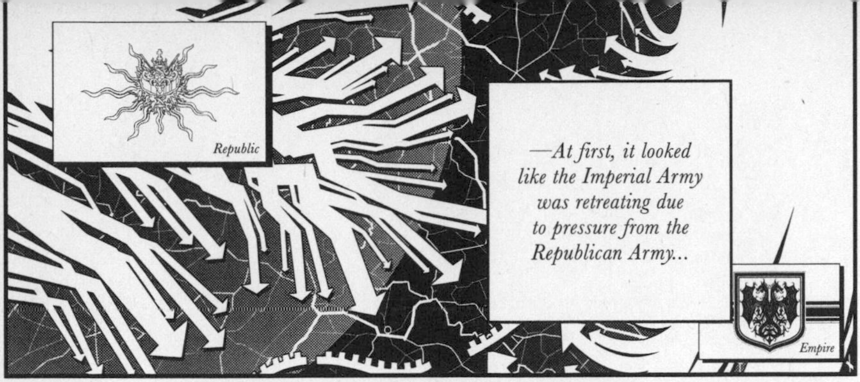
—At first, it looked like the Imperial Army was retreating due to pressure from the Republican Army...
Republic
Empire

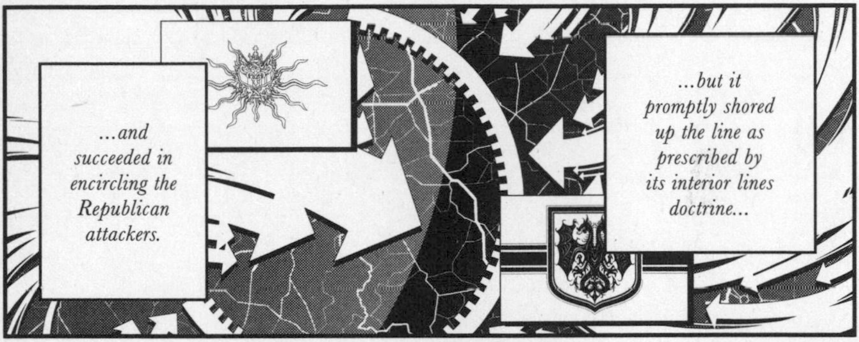
...but it promptly shored up the line as prescribed by its interior lines doctrine...
...and succeeded in encircling the Republican attackers.

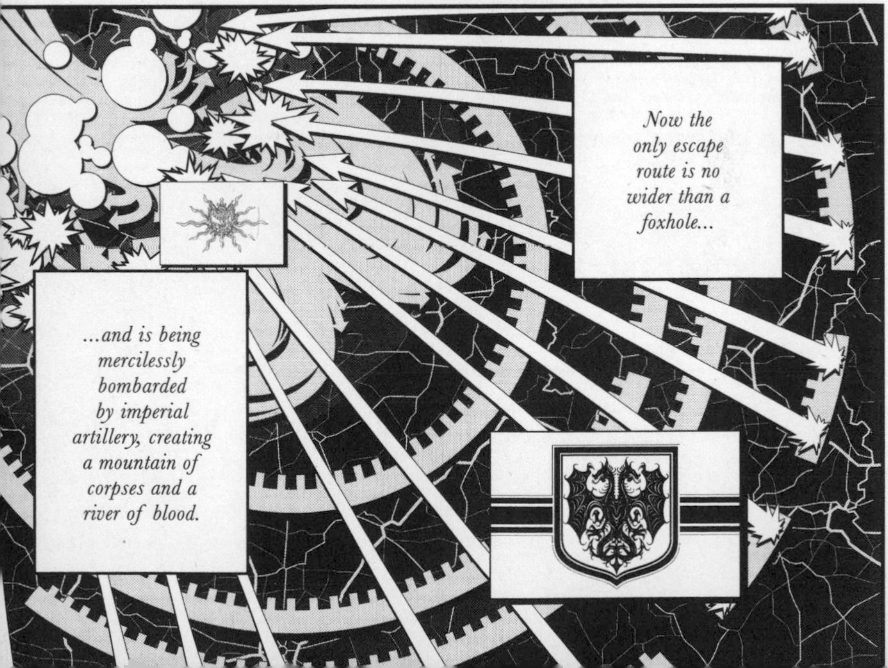
Now the only escape route is no wider than a foxhole...
...and is being mercilessly bombarded by imperial artillery, creating a mountain of corpses and a river of blood.

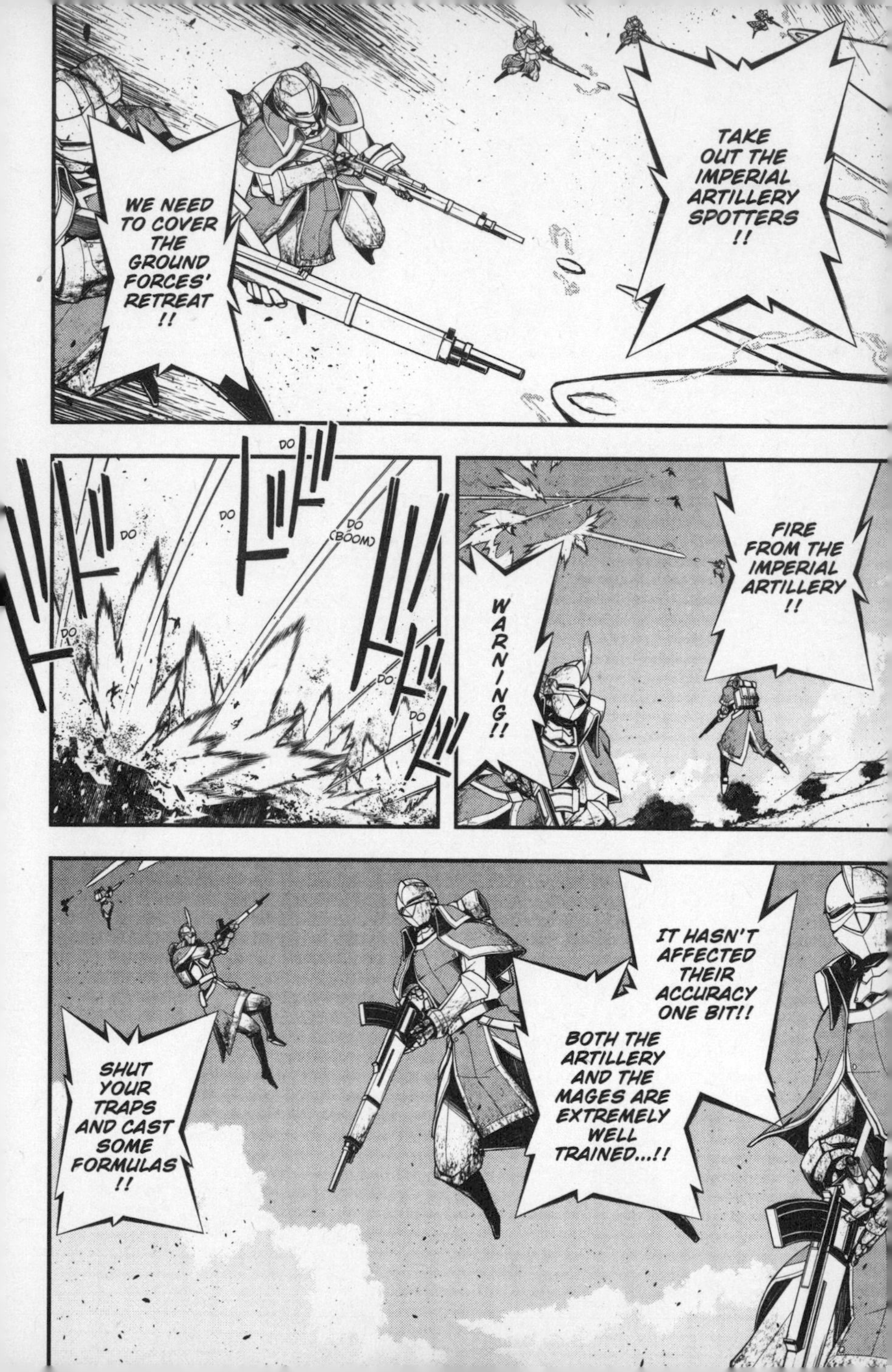
TAKE OUT THE IMPERIAL ARTILLERY SPOTTERS!!
WE NEED TO COVER THE GROUND FORCES' RETREAT!!
FIRE FROM THE IMPERIAL ARTILLERY!!
WARNING!!
DO
DO
DO (BOOM)
DO
DO
DO
DO
IT HASN'T AFFECTED THEIR ACCURACY ONE BIT!!
BOTH THE ARTILLERY AND THE MAGES ARE EXTREMELY WELL TRAINED...!!
SHUT YOUR TRAPS AND CAST SOME FORMULAS!!

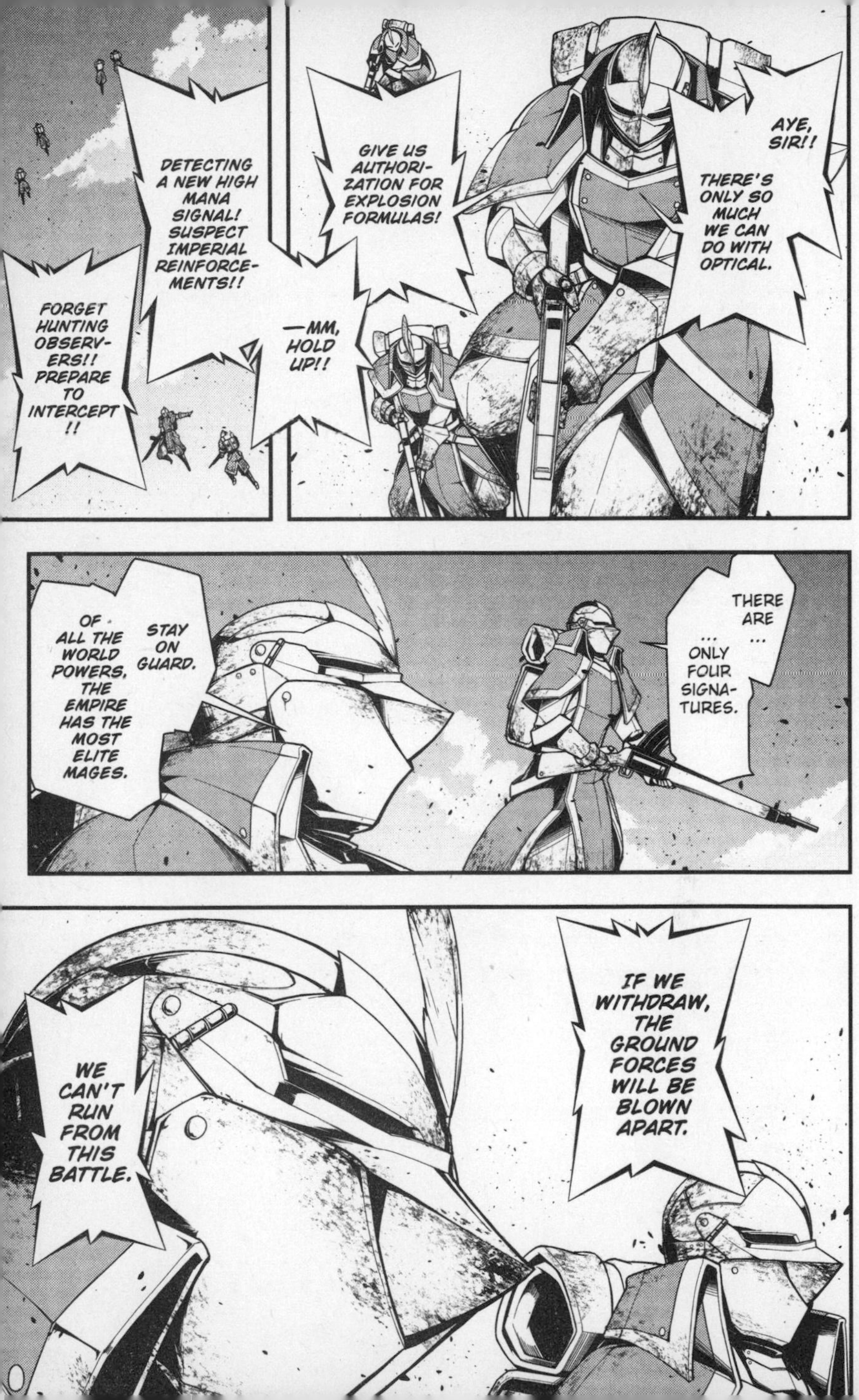
AYE, SIR!!
THERE'S ONLY SO MUCH WE CAN DO WITH OPTICAL.
GIVE US AUTHORIZATION FOR EXPLOSION FORMULAS!
—MM, HOLD UP!!
DETECTING A NEW HIGH MANA SIGNAL! SUSPECT IMPERIAL REINFORCEMENTS!!
FORGET HUNTING OBSERVERS!! PREPARE TO INTERCEPT!!
THERE ARE ... ... ONLY FOUR SIGNATURES.
STAY ON GUARD.
OF ALL THE WORLD POWERS, THE EMPIRE HAS THE MOST ELITE MAGES.
IF WE WITHDRAW, THE GROUND FORCES WILL BE BLOWN APART.
WE CAN'T RUN FROM THIS BATTLE.

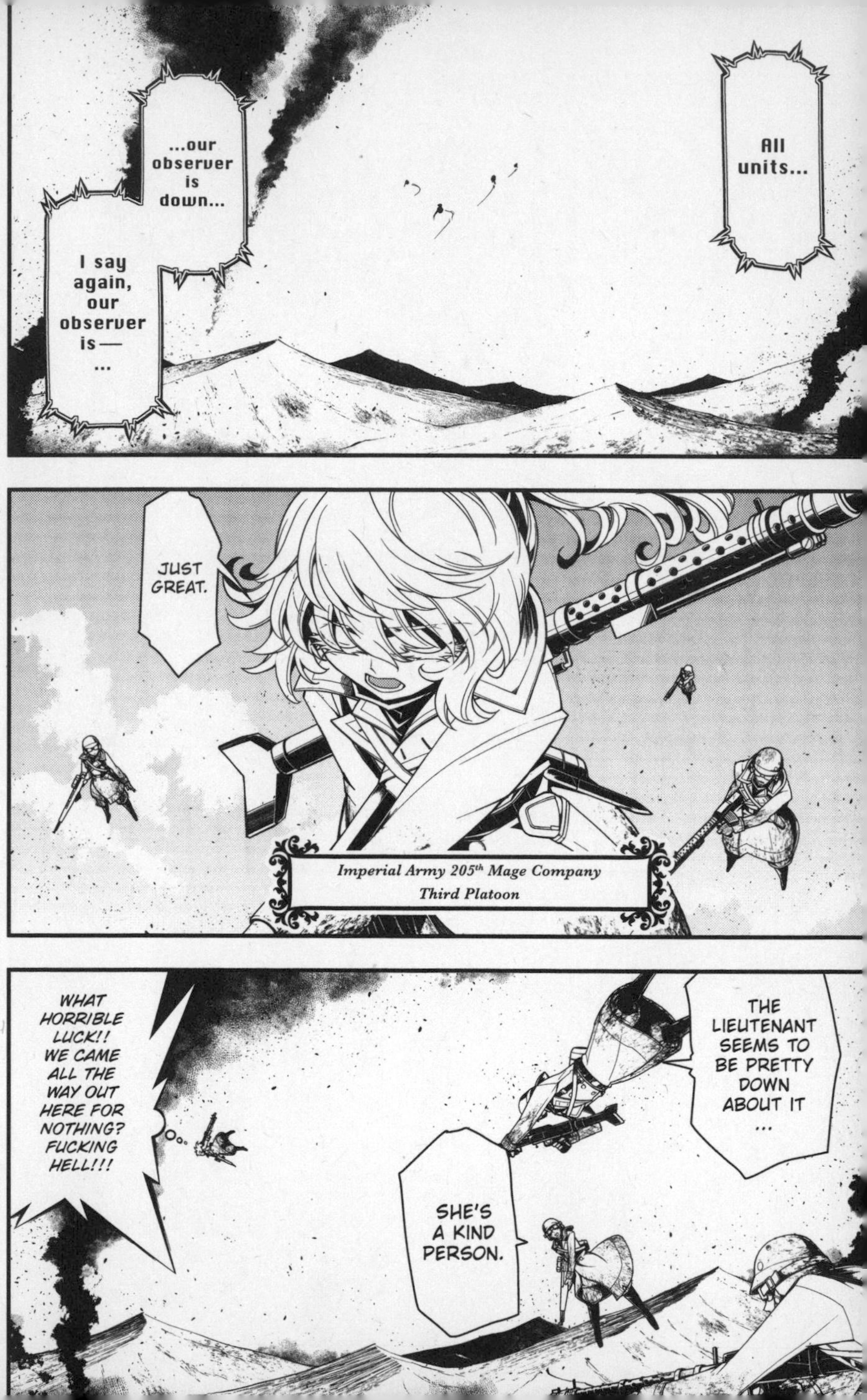
All units...
...our observer is down...
I say again, our observer is— ...
JUST GREAT.
Imperial Army 205th Mage Company
Third Platoon
THE LIEUTENANT SEEMS TO BE PRETTY DOWN ABOUT IT ...
WHAT HORRIBLE LUCK!! WE CAME ALL THE WAY OUT HERE FOR NOTHING? FUCKING HELL!!!
SHE'S A KIND PERSON.

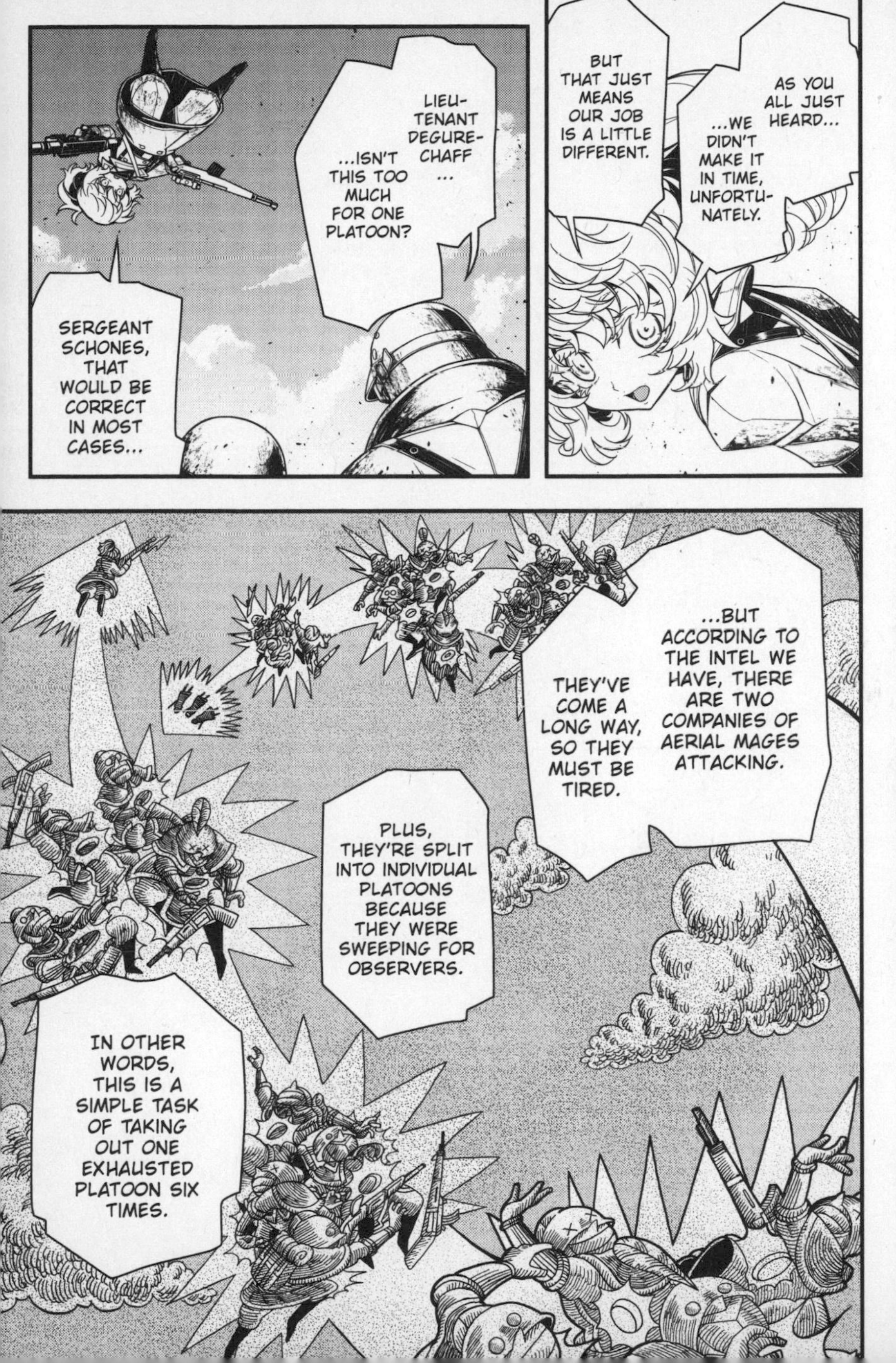
AS YOU ALL JUST HEARD...
...WE DIDN'T MAKE IT IN TIME, UNFORTUNATELY.
BUT THAT JUST MEANS OUR JOB IS A LITTLE DIFFERENT.
LIEU-TENANT DEGURE-CHAFF ...
...ISN'T THIS TOO MUCH FOR ONE PLATOON?
SERGEANT SCHONES, THAT WOULD BE CORRECT IN MOST CASES...
...BUT ACCORDING TO THE INTEL WE HAVE, THERE ARE TWO COMPANIES OF AERIAL MAGES ATTACKING.
THEY'VE COME A LONG WAY, SO THEY MUST BE TIRED.
PLUS, THEY'RE SPLIT INTO INDIVIDUAL PLATOONS BECAUSE THEY WERE SWEEPING FOR OBSERVERS.
IN OTHER WORDS, THIS IS A SIMPLE TASK OF TAKING OUT ONE EXHAUSTED PLATOON SIX TIMES.

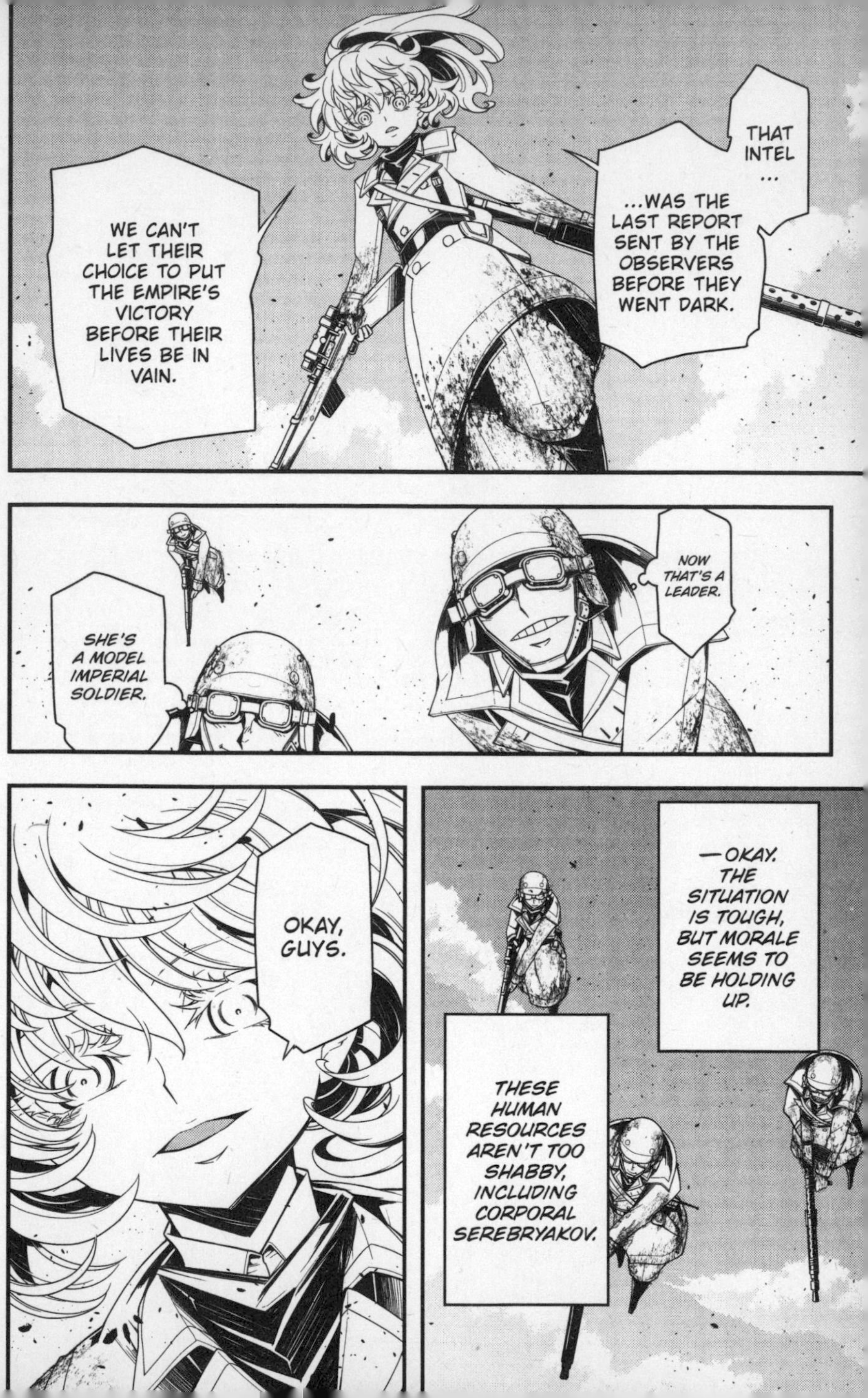
THAT INTEL ...
...WAS THE LAST REPORT SENT BY THE OBSERVERS BEFORE THEY WENT DARK.
WE CAN'T LET THEIR CHOICE TO PUT THE EMPIRE'S VICTORY BEFORE THEIR LIVES BE IN VAIN.
NOW THAT'S A LEADER.
SHE'S A MODEL IMPERIAL SOLDIER.
—OKAY. THE SITUATION IS TOUGH, BUT MORALE SEEMS TO BE HOLDING UP.
THESE HUMAN RESOURCES AREN'T TOO SHABBY, INCLUDING CORPORAL SEREBRYAKOV.
OKAY, GUYS.

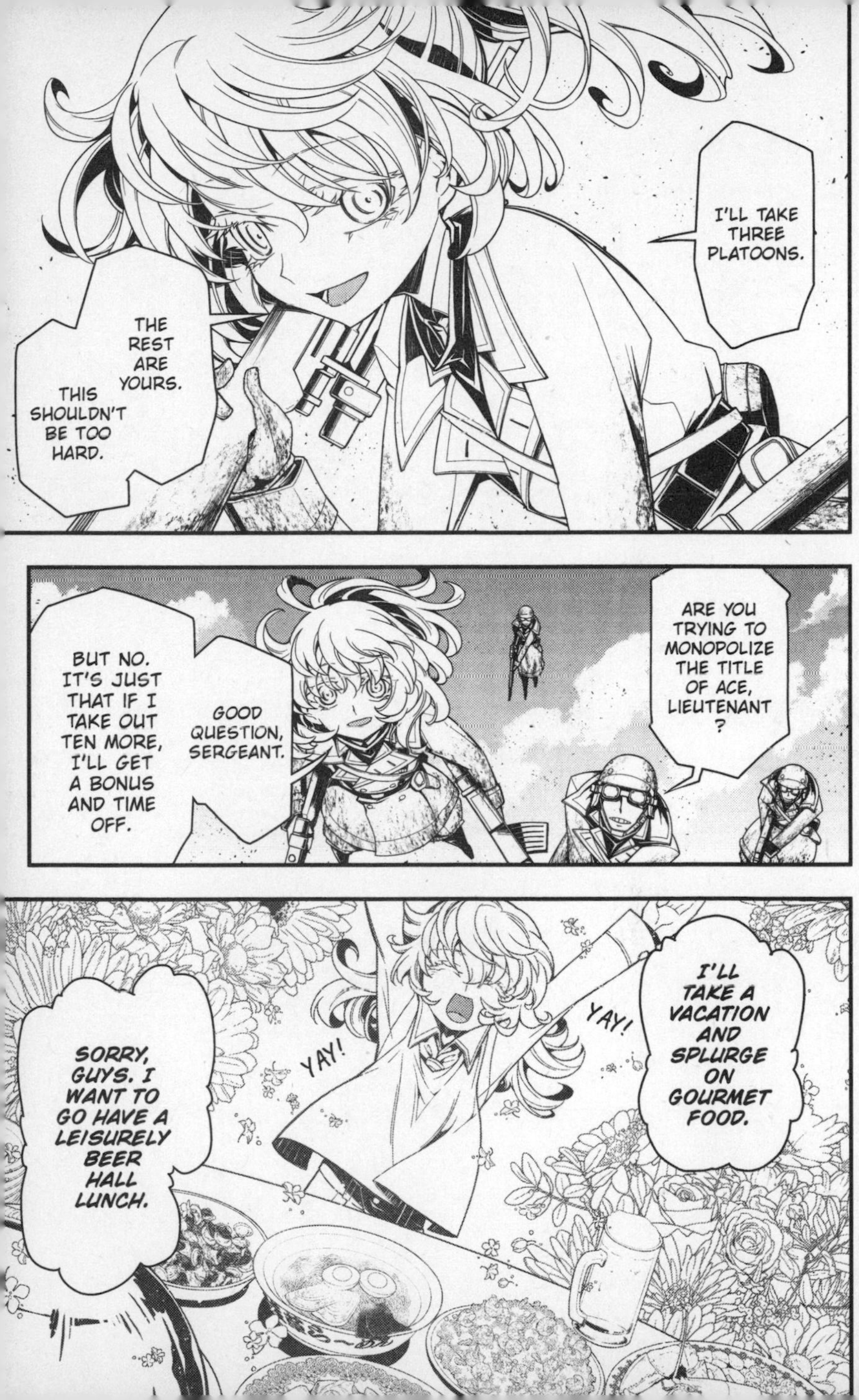
I'LL TAKE THREE PLATOONS.
THE REST ARE YOURS.
THIS SHOULDN'T BE TOO HARD.
ARE YOU TRYING TO MONOPOLIZE THE TITLE OF ACE, LIEUTENANT?
GOOD QUESTION, SERGEANT.
BUT NO. IT'S JUST THAT IF I TAKE OUT TEN MORE, I'LL GET A BONUS AND TIME OFF.
I'LL TAKE A VACATION AND SPLURGE ON GOURMET FOOD.
YAY!
YAY!
SORRY, GUYS. I WANT TO GO HAVE A LEISURELY BEER HALL LUNCH.

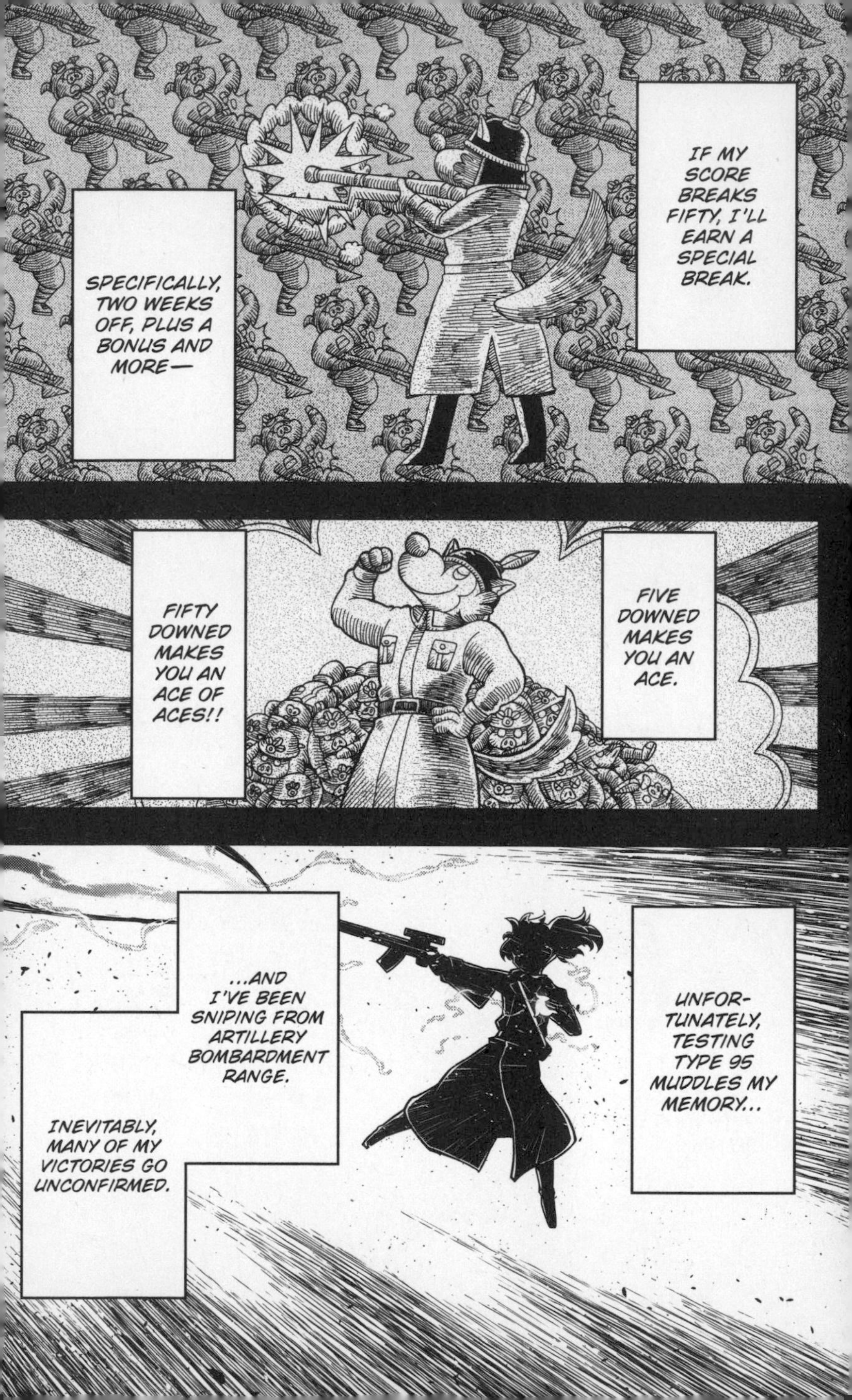
IF MY SCORE BREAKS FIFTY, I'LL EARN A SPECIAL BREAK.
SPECIFICALLY, TWO WEEKS OFF, PLUS A BONUS AND MORE—
FIVE DOWNED MAKES YOU AN ACE.
FIFTY DOWNED MAKES YOU AN ACE OF ACES!!
UNFOR-TUNATELY, TESTING TYPE 95 MUDDLES MY MEMORY...
...AND I'VE BEEN SNIPING FROM ARTILLERY BOMBARDMENT RANGE.
INEVITABLY, MANY OF MY VICTORIES GO UNCONFIRMED.

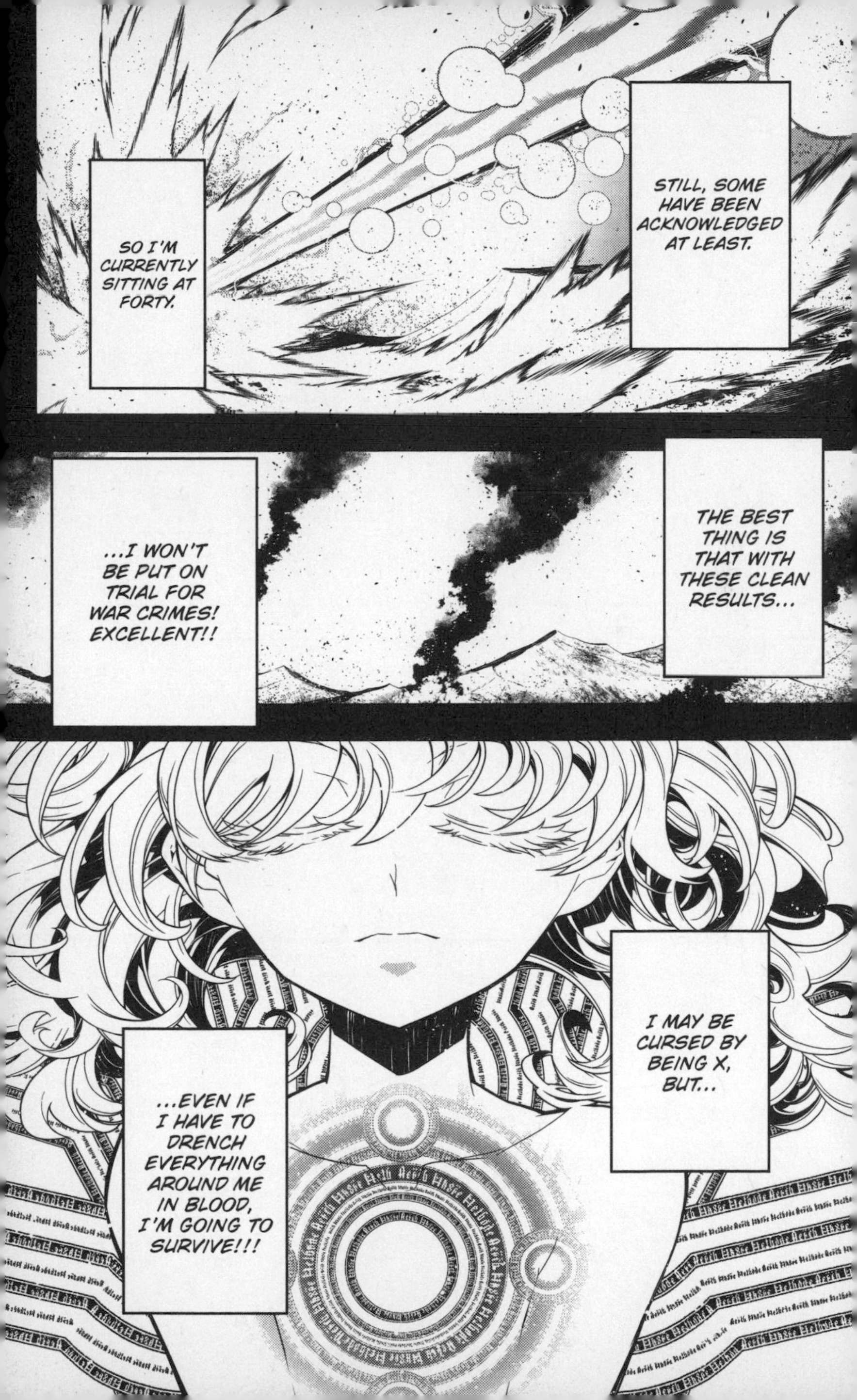
STILL, SOME HAVE BEEN ACKNOWLEDGED AT LEAST.
SO I'M CURRENTLY SITTING AT FORTY.
THE BEST THING IS THAT WITH THESE CLEAN RESULTS...
...I WON'T BE PUT ON TRIAL FOR WAR CRIMES! EXCELLENT!!
I MAY BE CURSED BY BEING X, BUT...
...EVEN IF I HAVE TO DRENCH EVERYTHING AROUND ME IN BLOOD, I'M GOING TO SURVIVE!!!

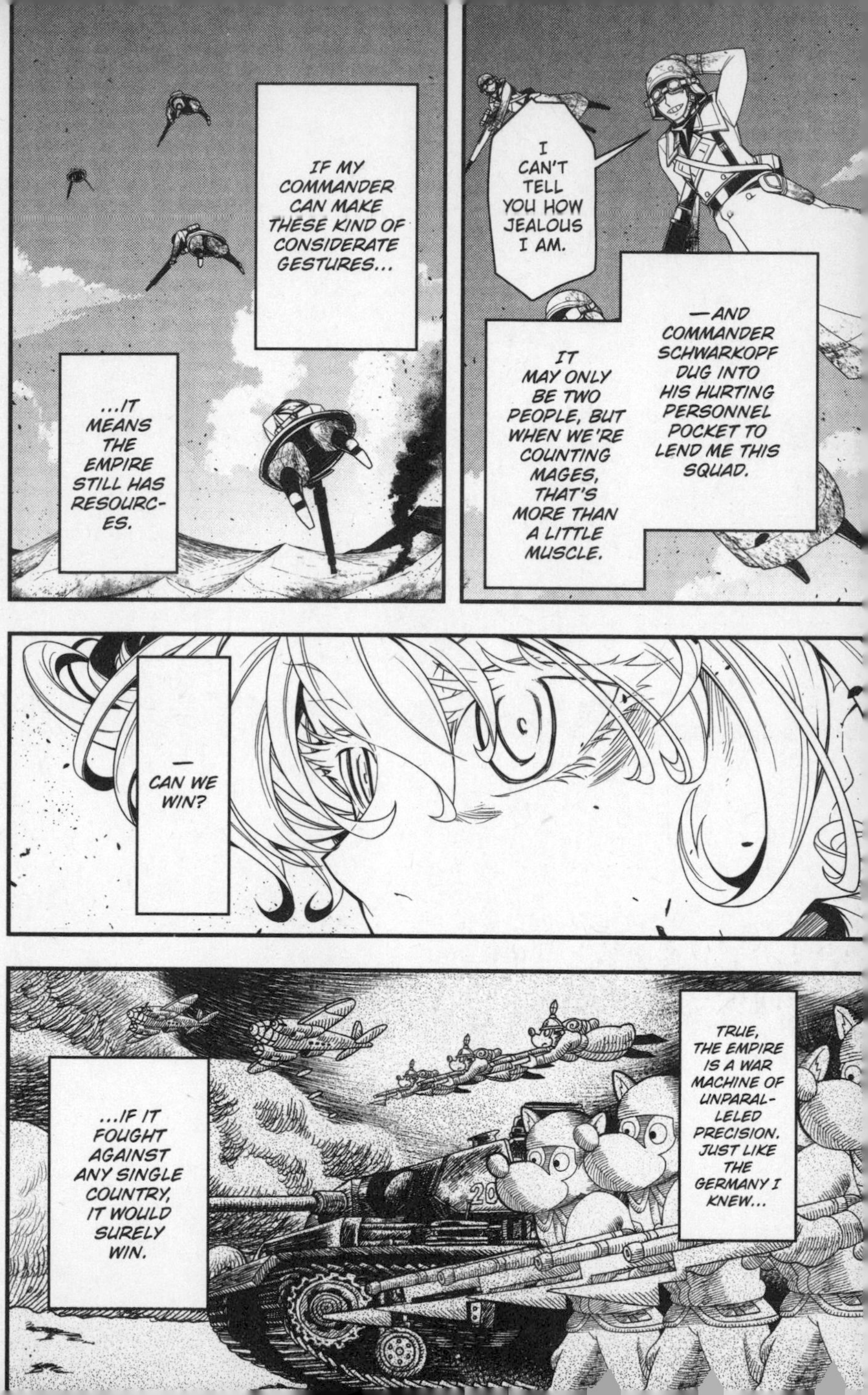
I CAN'T TELL YOU HOW JEALOUS I AM.
—AND COMMANDER SCHWARKOPF DUG INTO HIS HURTING PERSONNEL POCKET TO LEND ME THIS SQUAD.
IT MAY ONLY BE TWO PEOPLE, BUT WHEN WE'RE COUNTING MAGES, THAT'S MORE THAN A LITTLE MUSCLE.
IF MY COMMANDER CAN MAKE THESE KIND OF CONSIDERATE GESTURES...
...IT MEANS THE EMPIRE STILL HAS RESOURC-ES.
— CAN WE WIN?
TRUE, THE EMPIRE IS A WAR MACHINE OF UNPARAL-LELED PRECISION. JUST LIKE THE GERMANY I KNEW...
...IF IT FOUGHT AGAINST ANY SINGLE COUNTRY, IT WOULD SURELY WIN.

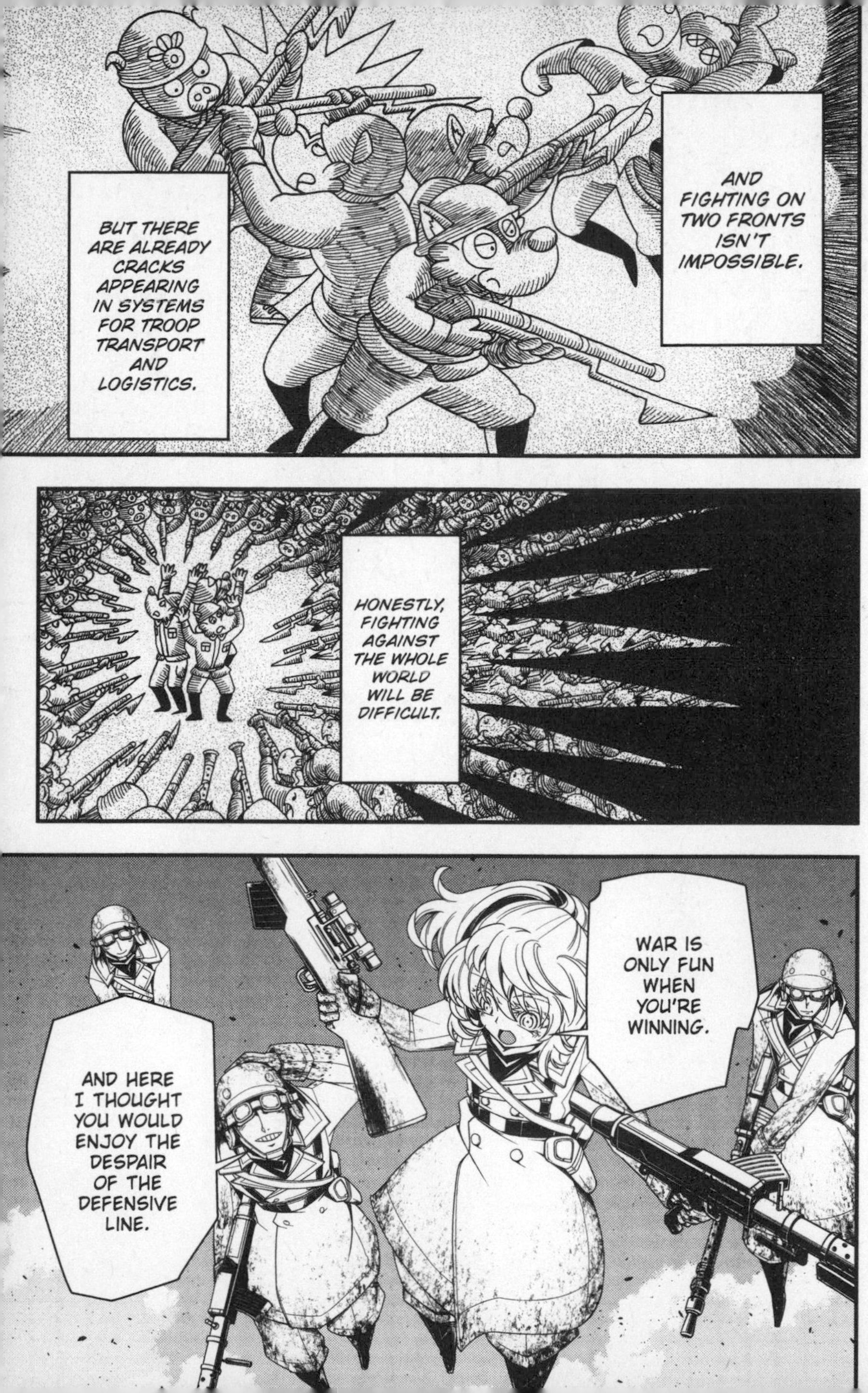
AND FIGHTING ON TWO FRONTS ISN'T IMPOSSIBLE.
BUT THERE ARE ALREADY CRACKS APPEARING IN SYSTEMS FOR TROOP TRANSPORT AND LOGISTICS.
HONESTLY, FIGHTING AGAINST THE WHOLE WORLD WILL BE DIFFICULT.
WAR IS ONLY FUN WHEN YOU'RE WINNING.
AND HERE I THOUGHT YOU WOULD ENJOY THE DESPAIR OF THE DEFENSIVE LINE.

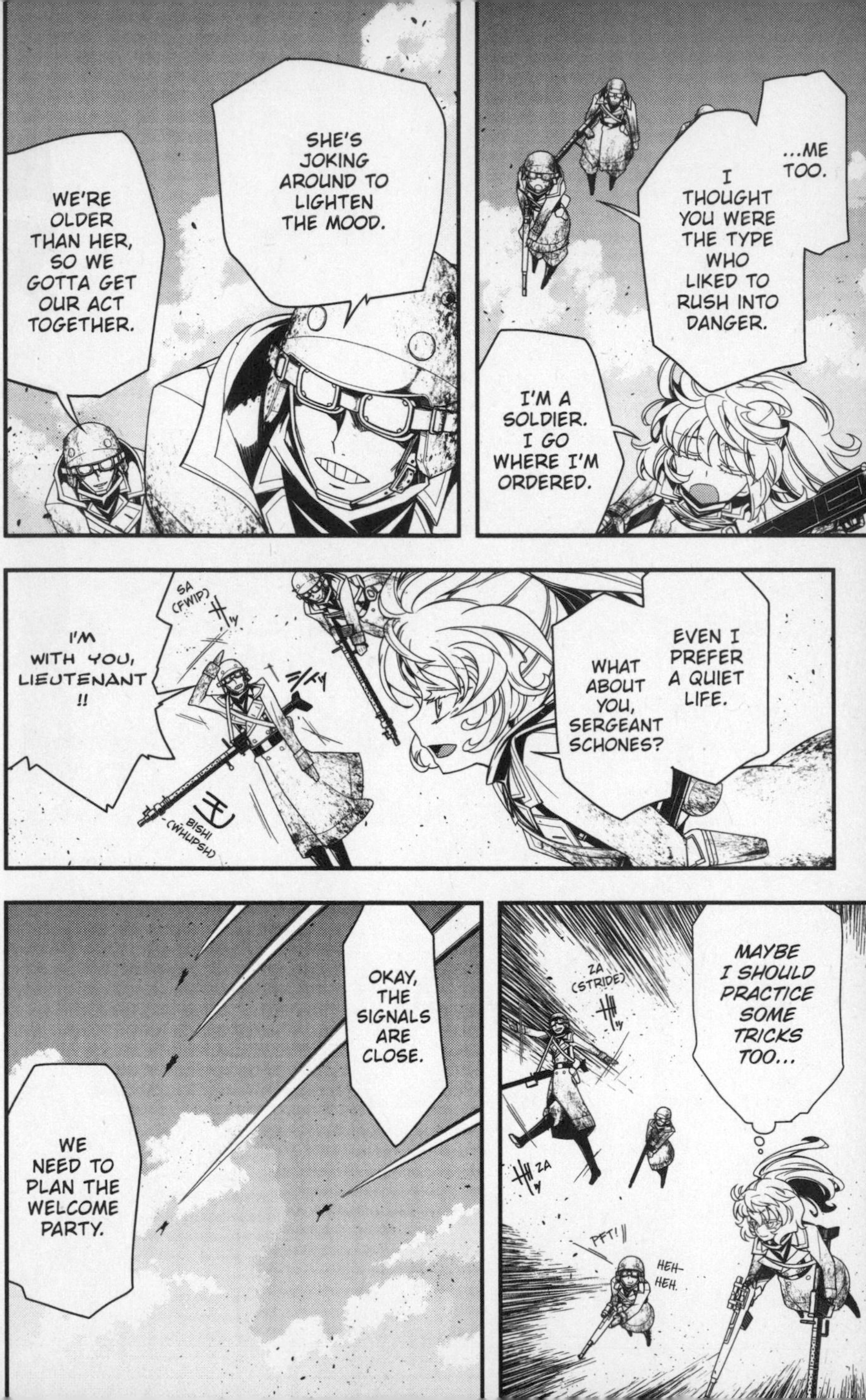
...ME TOO.
I THOUGHT YOU WERE THE TYPE WHO LIKED TO RUSH INTO DANGER.
I'M A SOLDIER. I GO WHERE I'M ORDERED.
SHE'S JOKING AROUND TO LIGHTEN THE MOOD.
WE'RE OLDER THAN HER, SO WE GOTTA GET OUR ACT TOGETHER.
EVEN I PREFER A QUIET LIFE.
WHAT ABOUT YOU, SERGEANT SCHONES?
SA (FWIP)
I'M WITH YOU, LIEUTENANT!!
BISHI (WHUPSH)
MAYBE I SHOULD PRACTICE SOME TRICKS TOO...
ZA (STRIDE)
ZA
HEH-HEH.
PFT!!
OKAY, THE SIGNALS ARE CLOSE.
WE NEED TO PLAN THE WELCOME PARTY.

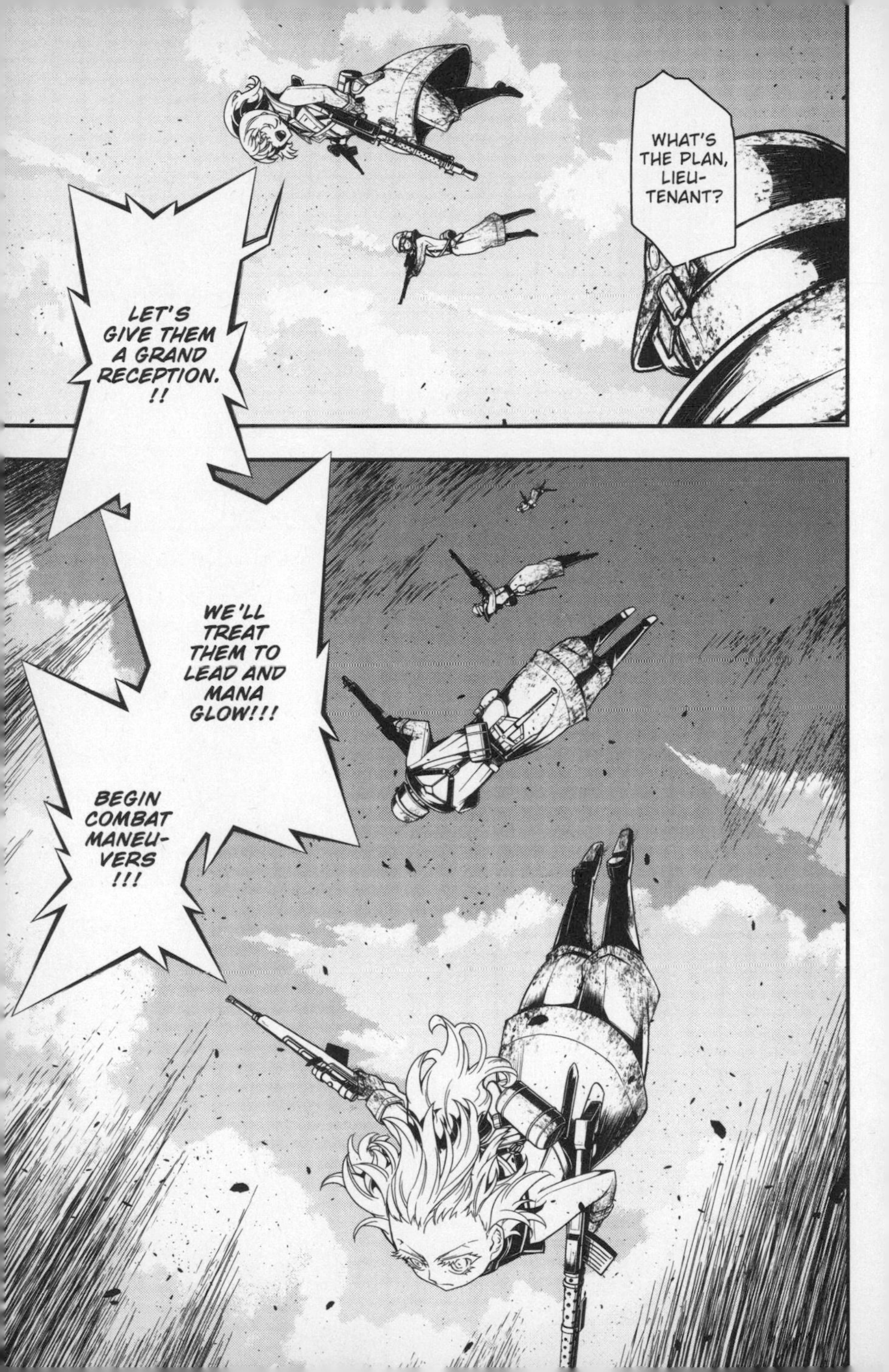
WHAT'S THE PLAN, LIEU-TENANT?
LET'S GIVE THEM A GRAND RECEPTION. !!
WE'LL TREAT THEM TO LEAD AND MANA GLOW!!!
BEGIN COMBAT MANEU-VERS!!!

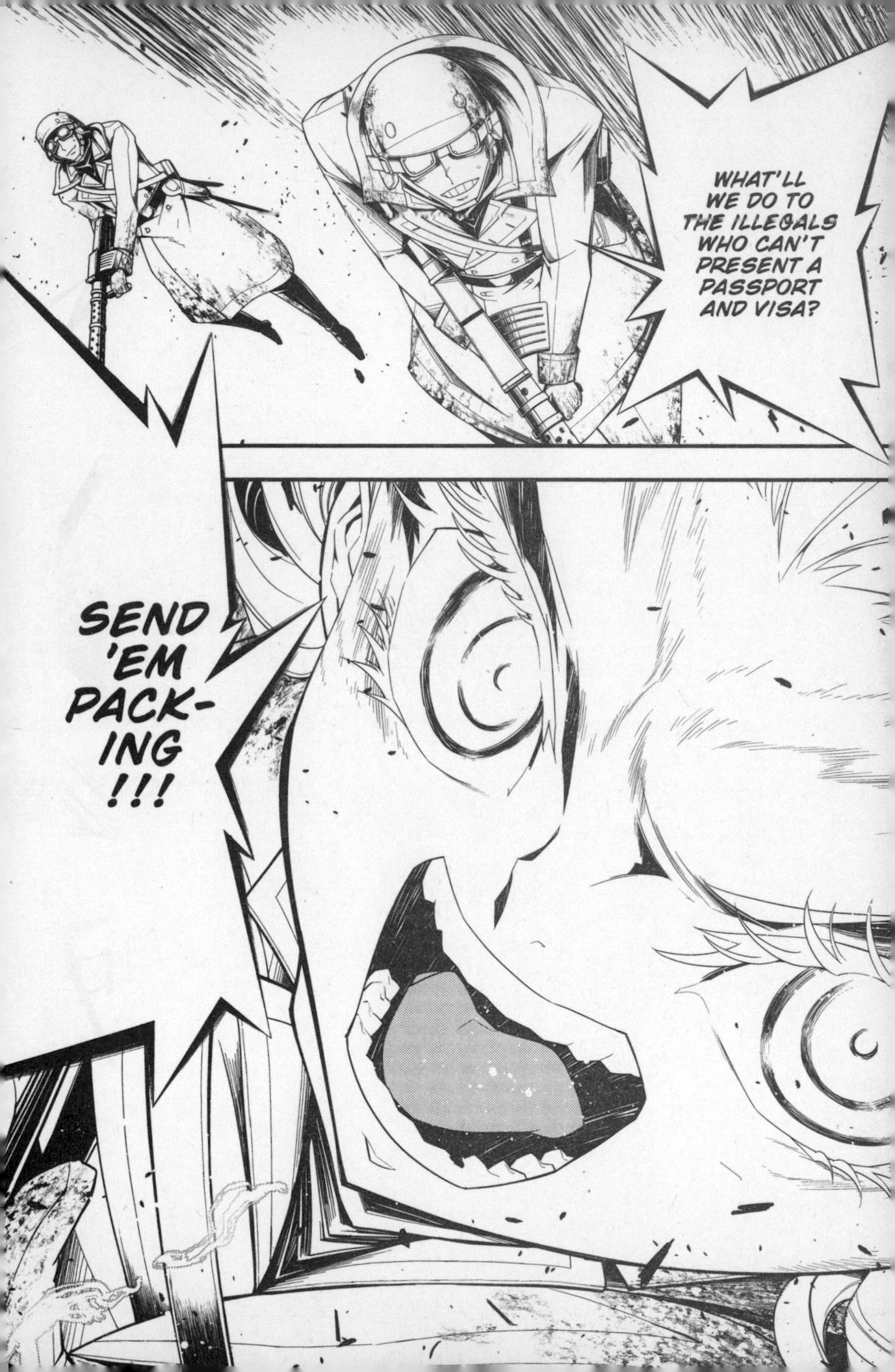
WHAT'LL WE DO TO THE ILLEGALS WHO CAN'T PRESENT A PASSPORT AND VISA?
SEND 'EM PACK-ING!!!

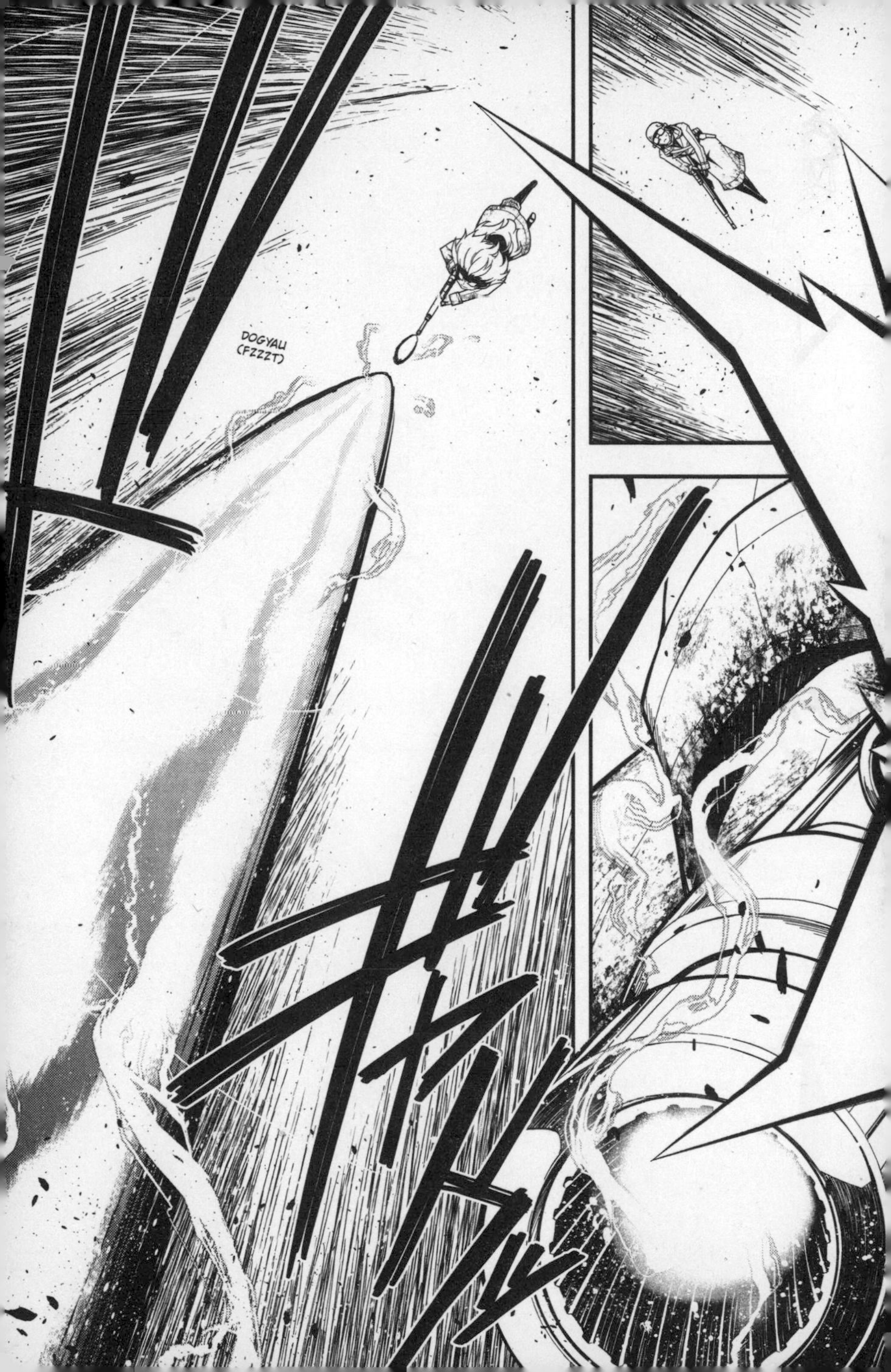
DOGYAU
(FZZZT)

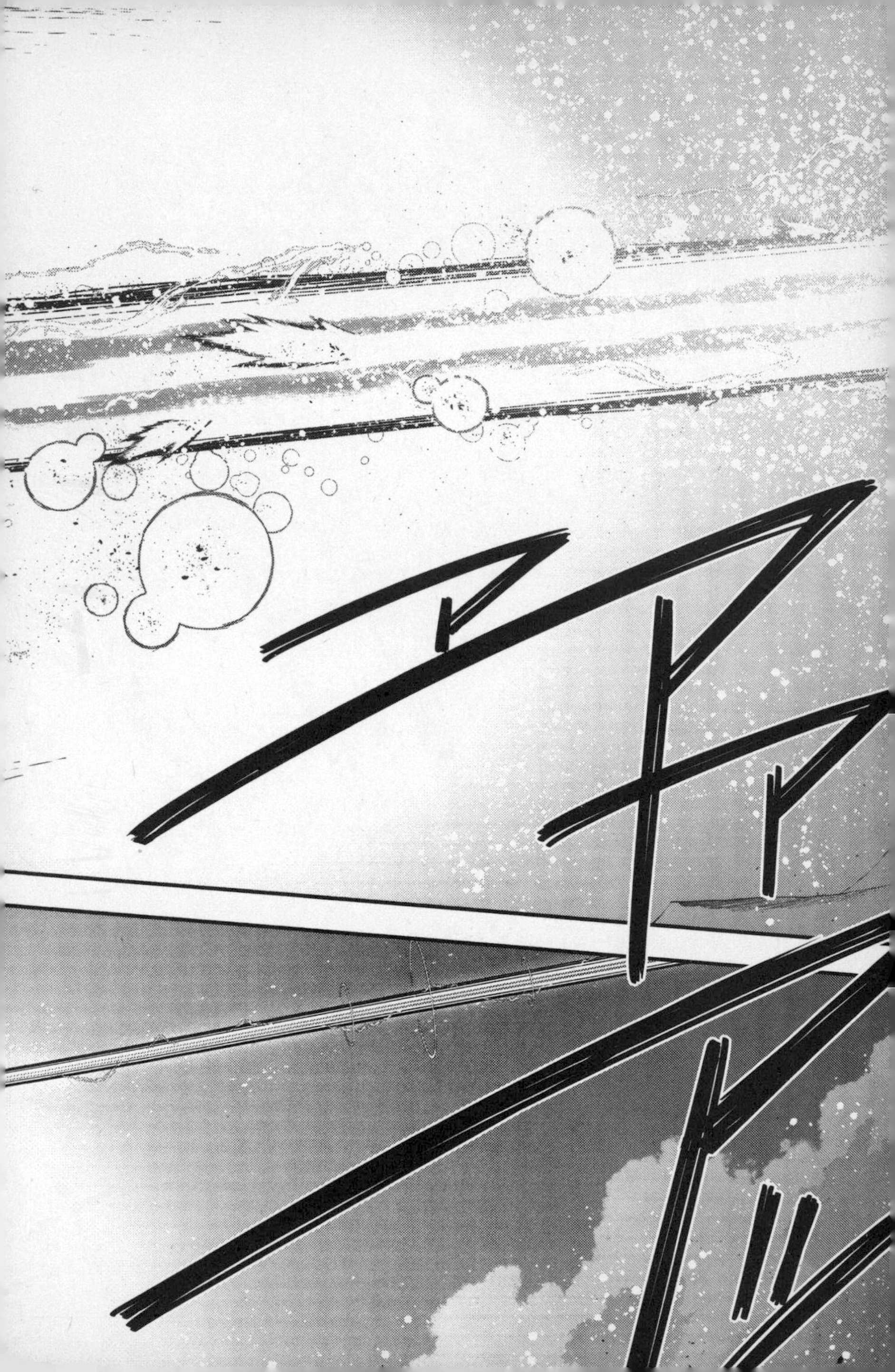

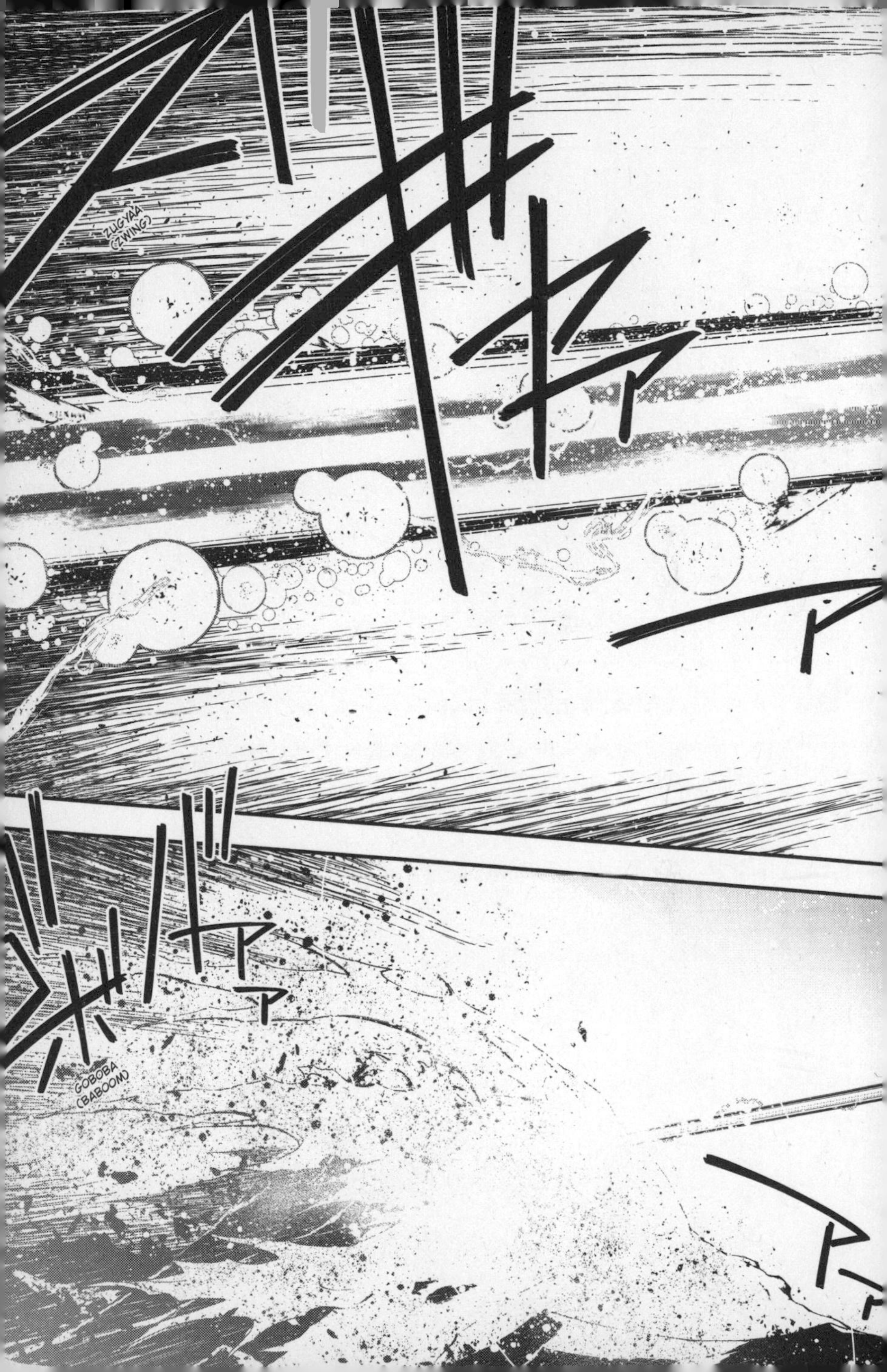
ZUGYAA
(ZWING)
GOBOBA
(BABOOM)

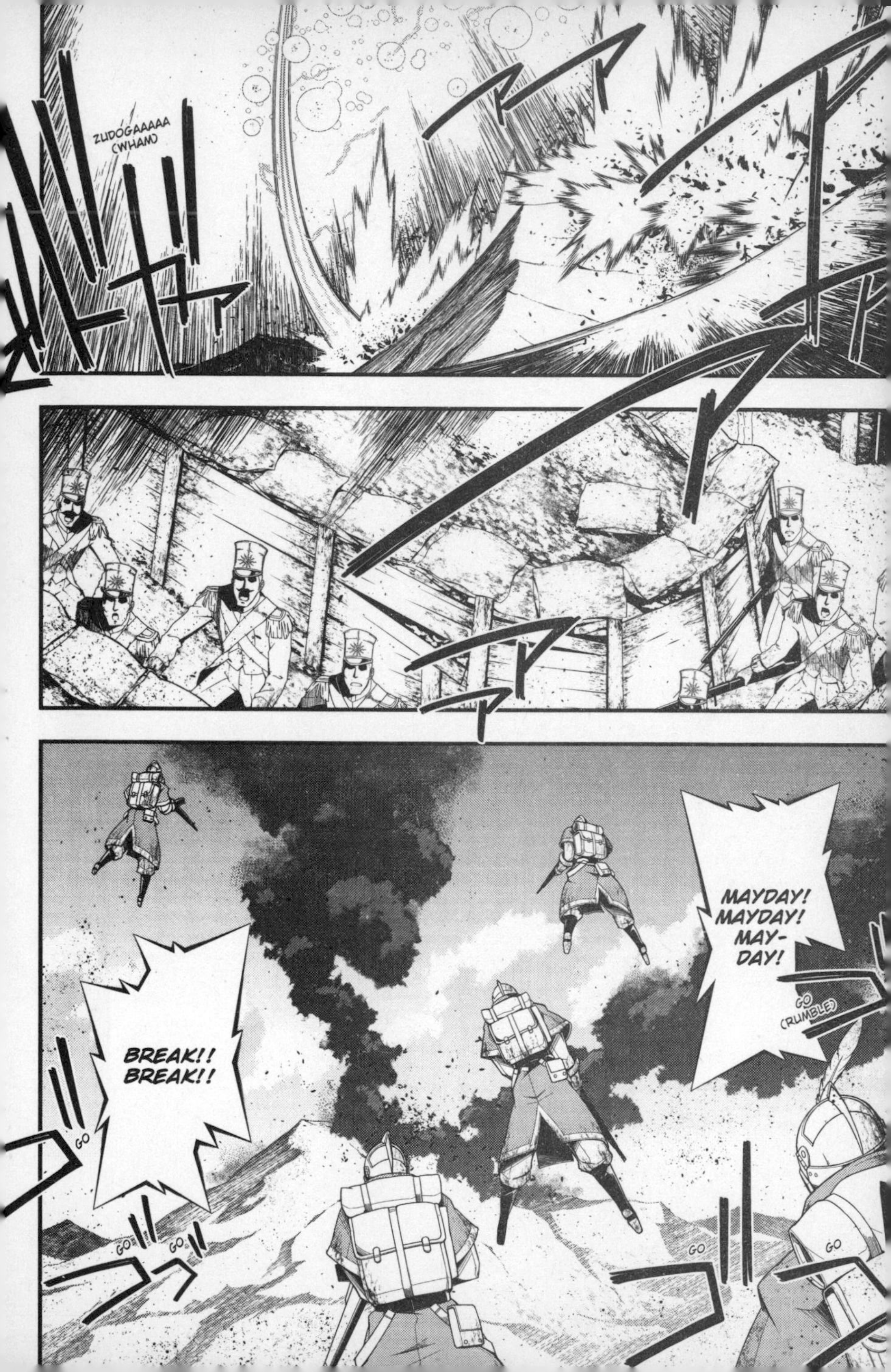
ZUDOGAAAAA
(WHAM)
MAYDAY! MAYDAY! MAY-DAY!
GO
(RUMBLE)
BREAK!! BREAK!!
GO
GO
GO
GO
GO

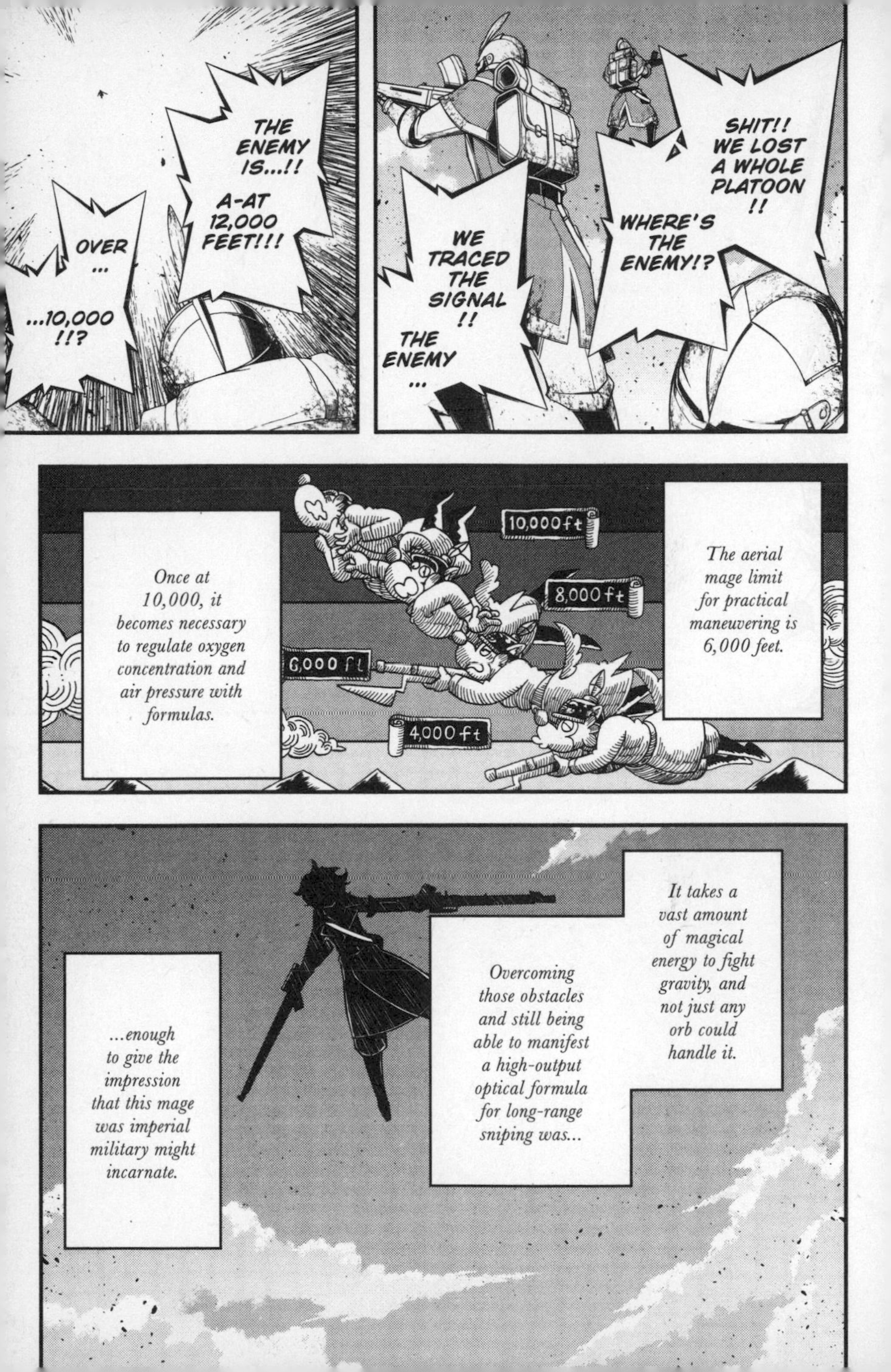
SHIT!! WE LOST A WHOLE PLATOON!!
WHERE'S THE ENEMY!?
WE TRACED THE SIGNAL!!
THE ENEMY...
THE ENEMY IS...!!
A-AT 12,000 FEET!!!
OVER...
...10,000!!?
The aerial mage limit for practical maneuvering is 6,000 feet.
10,000ft
8,000ft
6,000ft
4,000ft
Once at 10,000, it becomes necessary to regulate oxygen concentration and air pressure with formulas.
It takes a vast amount of magical energy to fight gravity, and not just any orb could handle it.
Overcoming those obstacles and still being able to manifest a high-output optical formula for long-range sniping was...
...enough to give the impression that this mage was imperial military might incarnate.

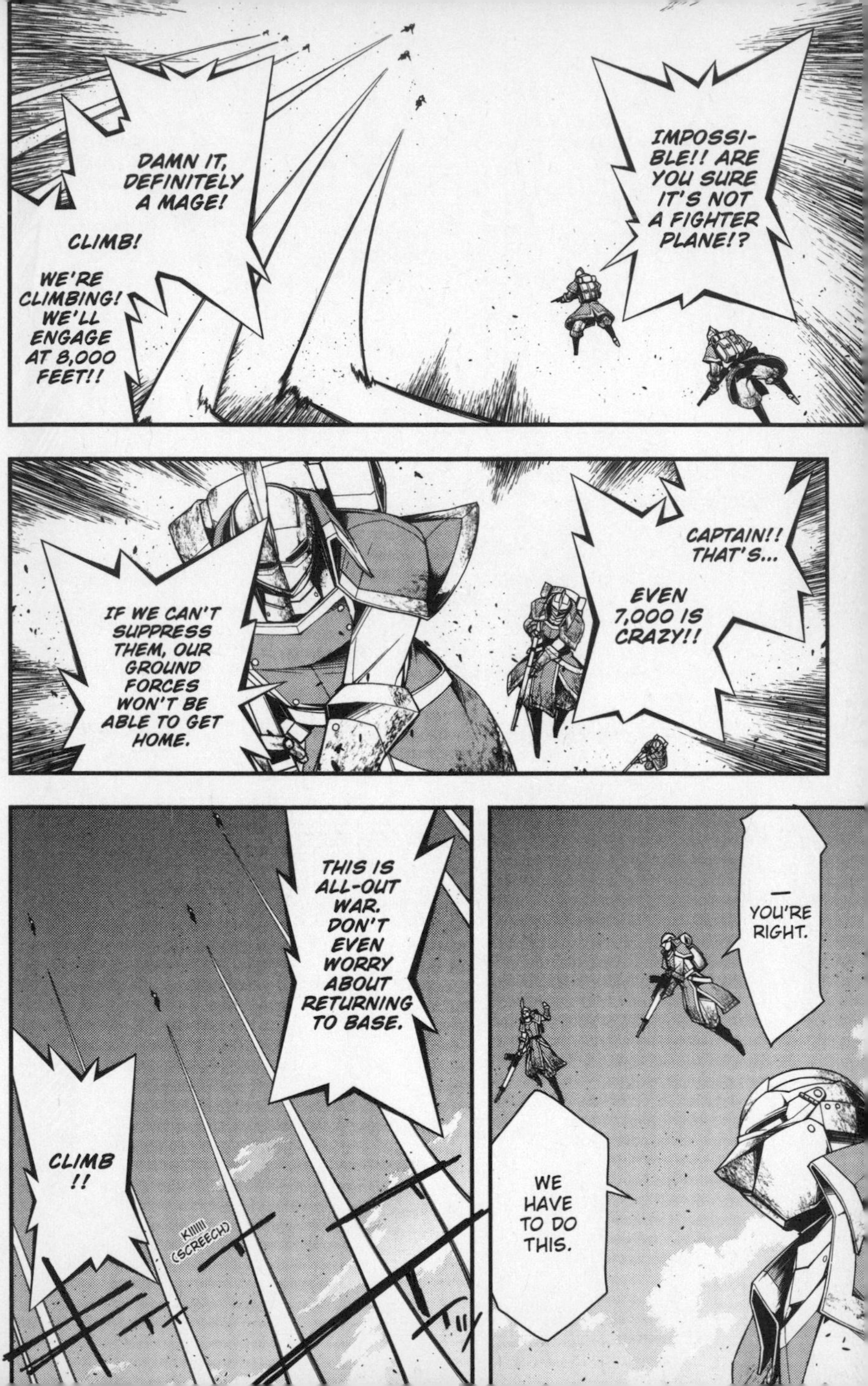
IMPOSSI-BLE!! ARE YOU SURE IT'S NOT A FIGHTER PLANE!?
DAMN IT, DEFINITELY A MAGE!
CLIMB!
WE'RE CLIMBING! WE'LL ENGAGE AT 8,000 FEET!!
CAPTAIN!! THAT'S...
EVEN 7,000 IS CRAZY!!
IF WE CAN'T SUPPRESS THEM, OUR GROUND FORCES WON'T BE ABLE TO GET HOME.
— YOU'RE RIGHT.
WE HAVE TO DO THIS.
THIS IS ALL-OUT WAR. DON'T EVEN WORRY ABOUT RETURNING TO BASE.
CLIMB !!
KIIIIII (SCREECH)

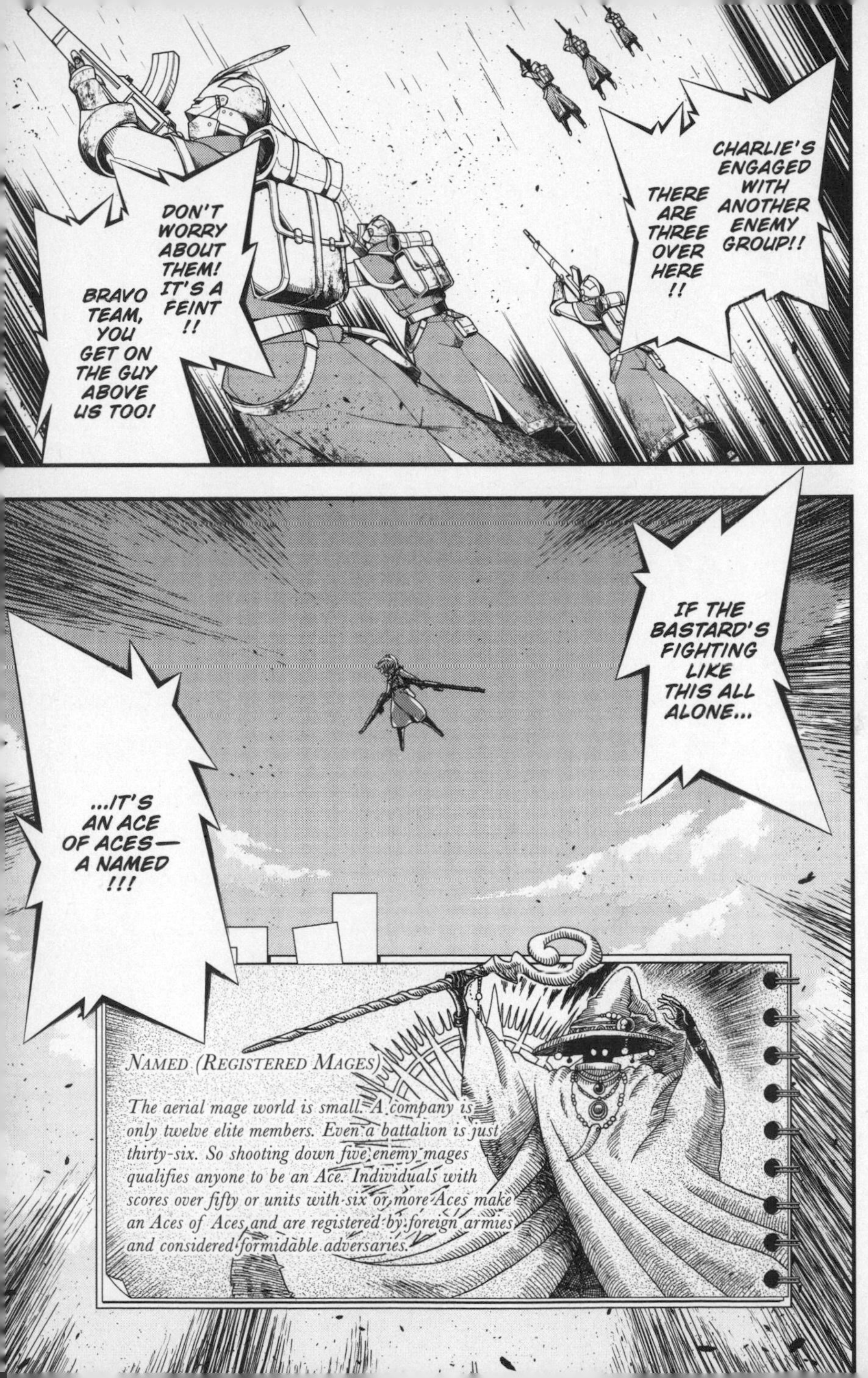
CHARLIE'S ENGAGED WITH ANOTHER ENEMY GROUP!!
THERE ARE THREE OVER HERE!!
DON'T WORRY ABOUT THEM! IT'S A FEINT!!
BRAVO TEAM, YOU GET ON THE GUY ABOVE US TOO!
IF THE BASTARD'S FIGHTING LIKE THIS ALL ALONE...
...IT'S AN ACE OF ACES—A NAMED!!!
NAMED (REGISTERED MAGES)
The aerial mage world is small. A company is only twelve elite members. Even a battalion is just thirty-six. So shooting down five enemy mages qualifies anyone to be an Ace. Individuals with scores over fifty or units with six or more Aces make an Aces of Aces and are registered by foreign armies and considered formidable adversaries.

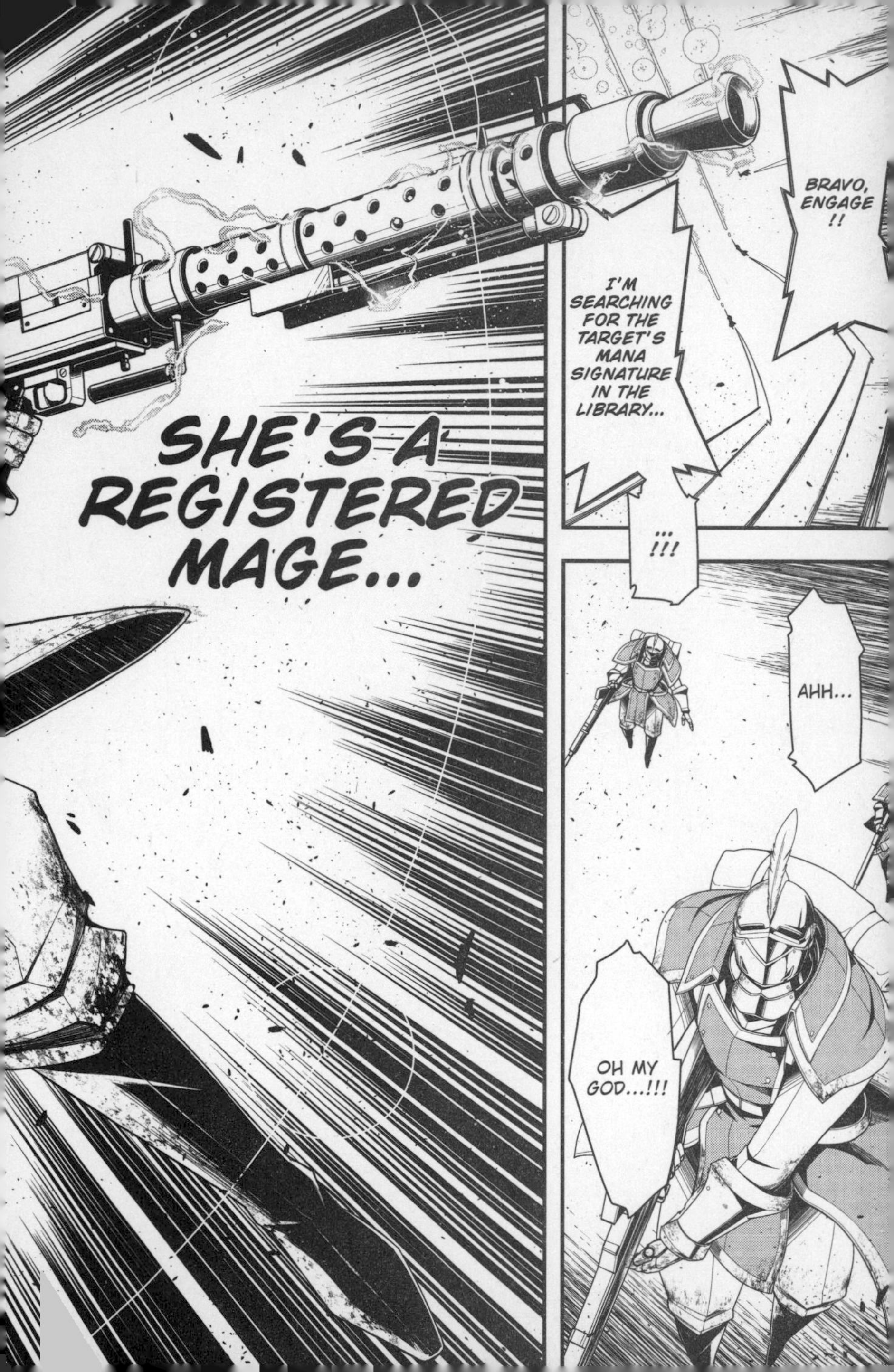

BRAVO, ENGAGE !!
I'M SEARCHING FOR THE TARGET'S MANA SIGNATURE IN THE LIBRARY...
... !!!
AHH...
OH MY GOD...!!!
SHE'S A REGISTERED MAGE...

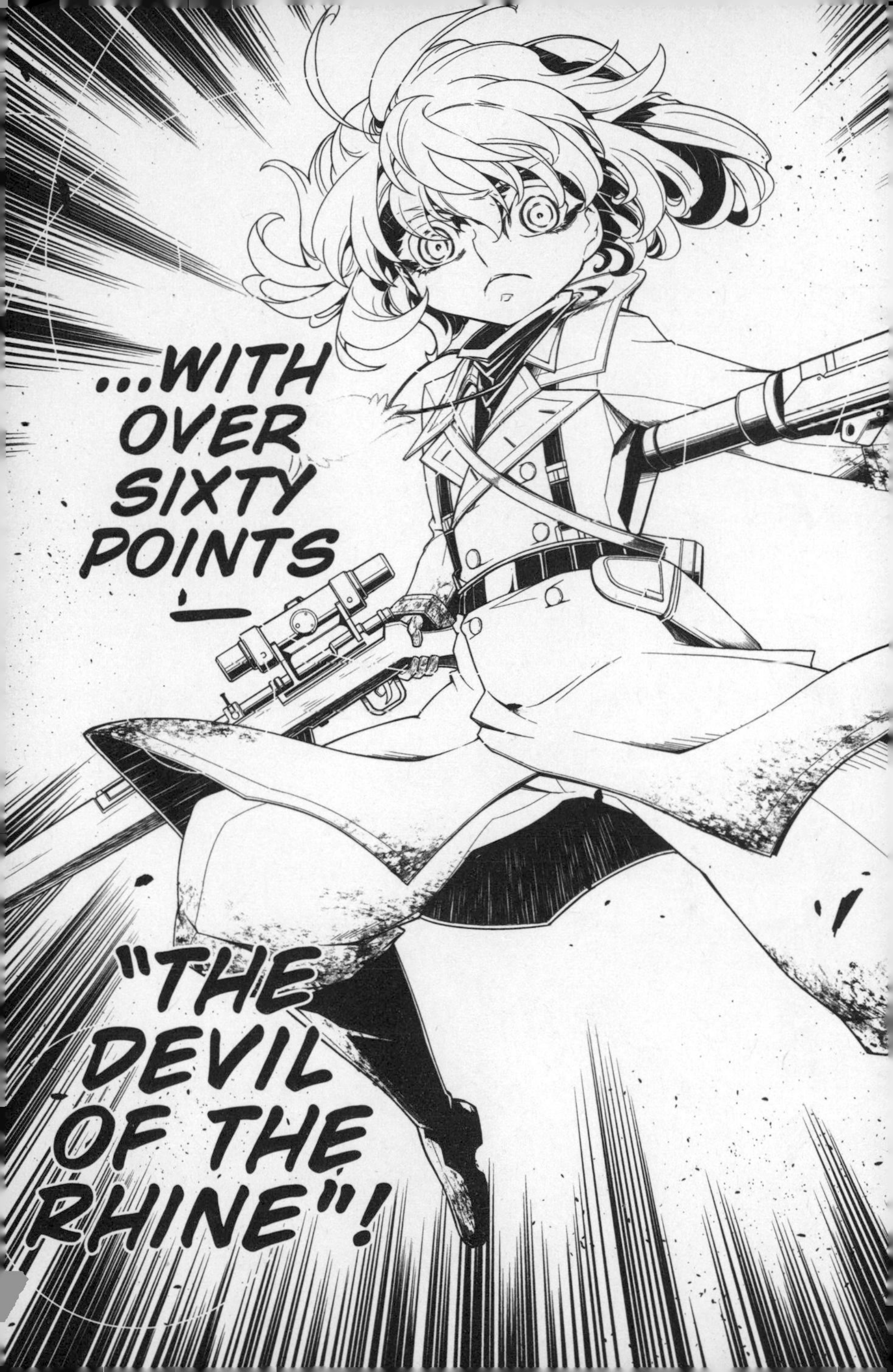
...WITH OVER SIXTY POINTS—
"THE DEVIL OF THE RHINE"!

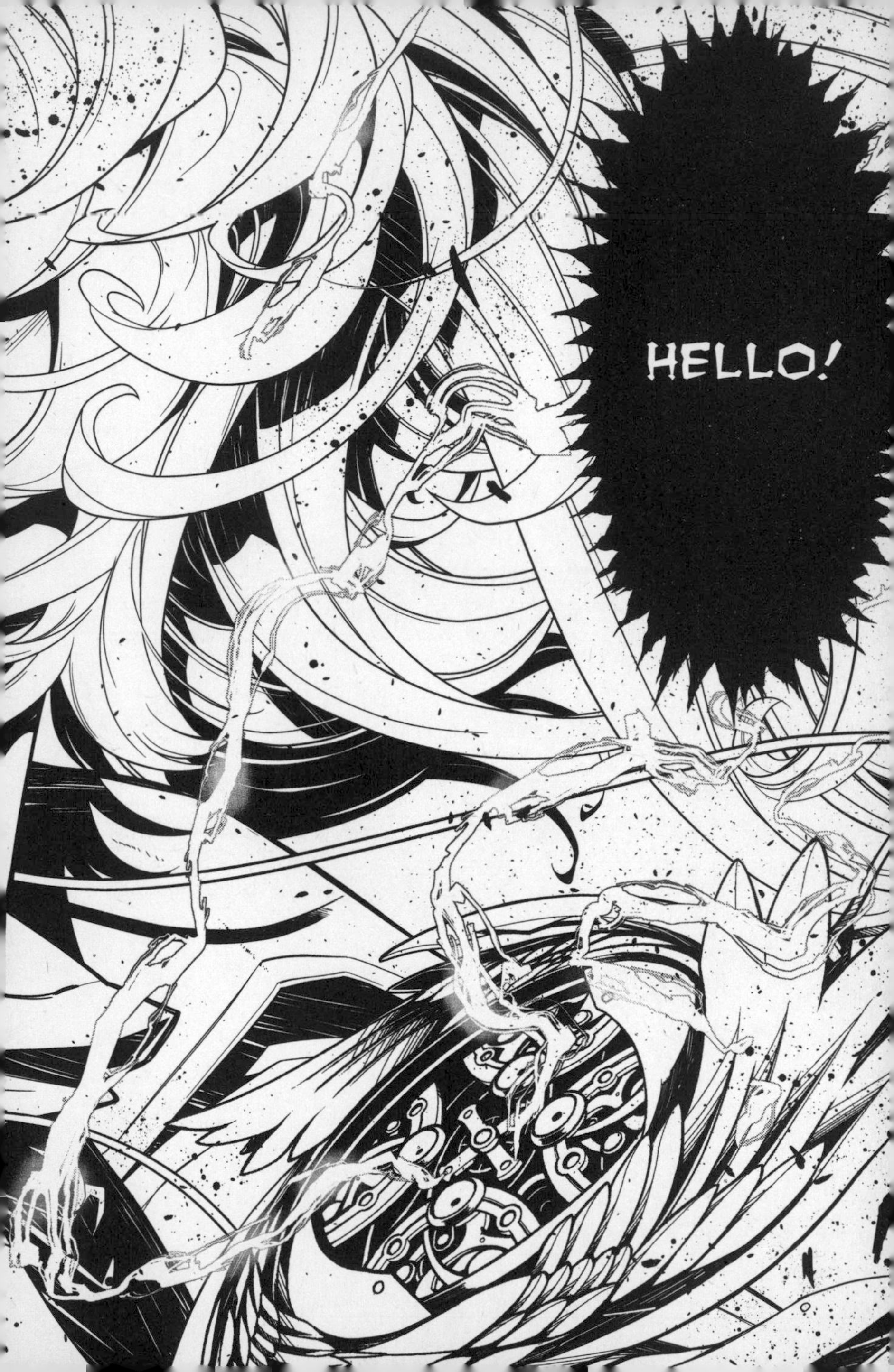
HELLO!

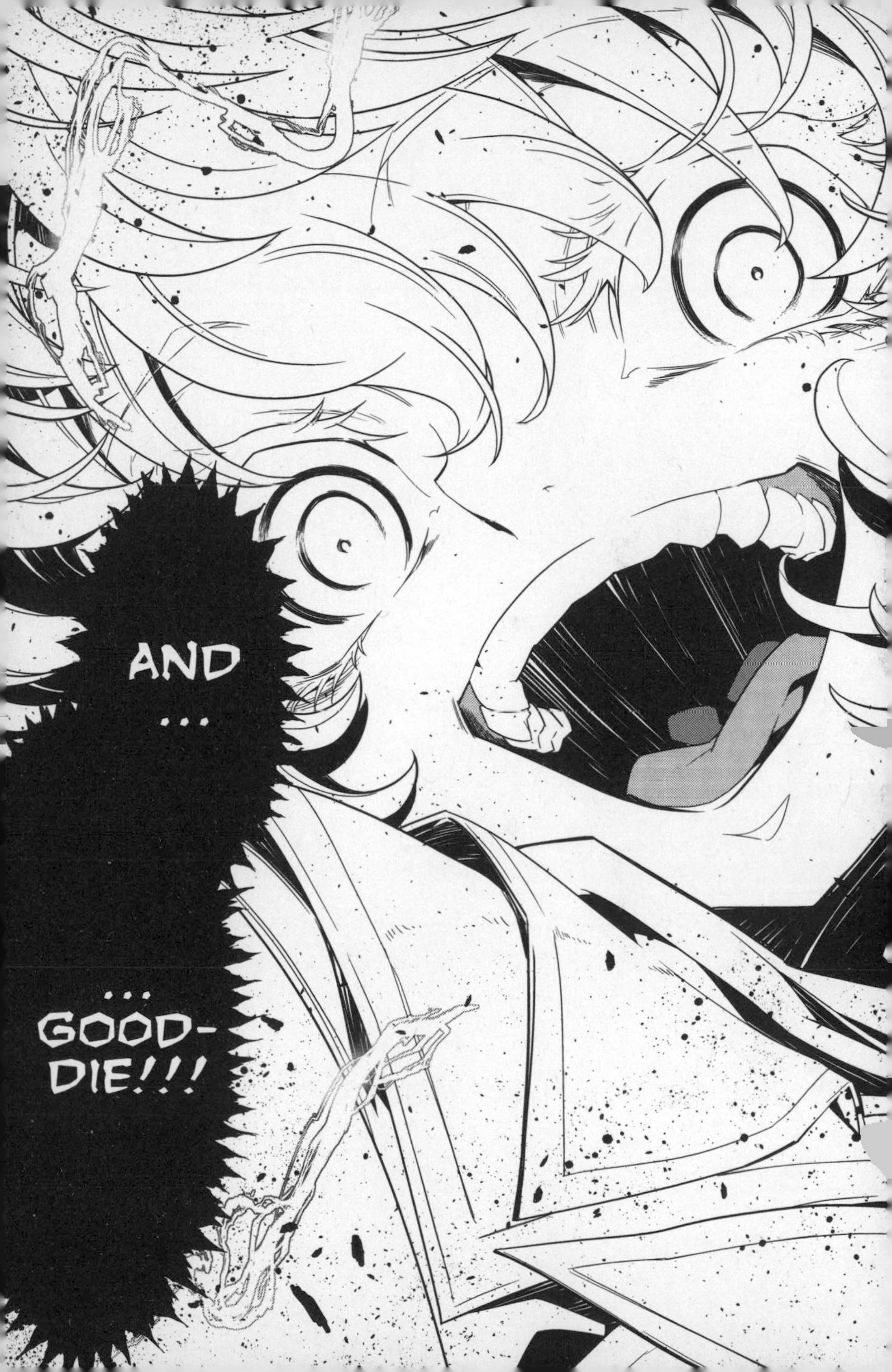
AND
...
...
GOOD-
DIE!!!

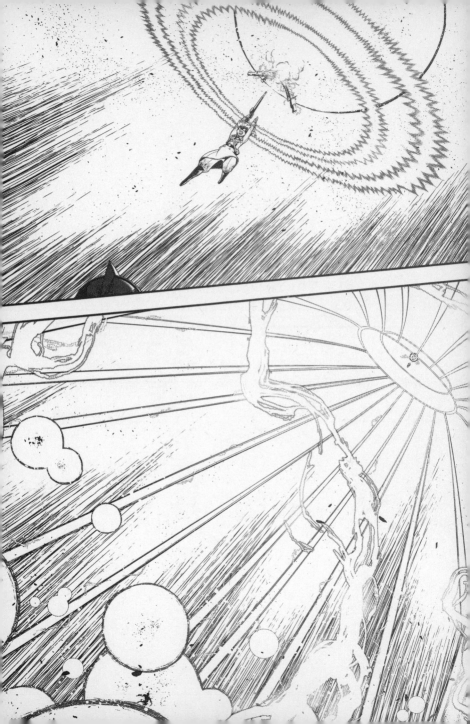

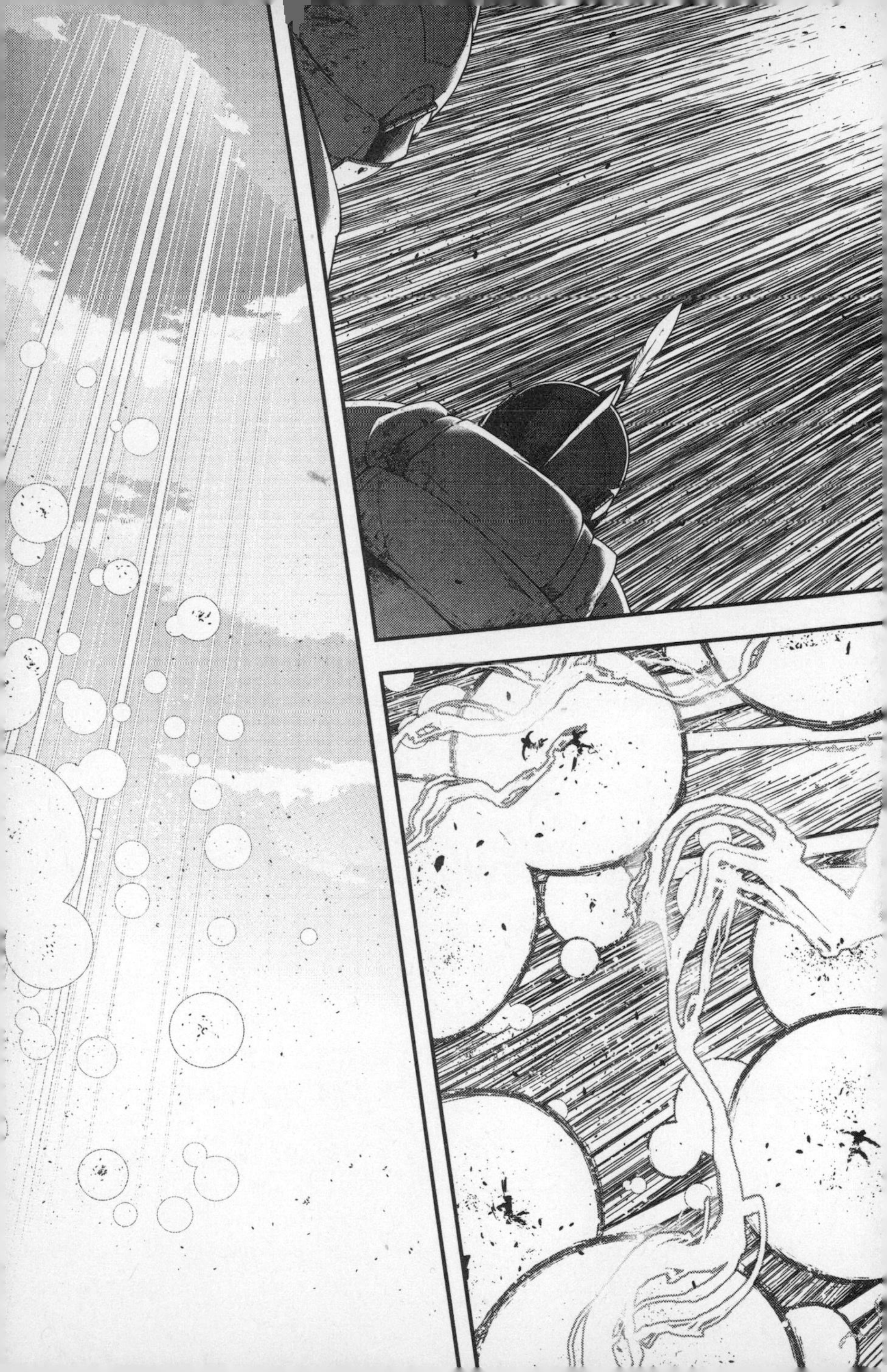

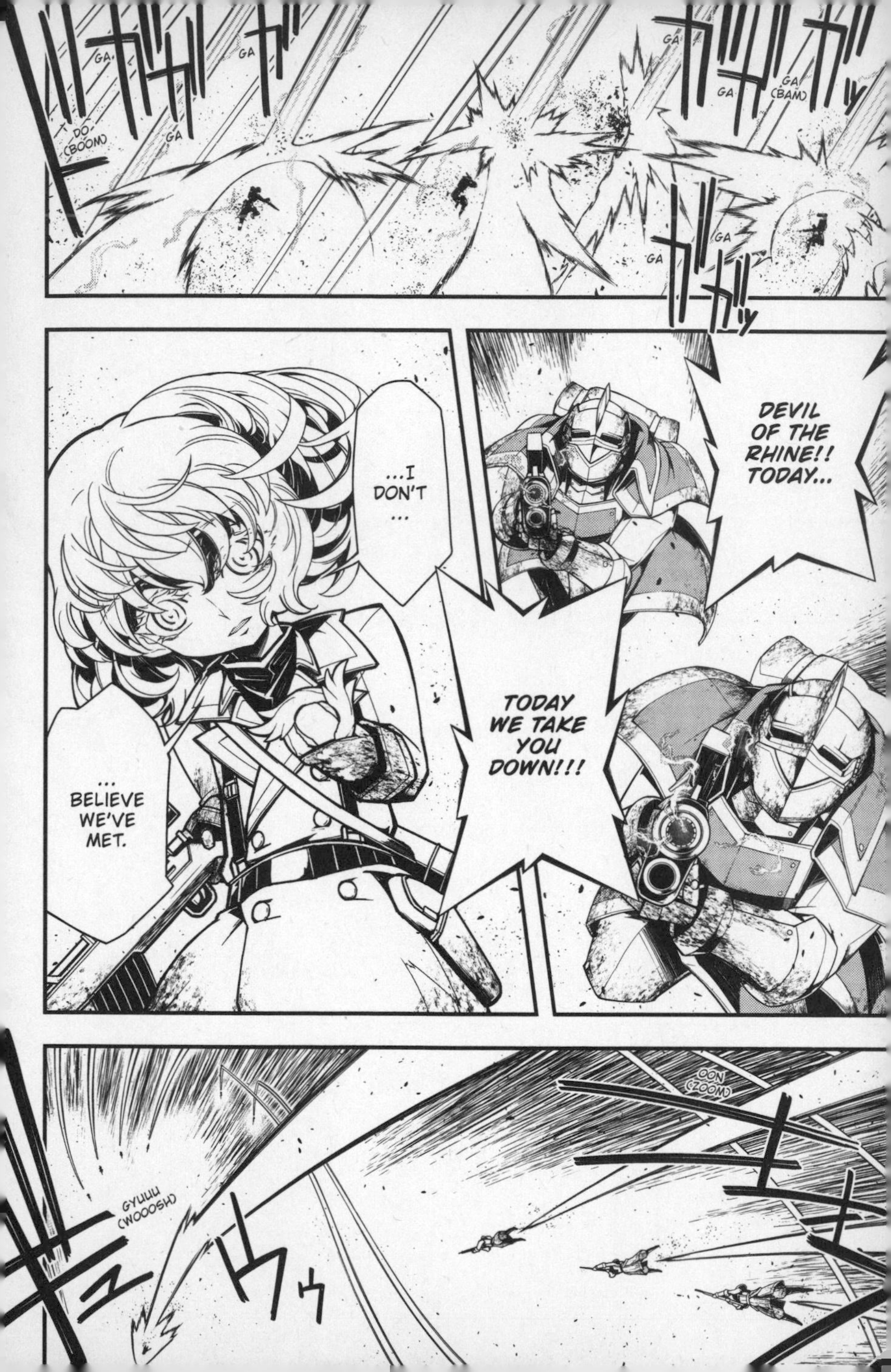
GA
GA (BAM)
GA
GA
GA
GA
GA
DO (BOOM)
GA
DEVIL OF THE RHINE!! TODAY...
TODAY WE TAKE YOU DOWN!!!
...I DON'T ...
... BELIEVE WE'VE MET.
OON (ZOOM)
GYUUU (WOOOSH)

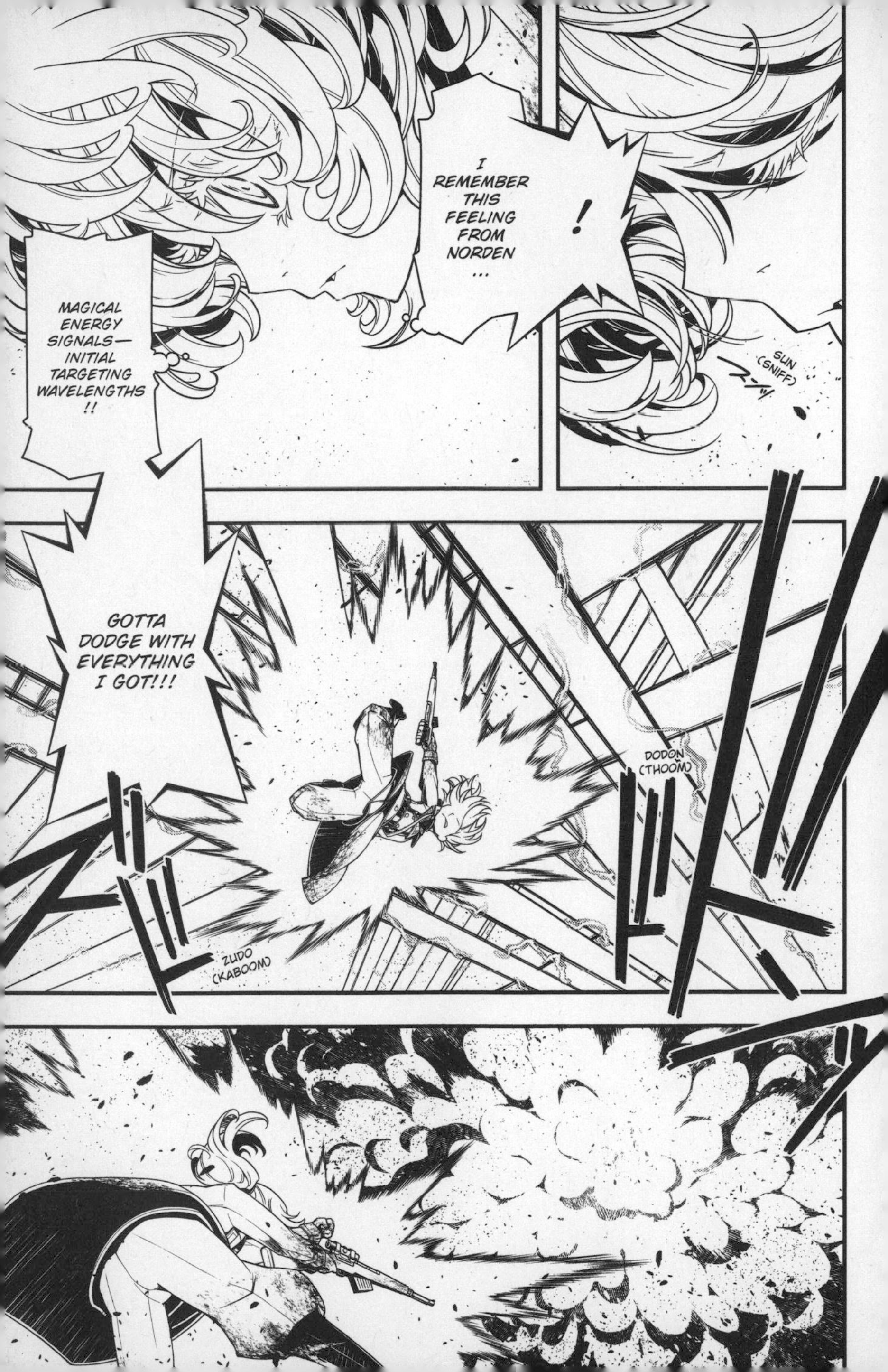
!
SUN (SNIFF)
I REMEMBER THIS FEELING FROM NORDEN ...
MAGICAL ENERGY SIGNALS— INITIAL TARGETING WAVELENGTHS !!
GOTTA DODGE WITH EVERYTHING I GOT!!!
DODON (THOOM)
ZUDO (KABOOM)

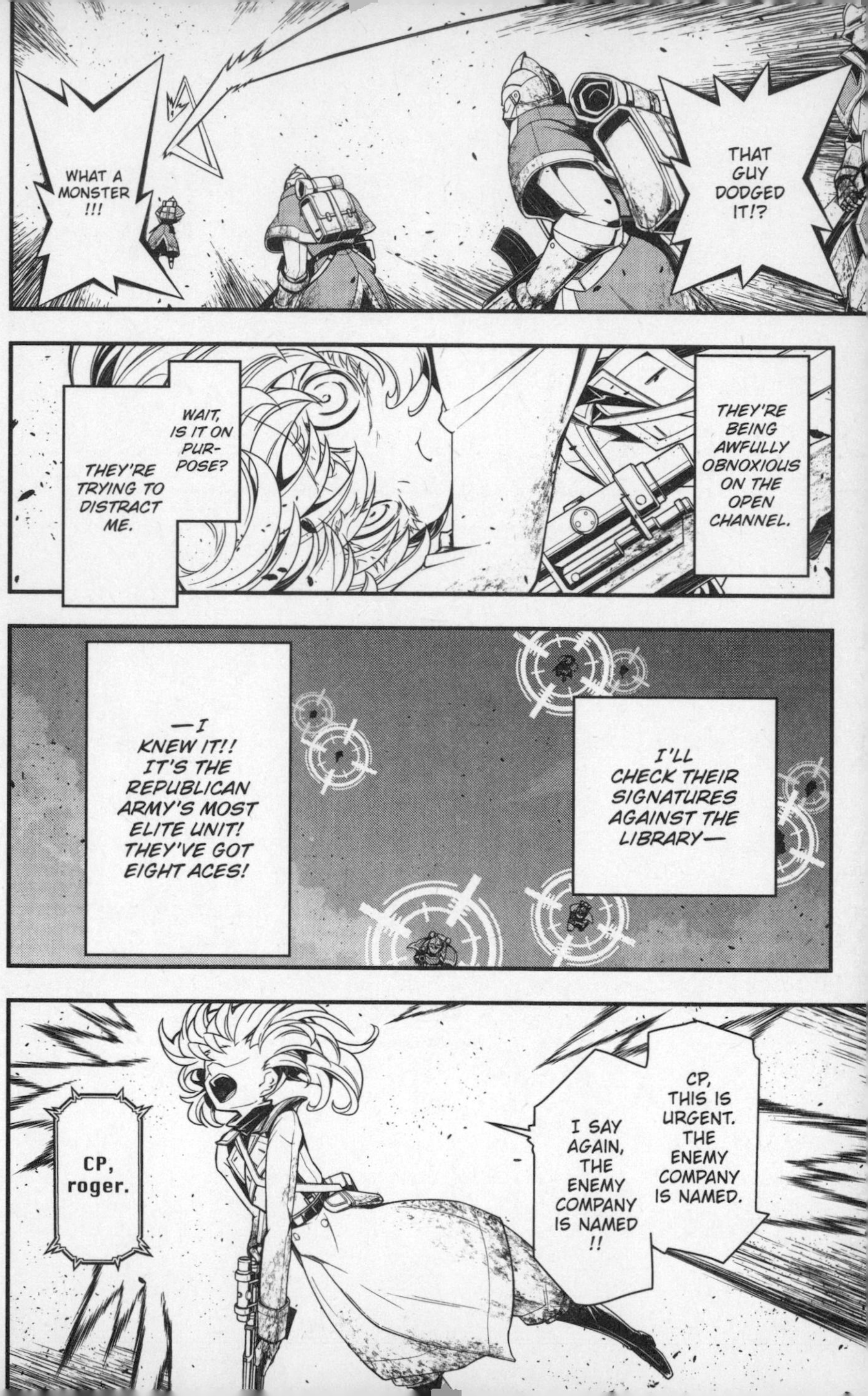
THAT GUY DODGED IT!?
WHAT A MONSTER !!!
THEY'RE BEING AWFULLY OBNOXIOUS ON THE OPEN CHANNEL.
WAIT, IS IT ON PUR-POSE?
THEY'RE TRYING TO DISTRACT ME.
I'LL CHECK THEIR SIGNATURES AGAINST THE LIBRARY—
—I KNEW IT!! IT'S THE REPUBLICAN ARMY'S MOST ELITE UNIT! THEY'VE GOT EIGHT ACES!
CP, THIS IS URGENT. THE ENEMY COMPANY IS NAMED.
I SAY AGAIN, THE ENEMY COMPANY IS NAMED !!
CP, roger.

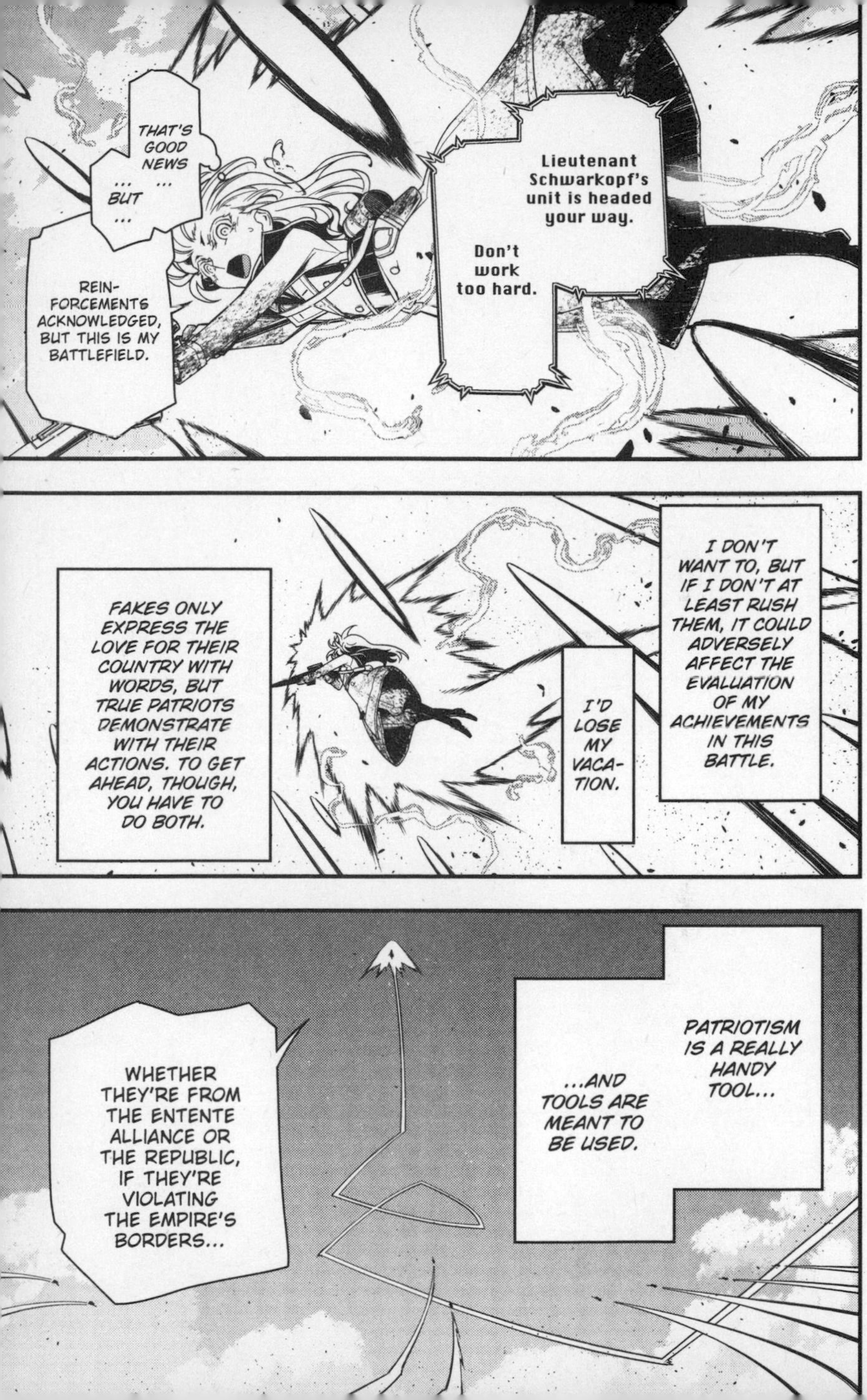
Lieutenant Schwarkopf's unit is headed your way.
Don't work too hard.
THAT'S GOOD NEWS ... ... BUT ...
REIN-FORCEMENTS ACKNOWLEDGED, BUT THIS IS MY BATTLEFIELD.
I DON'T WANT TO, BUT IF I DON'T AT LEAST RUSH THEM, IT COULD ADVERSELY AFFECT THE EVALUATION OF MY ACHIEVEMENTS IN THIS BATTLE.
I'D LOSE MY VACA-TION.
FAKES ONLY EXPRESS THE LOVE FOR THEIR COUNTRY WITH WORDS, BUT TRUE PATRIOTS DEMONSTRATE WITH THEIR ACTIONS. TO GET AHEAD, THOUGH, YOU HAVE TO DO BOTH.
PATRIOTISM IS A REALLY HANDY TOOL...
...AND TOOLS ARE MEANT TO BE USED.
WHETHER THEY'RE FROM THE ENTENTE ALLIANCE OR THE REPUBLIC, IF THEY'RE VIOLATING THE EMPIRE'S BORDERS...

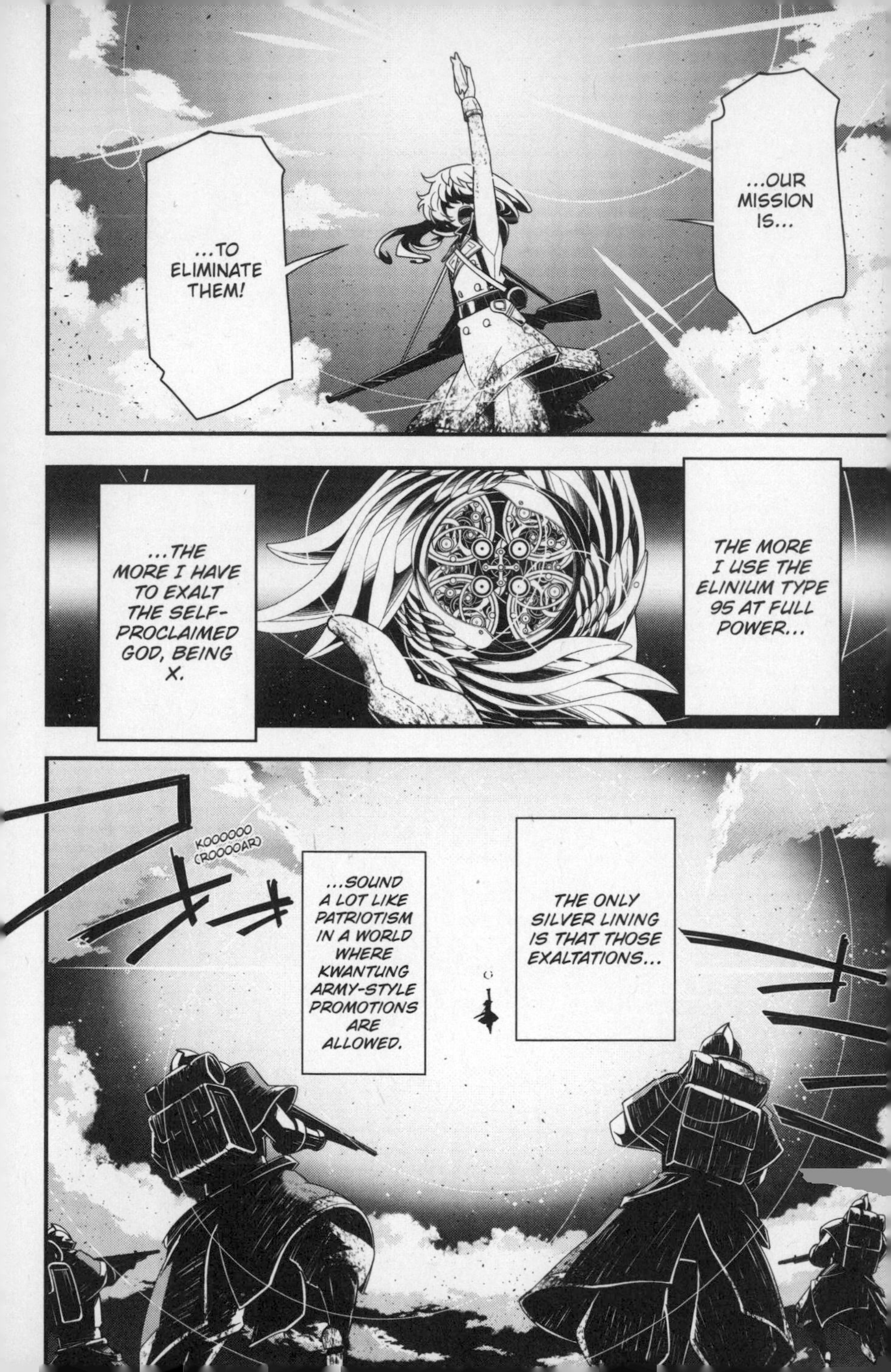
...OUR MISSION IS...
...TO ELIMINATE THEM!
THE MORE I USE THE ELINIUM TYPE 95 AT FULL POWER...
...THE MORE I HAVE TO EXALT THE SELF-PROCLAIMED GOD, BEING X.
THE ONLY SILVER LINING IS THAT THOSE EXALTATIONS...
...SOUND A LOT LIKE PATRIOTISM IN A WORLD WHERE KWANTUNG ARMY-STYLE PROMOTIONS ARE ALLOWED.
KOOOOOO (ROOOOAR)

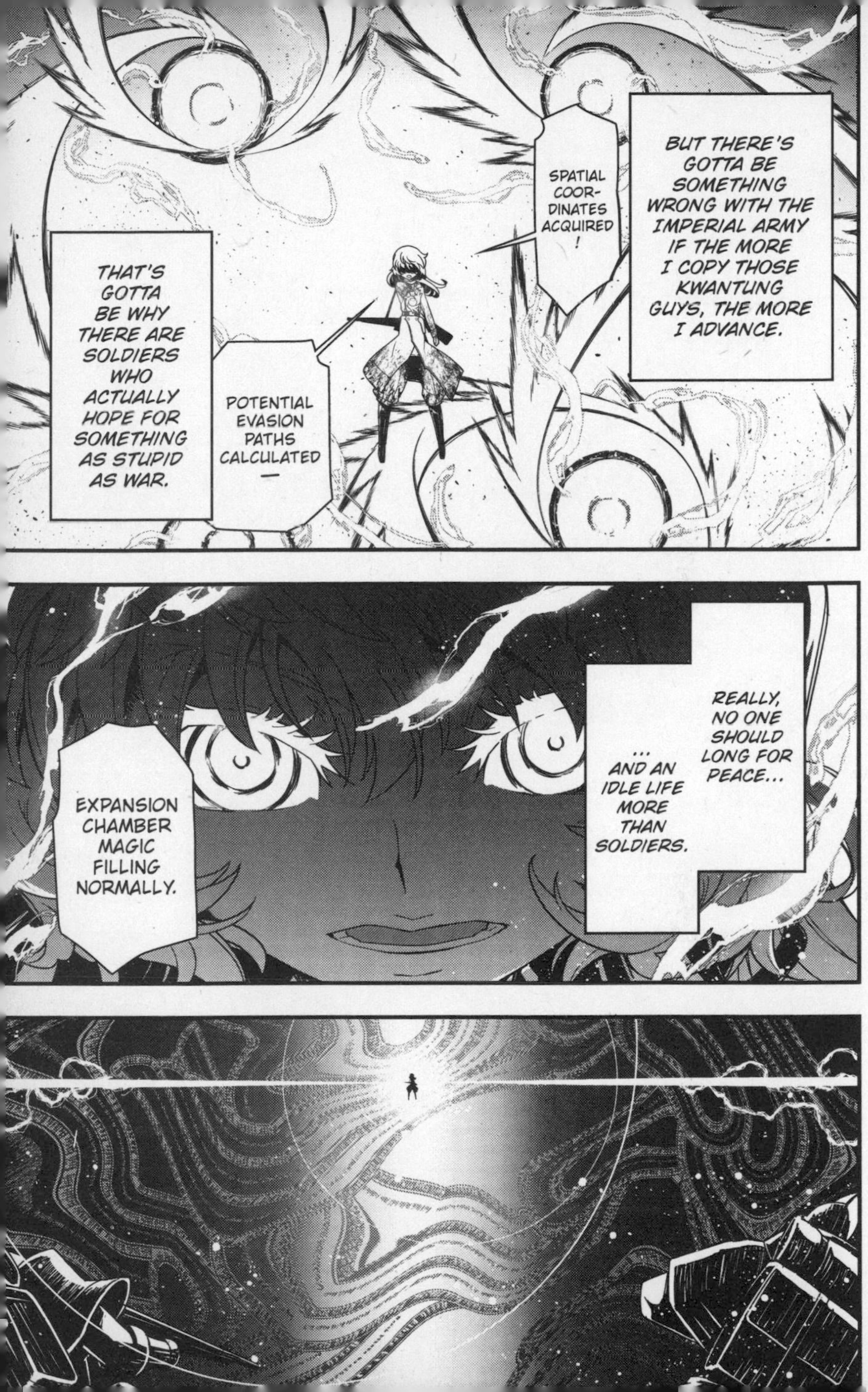
BUT THERE'S GOTTA BE SOMETHING WRONG WITH THE IMPERIAL ARMY IF THE MORE I COPY THOSE KWANTUNG GUYS, THE MORE I ADVANCE.
SPATIAL COORDINATES ACQUIRED!
POTENTIAL EVASION PATHS CALCULATED—
THAT'S GOTTA BE WHY THERE ARE SOLDIERS WHO ACTUALLY HOPE FOR SOMETHING AS STUPID AS WAR.
REALLY, NO ONE SHOULD LONG FOR PEACE...
...AND AN IDLE LIFE MORE THAN SOLDIERS.
EXPANSION CHAMBER MAGIC FILLING NORMALLY.

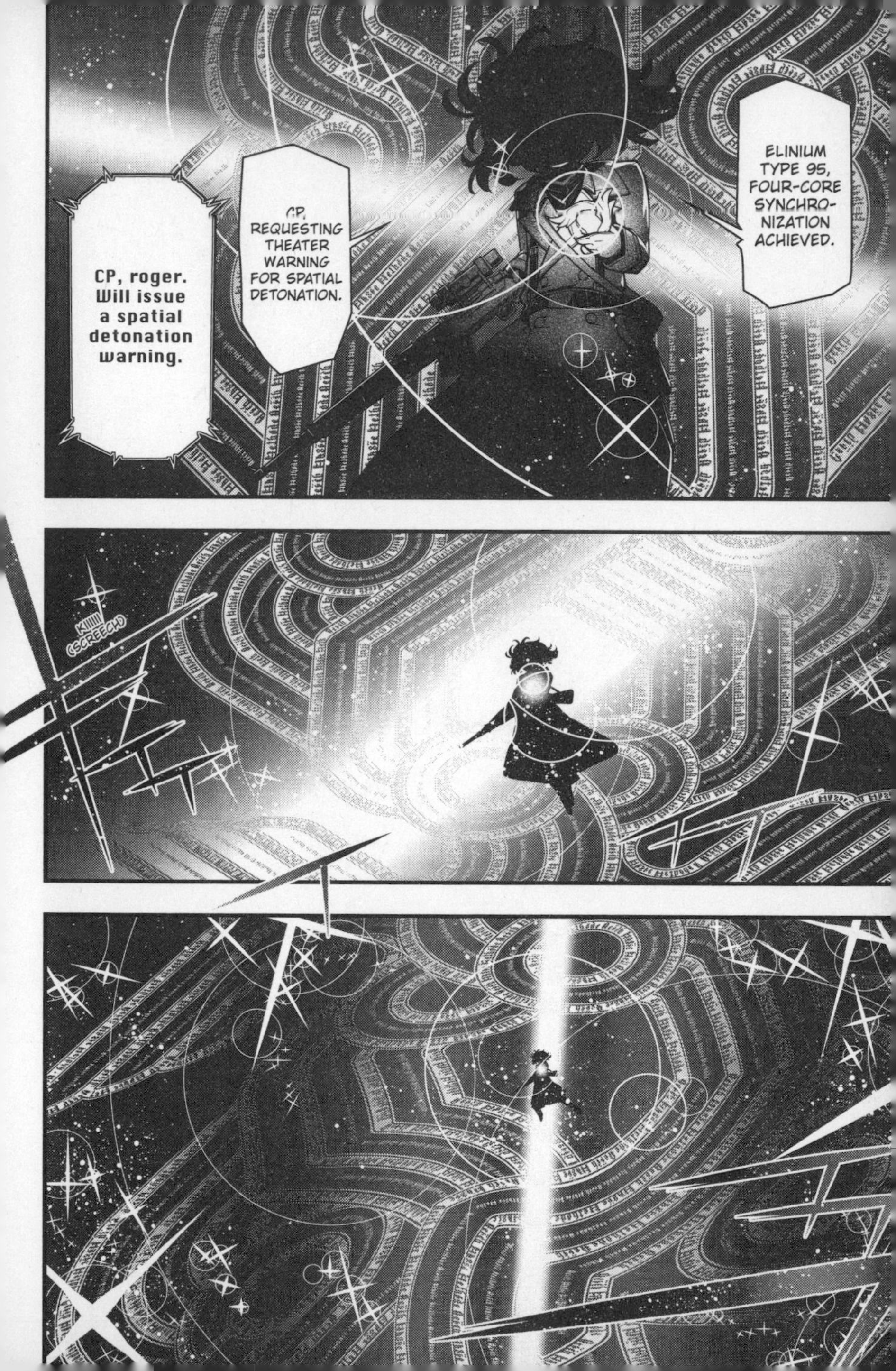
ELINIUM TYPE 95, FOUR-CORE SYNCHRONIZATION ACHIEVED.
CP, REQUESTING THEATER WARNING FOR SPATIAL DETONATION.
CP, roger. Will issue a spatial detonation warning.
KIIIIII (SCREECH)

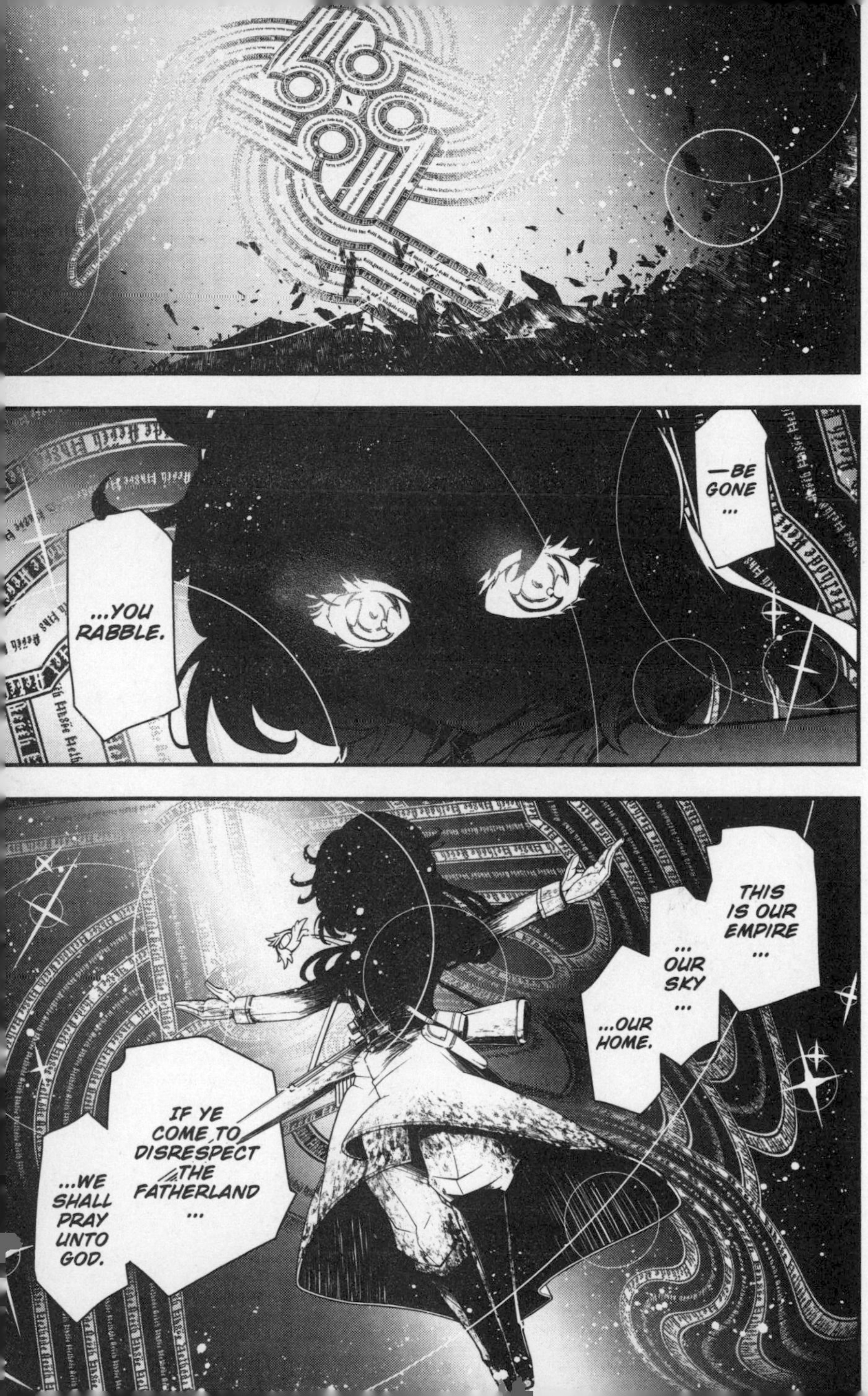
—BE GONE ...
...YOU RABBLE.
THIS IS OUR EMPIRE ...
... OUR SKY ...
...OUR HOME.
IF YE COME TO DISRESPECT THE FATHERLAND ...
...WE SHALL PRAY UNTO GOD.

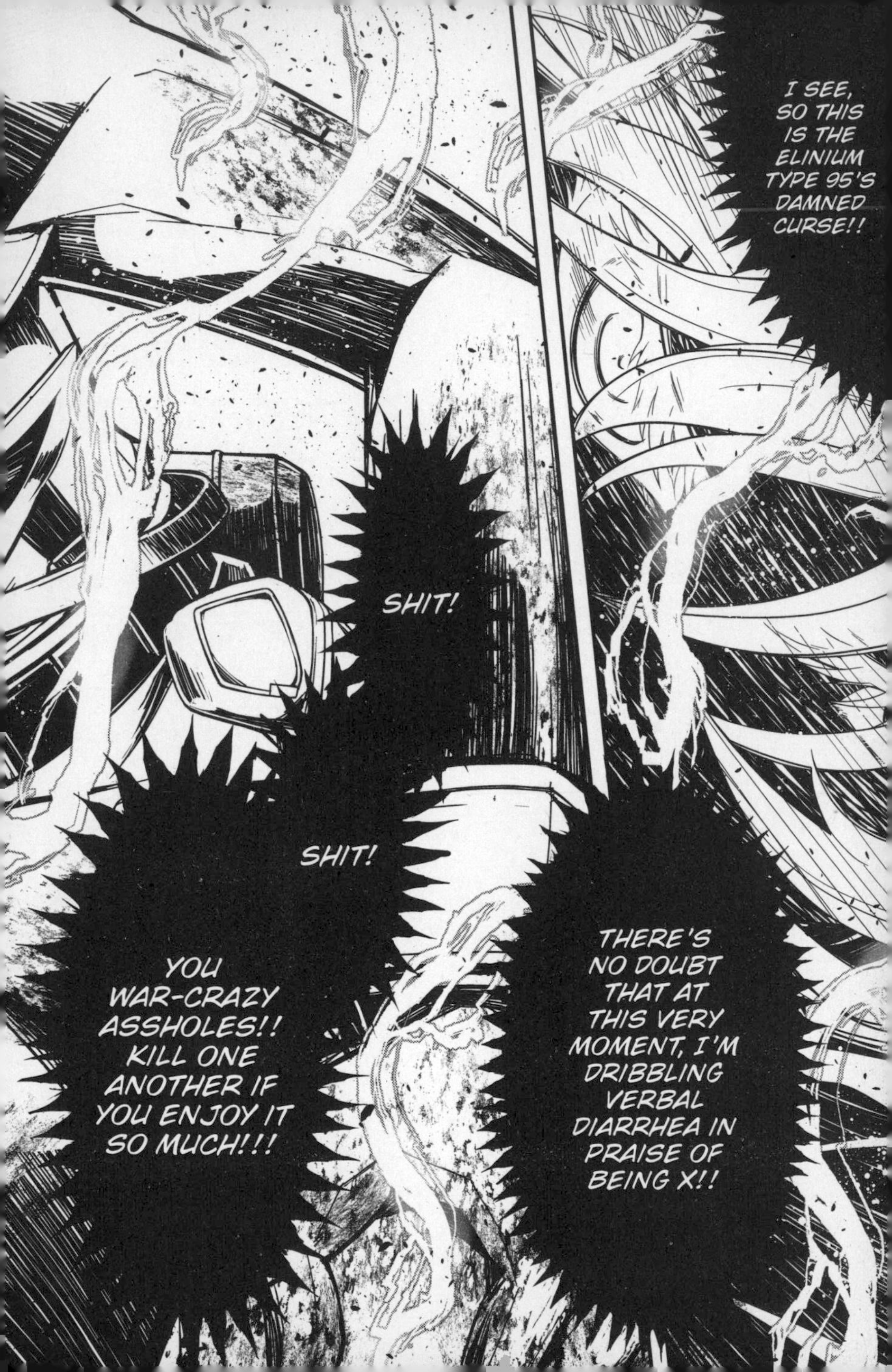
I SEE, SO THIS IS THE ELINIUM TYPE 95'S DAMNED CURSE!!
SHIT!
SHIT!
THERE'S NO DOUBT THAT AT THIS VERY MOMENT, I'M DRIBBLING VERBAL DIARRHEA IN PRAISE OF BEING X!!
YOU WAR-CRAZY ASSHOLES!! KILL ONE ANOTHER IF YOU ENJOY IT SO MUCH!!!

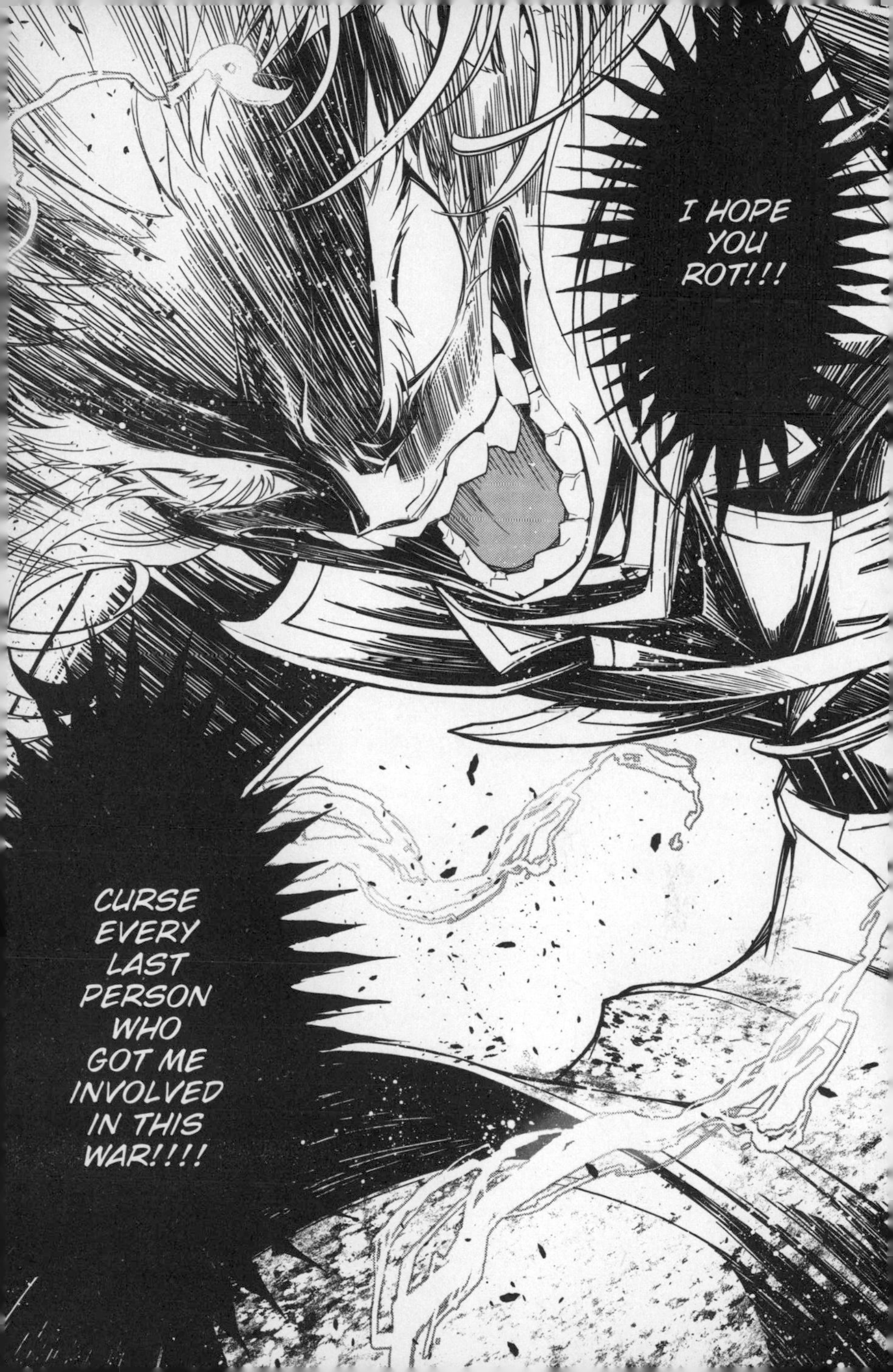
I HOPE YOU ROT!!!
CURSE EVERY LAST PERSON WHO GOT ME INVOLVED IN THIS WAR!!!!

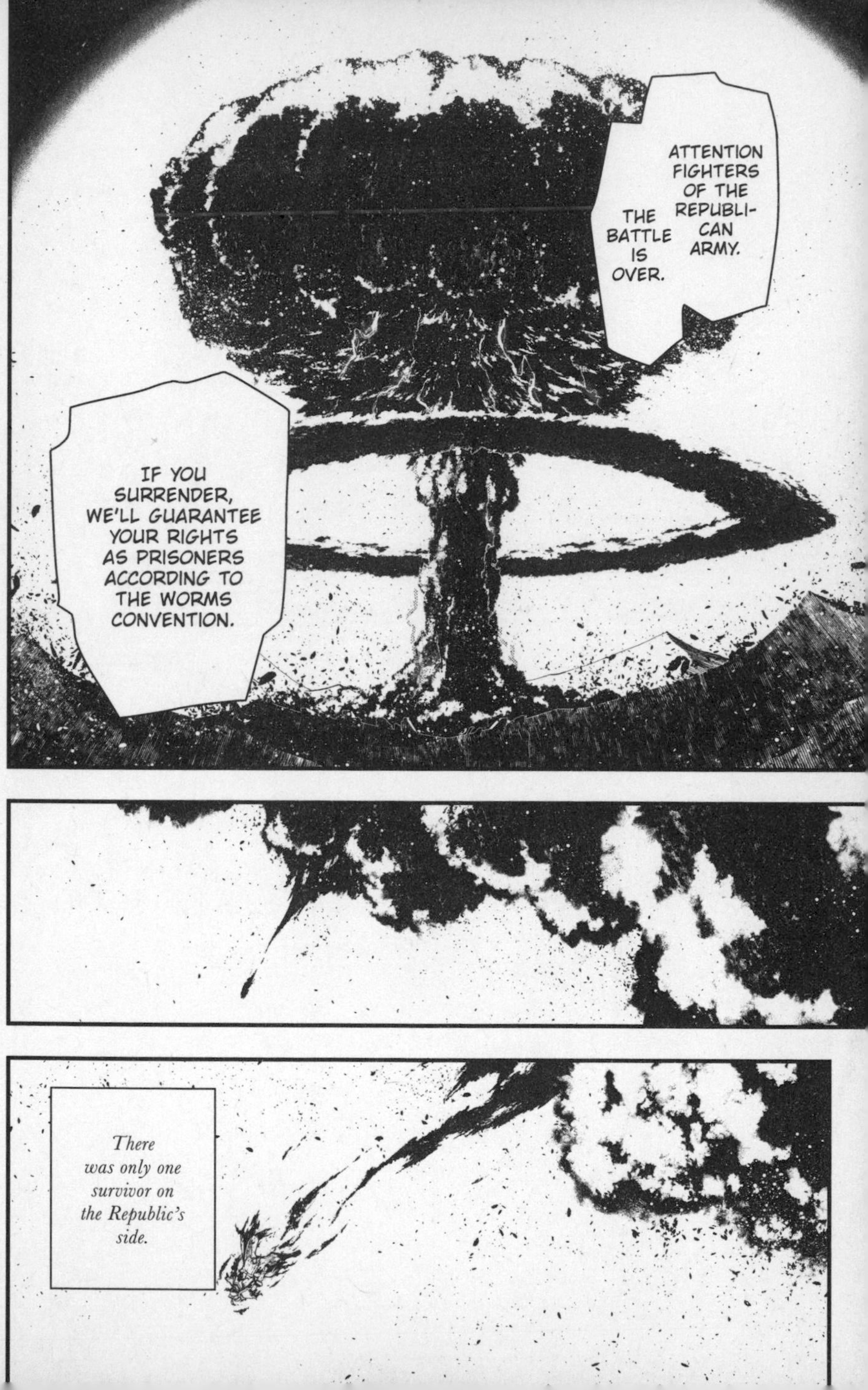
ATTENTION FIGHTERS OF THE REPUBLI-CAN ARMY.
THE BATTLE IS OVER.
IF YOU SURRENDER, WE'LL GUARANTEE YOUR RIGHTS AS PRISONERS ACCORDING TO THE WORMS CONVENTION.
There was only one survivor on the Republic's side.

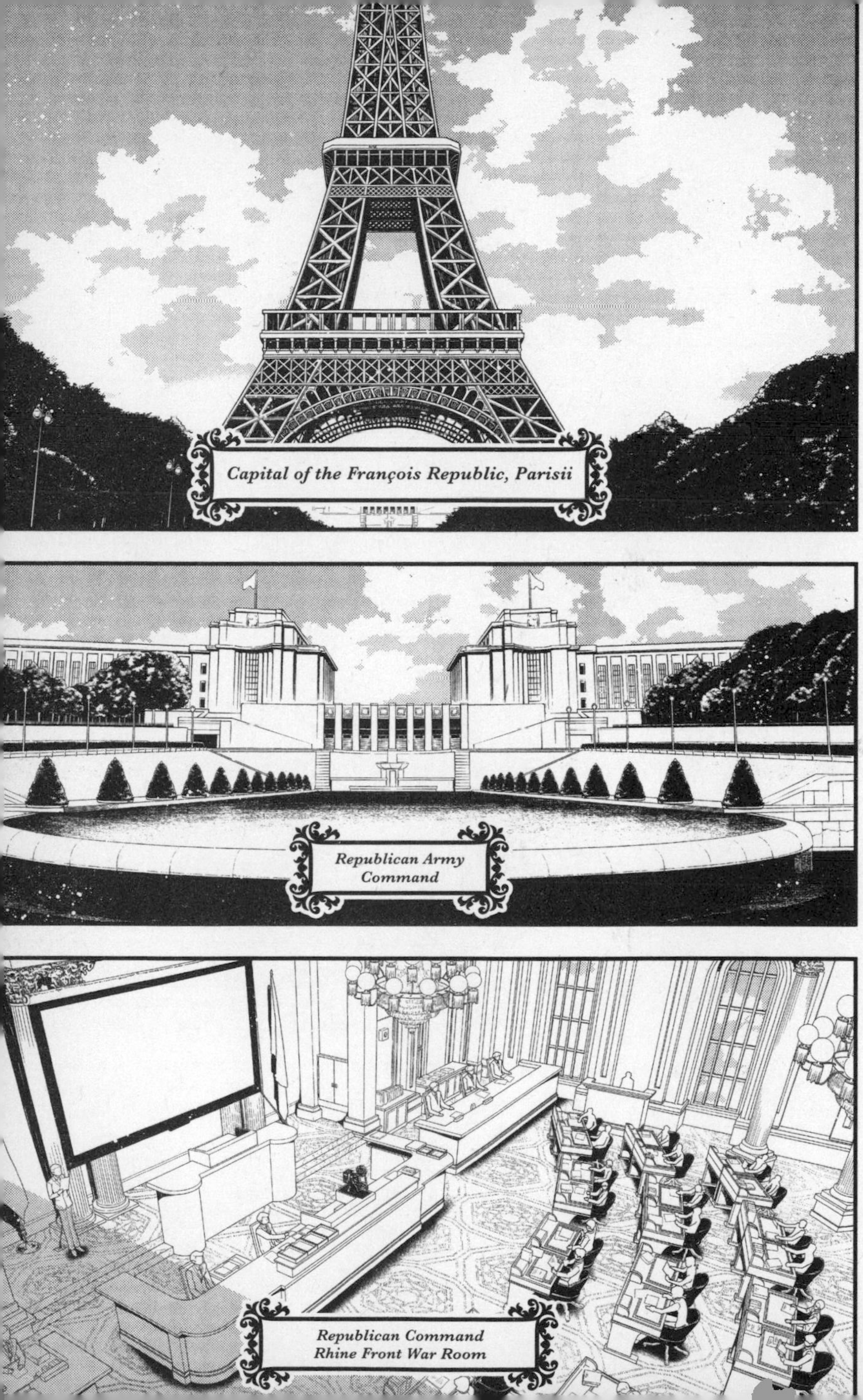
Capital of the François Republic, Parisii
Republican Army Command
Republican Command Rhine Front War Room

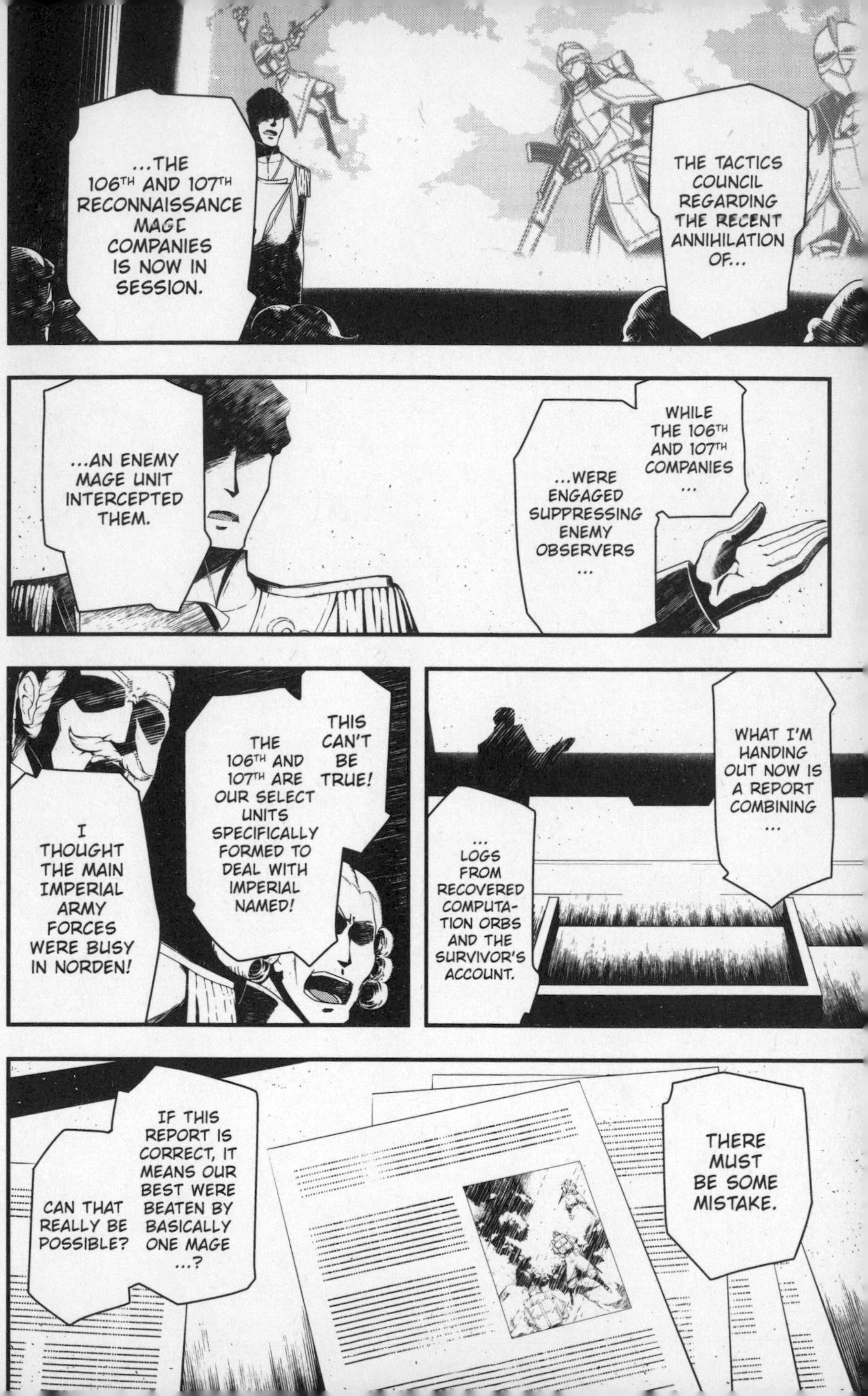
THE TACTICS COUNCIL REGARDING THE RECENT ANNIHILATION OF...
...THE 106TH AND 107TH RECONNAISSANCE MAGE COMPANIES IS NOW IN SESSION.
WHILE THE 106TH AND 107TH COMPANIES ...
...WERE ENGAGED SUPPRESSING ENEMY OBSERVERS ...
...AN ENEMY MAGE UNIT INTERCEPTED THEM.
WHAT I'M HANDING OUT NOW IS A REPORT COMBINING ...
... LOGS FROM RECOVERED COMPUTATION ORBS AND THE SURVIVOR'S ACCOUNT.
THIS CAN'T BE TRUE!
THE 106TH AND 107TH ARE OUR SELECT UNITS SPECIFICALLY FORMED TO DEAL WITH IMPERIAL NAMED!
I THOUGHT THE MAIN IMPERIAL ARMY FORCES WERE BUSY IN NORDEN!
THERE MUST BE SOME MISTAKE.
IF THIS REPORT IS CORRECT, IT MEANS OUR BEST WERE BEATEN BY BASICALLY ONE MAGE ...?
CAN THAT REALLY BE POSSIBLE?

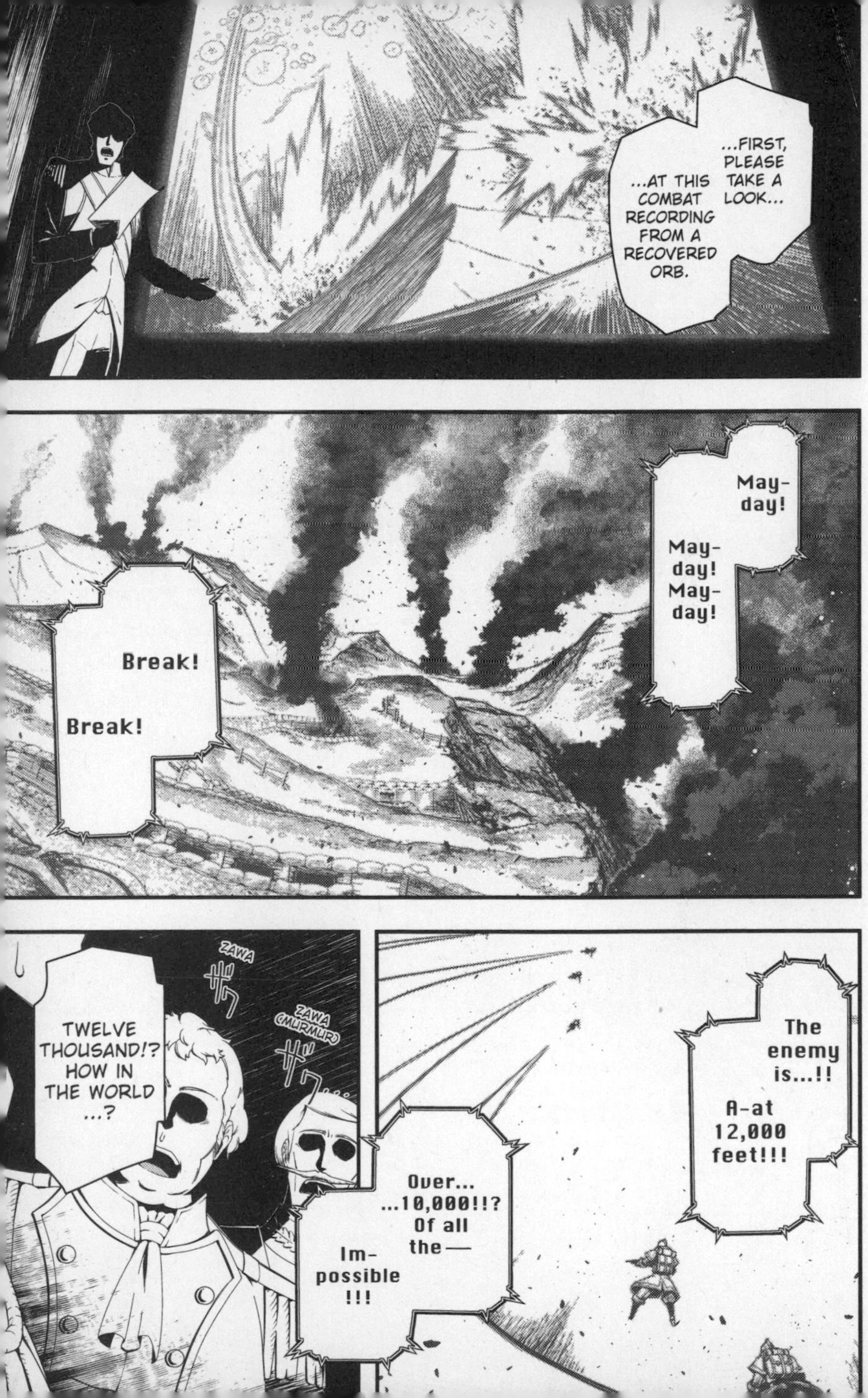

...FIRST, PLEASE TAKE A LOOK...
...AT THIS COMBAT RECORDING FROM A RECOVERED ORB.
May-day!
May-day! May-day!
Break!
Break!
The enemy is...!!
A-at 12,000 feet!!!
ZAWA
ZAWA (MURMUR)
TWELVE THOUSAND!? HOW IN THE WORLD ...?
Over... ...10,000!!? Of all the—
Im-possible!!!

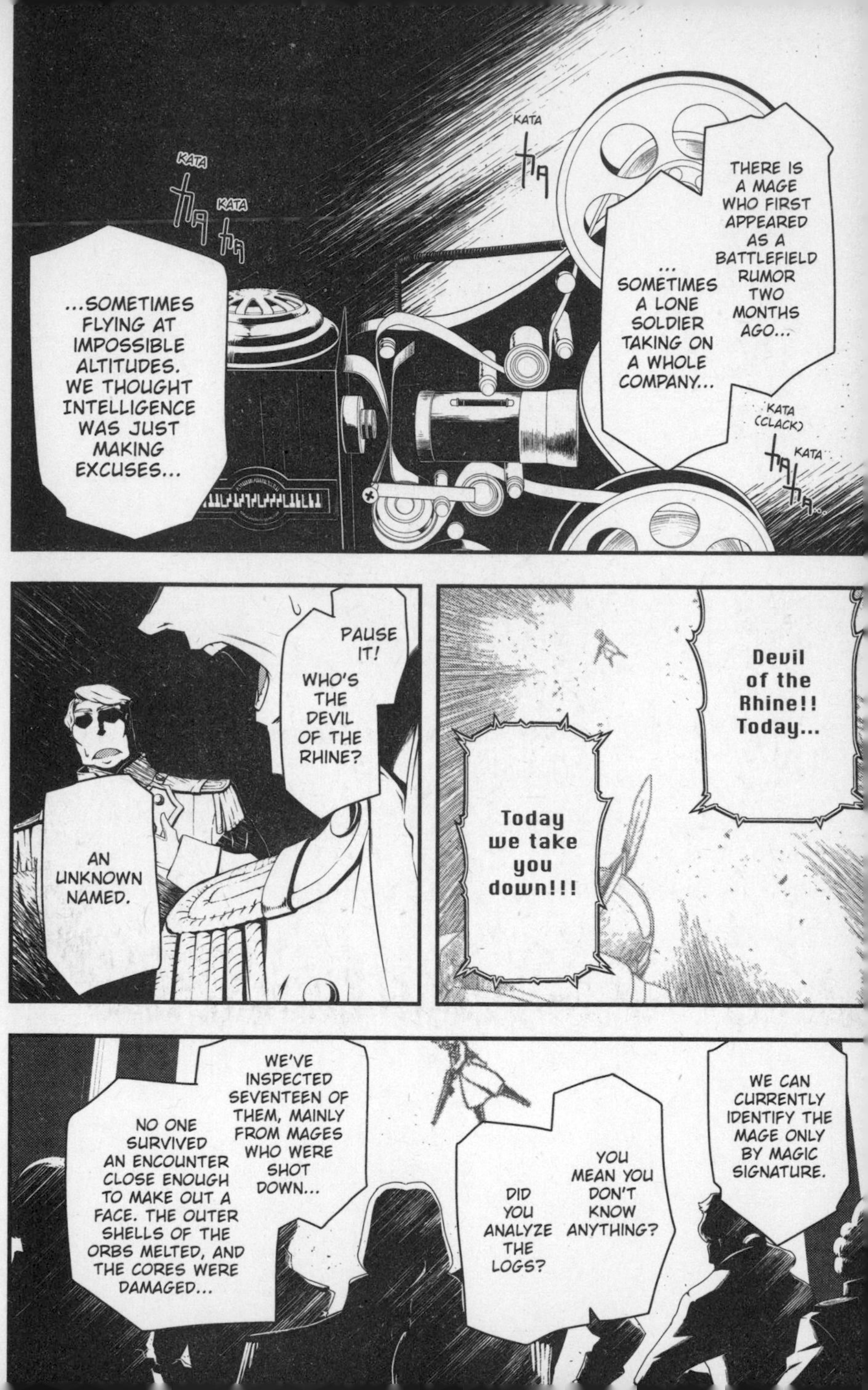
KATA
KATA (CLACK)
KATA
THERE IS A MAGE WHO FIRST APPEARED AS A BATTLEFIELD RUMOR TWO MONTHS AGO...
...SOMETIMES A LONE SOLDIER TAKING ON A WHOLE COMPANY...
KATA
KATA
KATA
...SOMETIMES FLYING AT IMPOSSIBLE ALTITUDES. WE THOUGHT INTELLIGENCE WAS JUST MAKING EXCUSES...
Devil of the Rhine!! Today...
Today we take you down!!!
PAUSE IT!
WHO'S THE DEVIL OF THE RHINE?
AN UNKNOWN NAMED.
WE CAN CURRENTLY IDENTIFY THE MAGE ONLY BY MAGIC SIGNATURE.
YOU MEAN YOU DON'T KNOW ANYTHING?
DID YOU ANALYZE THE LOGS?
WE'VE INSPECTED SEVENTEEN OF THEM, MAINLY FROM MAGES WHO WERE SHOT DOWN...
NO ONE SURVIVED AN ENCOUNTER CLOSE ENOUGH TO MAKE OUT A FACE. THE OUTER SHELLS OF THE ORBS MELTED, AND THE CORES WERE DAMAGED...

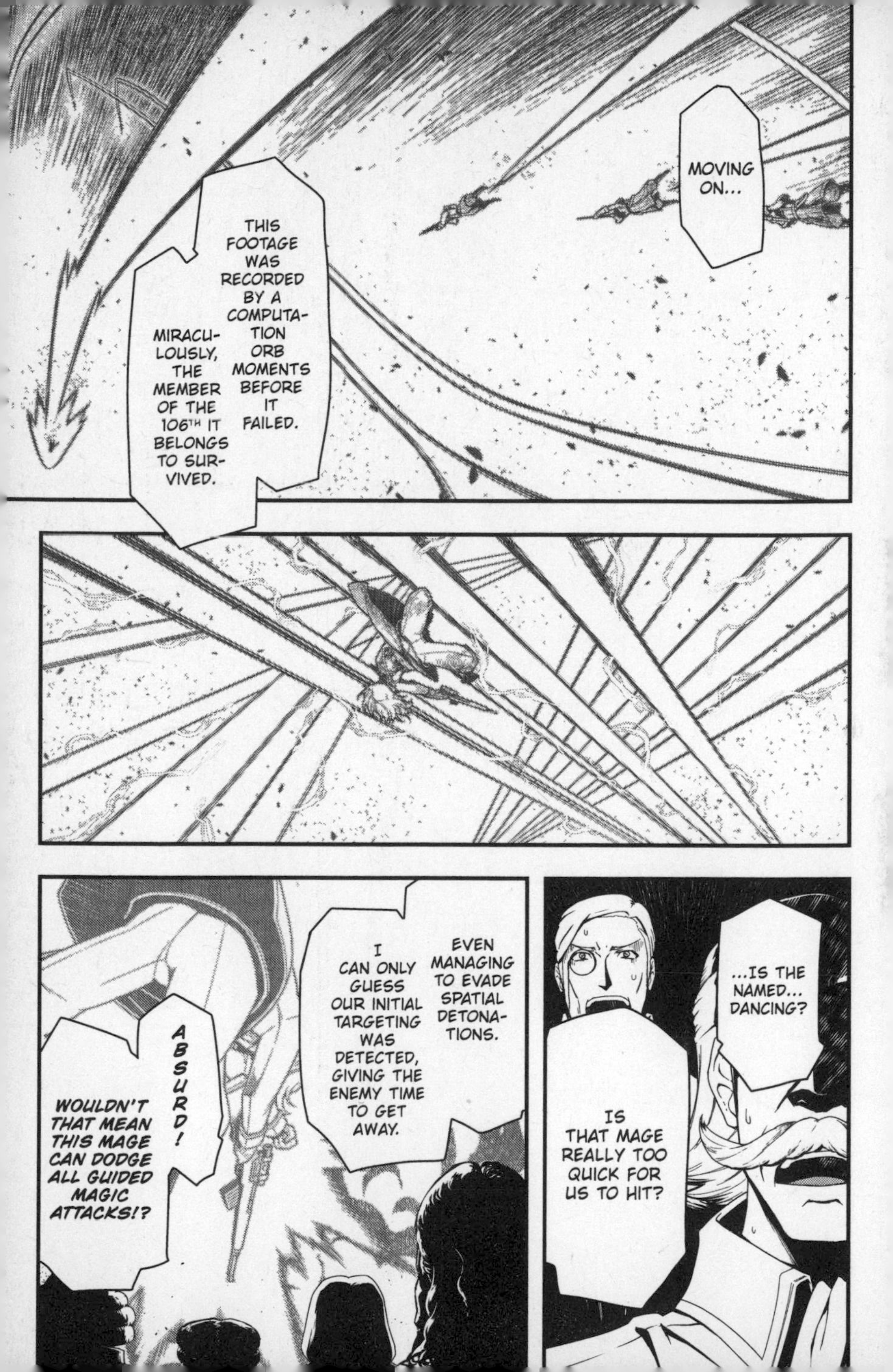
MOVING ON...
THIS FOOTAGE WAS RECORDED BY A COMPUTATION ORB MOMENTS BEFORE IT FAILED.
MIRACULOUSLY, THE MEMBER OF THE 106TH IT BELONGS TO SURVIVED.
...IS THE NAMED... DANCING?
IS THAT MAGE REALLY TOO QUICK FOR US TO HIT?
EVEN MANAGING TO EVADE SPATIAL DETONATIONS.
I CAN ONLY GUESS OUR INITIAL TARGETING WAS DETECTED, GIVING THE ENEMY TIME TO GET AWAY.
ABSURD!
WOULDN'T THAT MEAN THIS MAGE CAN DODGE ALL GUIDED MAGIC ATTACKS!?

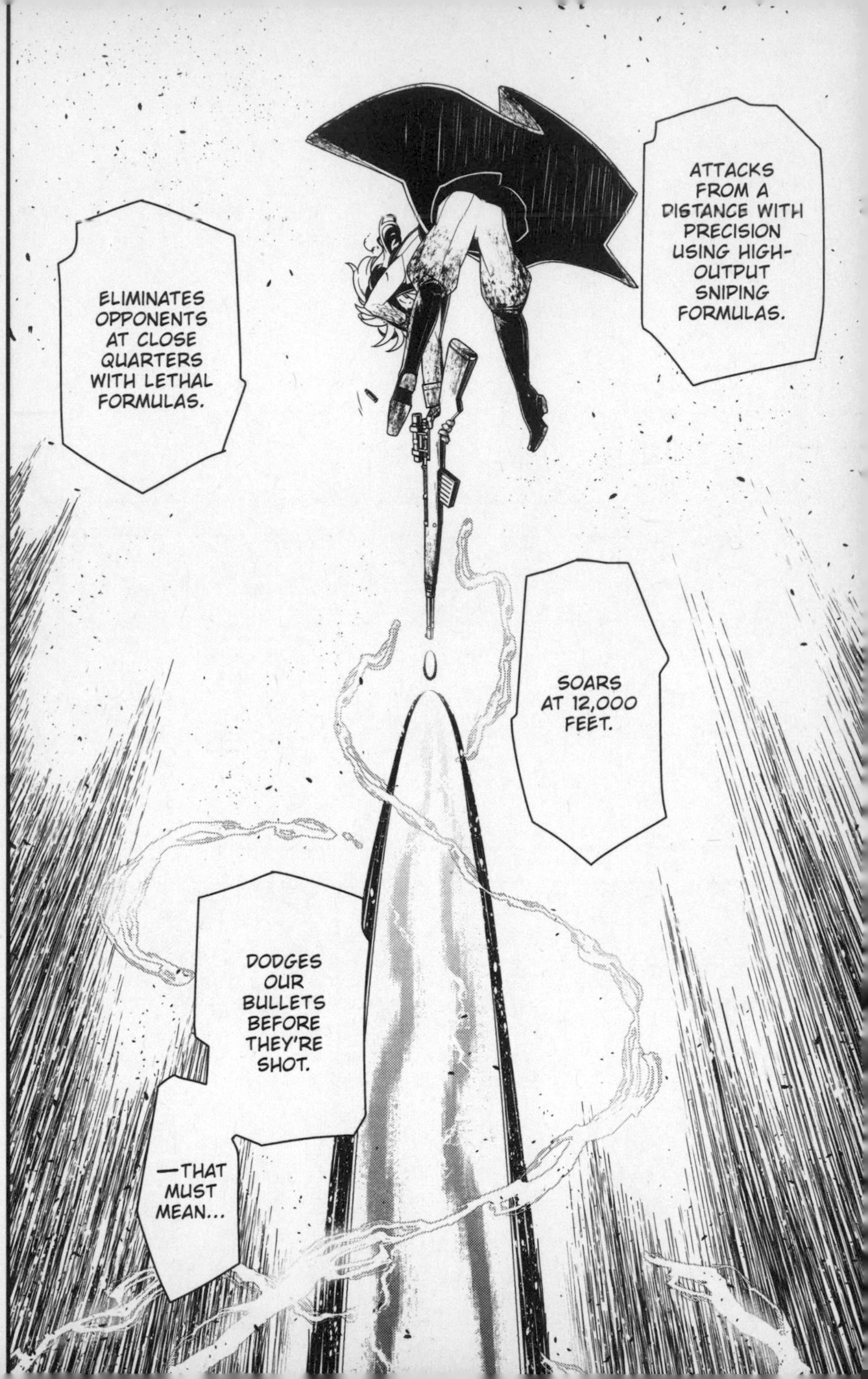
ATTACKS FROM A DISTANCE WITH PRECISION USING HIGH-OUTPUT SNIPING FORMULAS.
ELIMINATES OPPONENTS AT CLOSE QUARTERS WITH LETHAL FORMULAS.
SOARS AT 12,000 FEET.
DODGES OUR BULLETS BEFORE THEY'RE SHOT.
—THAT MUST MEAN...

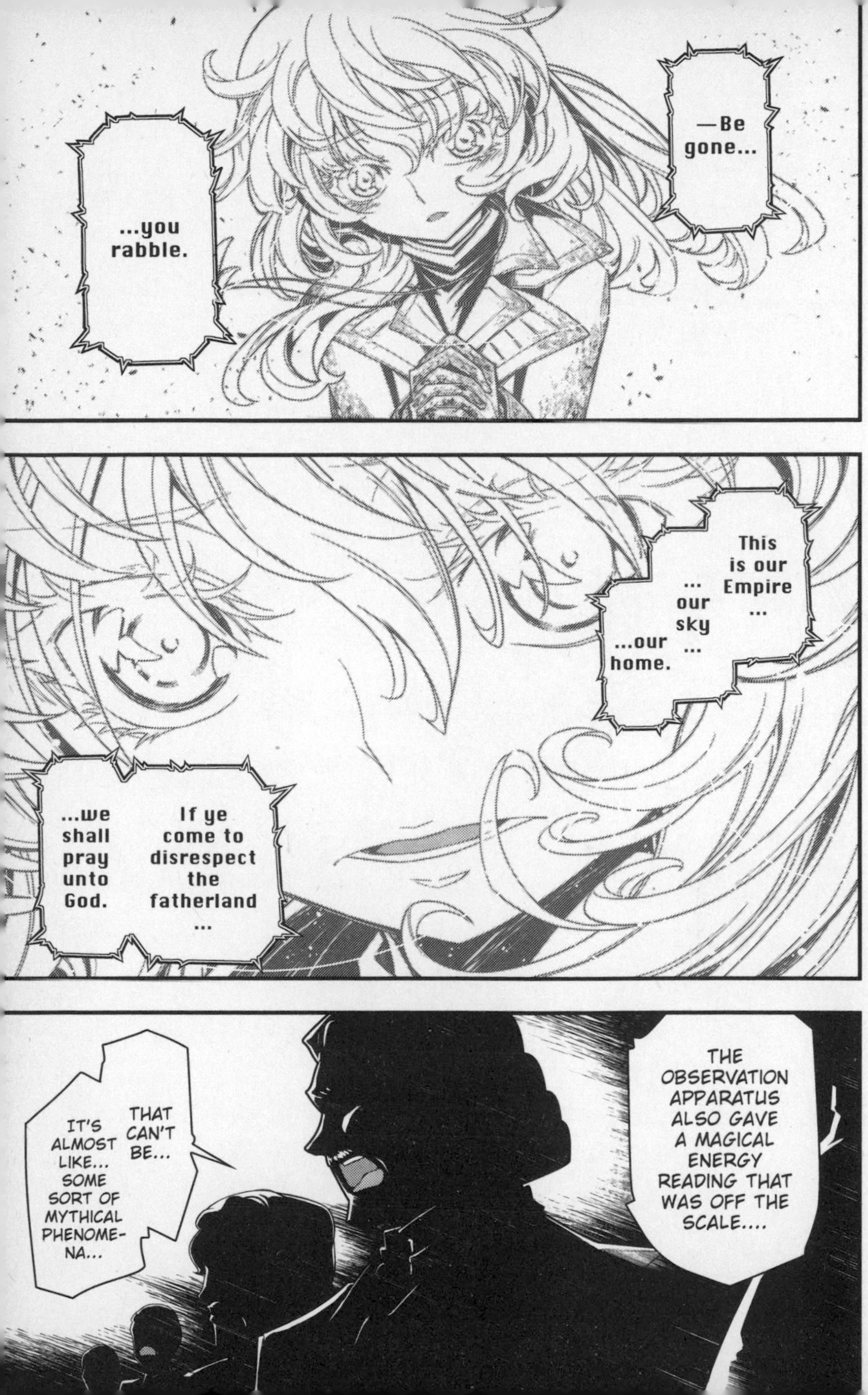
—Be gone...
...you rabble.
This is our Empire ... ... our sky ... ...our home.
If ye come to disrespect the fatherland ...
...we shall pray unto God.
THE OBSERVATION APPARATUS ALSO GAVE A MAGICAL ENERGY READING THAT WAS OFF THE SCALE....
THAT CAN'T BE...
IT'S ALMOST LIKE... SOME SORT OF MYTHICAL PHENOME-NA...

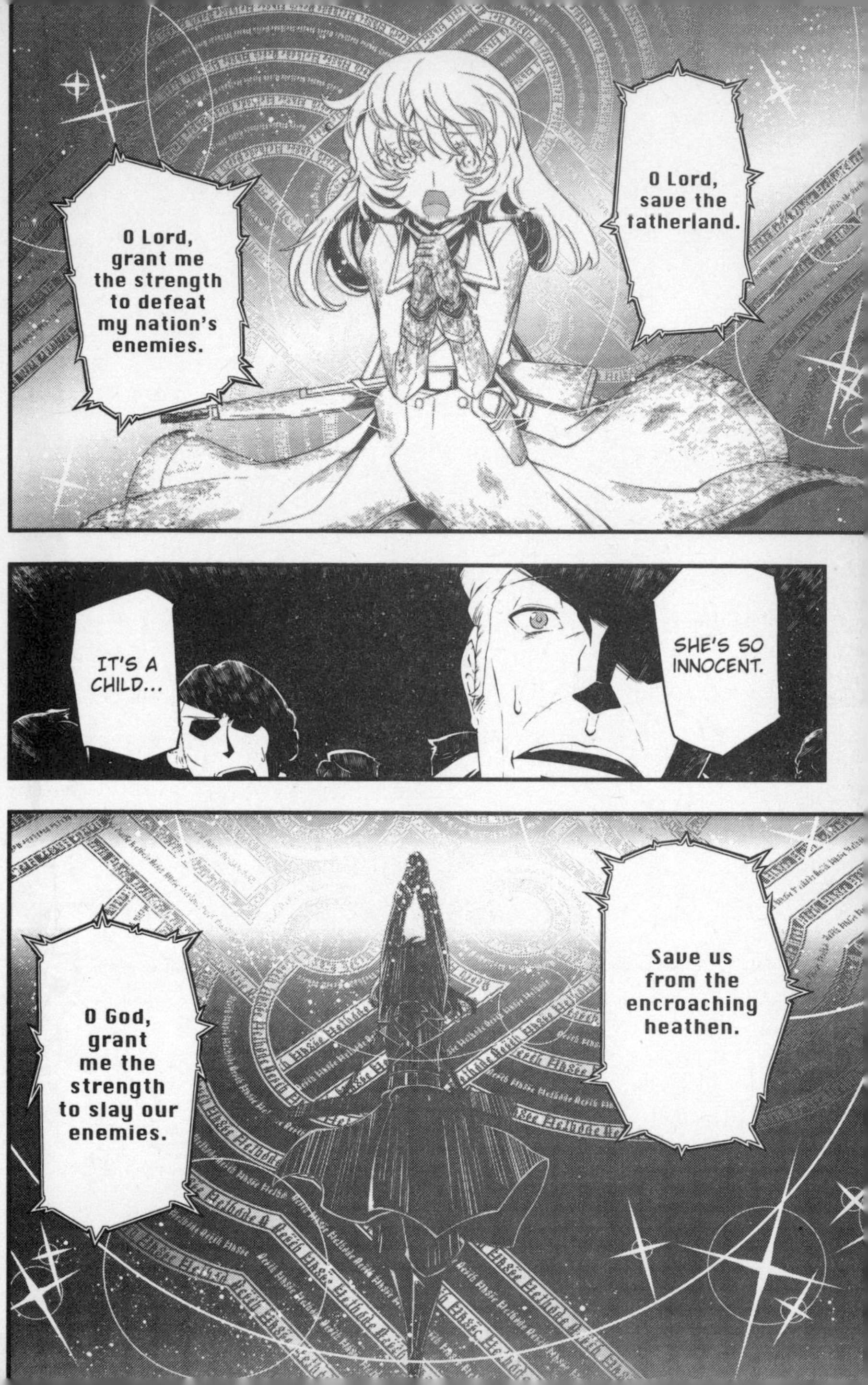
O Lord, save the fatherland.
O Lord, grant me the strength to defeat my nation's enemies.
SHE'S SO INNOCENT.
IT'S A CHILD...
Save us from the encroaching heathen.
O God, grant me the strength to slay our enemies.

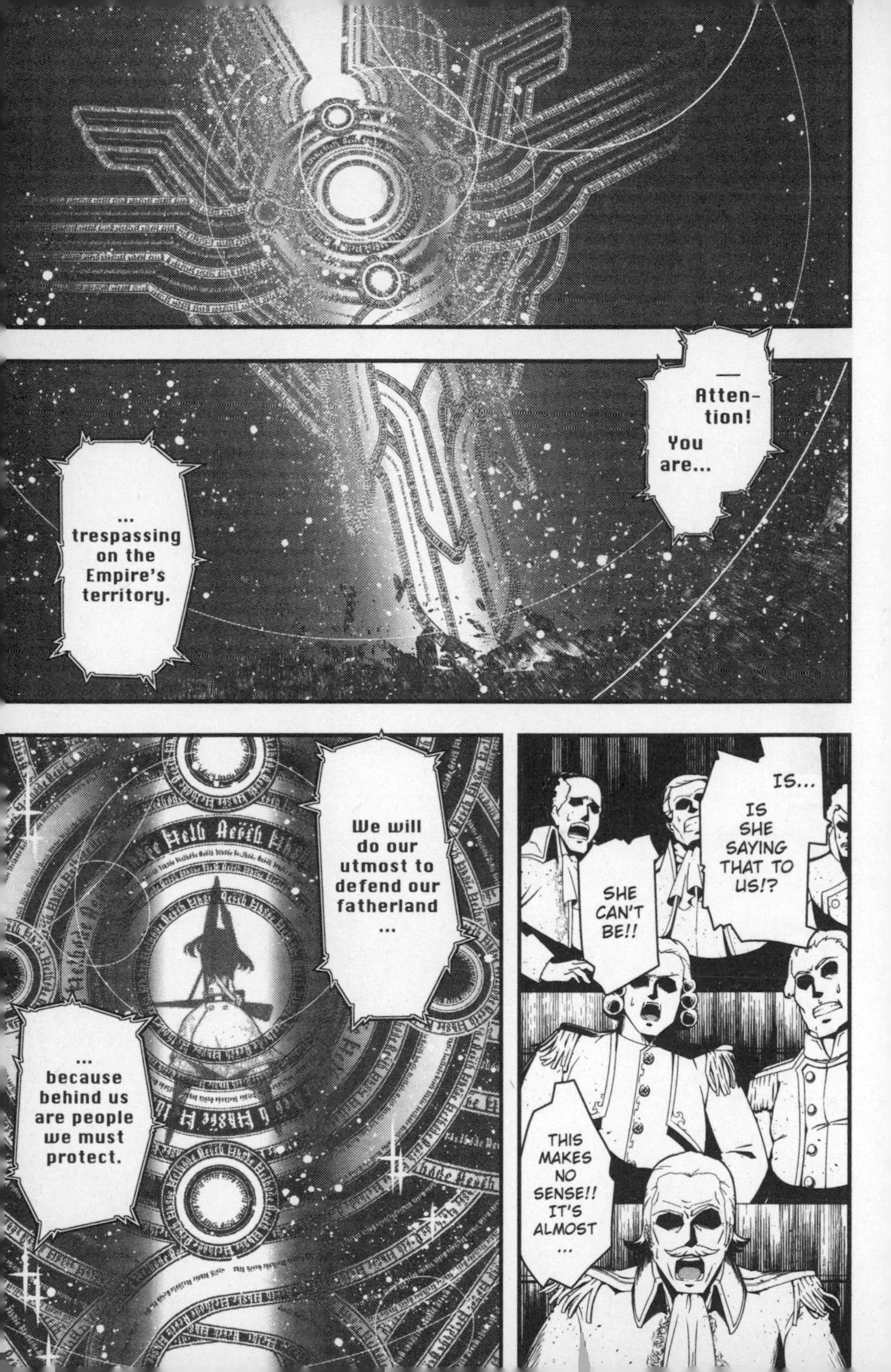
— Attention! You are...
... trespassing on the Empire's territory.
IS... IS SHE SAYING THAT TO US!?
SHE CAN'T BE!!
THIS MAKES NO SENSE!! IT'S ALMOST ...
We will do our utmost to defend our fatherland ...
... because behind us are people we must protect.

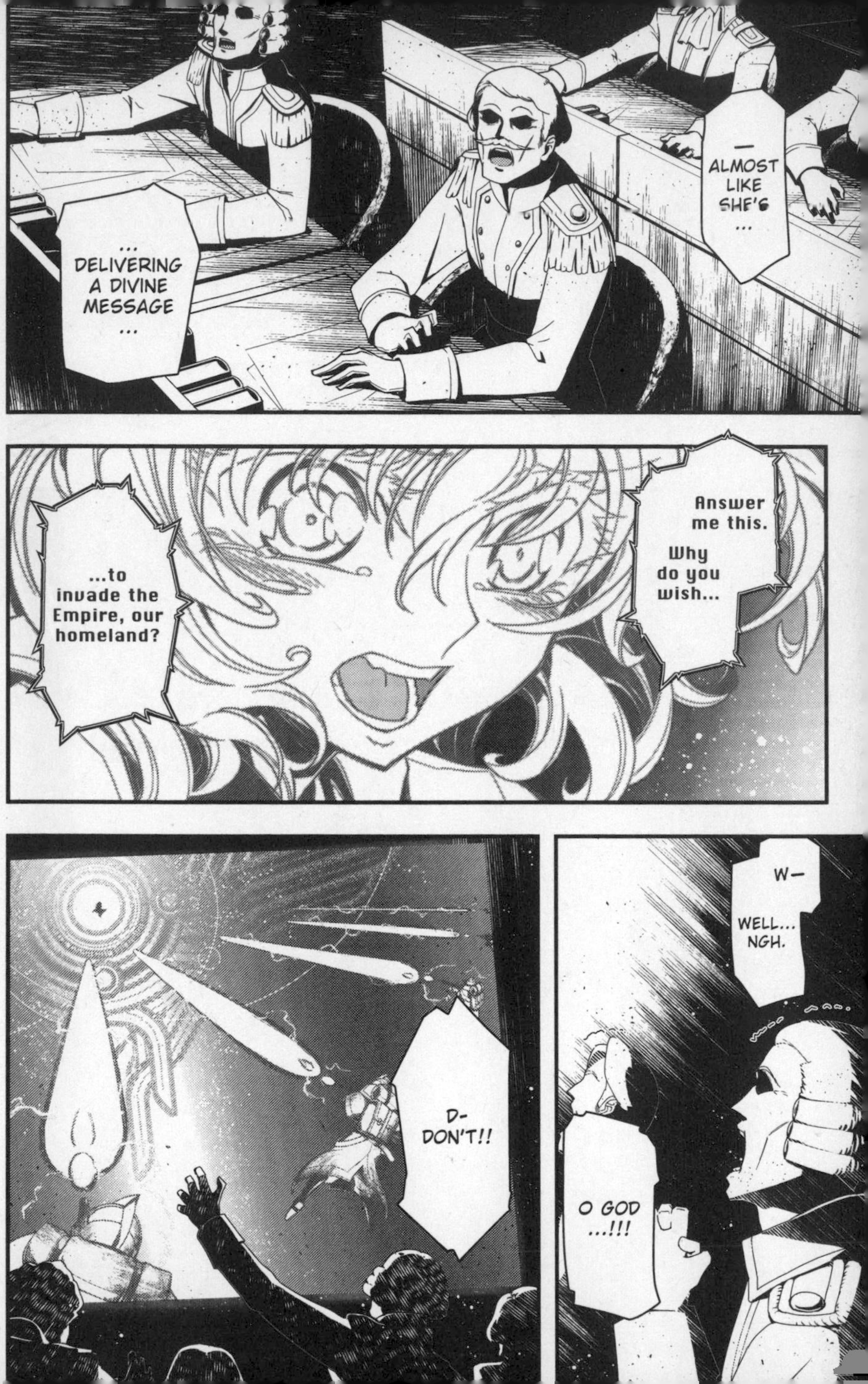
—ALMOST LIKE SHE'S ...
...DELIVERING A DIVINE MESSAGE ...
Answer me this.
Why do you wish...
...to invade the Empire, our homeland?
W—
WELL... NGH.
O GOD ...!!!
D-DON'T!!

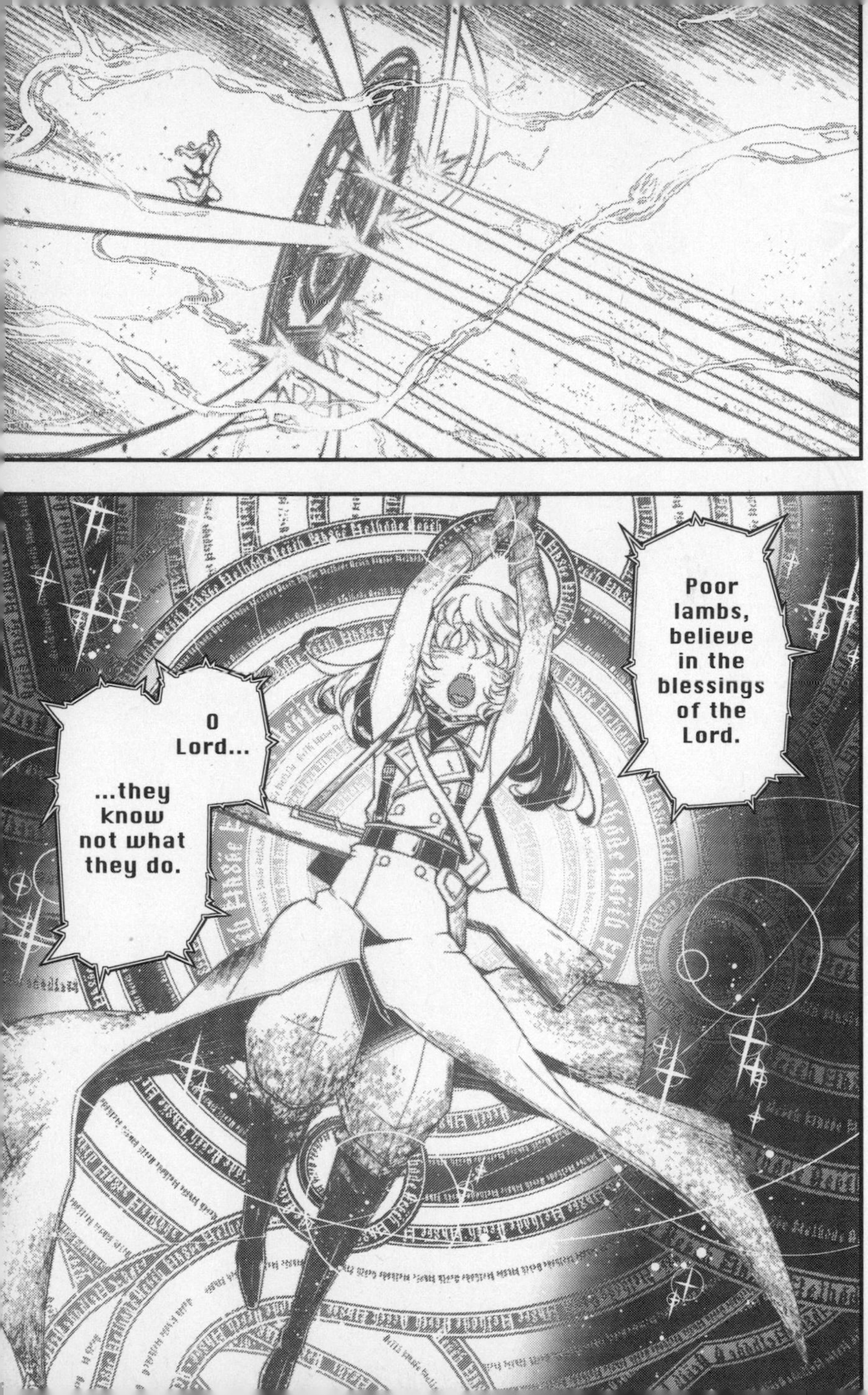
Poor lambs, believe in the blessings of the Lord.
O Lord...
...they know not what they do.

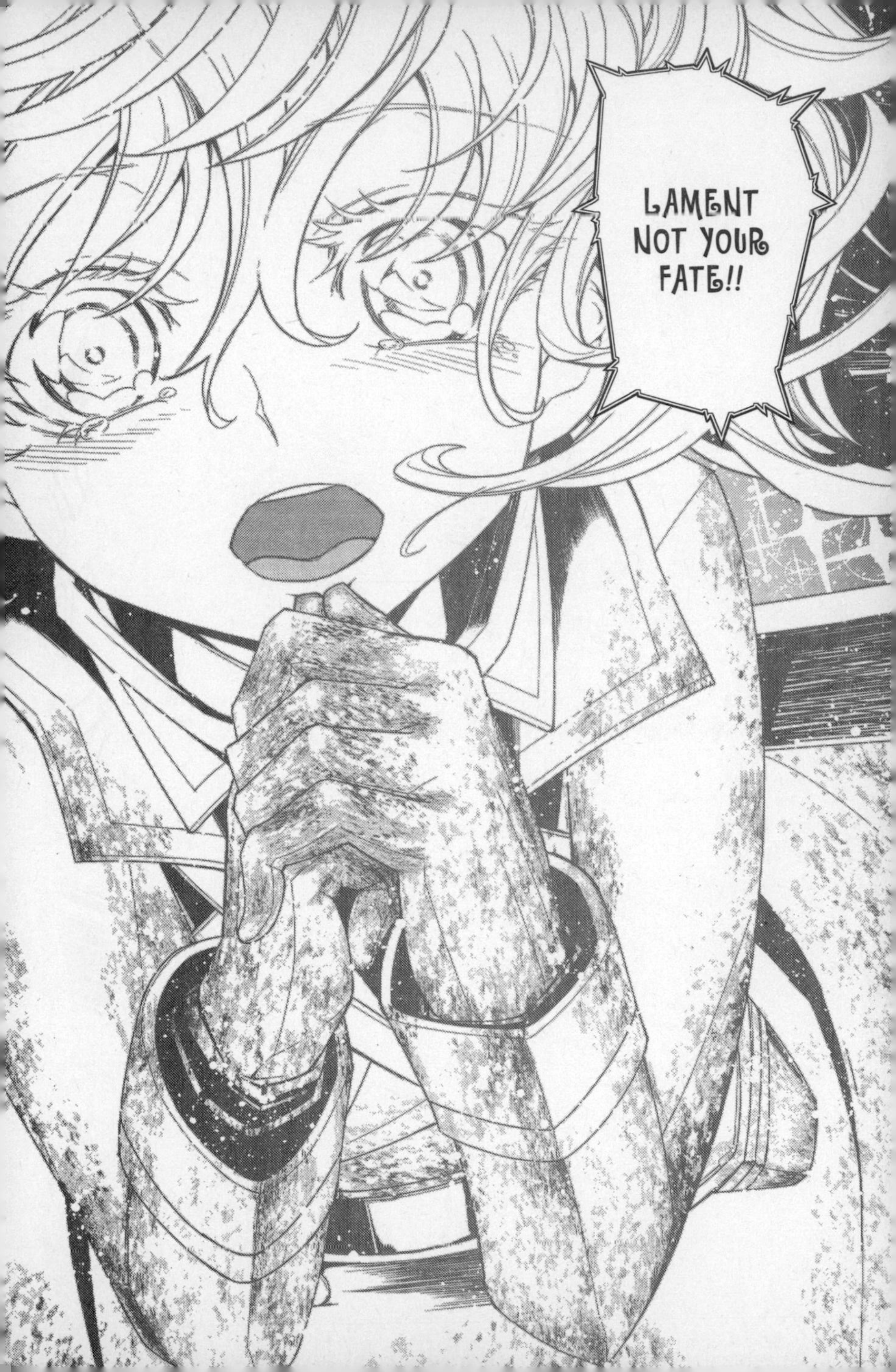
LAMENT NOT YOUR FATE!!

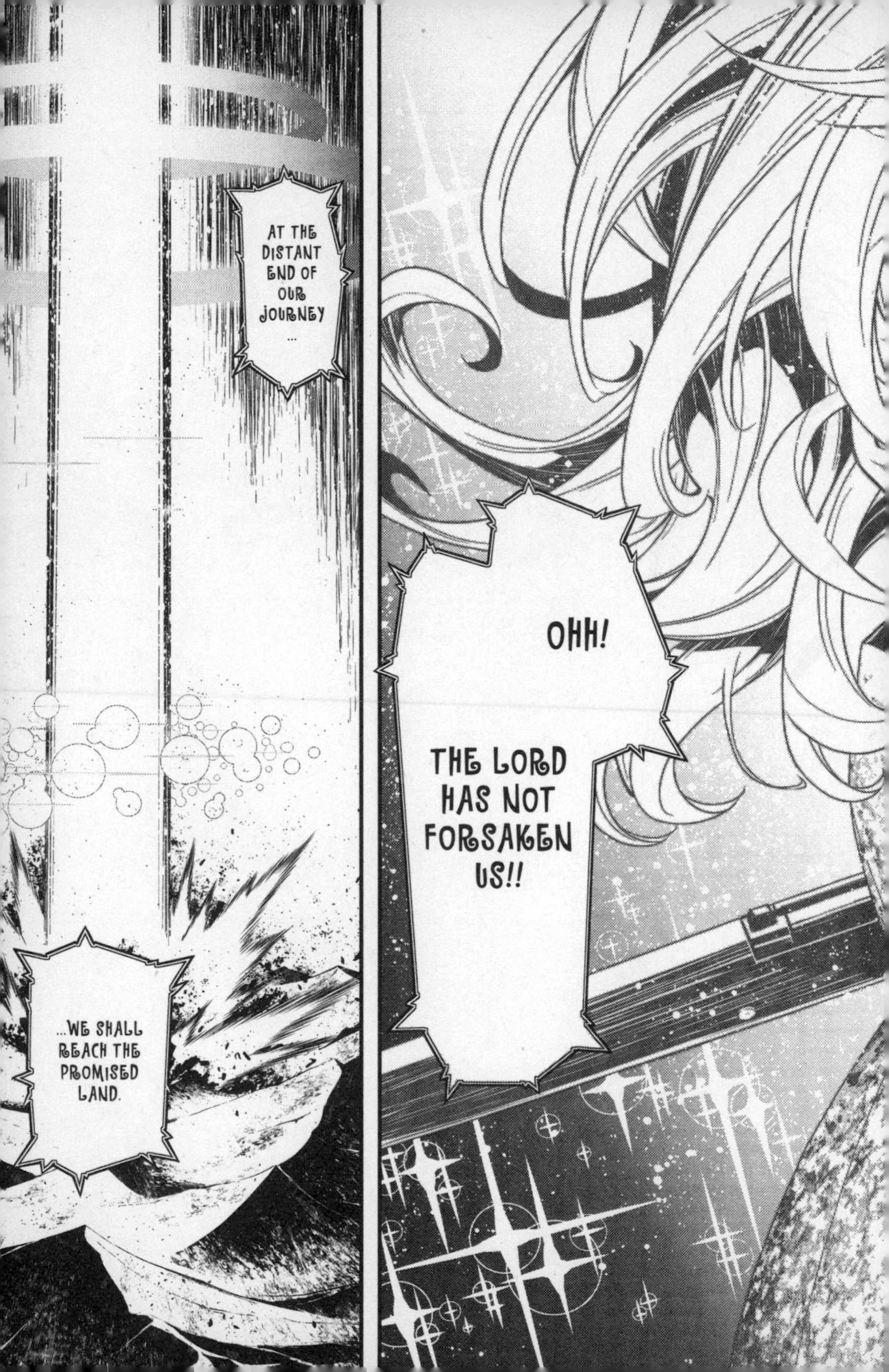
OHH! THE LORD HAS NOT FORSAKEN US!!
AT THE DISTANT END OF OUR JOURNEY ...
...WE SHALL REACH THE PROMISED LAND.

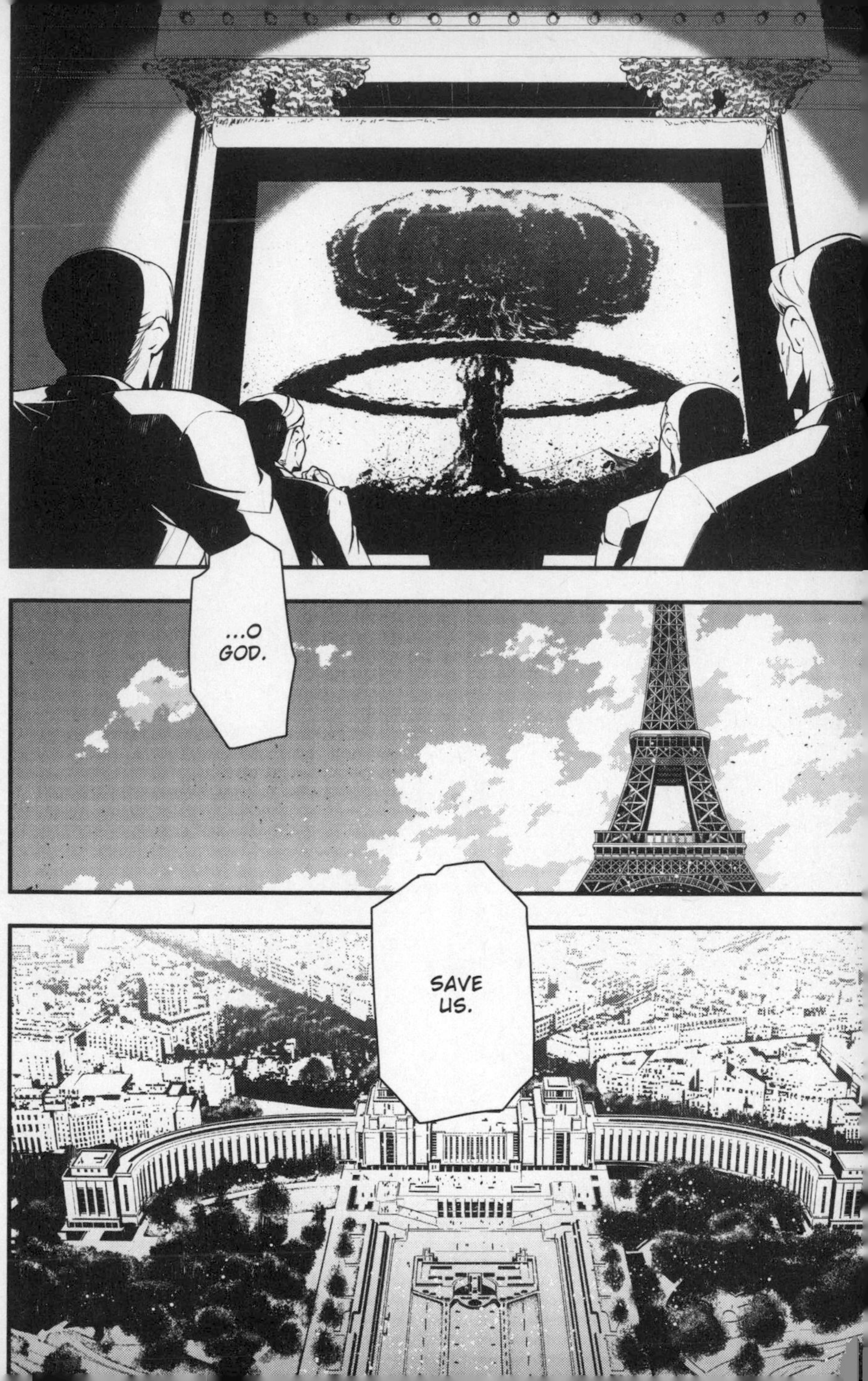
...O GOD.
SAVE US.

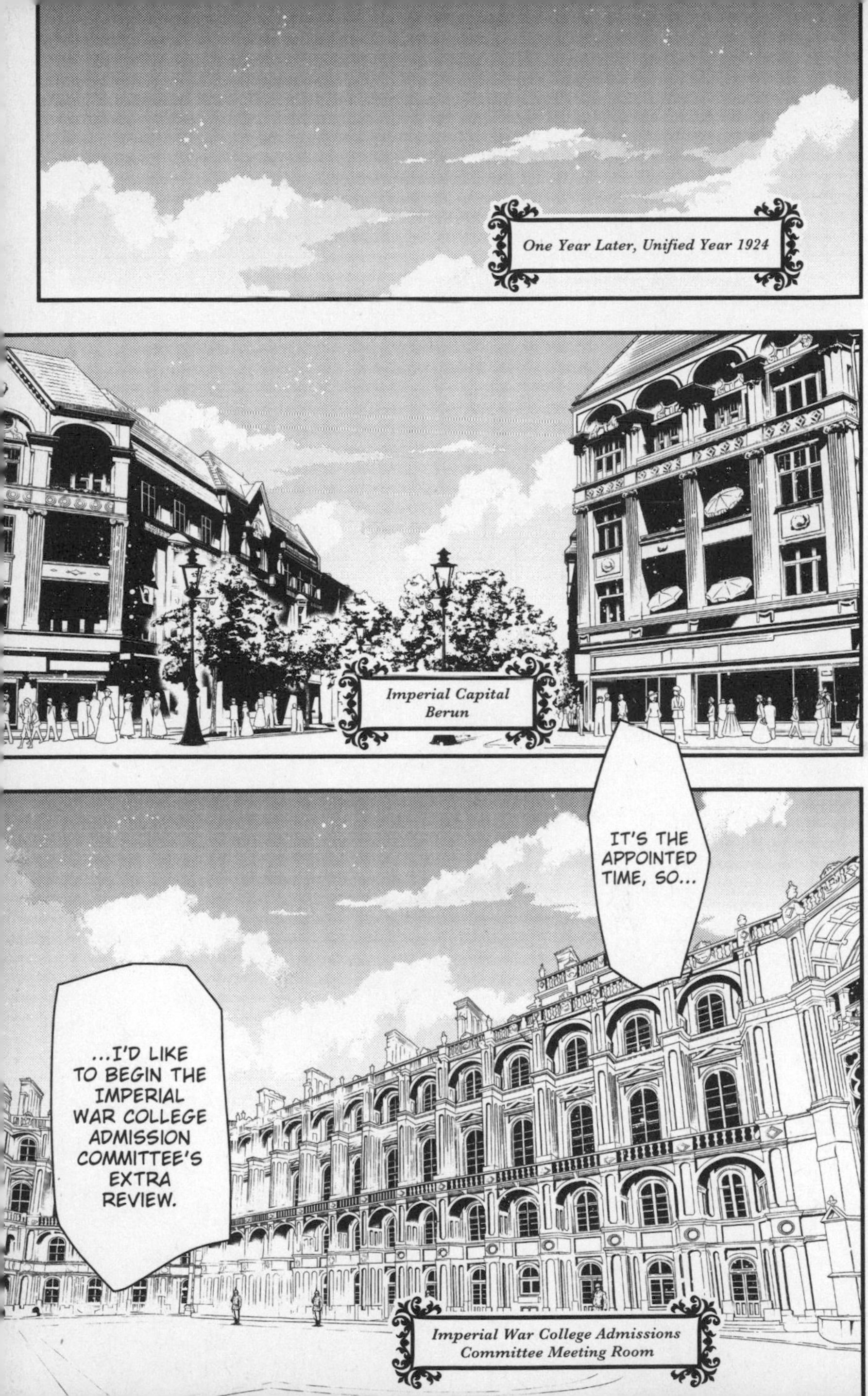
One Year Later, Unified Year 1924
Imperial Capital Berun
IT'S THE APPOINTED TIME, SO...
...I'D LIKE TO BEGIN THE IMPERIAL WAR COLLEGE ADMISSION COMMITTEE'S EXTRA REVIEW.
Imperial War College Admissions Committee Meeting Room

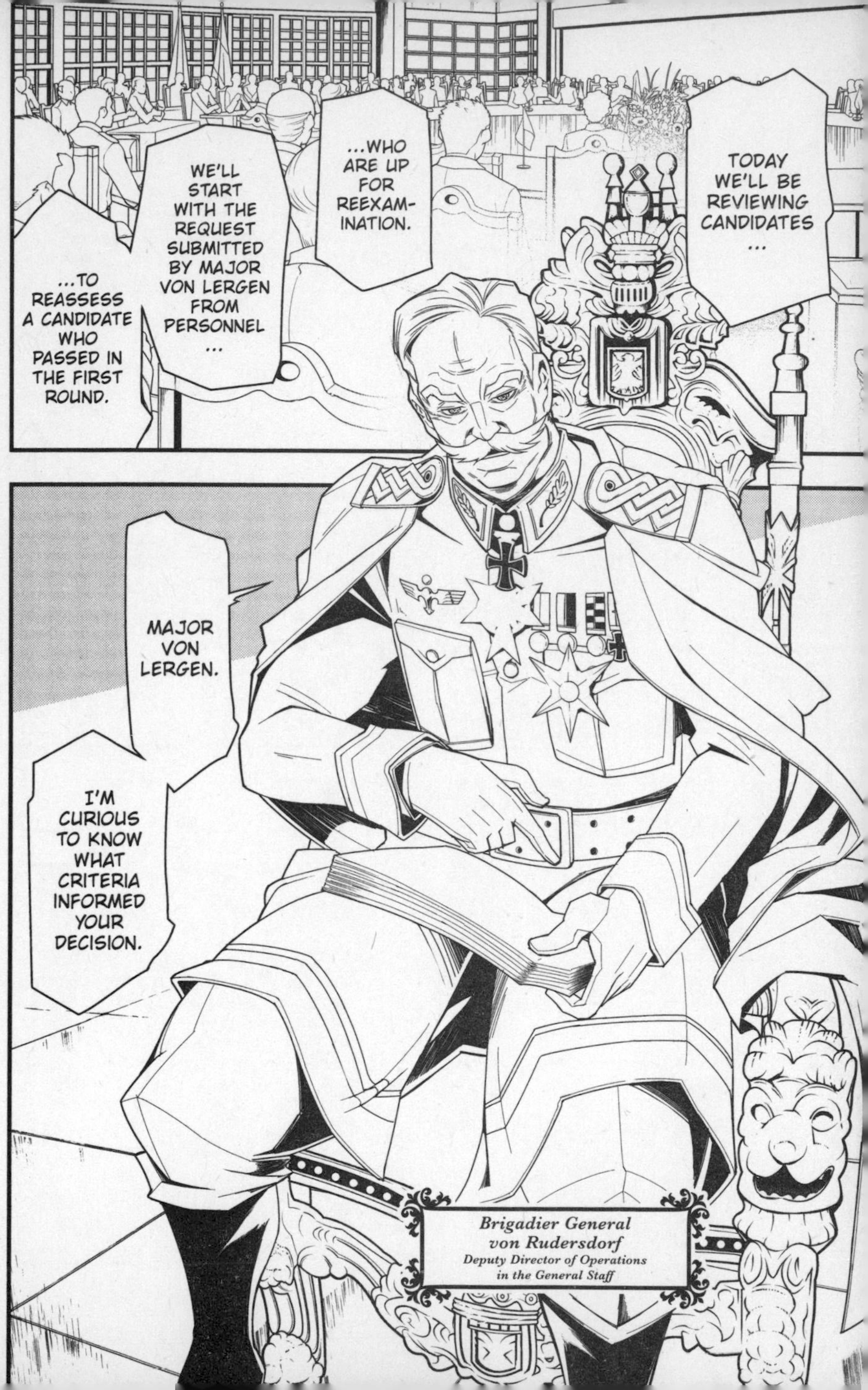
TODAY WE'LL BE REVIEWING CANDIDATES...
...WHO ARE UP FOR REEXAMINATION.
WE'LL START WITH THE REQUEST SUBMITTED BY MAJOR VON LERGEN FROM PERSONNEL...
...TO REASSESS A CANDIDATE WHO PASSED IN THE FIRST ROUND.
MAJOR VON LERGEN.
I'M CURIOUS TO KNOW WHAT CRITERIA INFORMED YOUR DECISION.
Brigadier General von Rudersdorf
Deputy Director of Operations in the General Staff

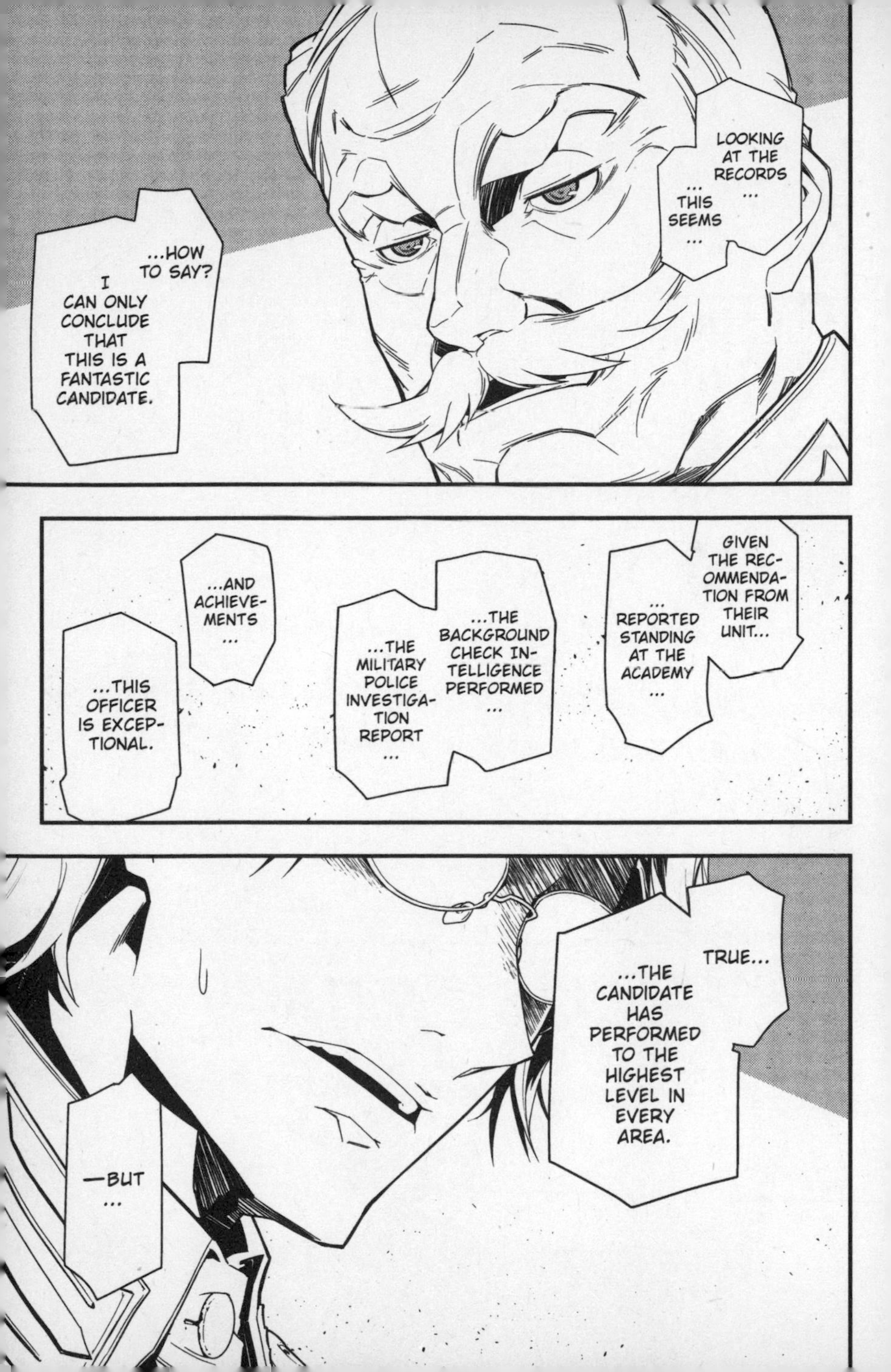
LOOKING AT THE RECORDS ... ... THIS SEEMS ...
...HOW TO SAY? I CAN ONLY CONCLUDE THAT THIS IS A FANTASTIC CANDIDATE.
GIVEN THE RECOMMENDATION FROM THEIR UNIT...
...REPORTED STANDING AT THE ACADEMY ...
...THE BACKGROUND CHECK INTELLIGENCE PERFORMED ...
...THE MILITARY POLICE INVESTIGATION REPORT ...
...AND ACHIEVEMENTS ...
...THIS OFFICER IS EXCEPTIONAL.
TRUE... ...THE CANDIDATE HAS PERFORMED TO THE HIGHEST LEVEL IN EVERY AREA.
—BUT ...

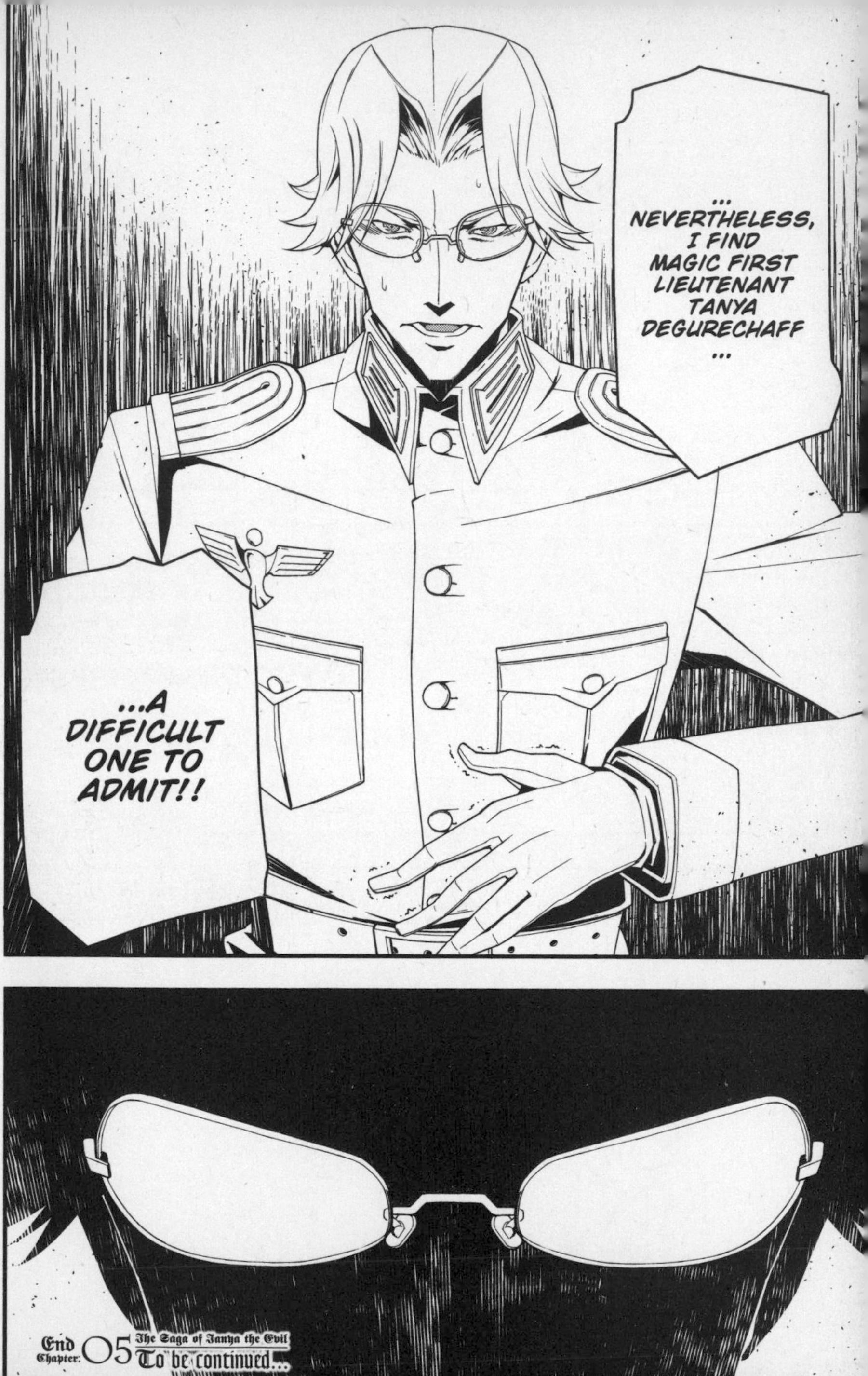
...NEVERTHELESS, I FIND MAGIC FIRST LIEUTENANT TANYA DEGURECHAFF ...
...A DIFFICULT ONE TO ADMIT!!
End Chapter: 05 The Saga of Tanya the Evil
To be continued...

Glossary Chapter O3

Trench

Ditches that soldiers dig to protect themselves from gunfire on the front line. To prevent soldiers from getting completely wiped out in an explosion when shells land inside, trenches are often dug in zigzag patterns. At the bottom are pits called "grenade sumps" into which enemy grenades can be dropped.

Trenches can't perfectly defend against trench mortar guns firing on a parabola, poison gas, or tanks, but countermeasures such as dugouts, gas masks, and anti-tank trenches can be taken to make it quite difficult to break through a well-prepared line.

While penetration is possible using an elaborate combination of methods such as artillery barrage, infantry charge, exploiting a weak point, and destroying communication lines, the advantage nevertheless lies with the defenders, and the battlefront tends to reach a stalemate.

Pillbox

A defensive position surrounded with stone or concrete. It's also possible to build simple ones with sandbags or logs. Firing slits are built into the walls to allow soldiers inside to spot and fire upon enemies, but due to defensive necessity, the openings are very small, so the field of view is limited. In order to compensate for blind spots, multiple pillboxes are sometimes built in a line.

Armored Division

A self-propelled division built around tanks. They are highly mobile, highly destructive, and specialize in rapid strikes.

Armored divisions can break through enemy trenches with tanks and swiftly penetrate deep into enemy territory, so they become the pivotal point of blitzkrieg strategies that throw enemy intelligence into confusion.

Glossary Chapter 04

Logistics

The replenishing of supplies such as food and fuel, monitoring hygiene, as well as preparing weapons or setting up bases so that the army can carry out its missions smoothly.

Armies consume an enormous amount of matériel each day, so logistics is their lifeline. Cutting off access to it means no food, fuel, ammunition, medical equipment, or other supplies can reach the front, so it becomes practically impossible to continue fighting.

It's even said, "War is comprised of strategy, tactics, and logistics."

If the army advances too quickly, or like in the Empire, the military is deployed to multiple fronts, sometimes logistics can't keep up, so the soldiers can't fight at their full strength. Ideally, the lines should only expand with proportional increases in logistics capability.

Battalion, Company, Platoon

An army is made of divisions, brigades, and other units of varying size.

It depends on the army, but generally, a handful to a few dozen soldiers make a platoon, two or more platoons form a company, and two or more companies are a battalion. A platoon is the smallest unit commanded by an officer (second lieutenant or higher). Battalions are usually commanded by at least a major.

Doctrine

Fundamental principles in politics, diplomacy, the military, and so on. In the military, it refers especially to various guidelines armies follow.

We say "war" so simply, but the focus differs between armies—will you aim for a quick, decisive fight or invest in matériel strategy? An army's doctrine describes what it values and focuses on.

An army is generally a top-down organization, but directives from the top don't always make it all the way to the bottom. When units need to act of their own accord, the doctrine acts as the basis for their decisions. For example, if a unit has sustained a certain amount of casualties, the commander decides whether to retreat or not based on doctrine.

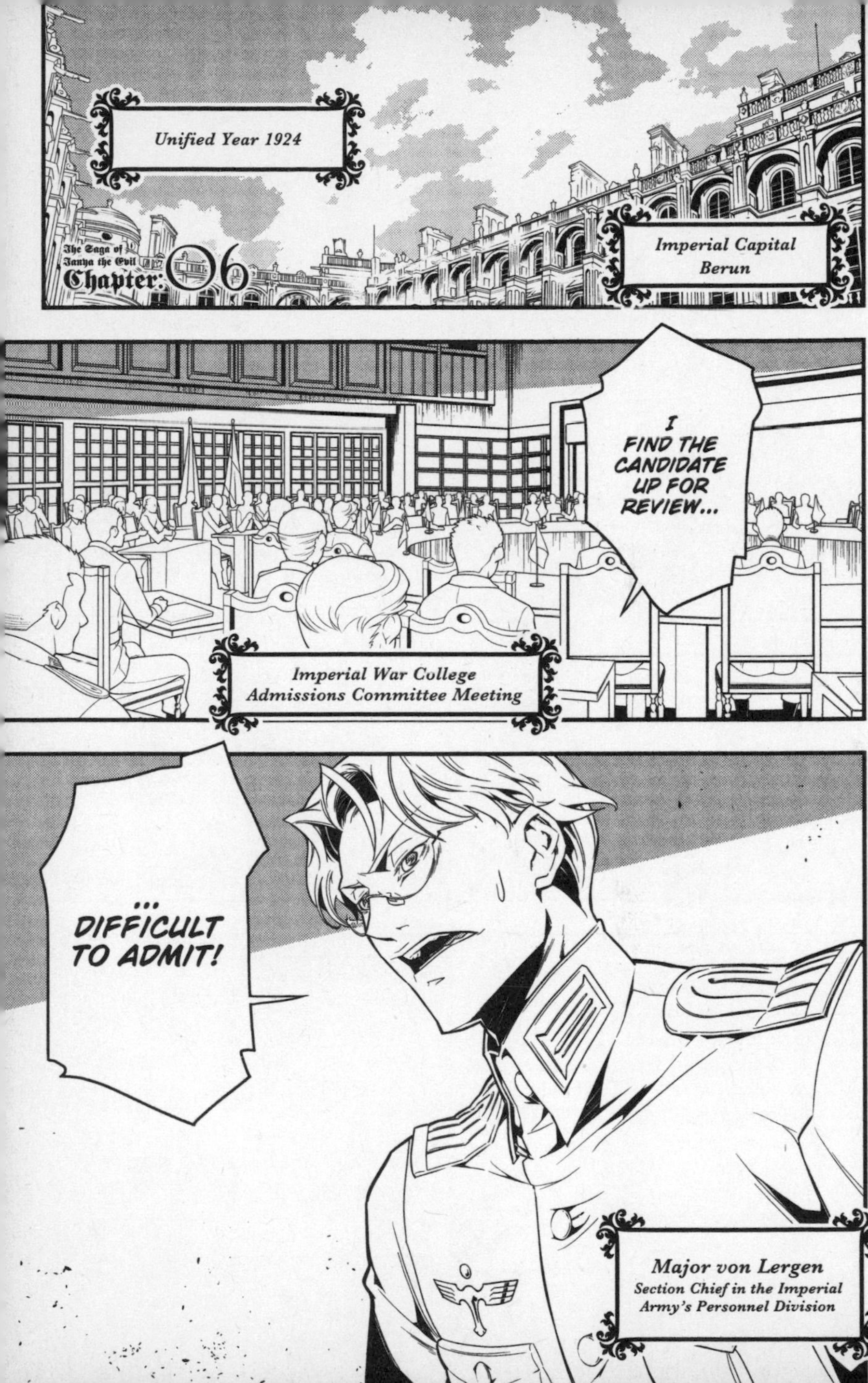

The Saga of Tanya the Evil
Chapter: 06
Unified Year 1924
Imperial Capital Berun
I FIND THE CANDIDATE UP FOR REVIEW...
Imperial War College Admissions Committee Meeting
...DIFFICULT TO ADMIT!
Major von Lergen
Section Chief in the Imperial Army's Personnel Division

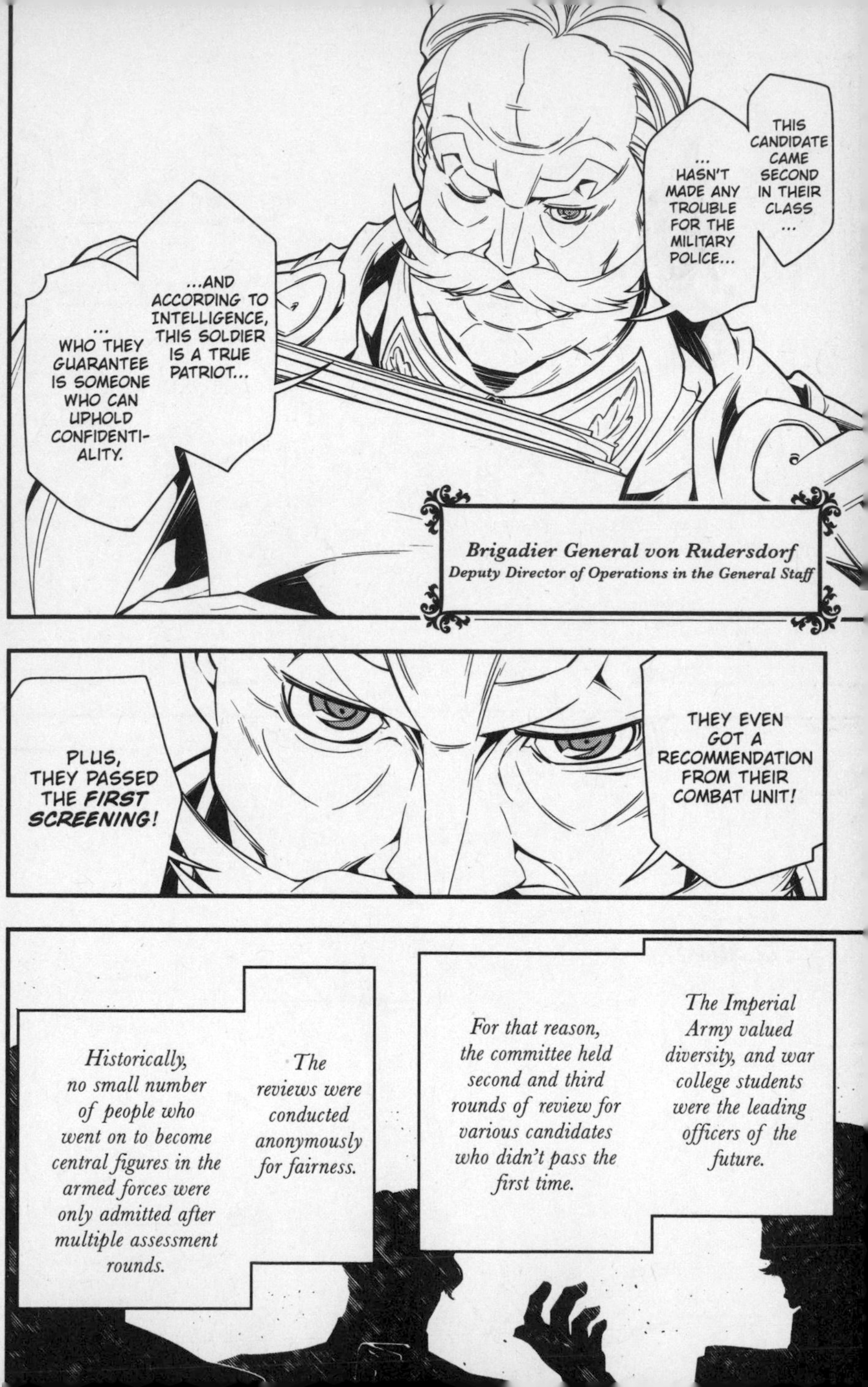
THIS CANDIDATE CAME SECOND IN THEIR CLASS...
...HASN'T MADE ANY TROUBLE FOR THE MILITARY POLICE...
...AND ACCORDING TO INTELLIGENCE, THIS SOLDIER IS A TRUE PATRIOT...
...WHO THEY GUARANTEE IS SOMEONE WHO CAN UPHOLD CONFIDENTIALITY.
Brigadier General von Rudersdorf
Deputy Director of Operations in the General Staff
THEY EVEN GOT A RECOMMENDATION FROM THEIR COMBAT UNIT!
PLUS, THEY PASSED THE FIRST SCREENING!
The Imperial Army valued diversity, and war college students were the leading officers of the future.
For that reason, the committee held second and third rounds of review for various candidates who didn't pass the first time.
The reviews were conducted anonymously for fairness.
Historically, no small number of people who went on to become central figures in the armed forces were only admitted after multiple assessment rounds.

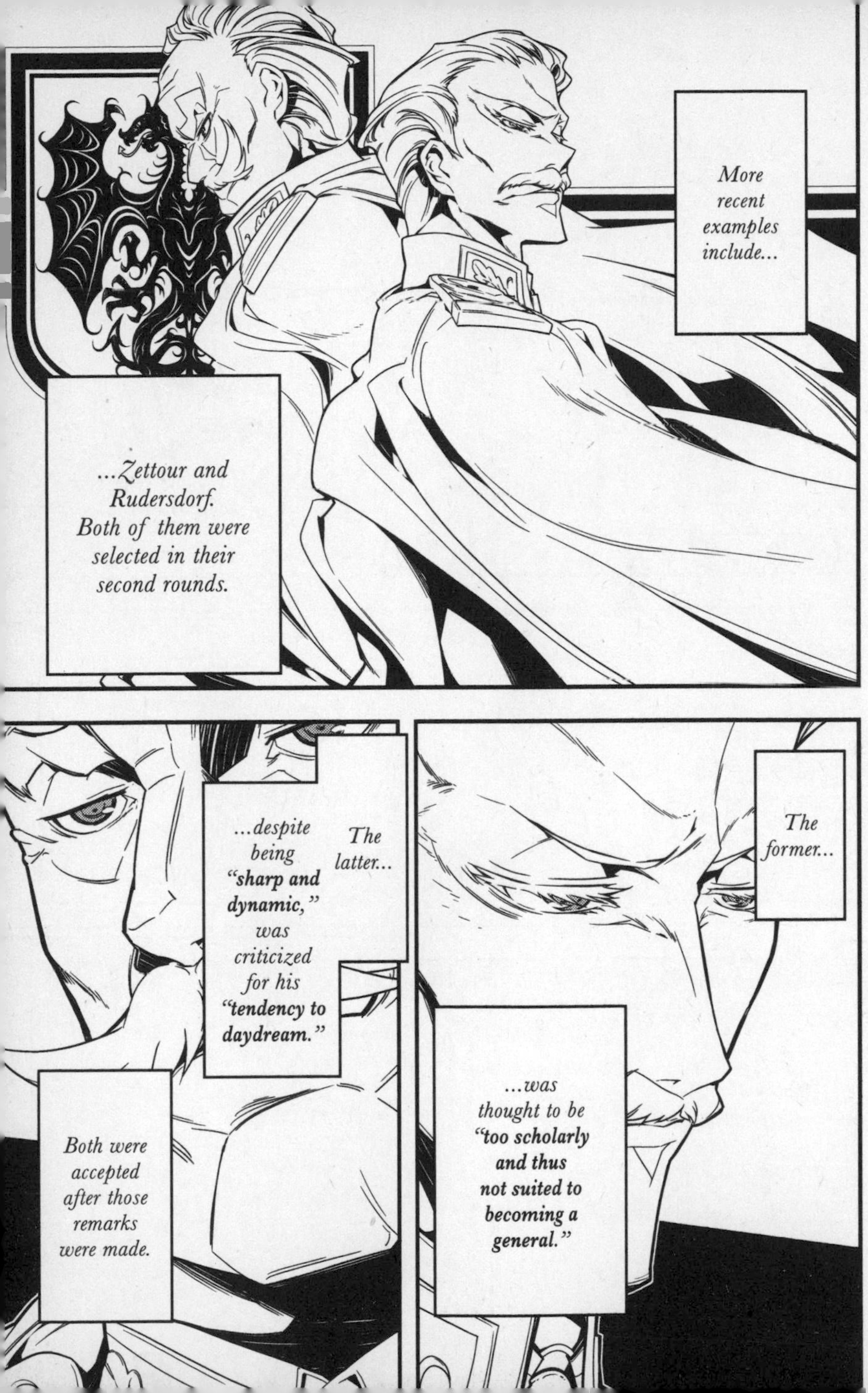
More recent examples include...
...Zettour and Rudersdorf. Both of them were selected in their second rounds.
The former...
...was thought to be **"too scholarly and thus not suited to becoming a general."**
The latter...
...despite being **"sharp and dynamic,"** was criticized for his **"tendency to daydream."**
Both were accepted after those remarks were made.

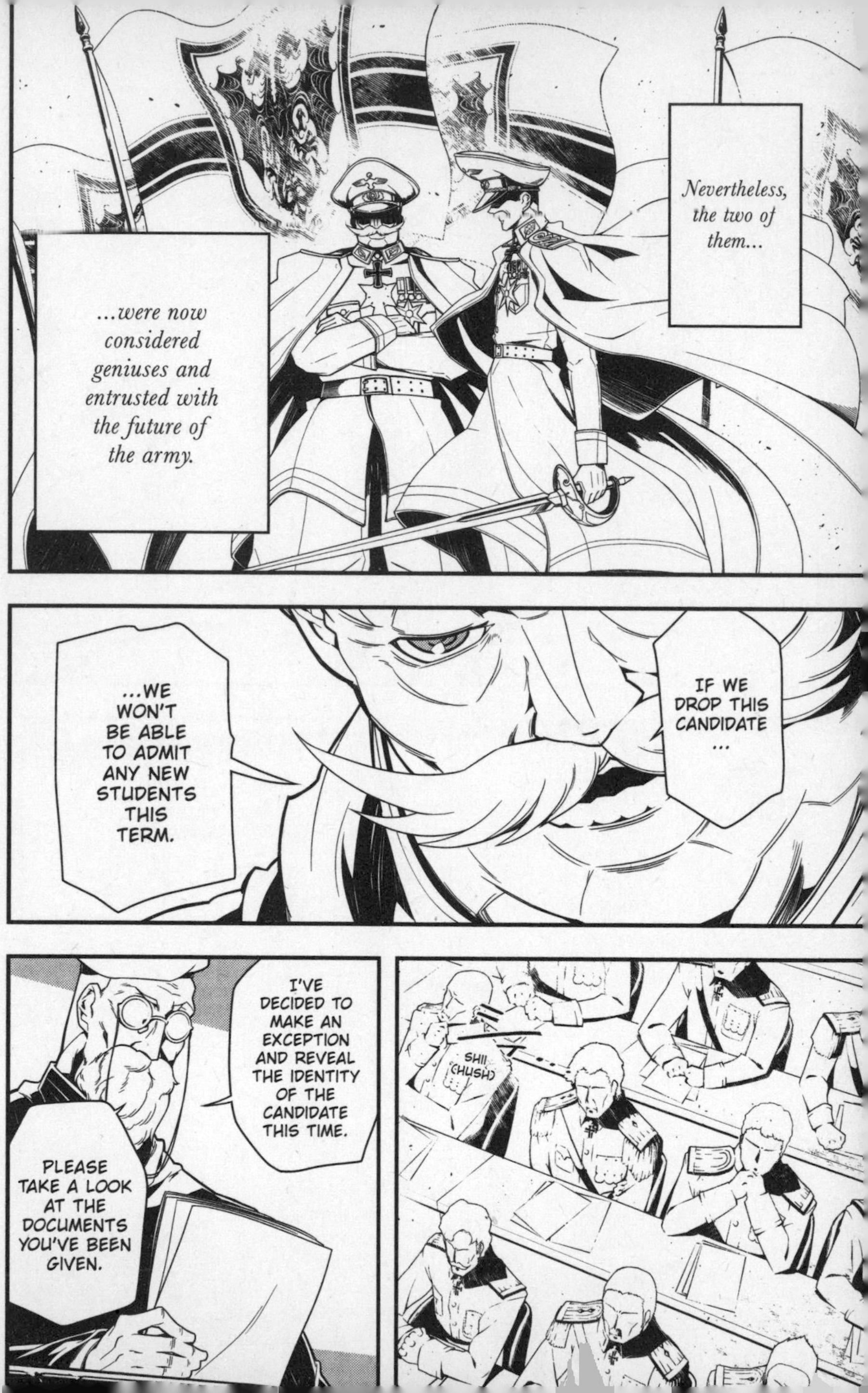
Nevertheless, the two of them...
...were now considered geniuses and entrusted with the future of the army.
IF WE DROP THIS CANDIDATE...
...WE WON'T BE ABLE TO ADMIT ANY NEW STUDENTS THIS TERM.
SHH (HUSH)
I'VE DECIDED TO MAKE AN EXCEPTION AND REVEAL THE IDENTITY OF THE CANDIDATE THIS TIME.
PLEASE TAKE A LOOK AT THE DOCUMENTS YOU'VE BEEN GIVEN.

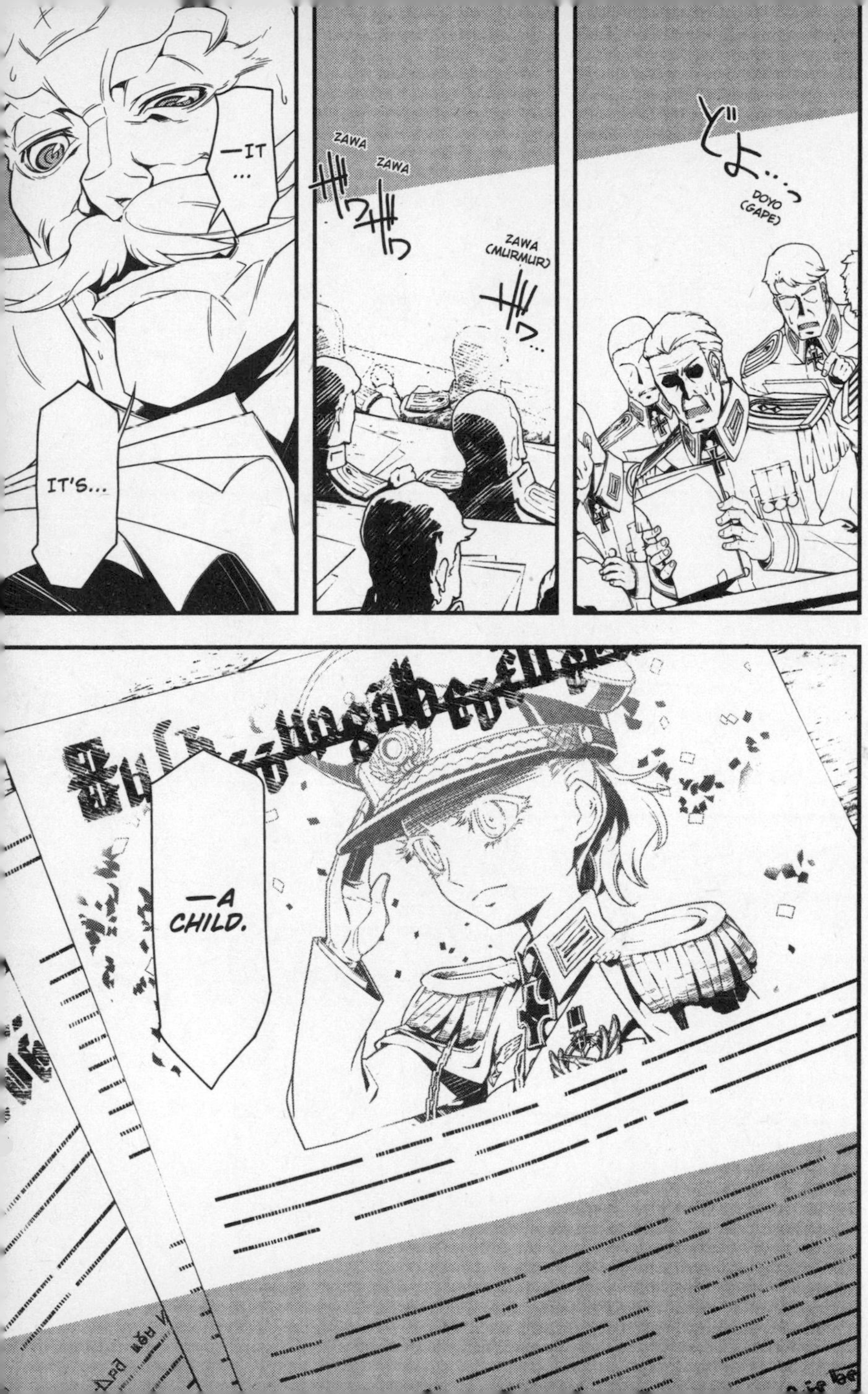

どよ…っ
DOYO (GAPE)
ZAWA
ZAWA
ZAWA (MURMUR)
—IT ...
IT'S...
—A CHILD.

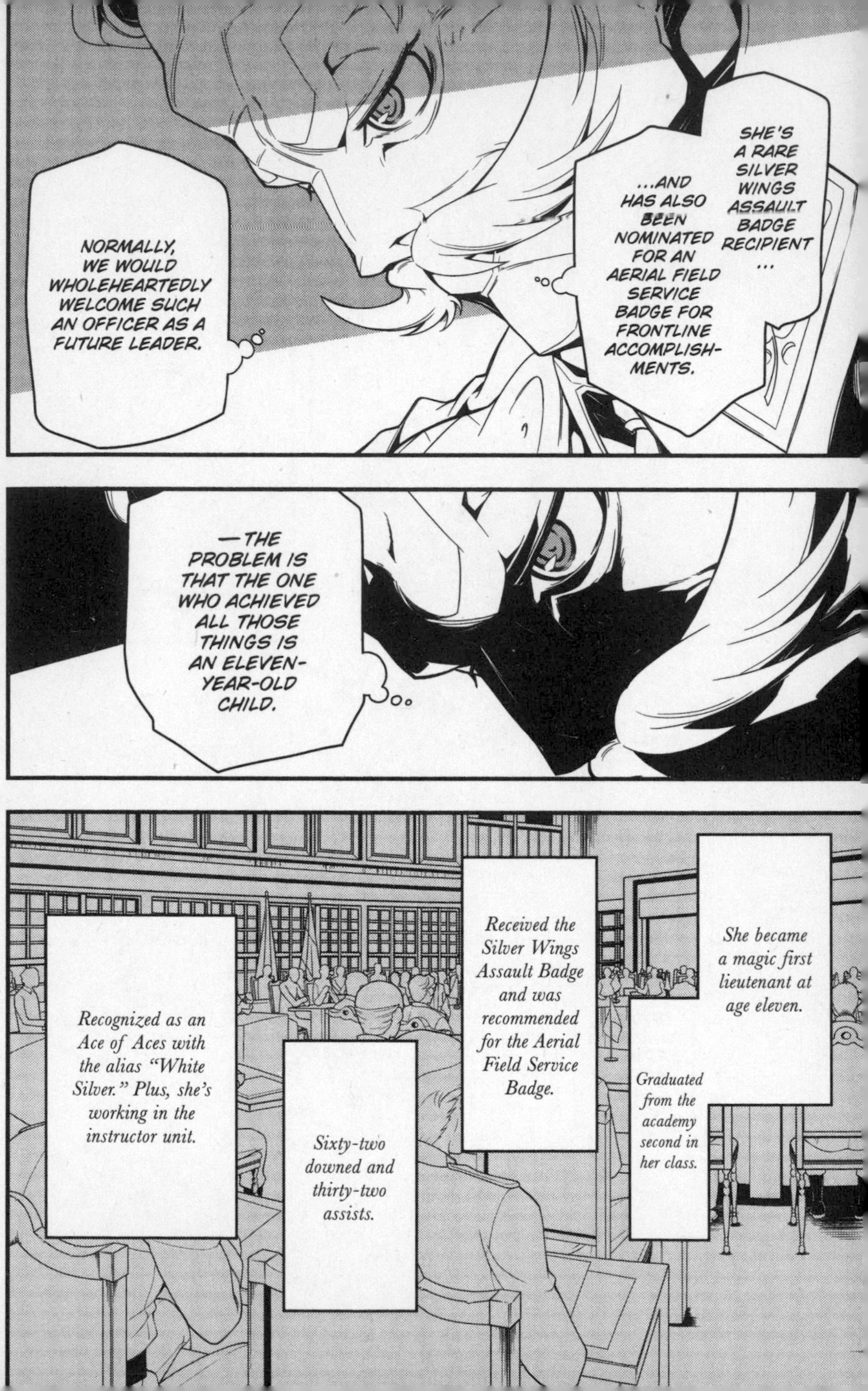
SHE'S A RARE SILVER WINGS ASSAULT BADGE RECIPIENT...
...AND HAS ALSO BEEN NOMINATED FOR AN AERIAL FIELD SERVICE BADGE FOR FRONTLINE ACCOMPLISH-MENTS.
NORMALLY, WE WOULD WHOLEHEARTEDLY WELCOME SUCH AN OFFICER AS A FUTURE LEADER.
—THE PROBLEM IS THAT THE ONE WHO ACHIEVED ALL THOSE THINGS IS AN ELEVEN-YEAR-OLD CHILD.
She became a magic first lieutenant at age eleven.
Graduated from the academy second in her class.
Received the Silver Wings Assault Badge and was recommended for the Aerial Field Service Badge.
Sixty-two downed and thirty-two assists.
Recognized as an Ace of Aces with the alias "White Silver." Plus, she's working in the instructor unit.

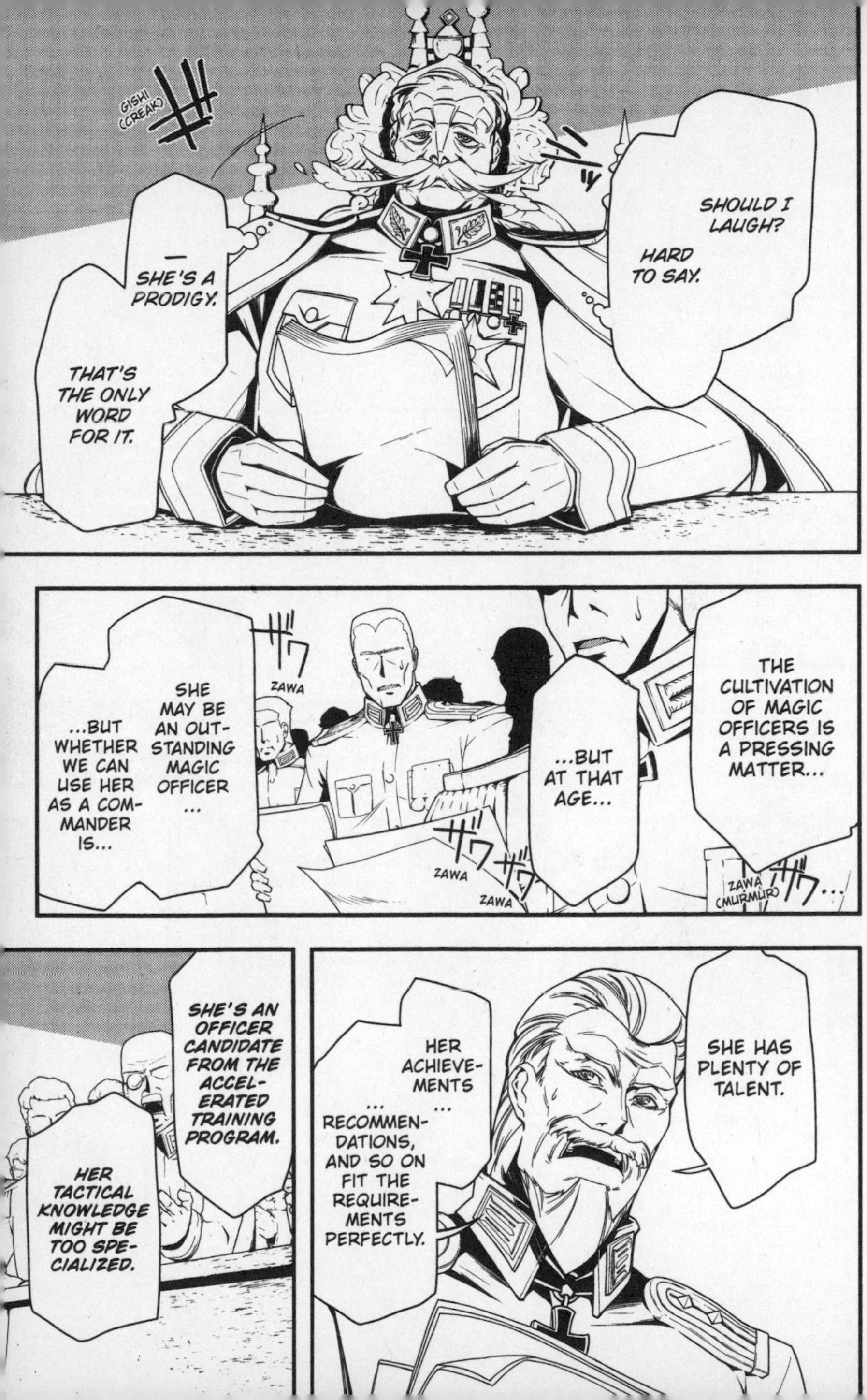
SHOULD I LAUGH?
HARD TO SAY.
GISHI (CREAK)
— SHE'S A PRODIGY.
THAT'S THE ONLY WORD FOR IT.
THE CULTIVATION OF MAGIC OFFICERS IS A PRESSING MATTER...
...BUT AT THAT AGE...
ZAWA (MURMUR)
ZAWA
ZAWA
ZAWA
SHE MAY BE AN OUTSTANDING MAGIC OFFICER ...
...BUT WHETHER WE CAN USE HER AS A COMMANDER IS...
SHE HAS PLENTY OF TALENT.
HER ACHIEVEMENTS ... RECOMMENDATIONS, AND SO ON FIT THE REQUIREMENTS PERFECTLY.
SHE'S AN OFFICER CANDIDATE FROM THE ACCELERATED TRAINING PROGRAM.
HER TACTICAL KNOWLEDGE MIGHT BE TOO SPECIALIZED.

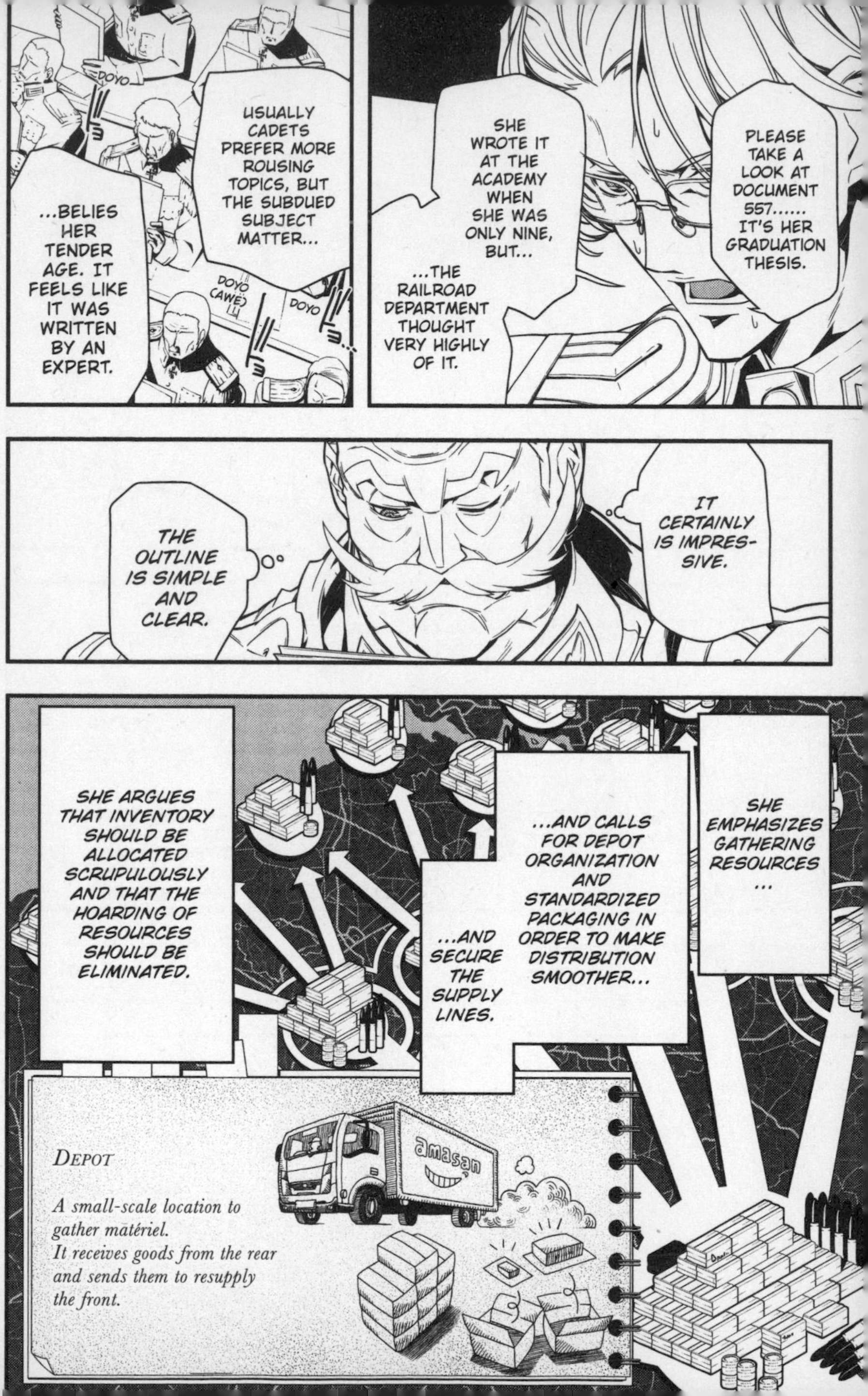
PLEASE TAKE A LOOK AT DOCUMENT 557...... IT'S HER GRADUATION THESIS.
SHE WROTE IT AT THE ACADEMY WHEN SHE WAS ONLY NINE, BUT...
...THE RAILROAD DEPARTMENT THOUGHT VERY HIGHLY OF IT.
DOYO
USUALLY CADETS PREFER MORE ROUSING TOPICS, BUT THE SUBDUED SUBJECT MATTER...
...BELIES HER TENDER AGE. IT FEELS LIKE IT WAS WRITTEN BY AN EXPERT.
DOYO (AWE)
DOYO
IT CERTAINLY IS IMPRESSIVE.
THE OUTLINE IS SIMPLE AND CLEAR.
SHE EMPHASIZES GATHERING RESOURCES ...
...AND CALLS FOR DEPOT ORGANIZATION AND STANDARDIZED PACKAGING IN ORDER TO MAKE DISTRIBUTION SMOOTHER...
...AND SECURE THE SUPPLY LINES.
SHE ARGUES THAT INVENTORY SHOULD BE ALLOCATED SCRUPULOUSLY AND THAT THE HOARDING OF RESOURCES SHOULD BE ELIMINATED.
DEPOT
A small-scale location to gather matériel.
It receives goods from the rear and sends them to resupply the front.
amasan

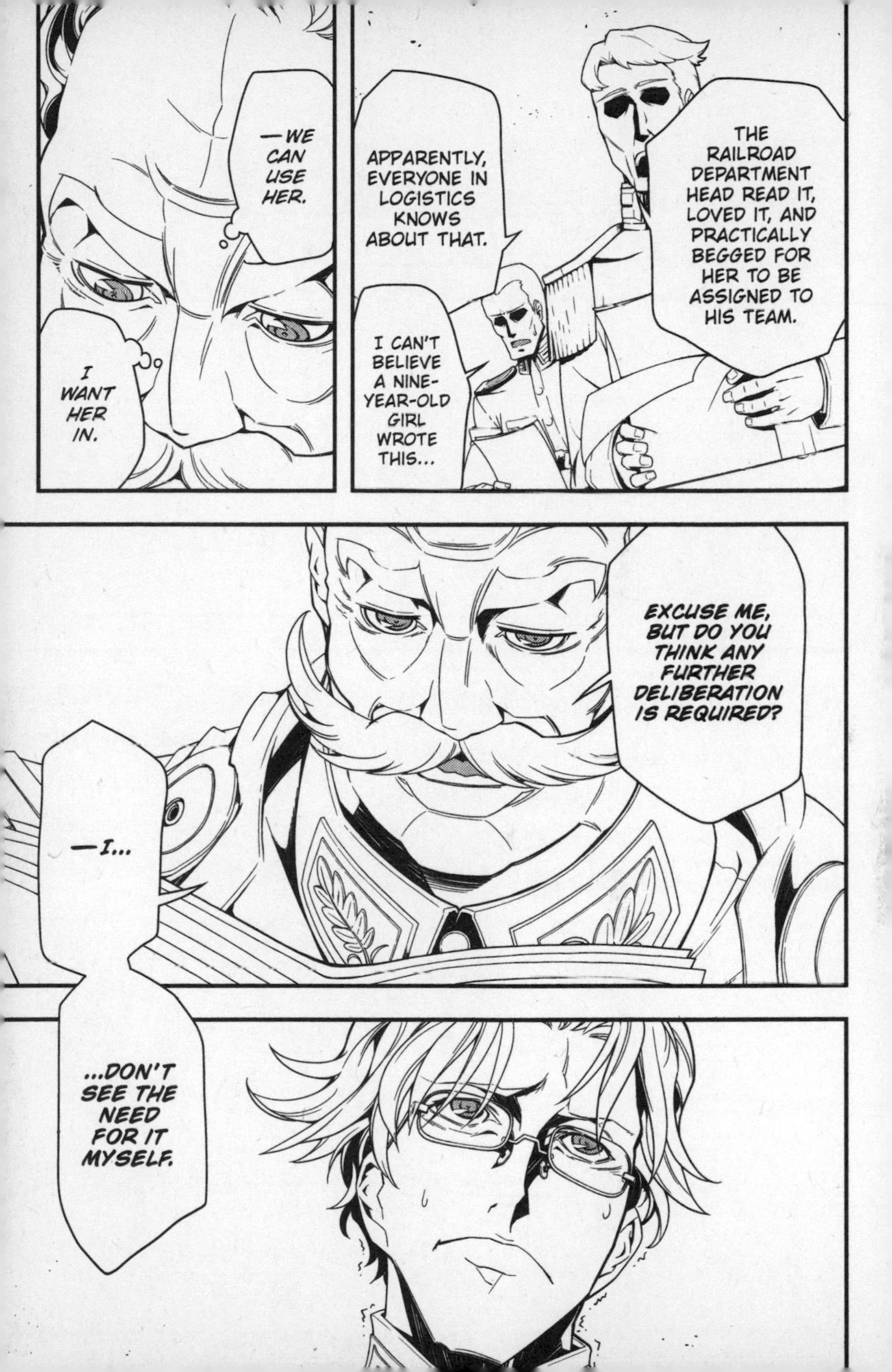
THE RAILROAD DEPARTMENT HEAD READ IT, LOVED IT, AND PRACTICALLY BEGGED FOR HER TO BE ASSIGNED TO HIS TEAM.
APPARENTLY, EVERYONE IN LOGISTICS KNOWS ABOUT THAT.
I CAN'T BELIEVE A NINE-YEAR-OLD GIRL WROTE THIS...
—WE CAN USE HER.
I WANT HER IN.
EXCUSE ME, BUT DO YOU THINK ANY FURTHER DELIBERATION IS REQUIRED?
—I...
...DON'T SEE THE NEED FOR IT MYSELF.

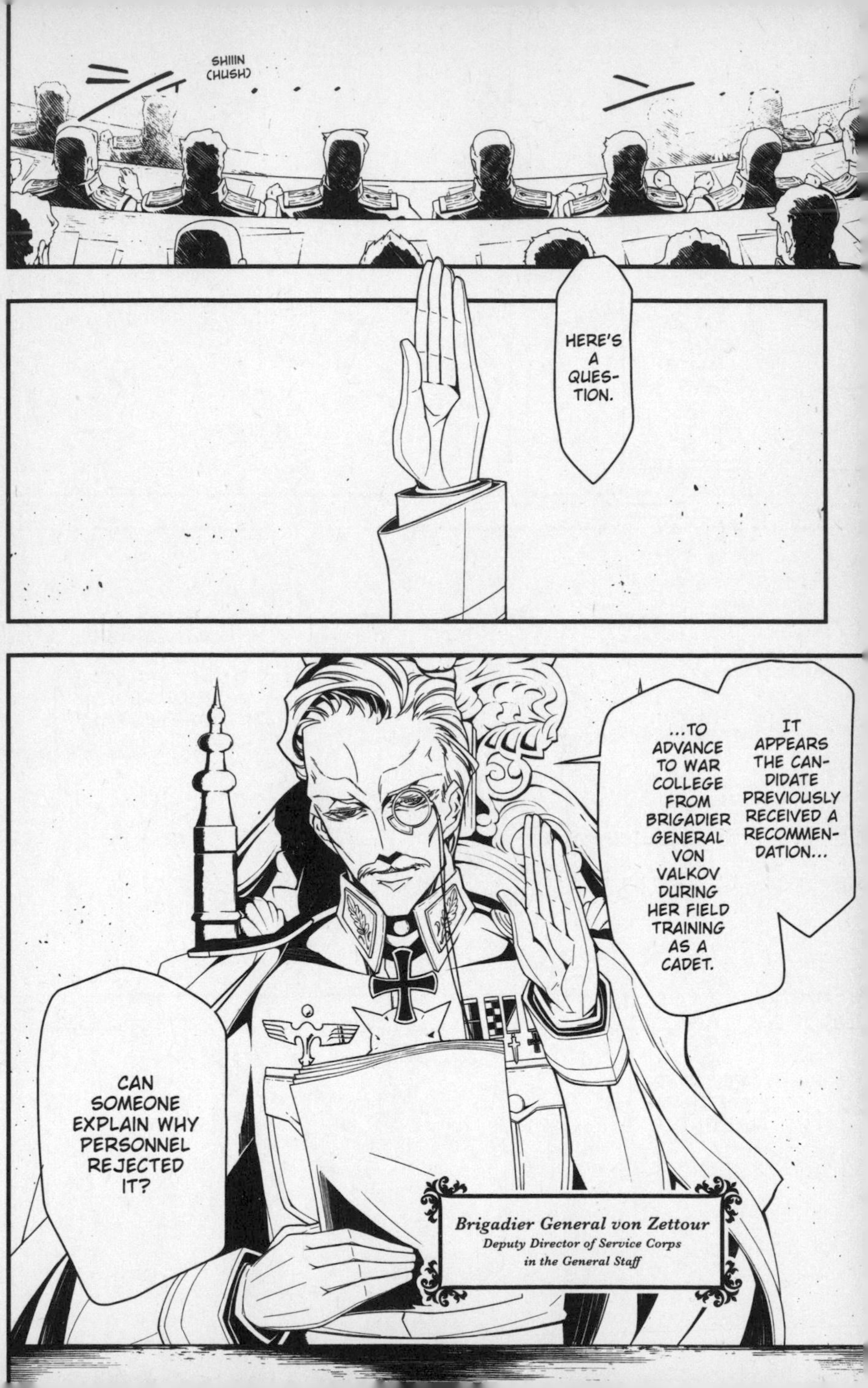
SHIIIN (HUSH)
HERE'S A QUESTION.
IT APPEARS THE CANDIDATE PREVIOUSLY RECEIVED A RECOMMENDATION...
...TO ADVANCE TO WAR COLLEGE FROM BRIGADIER GENERAL VON VALKOV DURING HER FIELD TRAINING AS A CADET.
CAN SOMEONE EXPLAIN WHY PERSONNEL REJECTED IT?
Brigadier General von Zettour
Deputy Director of Service Corps in the General Staff

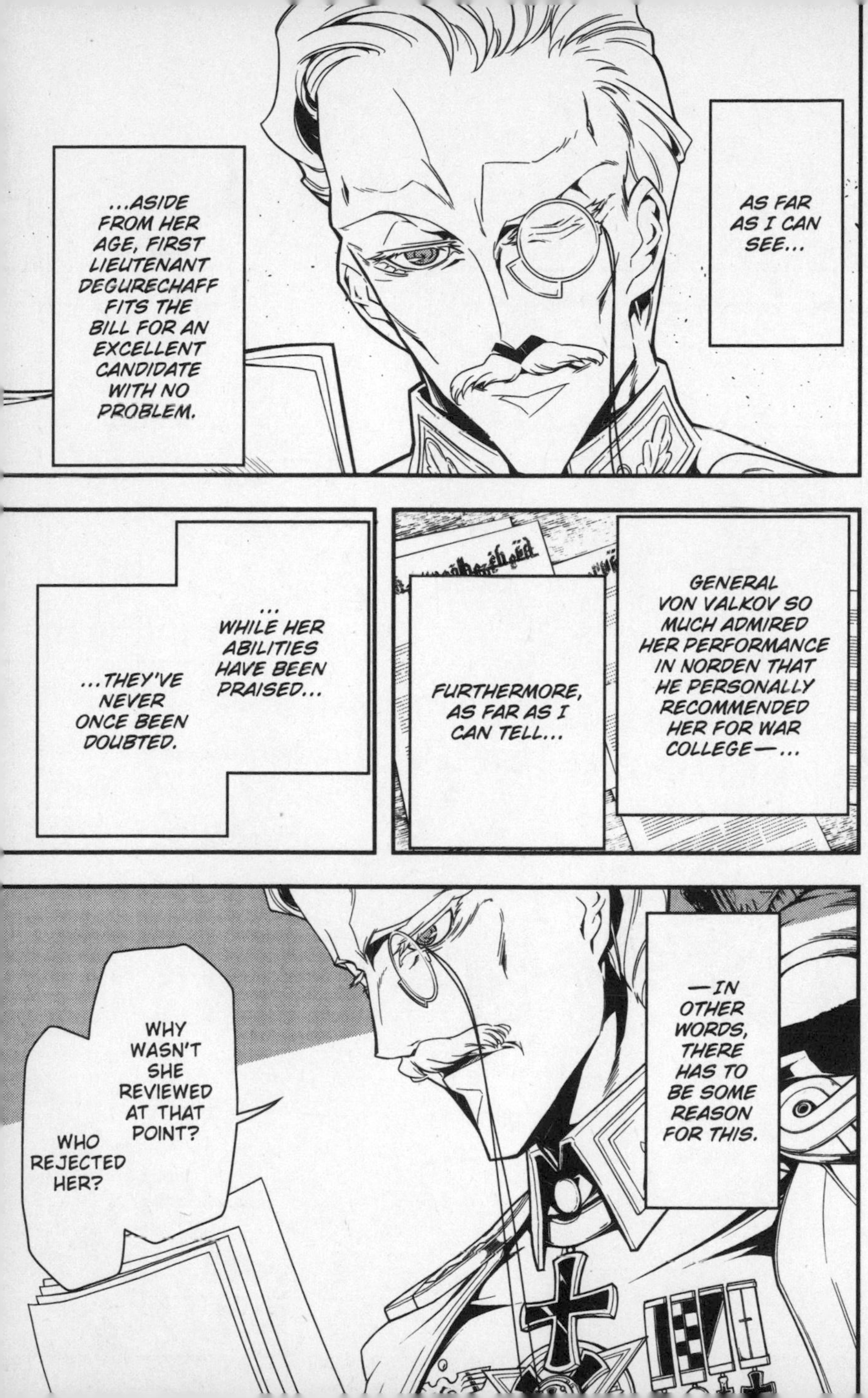
AS FAR AS I CAN SEE...
...ASIDE FROM HER AGE, FIRST LIEUTENANT DEGURECHAFF FITS THE BILL FOR AN EXCELLENT CANDIDATE WITH NO PROBLEM.
GENERAL VON VALKOV SO MUCH ADMIRED HER PERFORMANCE IN NORDEN THAT HE PERSONALLY RECOMMENDED HER FOR WAR COLLEGE—...
FURTHERMORE, AS FAR AS I CAN TELL...
... WHILE HER ABILITIES HAVE BEEN PRAISED...
...THEY'VE NEVER ONCE BEEN DOUBTED.
—IN OTHER WORDS, THERE HAS TO BE SOME REASON FOR THIS.
WHY WASN'T SHE REVIEWED AT THAT POINT?
WHO REJECTED HER?

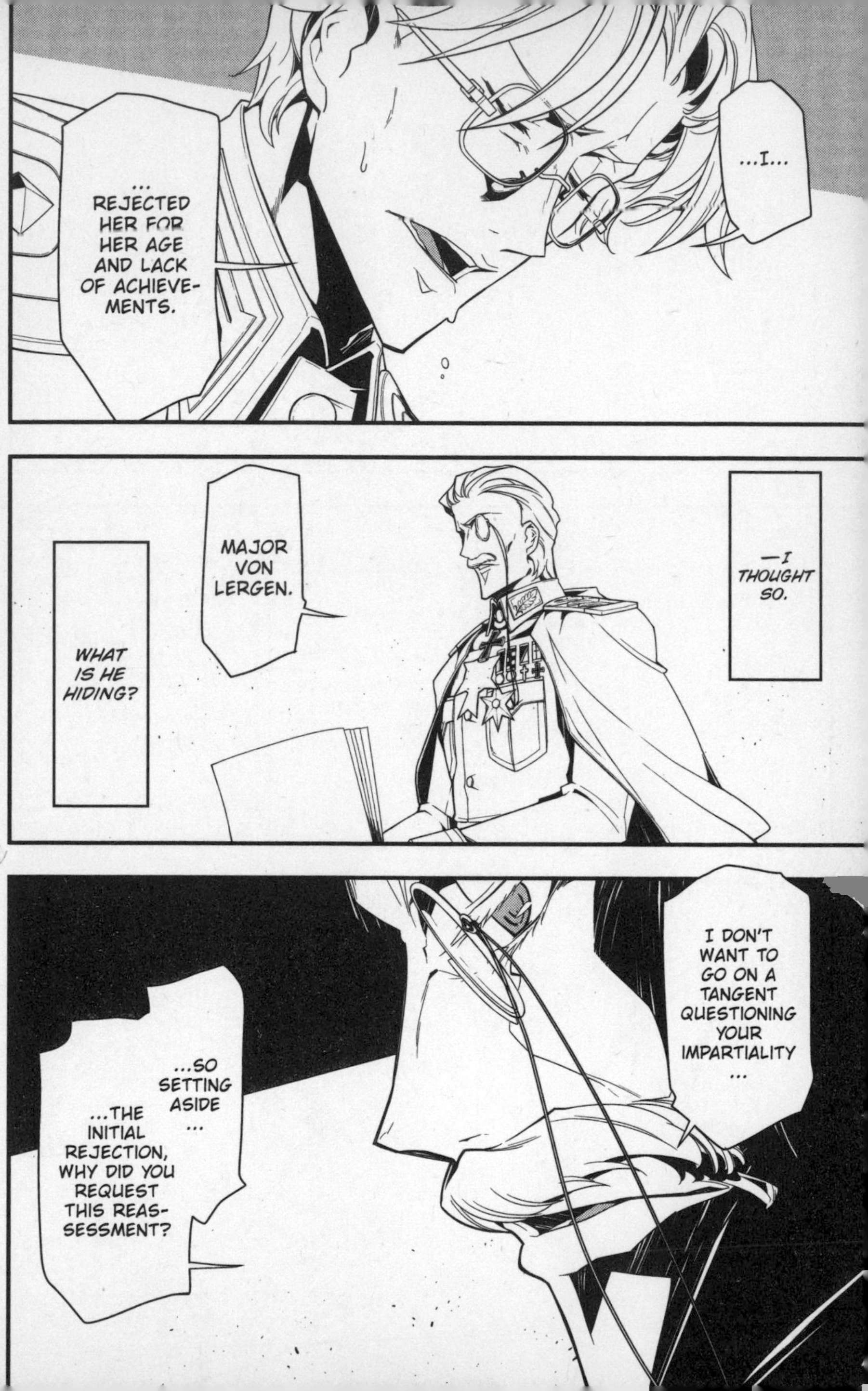
...I...
... REJECTED HER FOR HER AGE AND LACK OF ACHIEVEMENTS.
—I THOUGHT SO.
MAJOR VON LERGEN.
WHAT IS HE HIDING?
I DON'T WANT TO GO ON A TANGENT QUESTIONING YOUR IMPARTIALITY ...
...SO SETTING ASIDE ...
...THE INITIAL REJECTION, WHY DID YOU REQUEST THIS REASSESSMENT?

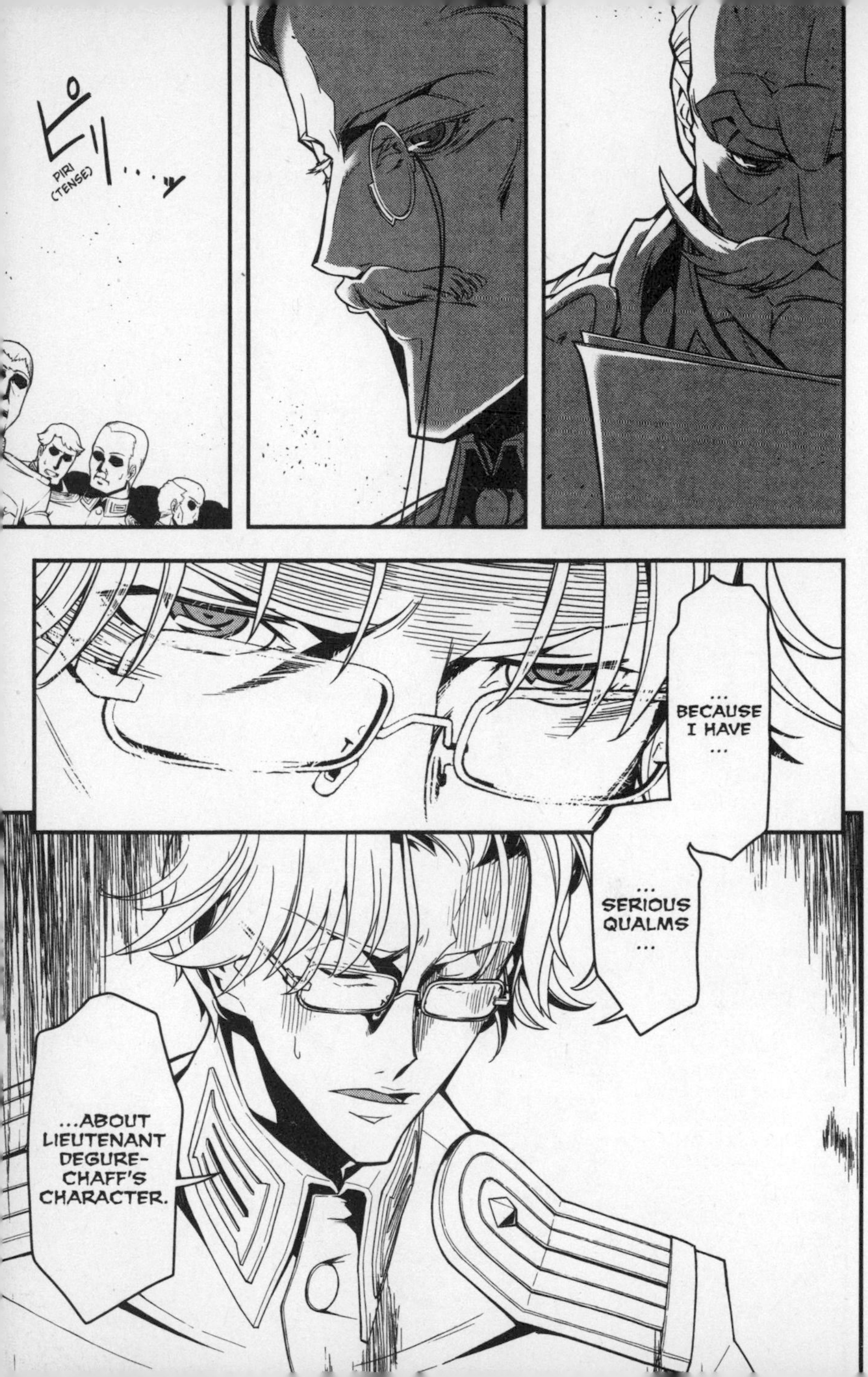
ピリ…ッ
PIRI (TENSE)
... BECAUSE I HAVE ...
... SERIOUS QUALMS ...
...ABOUT LIEUTENANT DEGURE-CHAFF'S CHARACTER.

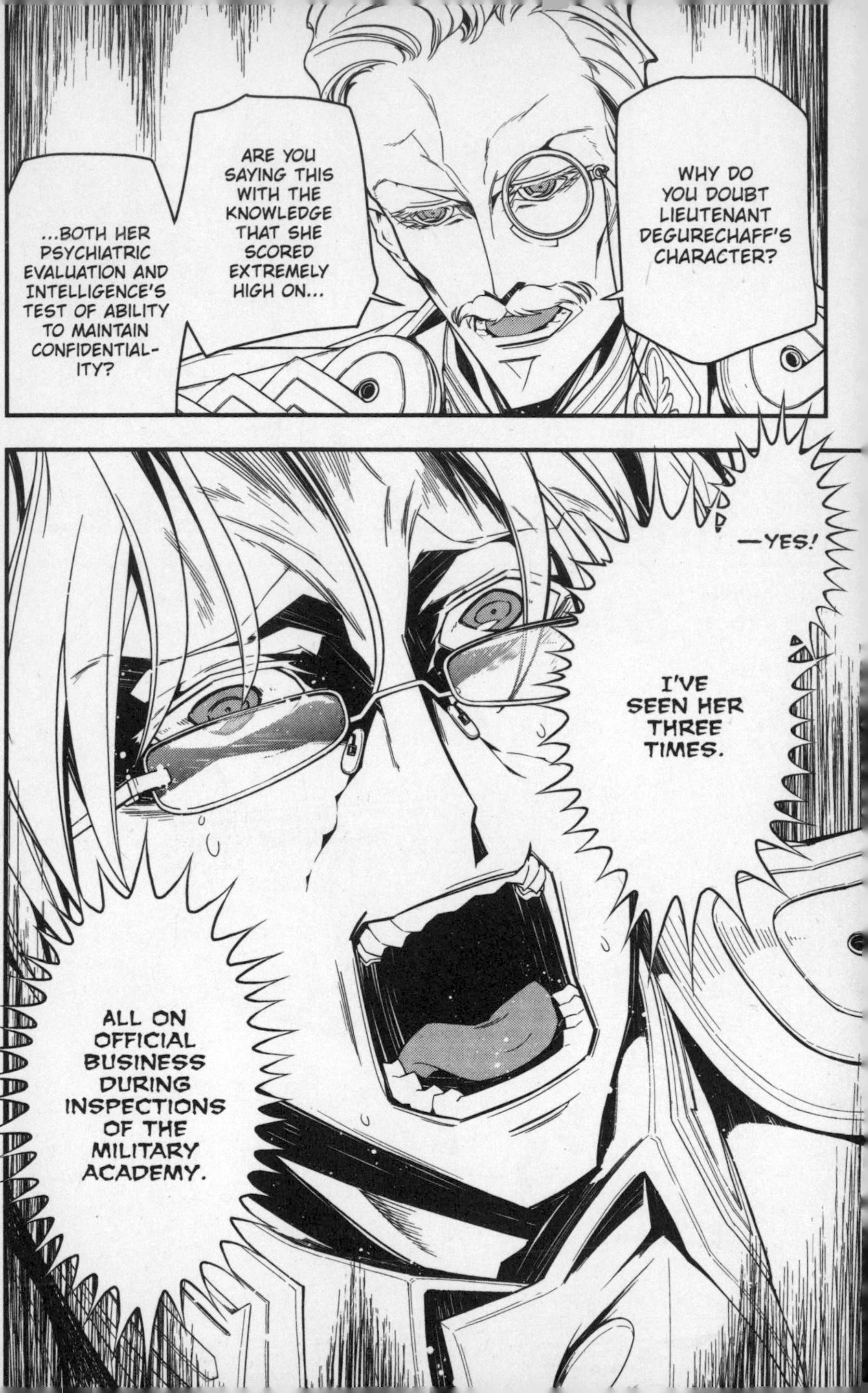
WHY DO YOU DOUBT LIEUTENANT DEGURECHAFF'S CHARACTER?
ARE YOU SAYING THIS WITH THE KNOWLEDGE THAT SHE SCORED EXTREMELY HIGH ON...
...BOTH HER PSYCHIATRIC EVALUATION AND INTELLIGENCE'S TEST OF ABILITY TO MAINTAIN CONFIDENTIAL-ITY?
—YES!
I'VE SEEN HER THREE TIMES.
ALL ON OFFICIAL BUSINESS DURING INSPECTIONS OF THE MILITARY ACADEMY.

Chapter 6 War College I Admissions Committee

The Saga of Tanya the Evil Chapter: 06

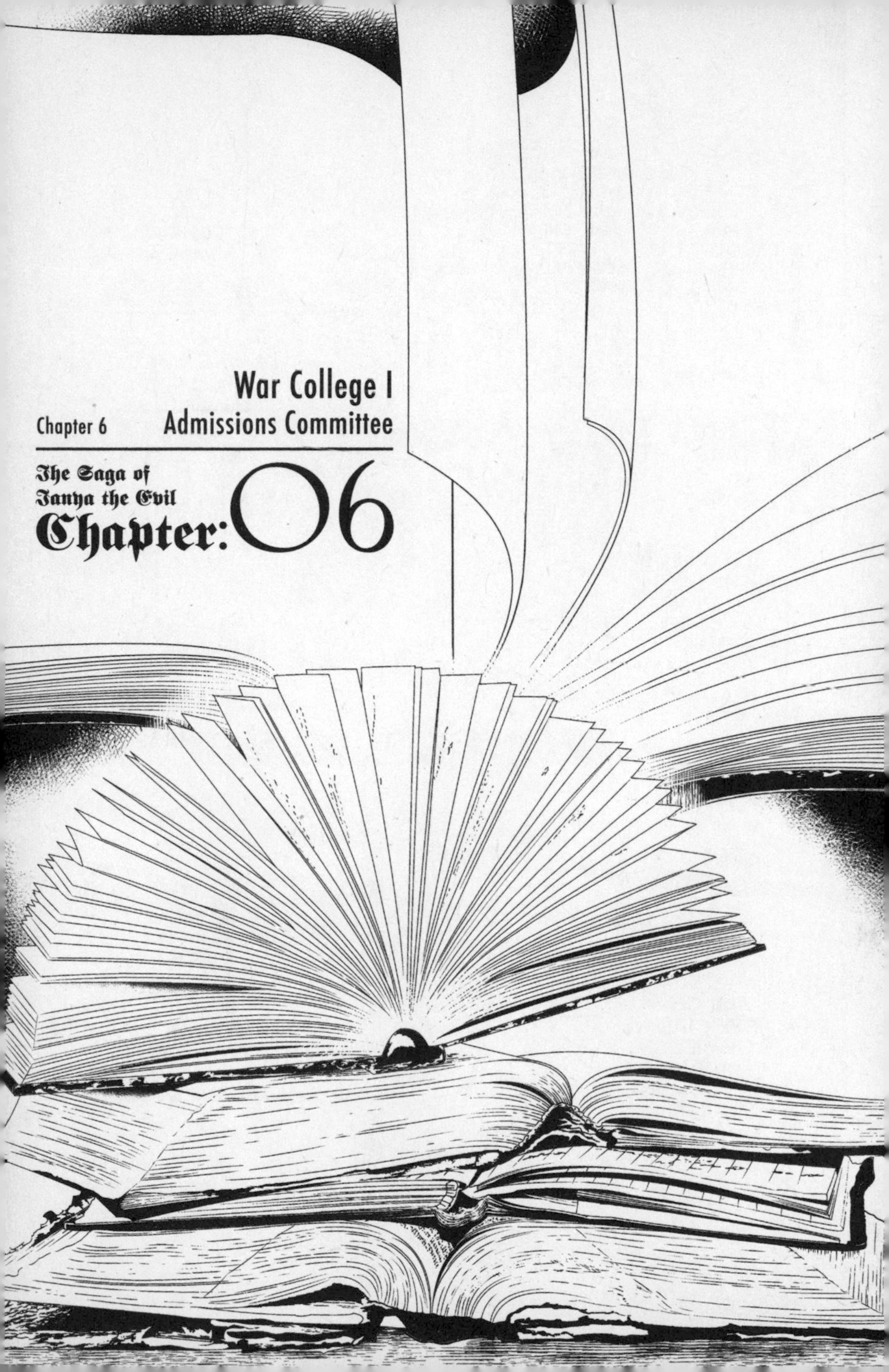

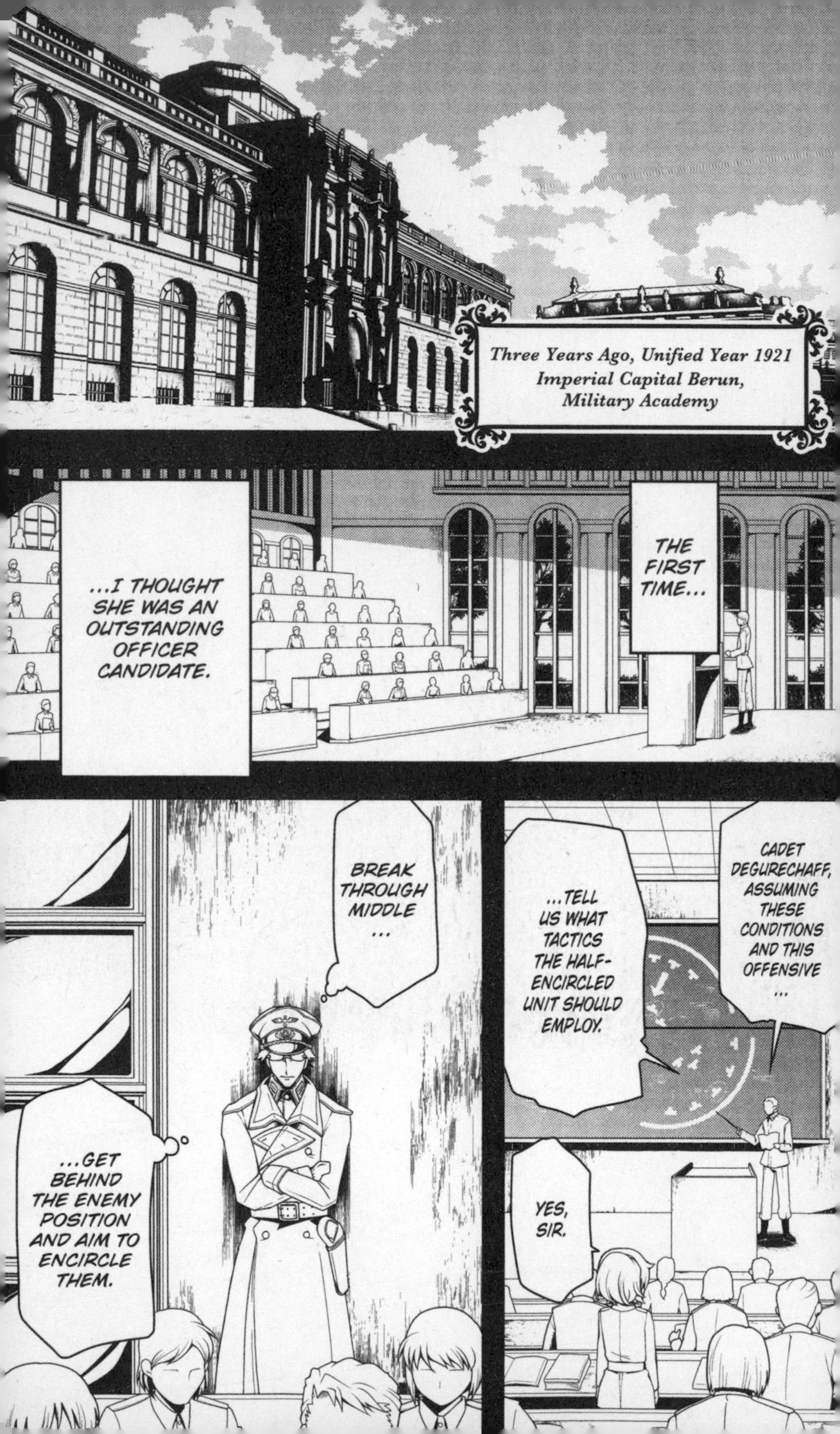
Three Years Ago, Unified Year 1921 Imperial Capital Berun, Military Academy
THE FIRST TIME...
...I THOUGHT SHE WAS AN OUTSTANDING OFFICER CANDIDATE.
CADET DEGURECHAFF, ASSUMING THESE CONDITIONS AND THIS OFFENSIVE...
...TELL US WHAT TACTICS THE HALF-ENCIRCLED UNIT SHOULD EMPLOY.
YES, SIR.
BREAK THROUGH MIDDLE...
...GET BEHIND THE ENEMY POSITION AND AIM TO ENCIRCLE THEM.

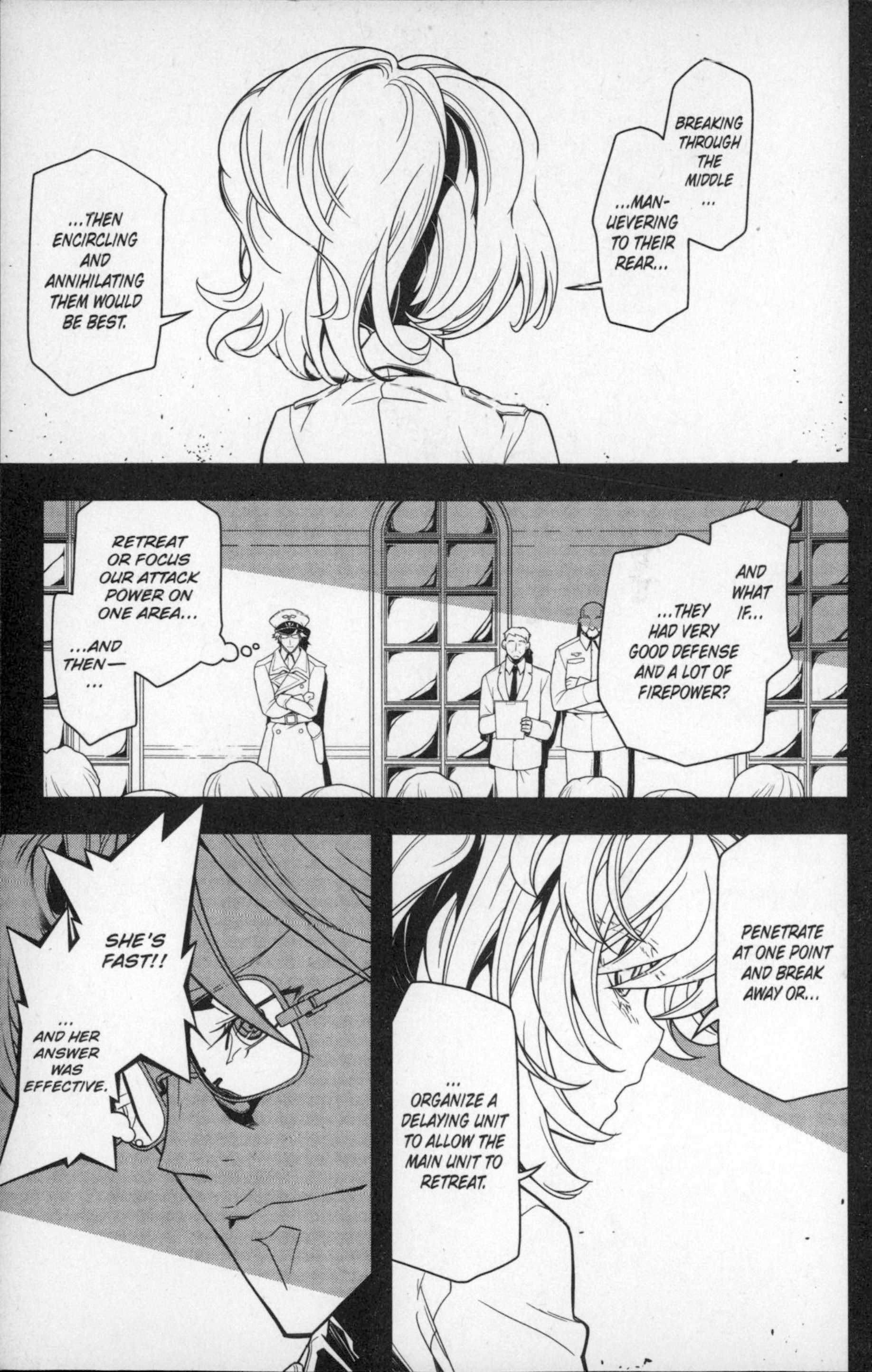
BREAKING THROUGH THE MIDDLE ...
...MAN-UEVERING TO THEIR REAR...
...THEN ENCIRCLING AND ANNIHILATING THEM WOULD BE BEST.
AND WHAT IF... ...THEY HAD VERY GOOD DEFENSE AND A LOT OF FIREPOWER?
RETREAT OR FOCUS OUR ATTACK POWER ON ONE AREA... ...AND THEN— ...
PENETRATE AT ONE POINT AND BREAK AWAY OR...
...ORGANIZE A DELAYING UNIT TO ALLOW THE MAIN UNIT TO RETREAT.
SHE'S FAST!!
...AND HER ANSWER WAS EFFECTIVE.

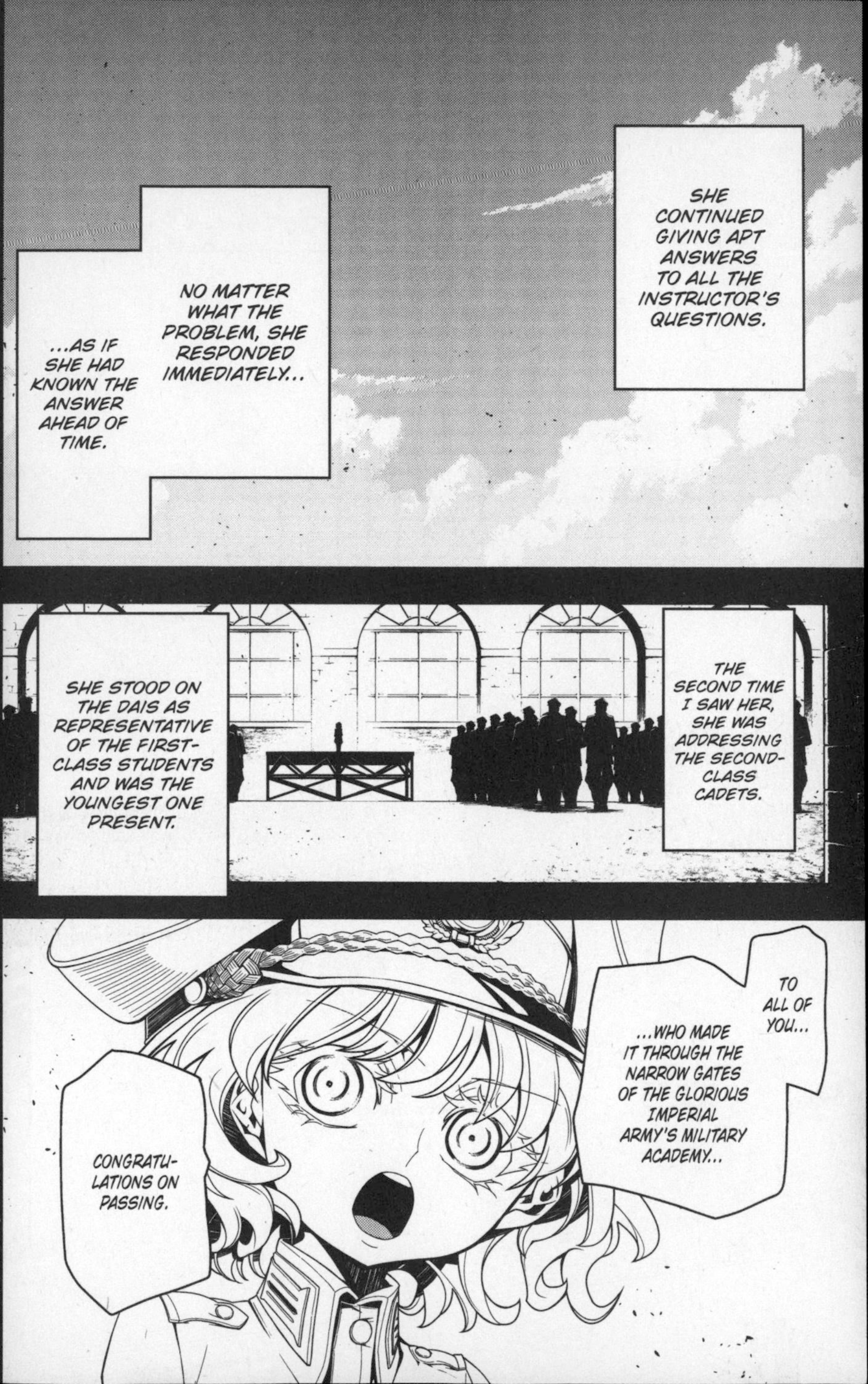
SHE CONTINUED GIVING APT ANSWERS TO ALL THE INSTRUCTOR'S QUESTIONS.
NO MATTER WHAT THE PROBLEM, SHE RESPONDED IMMEDIATELY...
...AS IF SHE HAD KNOWN THE ANSWER AHEAD OF TIME.
THE SECOND TIME I SAW HER, SHE WAS ADDRESSING THE SECOND-CLASS CADETS.
SHE STOOD ON THE DAIS AS REPRESENTATIVE OF THE FIRST-CLASS STUDENTS AND WAS THE YOUNGEST ONE PRESENT.
TO ALL OF YOU...
...WHO MADE IT THROUGH THE NARROW GATES OF THE GLORIOUS IMPERIAL ARMY'S MILITARY ACADEMY...
CONGRATULATIONS ON PASSING.

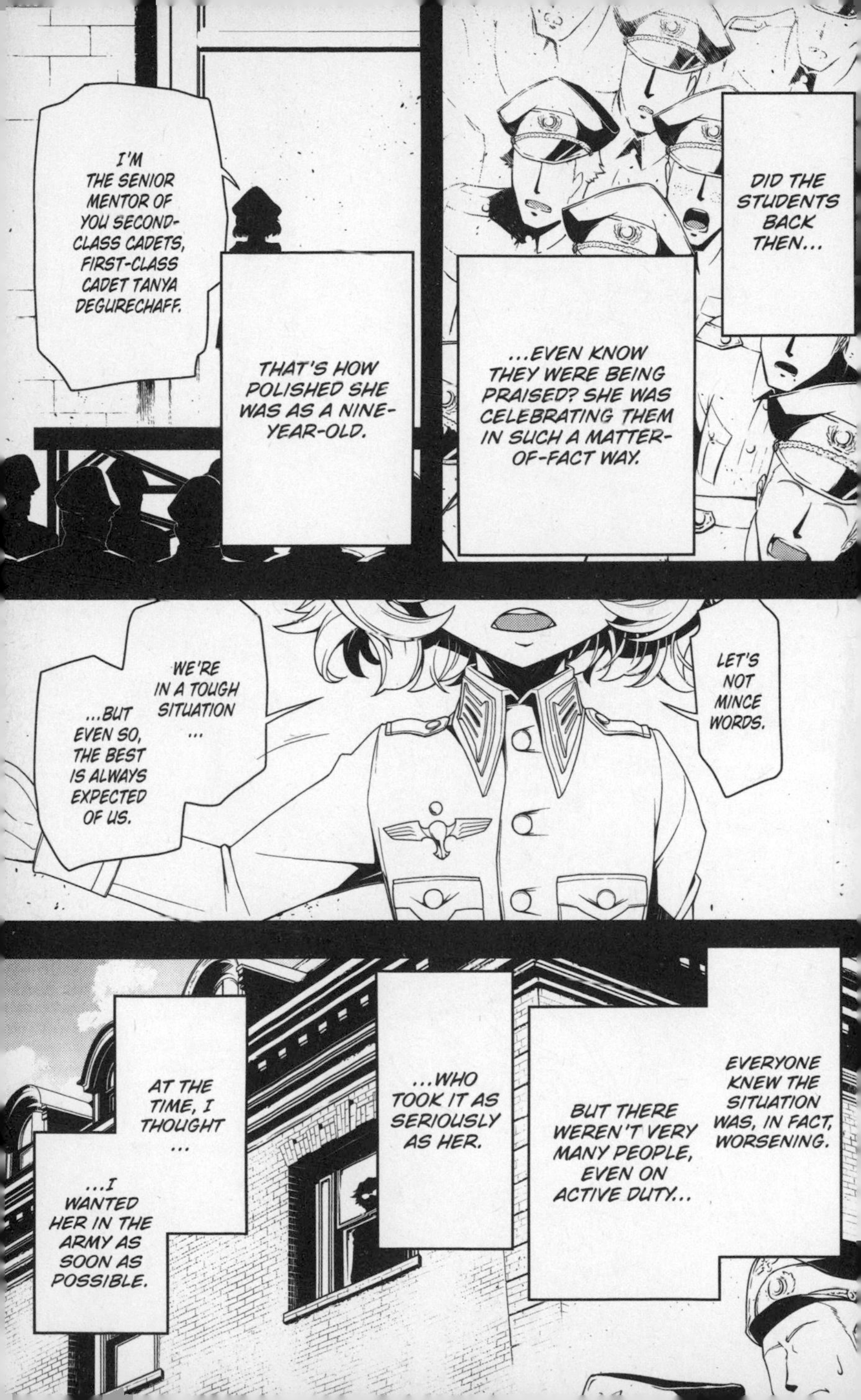

DID THE STUDENTS BACK THEN...
...EVEN KNOW THEY WERE BEING PRAISED? SHE WAS CELEBRATING THEM IN SUCH A MATTER-OF-FACT WAY.
I'M THE SENIOR MENTOR OF YOU SECOND-CLASS CADETS, FIRST-CLASS CADET TANYA DEGURECHAFF.
THAT'S HOW POLISHED SHE WAS AS A NINE-YEAR-OLD.
LET'S NOT MINCE WORDS.
WE'RE IN A TOUGH SITUATION...
...BUT EVEN SO, THE BEST IS ALWAYS EXPECTED OF US.
EVERYONE KNEW THE SITUATION WAS, IN FACT, WORSENING.
BUT THERE WEREN'T VERY MANY PEOPLE, EVEN ON ACTIVE DUTY...
...WHO TOOK IT AS SERIOUSLY AS HER.
AT THE TIME, I THOUGHT...
...I WANTED HER IN THE ARMY AS SOON AS POSSIBLE.

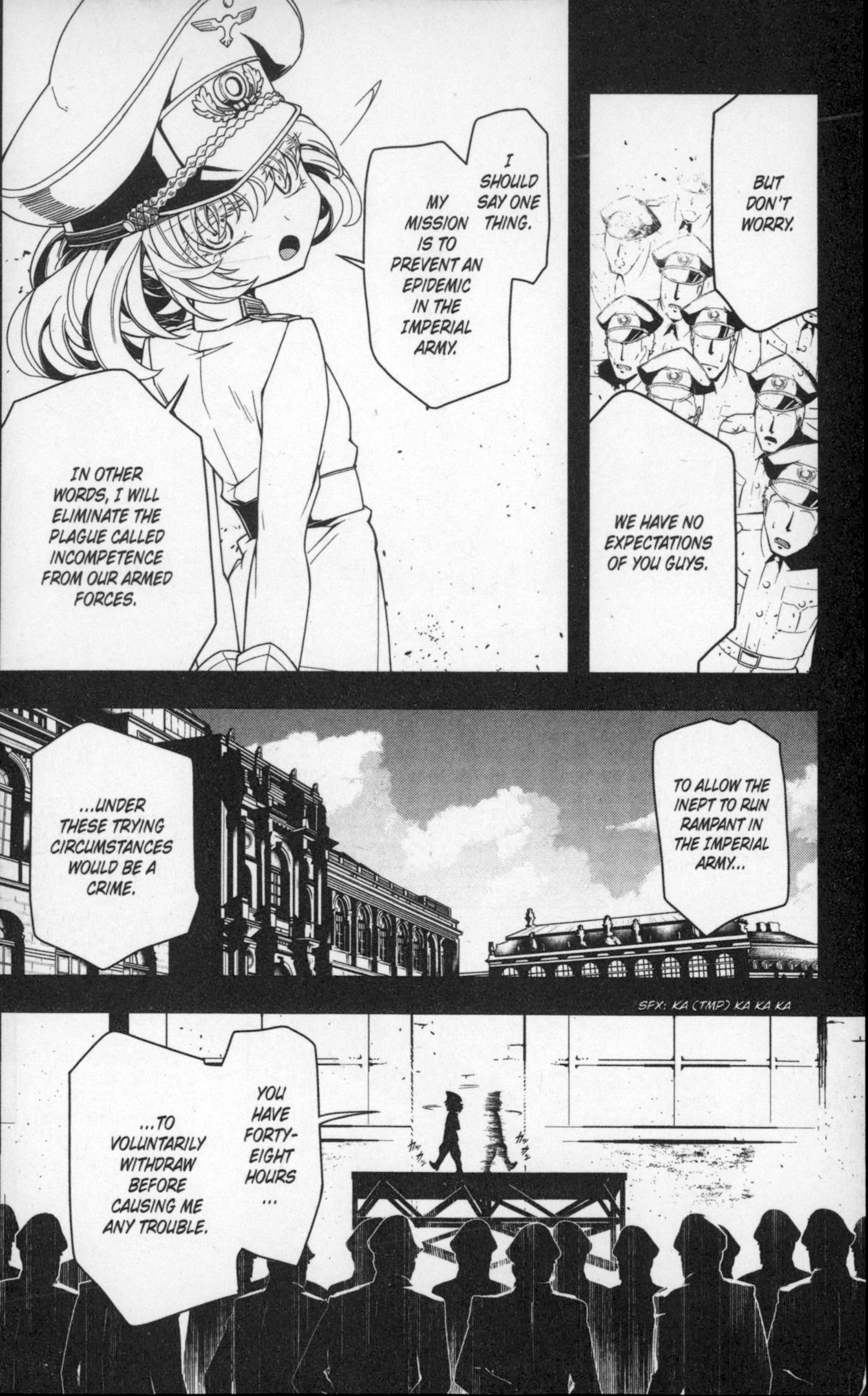
BUT DON'T WORRY.
WE HAVE NO EXPECTATIONS OF YOU GUYS.
I SHOULD SAY ONE THING.
MY MISSION IS TO PREVENT AN EPIDEMIC IN THE IMPERIAL ARMY.
IN OTHER WORDS, I WILL ELIMINATE THE PLAGUE CALLED INCOMPETENCE FROM OUR ARMED FORCES.
TO ALLOW THE INEPT TO RUN RAMPANT IN THE IMPERIAL ARMY...
...UNDER THESE TRYING CIRCUMSTANCES WOULD BE A CRIME.
SFX: KA (TMP) KA KA KA
YOU HAVE FORTY-EIGHT HOURS ...
...TO VOLUNTARILY WITHDRAW BEFORE CAUSING ME ANY TROUBLE.

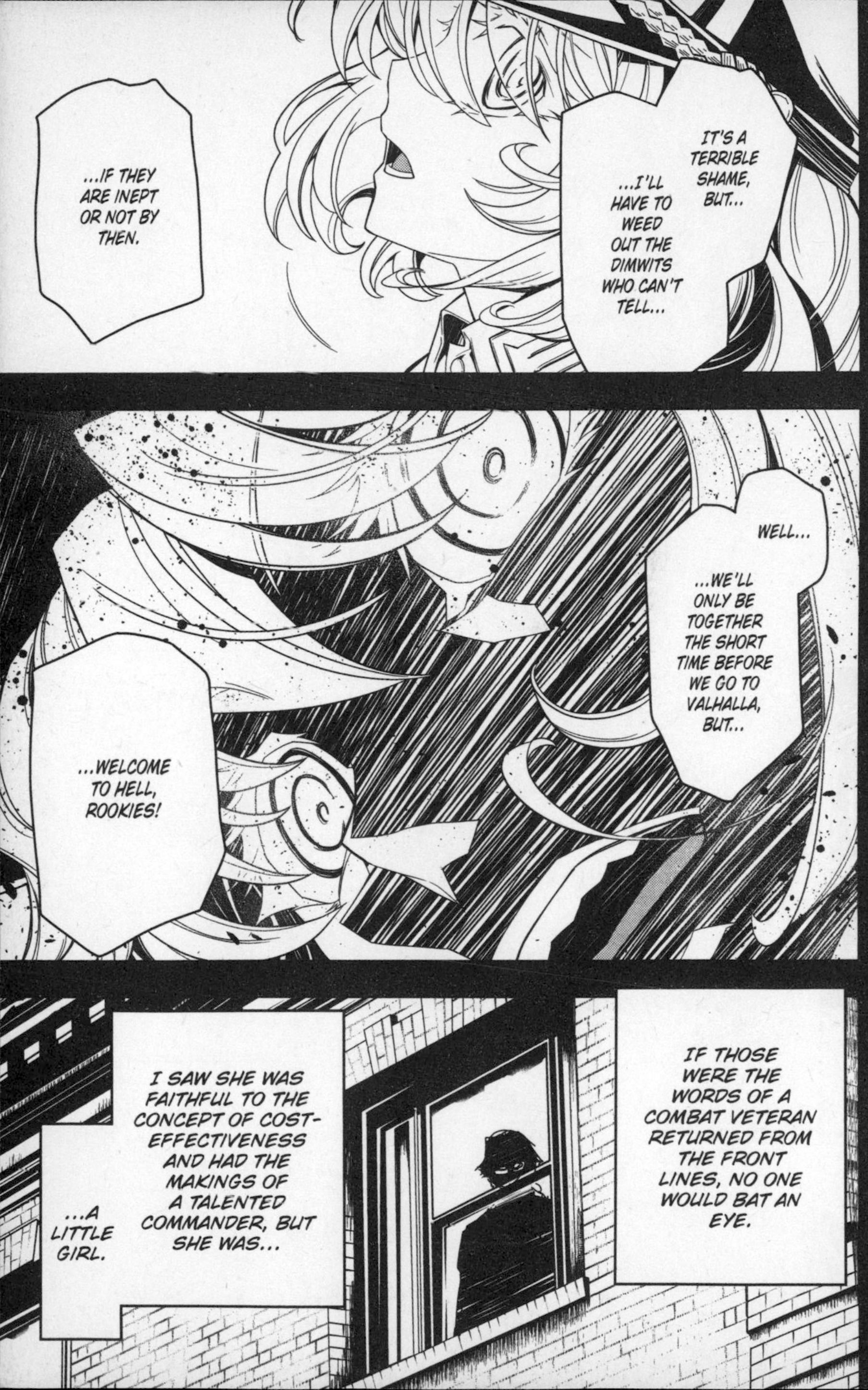
IT'S A TERRIBLE SHAME, BUT...
...I'LL HAVE TO WEED OUT THE DIMWITS WHO CAN'T TELL...
...IF THEY ARE INEPT OR NOT BY THEN.
WELL...
...WE'LL ONLY BE TOGETHER THE SHORT TIME BEFORE WE GO TO VALHALLA, BUT...
...WELCOME TO HELL, ROOKIES!
IF THOSE WERE THE WORDS OF A COMBAT VETERAN RETURNED FROM THE FRONT LINES, NO ONE WOULD BAT AN EYE.
I SAW SHE WAS FAITHFUL TO THE CONCEPT OF COST-EFFECTIVENESS AND HAD THE MAKINGS OF A TALENTED COMMANDER, BUT SHE WAS...
...A LITTLE GIRL.

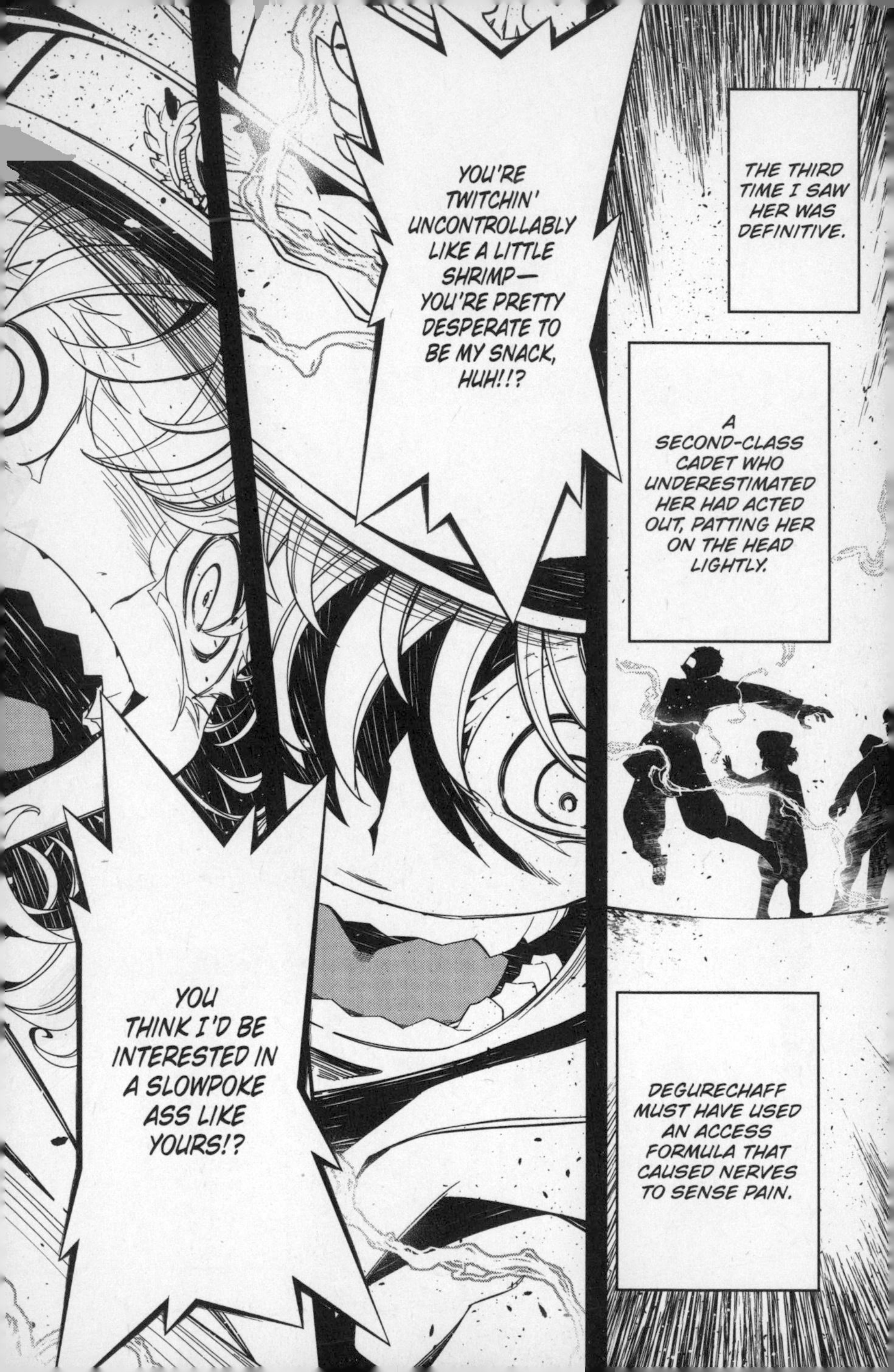
THE THIRD TIME I SAW HER WAS DEFINITIVE.
A SECOND-CLASS CADET WHO UNDERESTIMATED HER HAD ACTED OUT, PATTING HER ON THE HEAD LIGHTLY.
DEGURECHAFF MUST HAVE USED AN ACCESS FORMULA THAT CAUSED NERVES TO SENSE PAIN.
YOU'RE TWITCHIN' UNCONTROLLABLY LIKE A LITTLE SHRIMP— YOU'RE PRETTY DESPERATE TO BE MY SNACK, HUH!!?
YOU THINK I'D BE INTERESTED IN A SLOWPOKE ASS LIKE YOURS!?

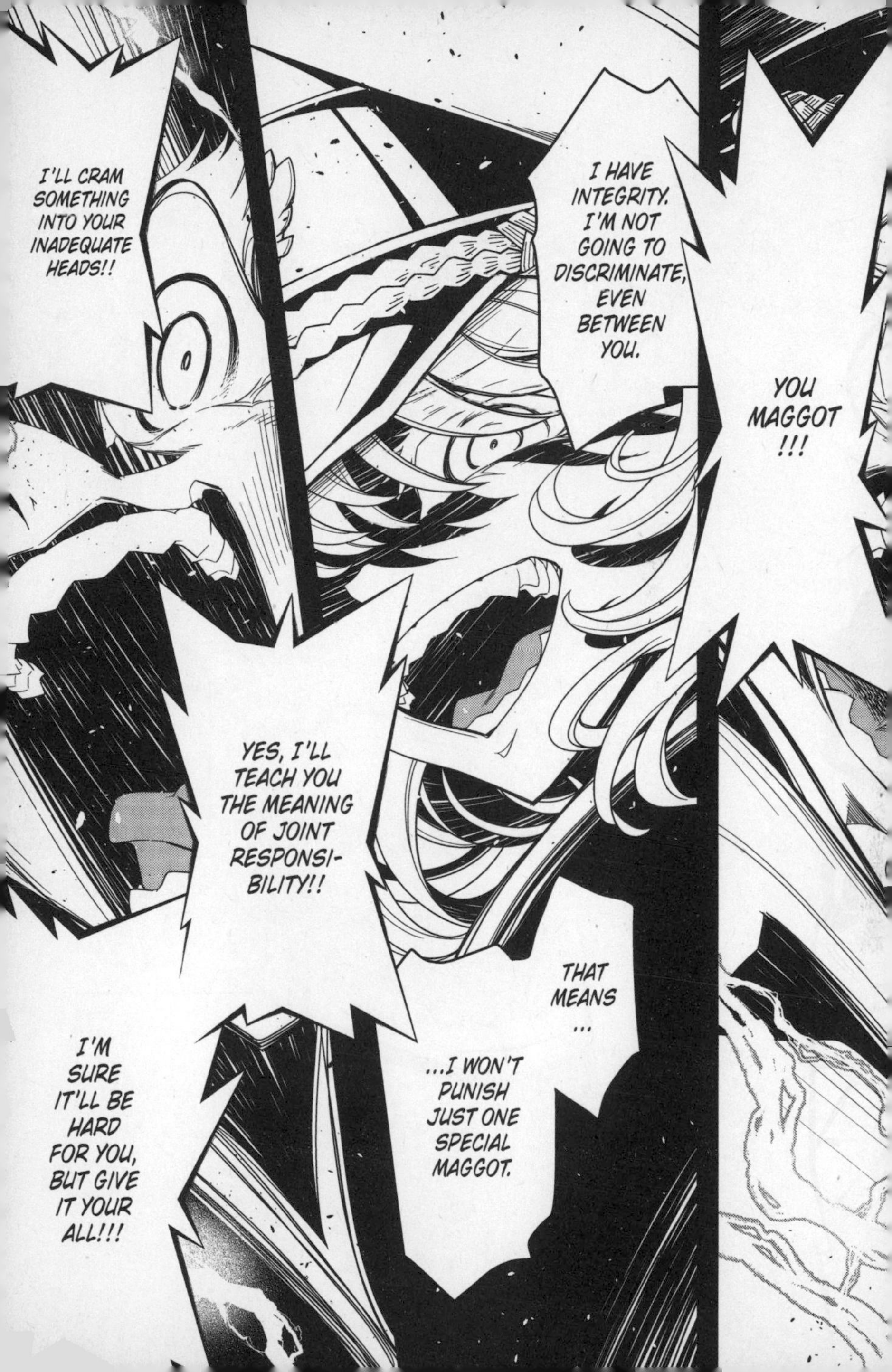
YOU MAGGOT!!!
I HAVE INTEGRITY. I'M NOT GOING TO DISCRIMINATE, EVEN BETWEEN YOU.
THAT MEANS...
...I WON'T PUNISH JUST ONE SPECIAL MAGGOT.
I'LL CRAM SOMETHING INTO YOUR INADEQUATE HEADS!!
YES, I'LL TEACH YOU THE MEANING OF JOINT RESPONSI-BILITY!!
I'M SURE IT'LL BE HARD FOR YOU, BUT GIVE IT YOUR ALL!!!

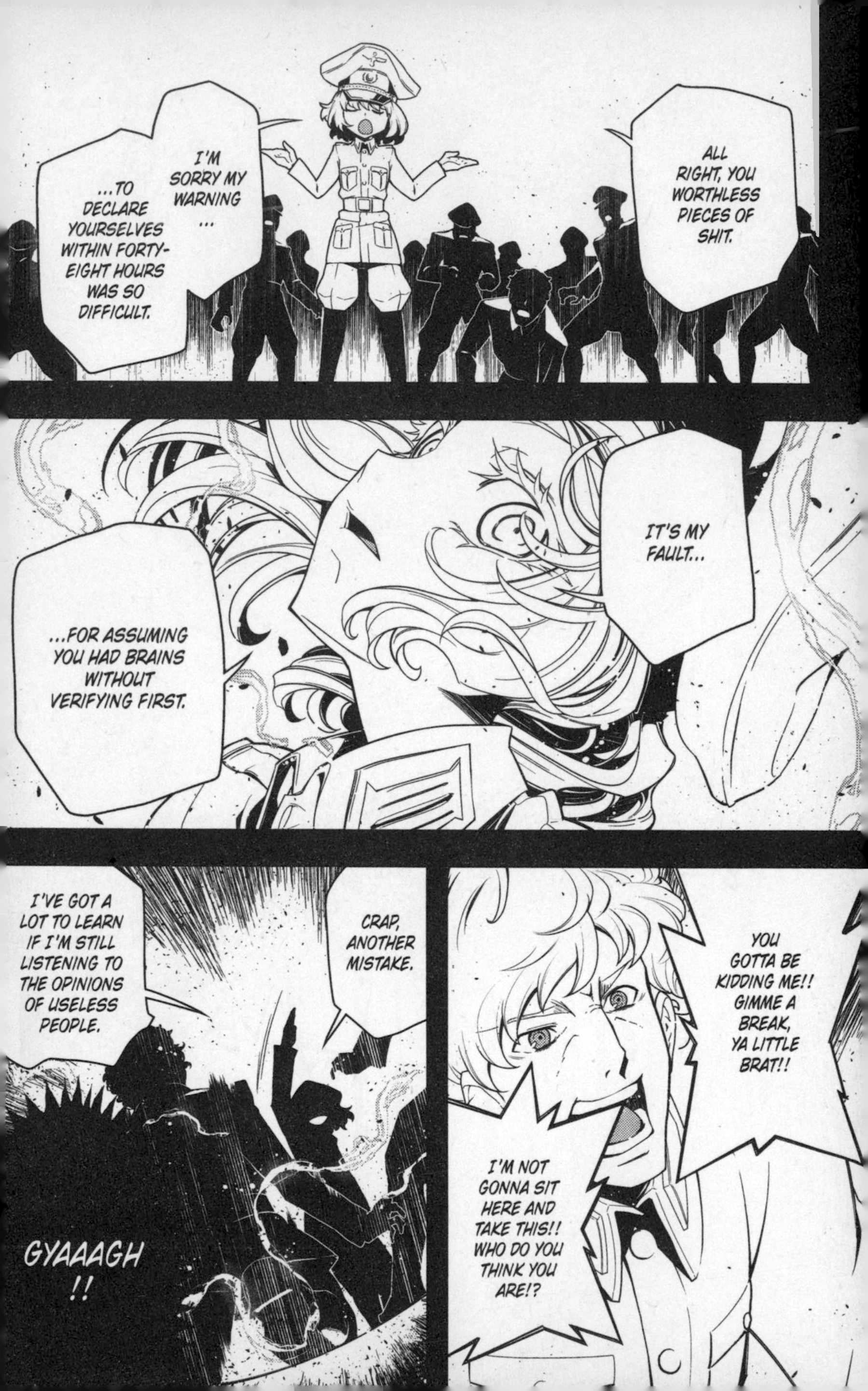
ALL RIGHT, YOU WORTHLESS PIECES OF SHIT.
I'M SORRY MY WARNING...
...TO DECLARE YOURSELVES WITHIN FORTY-EIGHT HOURS WAS SO DIFFICULT.
IT'S MY FAULT...
...FOR ASSUMING YOU HAD BRAINS WITHOUT VERIFYING FIRST.
YOU GOTTA BE KIDDING ME!! GIMME A BREAK, YA LITTLE BRAT!!
I'M NOT GONNA SIT HERE AND TAKE THIS!! WHO DO YOU THINK YOU ARE!?
CRAP, ANOTHER MISTAKE.
I'VE GOT A LOT TO LEARN IF I'M STILL LISTENING TO THE OPINIONS OF USELESS PEOPLE.
GYAAAGH!!

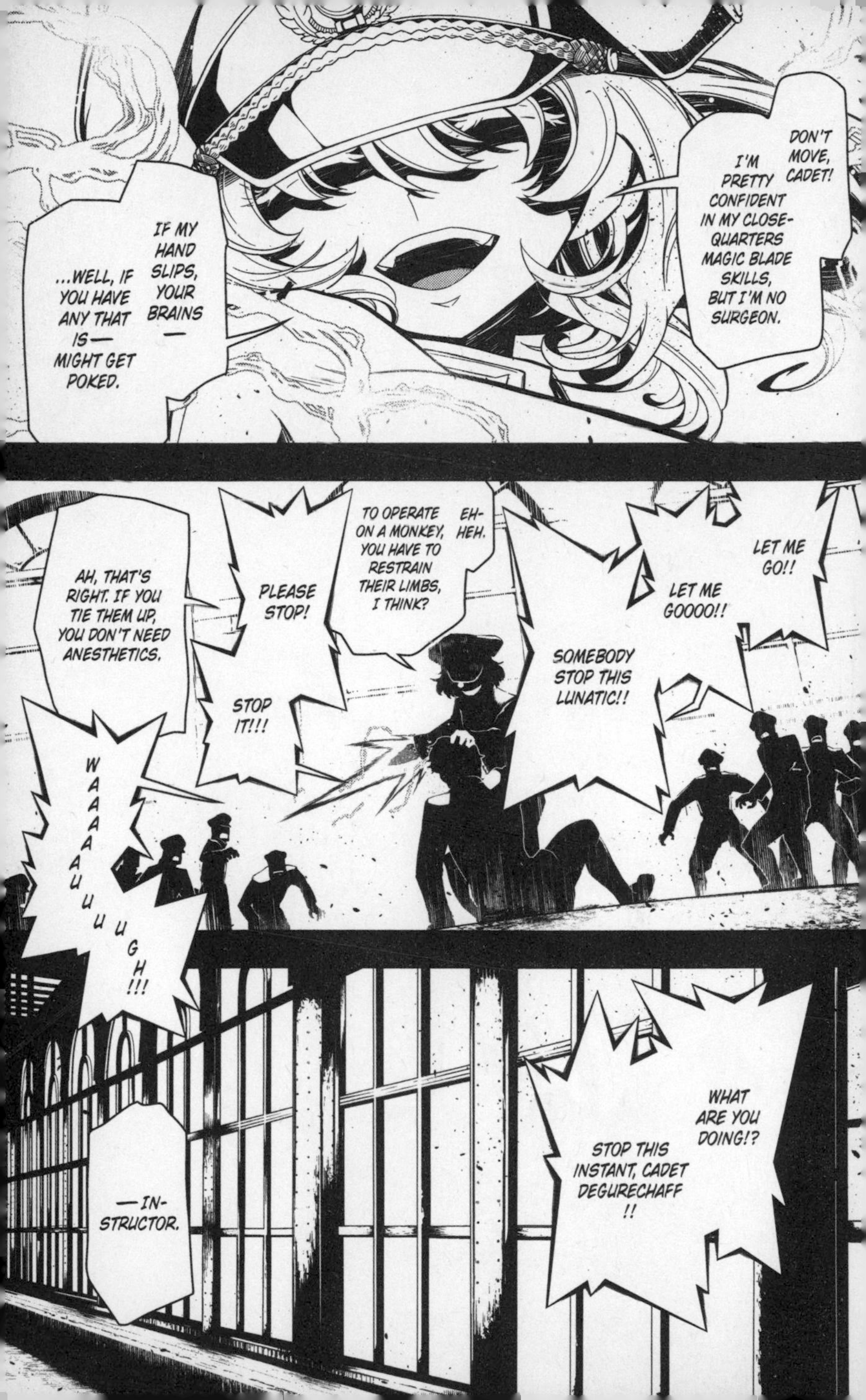
DON'T MOVE, CADET!
I'M PRETTY CONFIDENT IN MY CLOSE-QUARTERS MAGIC BLADE SKILLS, BUT I'M NO SURGEON.
IF MY HAND SLIPS, YOUR BRAINS—
...WELL, IF YOU HAVE ANY THAT IS—MIGHT GET POKED.
LET ME GO!!
LET ME GOOOO!!
SOMEBODY STOP THIS LUNATIC!!
EH-HEH.
TO OPERATE ON A MONKEY, YOU HAVE TO RESTRAIN THEIR LIMBS, I THINK?
PLEASE STOP!
STOP IT!!!
AH, THAT'S RIGHT. IF YOU TIE THEM UP, YOU DON'T NEED ANESTHETICS.
WAAAAAUUUUGH!!!
WHAT ARE YOU DOING!?
STOP THIS INSTANT, CADET DEGURECHAFF!!
—IN-STRUCTOR.

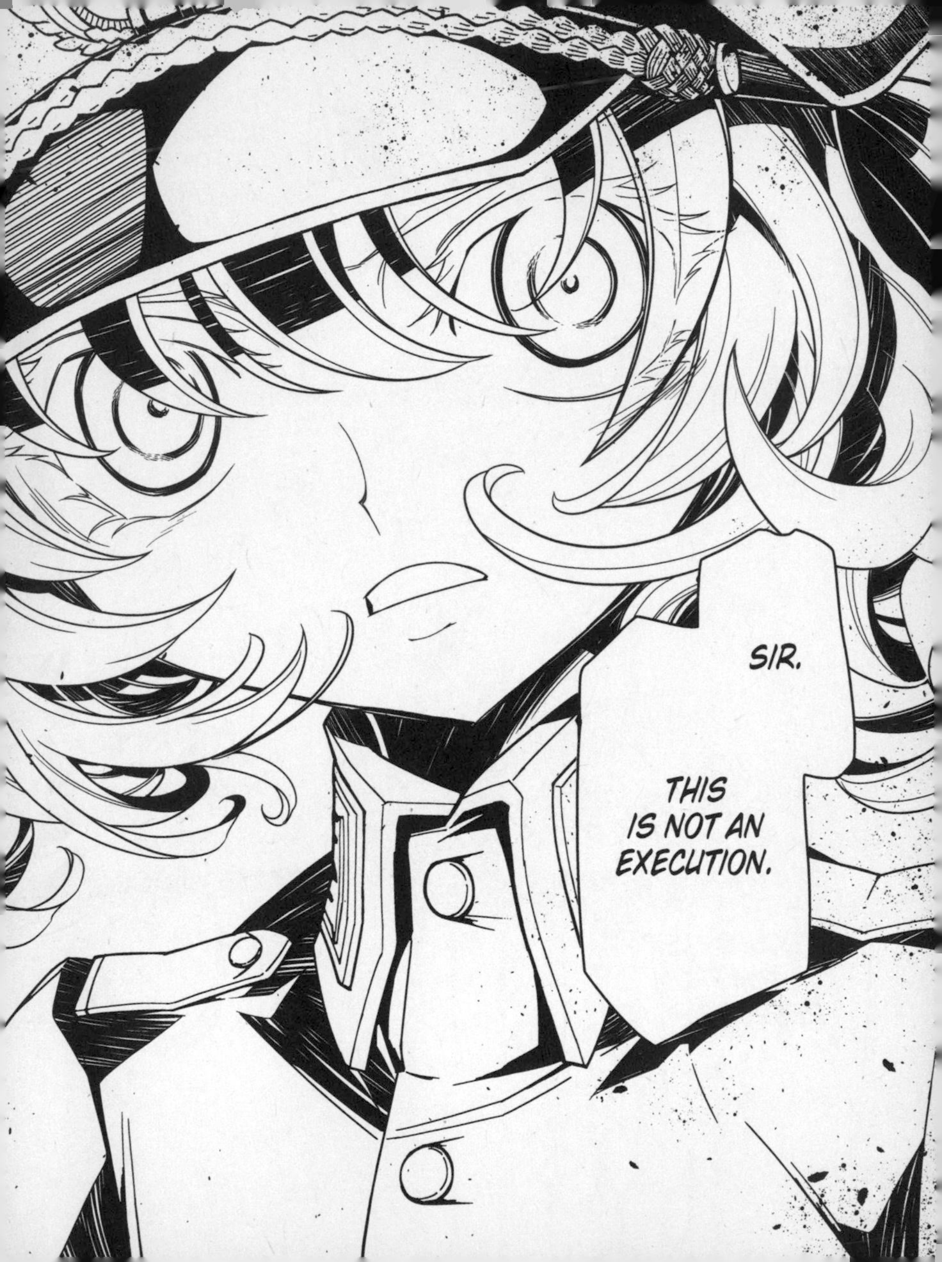
SIR.
THIS IS NOT AN EXECUTION.

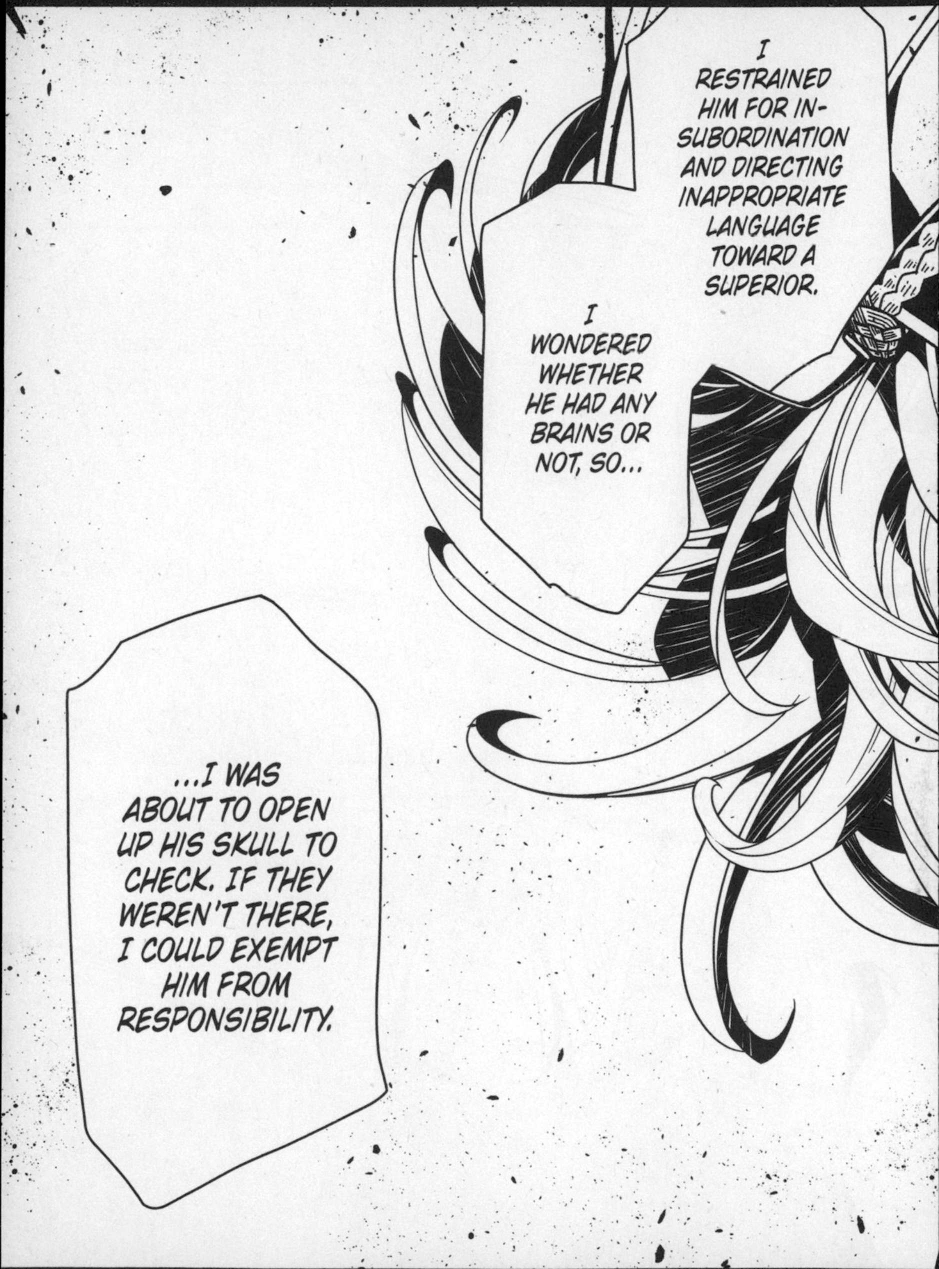
I RESTRAINED HIM FOR IN-SUBORDINATION AND DIRECTING INAPPROPRIATE LANGUAGE TOWARD A SUPERIOR.
I WONDERED WHETHER HE HAD ANY BRAINS OR NOT, SO...
...I WAS ABOUT TO OPEN UP HIS SKULL TO CHECK. IF THEY WEREN'T THERE, I COULD EXEMPT HIM FROM RESPONSIBILITY.

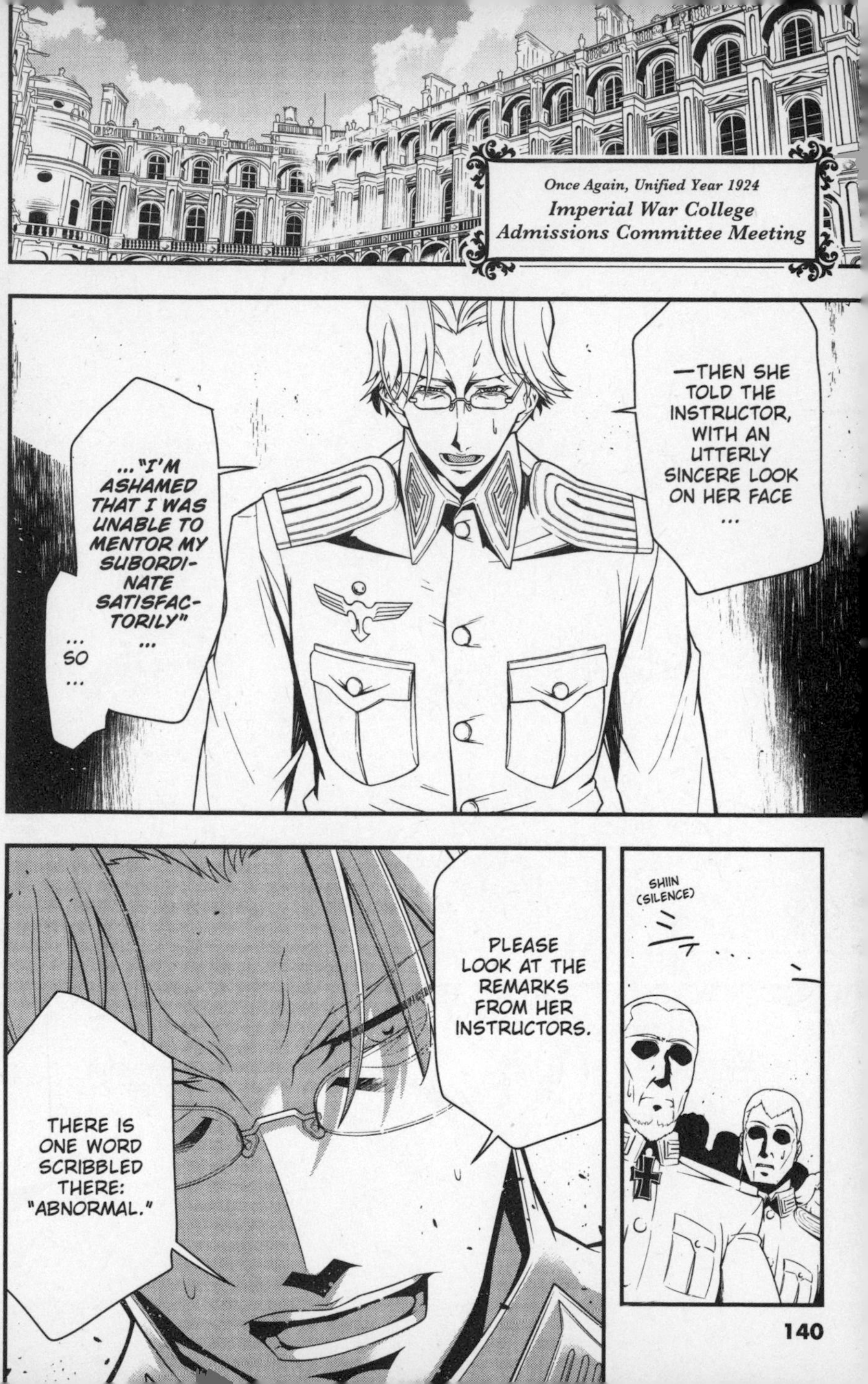
Once Again, Unified Year 1924
Imperial War College Admissions Committee Meeting
—THEN SHE TOLD THE INSTRUCTOR, WITH AN UTTERLY SINCERE LOOK ON HER FACE ...
..."I'M ASHAMED THAT I WAS UNABLE TO MENTOR MY SUBORDI-NATE SATISFAC-TORILY" ... ... SO ...
SHIIN (SILENCE)
PLEASE LOOK AT THE REMARKS FROM HER INSTRUCTORS.
THERE IS ONE WORD SCRIBBLED THERE: "ABNORMAL."

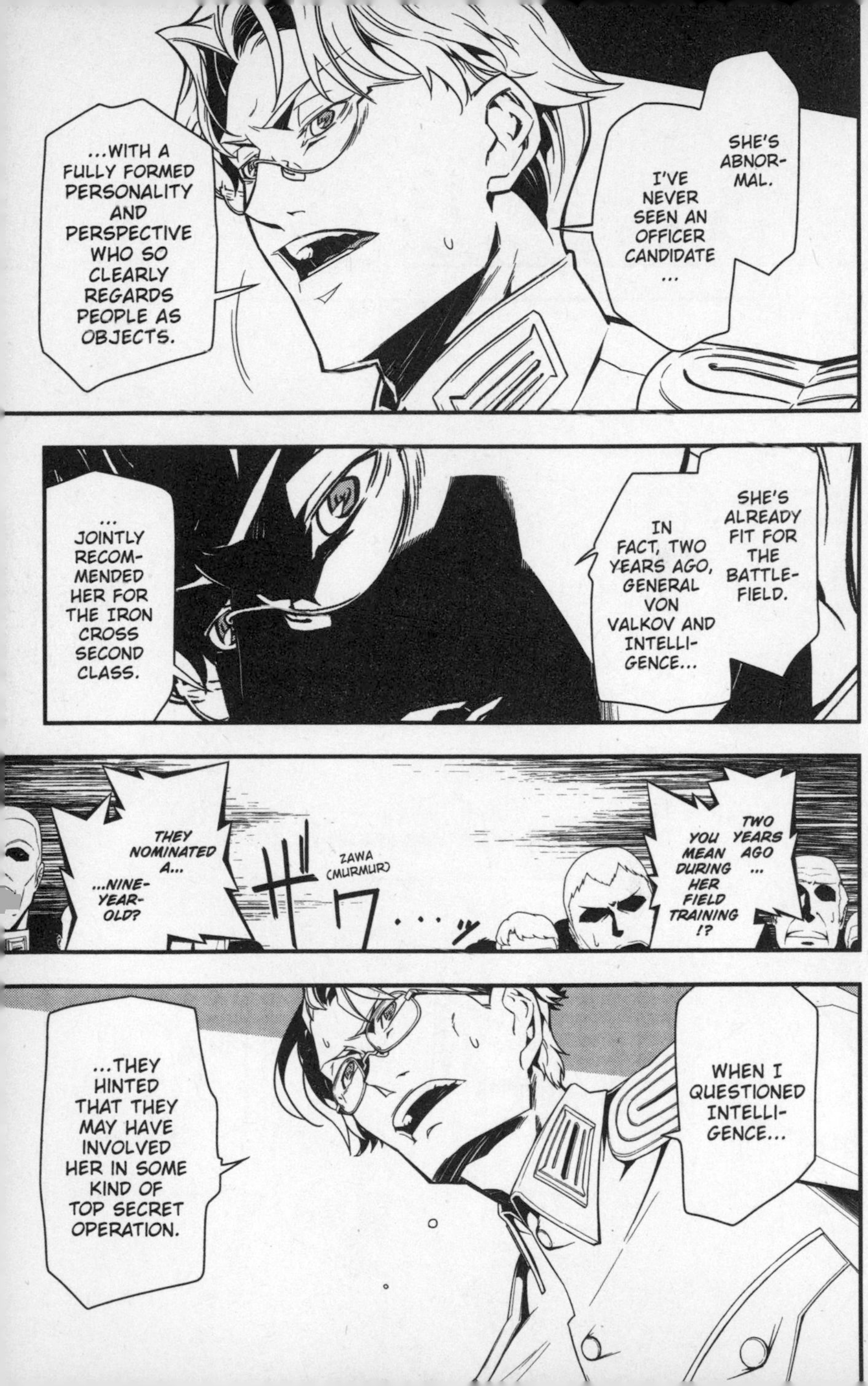
SHE'S ABNORMAL.
I'VE NEVER SEEN AN OFFICER CANDIDATE...
...WITH A FULLY FORMED PERSONALITY AND PERSPECTIVE WHO SO CLEARLY REGARDS PEOPLE AS OBJECTS.
SHE'S ALREADY FIT FOR THE BATTLEFIELD.
IN FACT, TWO YEARS AGO, GENERAL VON VALKOV AND INTELLIGENCE...
...JOINTLY RECOMMENDED HER FOR THE IRON CROSS SECOND CLASS.
TWO YEARS AGO...
YOU MEAN DURING HER FIELD TRAINING!?
ザワ…ッ
ZAWA (MURMUR)
THEY NOMINATED A... ...NINE-YEAR-OLD?
WHEN I QUESTIONED INTELLIGENCE...
...THEY HINTED THAT THEY MAY HAVE INVOLVED HER IN SOME KIND OF TOP SECRET OPERATION.

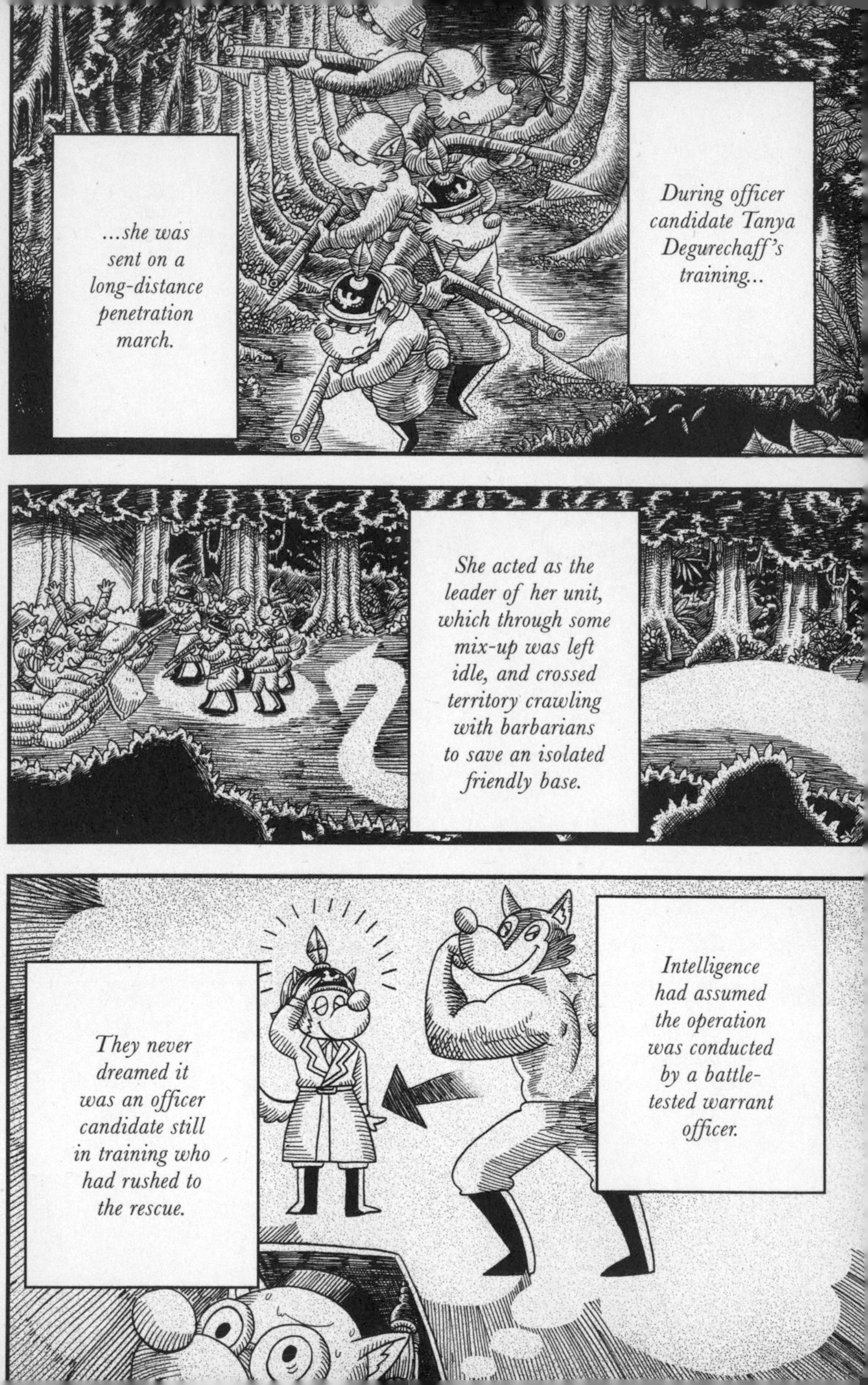
During officer candidate Tanya Degurechaff's training...
...she was sent on a long-distance penetration march.
She acted as the leader of her unit, which through some mix-up was left idle, and crossed territory crawling with barbarians to save an isolated friendly base.
Intelligence had assumed the operation was conducted by a battle-tested warrant officer.
They never dreamed it was an officer candidate still in training who had rushed to the rescue.

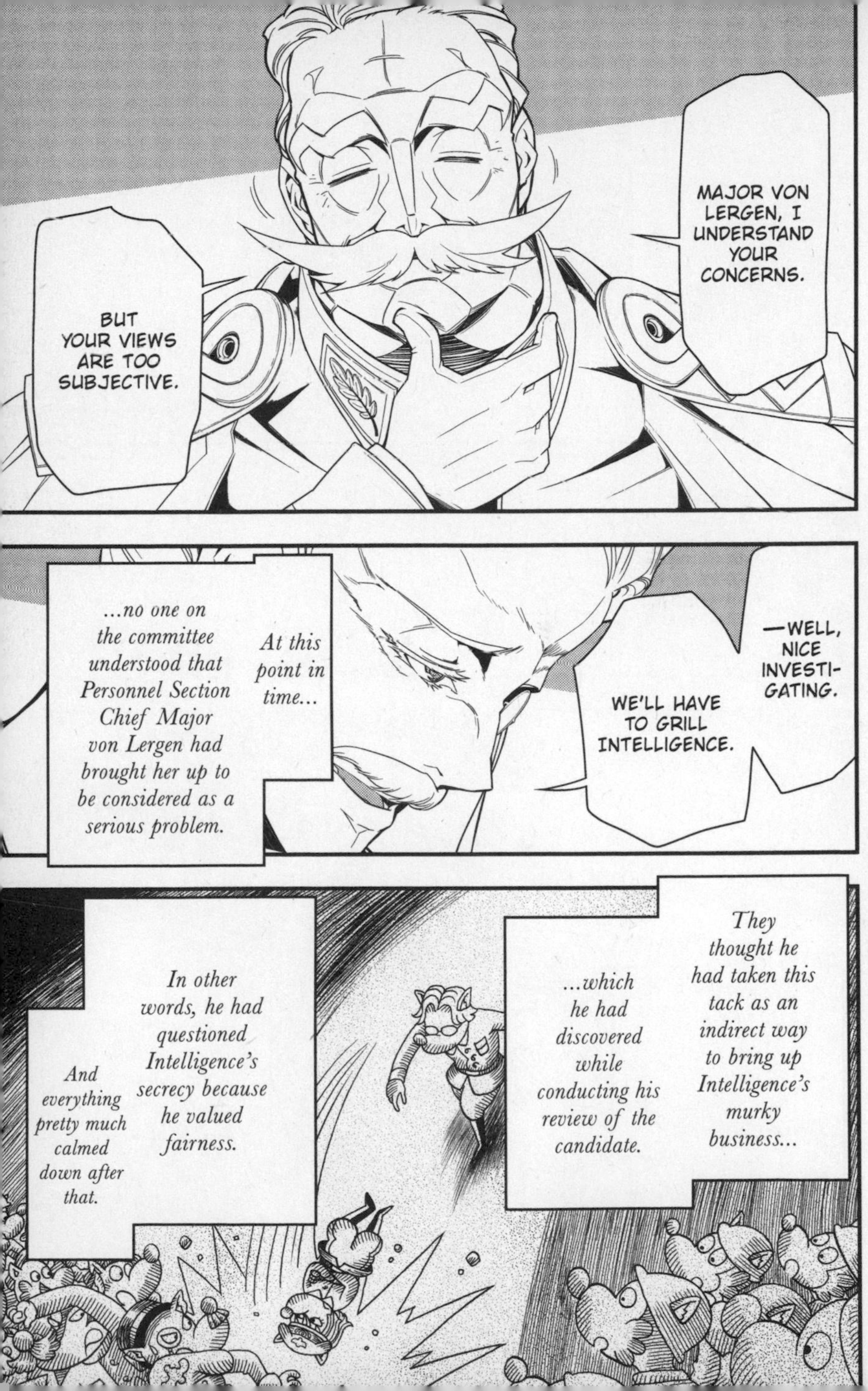
MAJOR VON LERGEN, I UNDERSTAND YOUR CONCERNS.
BUT YOUR VIEWS ARE TOO SUBJECTIVE.
—WELL, NICE INVESTIGATING.
WE'LL HAVE TO GRILL INTELLIGENCE.
At this point in time...
...no one on the committee understood that Personnel Section Chief Major von Lergen had brought her up to be considered as a serious problem.
They thought he had taken this tack as an indirect way to bring up Intelligence's murky business...
...which he had discovered while conducting his review of the candidate.
In other words, he had questioned Intelligence's secrecy because he valued fairness.
And everything pretty much calmed down after that.

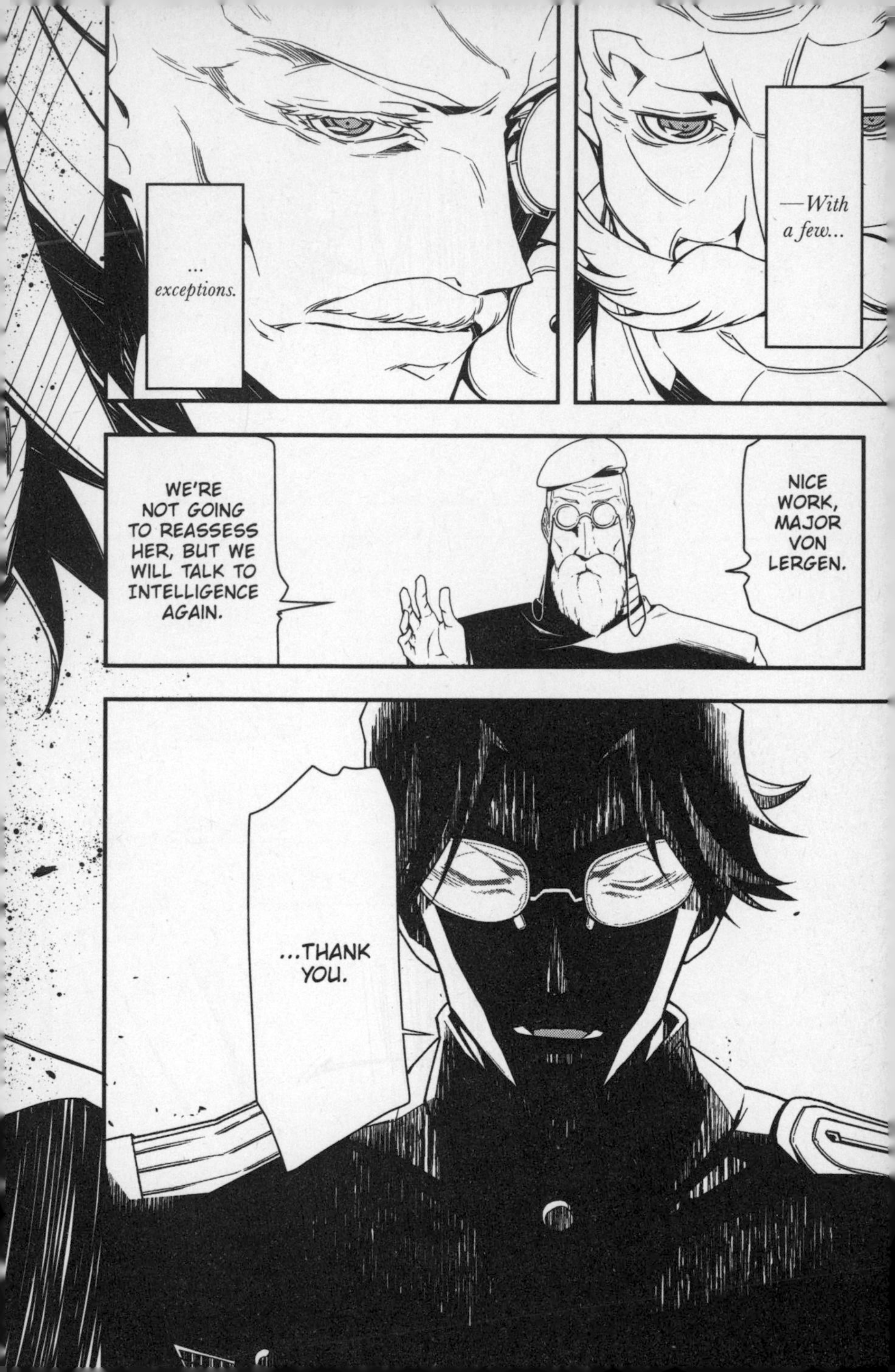
—With a few...
...exceptions.
NICE WORK, MAJOR VON LERGEN.
WE'RE NOT GOING TO REASSESS HER, BUT WE WILL TALK TO INTELLIGENCE AGAIN.
...THANK YOU.

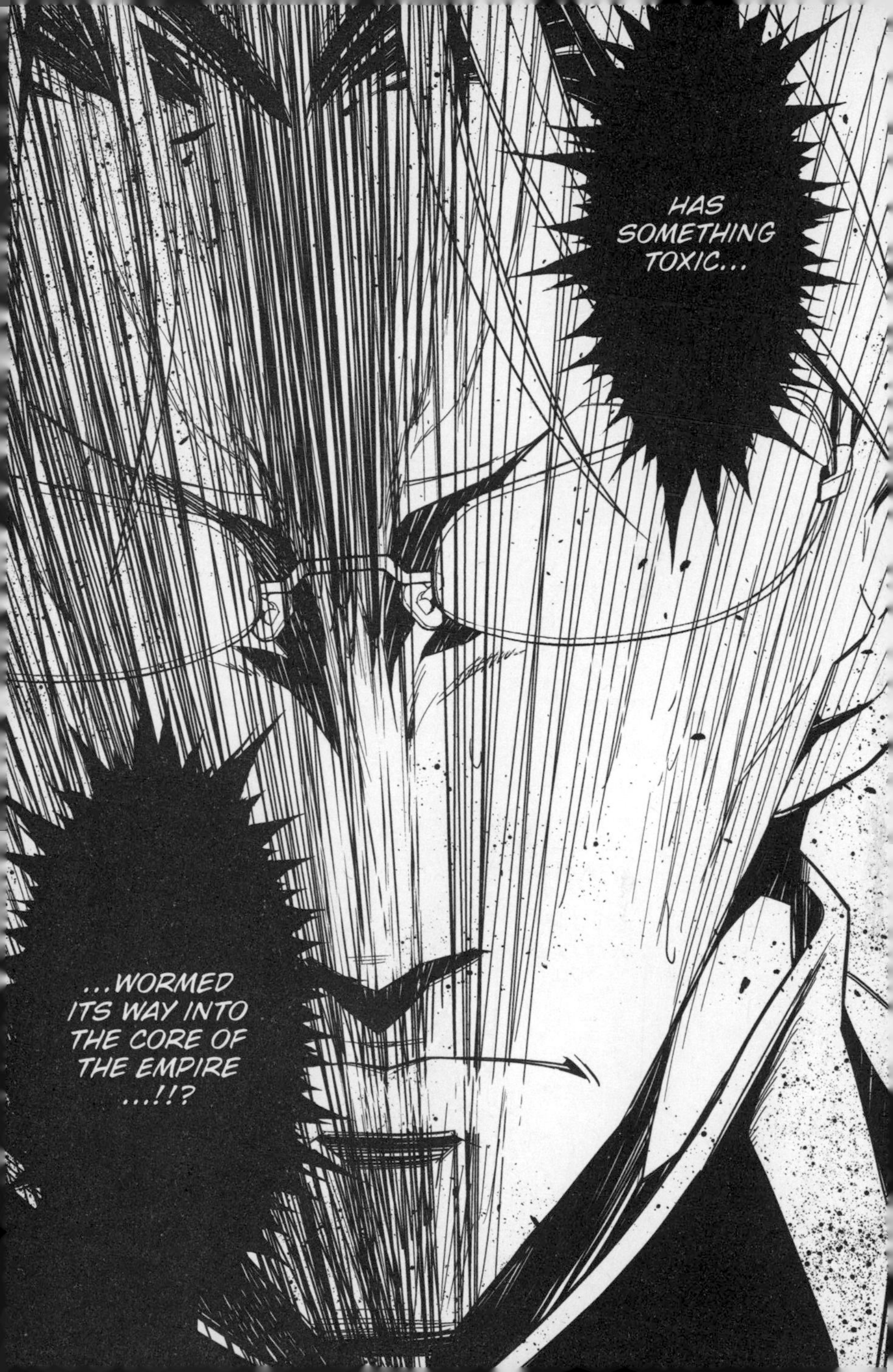
HAS SOMETHING TOXIC...
...WORMED ITS WAY INTO THE CORE OF THE EMPIRE ...!!?

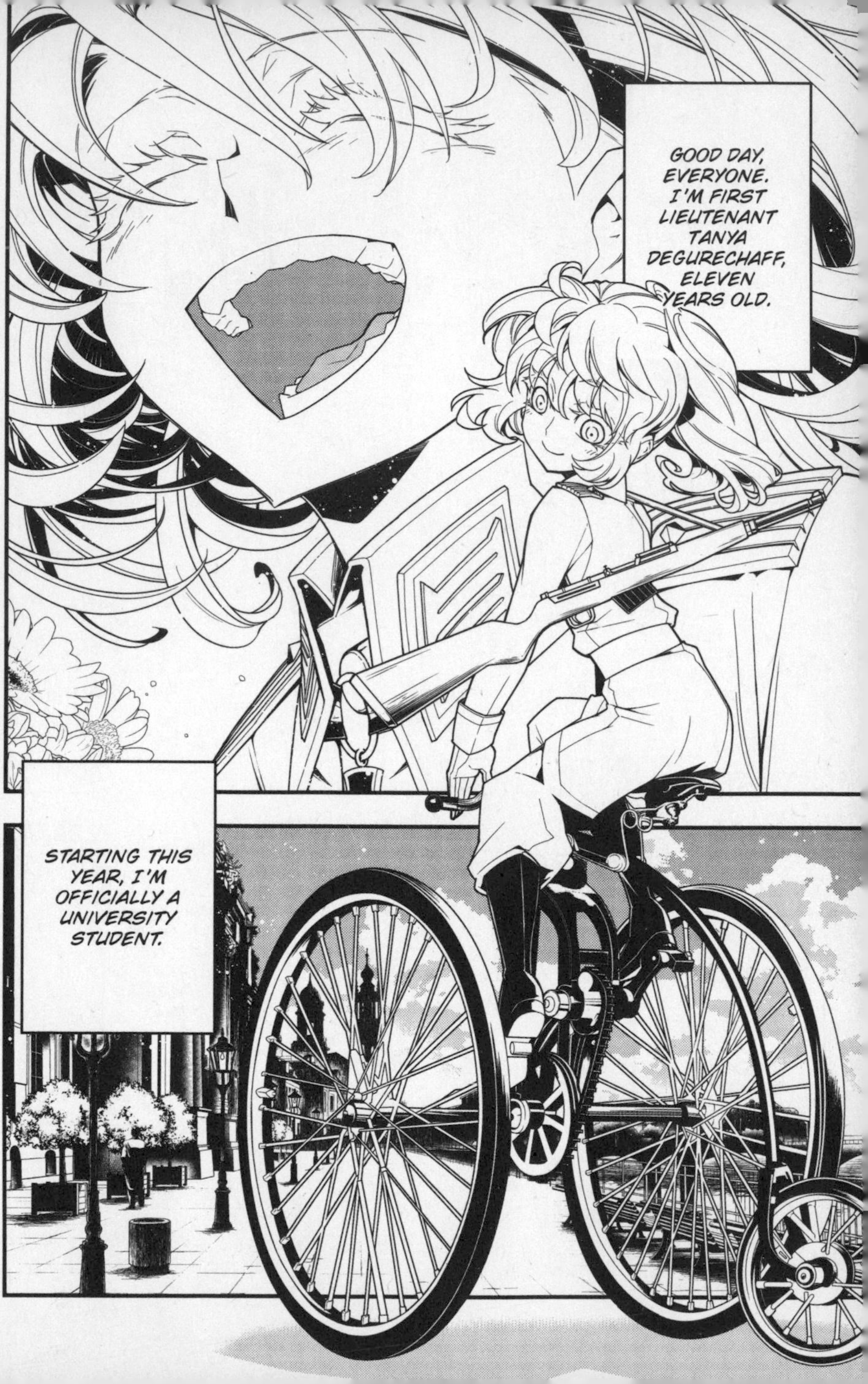
GOOD DAY, EVERYONE. I'M FIRST LIEUTENANT TANYA DEGURECHAFF, ELEVEN YEARS OLD.
STARTING THIS YEAR, I'M OFFICIALLY A UNIVERSITY STUDENT.

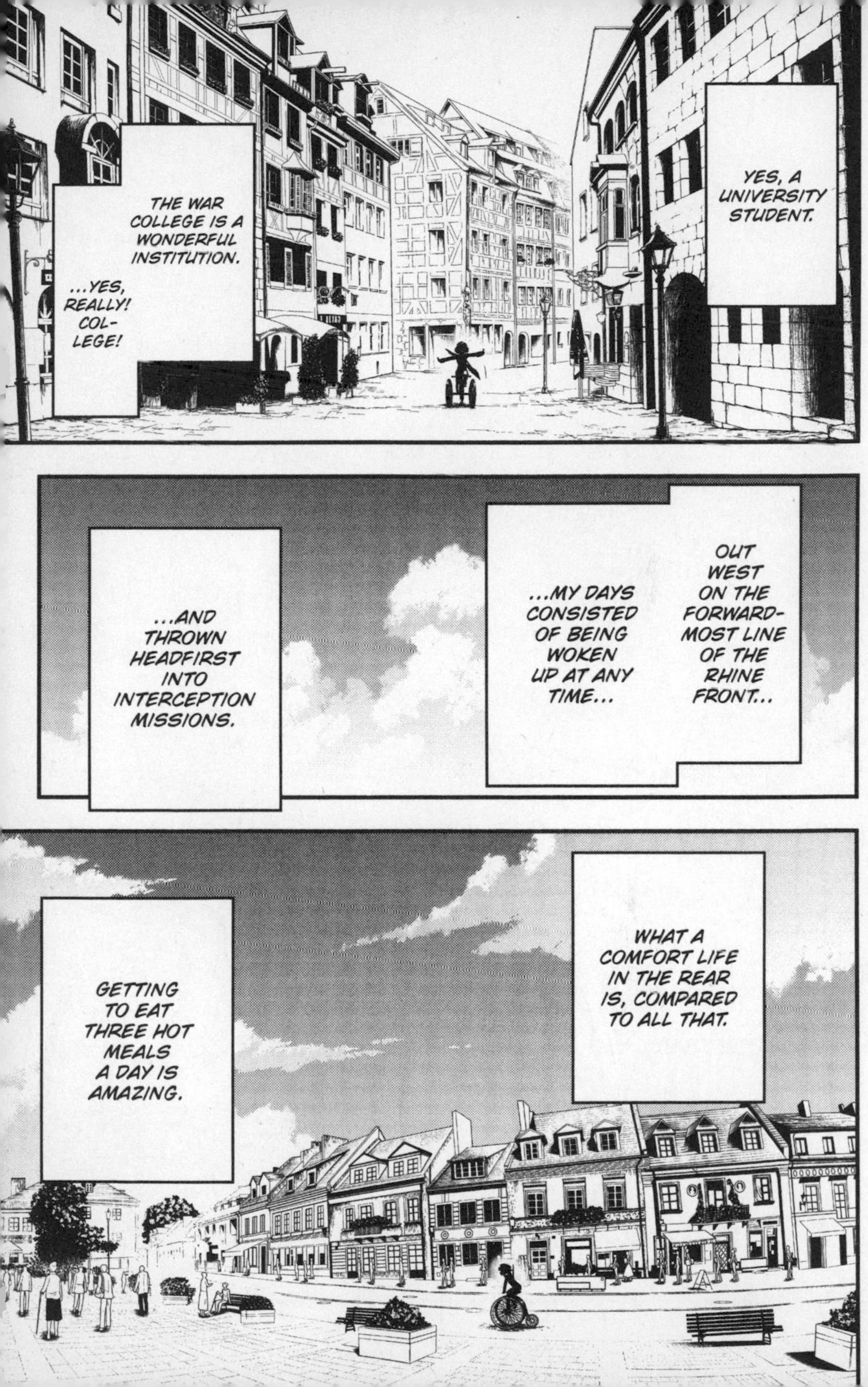
YES, A UNIVERSITY STUDENT.
THE WAR COLLEGE IS A WONDERFUL INSTITUTION.
...YES, REALLY! COL-LEGE!
OUT WEST ON THE FORWARD-MOST LINE OF THE RHINE FRONT...
...MY DAYS CONSISTED OF BEING WOKEN UP AT ANY TIME...
...AND THROWN HEADFIRST INTO INTERCEPTION MISSIONS.
WHAT A COMFORT LIFE IN THE REAR IS, COMPARED TO ALL THAT.
GETTING TO EAT THREE HOT MEALS A DAY IS AMAZING.

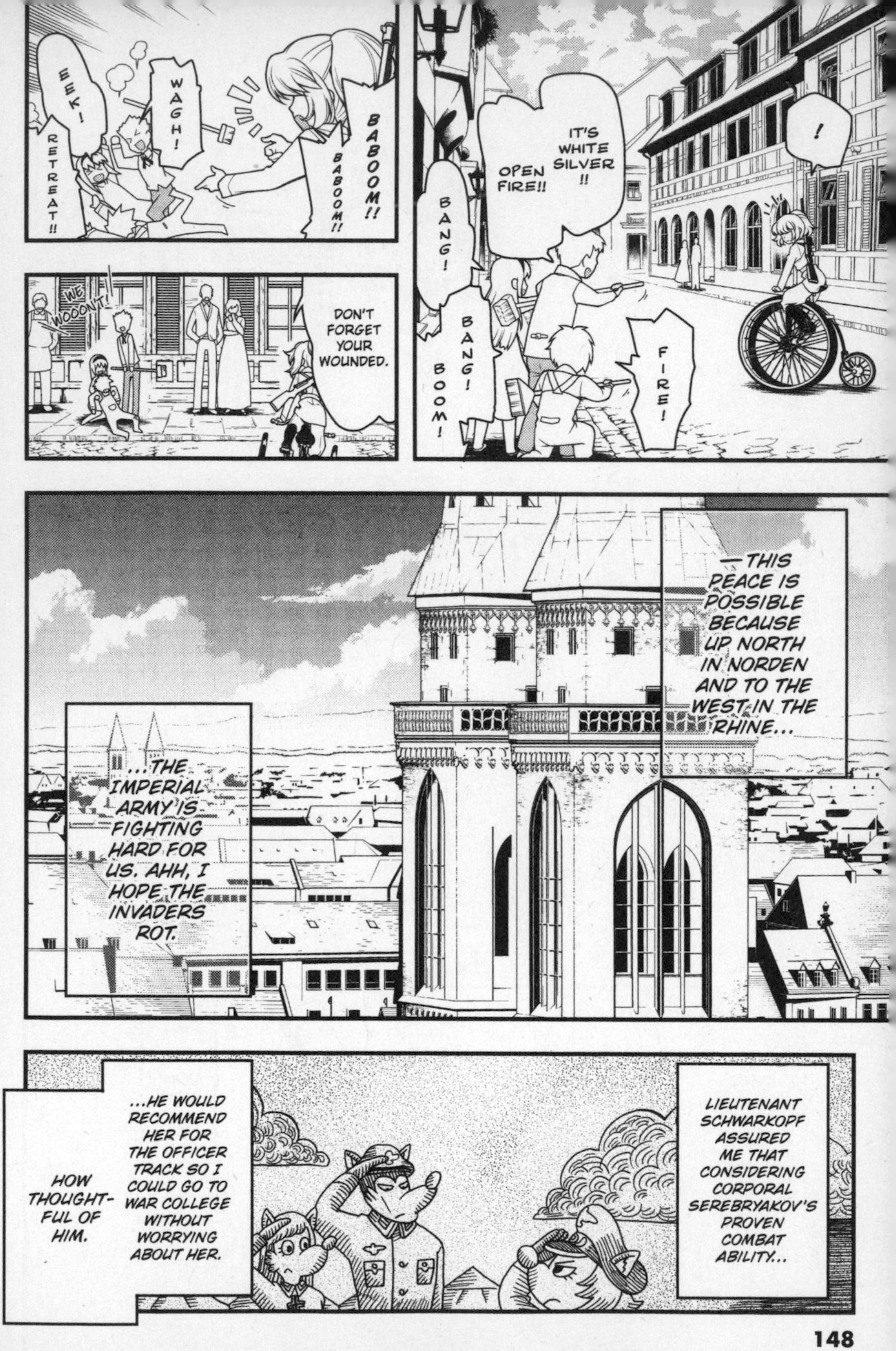
!
IT'S WHITE SILVER!!
OPEN FIRE!!
FIRE!
BANG! BANG! BOOM!
BABOOM!! BABOOM!!
WAGH!
EEK! RETREAT!!
DON'T FORGET YOUR WOUNDED.
WE WOOON'T!
—THIS PEACE IS POSSIBLE BECAUSE UP NORTH IN NORDEN AND TO THE WEST IN THE RHINE...
...THE IMPERIAL ARMY IS FIGHTING HARD FOR US. AHH, I HOPE THE INVADERS ROT.
LIEUTENANT SCHWARKOPF ASSURED ME THAT CONSIDERING CORPORAL SEREBRYAKOV'S PROVEN COMBAT ABILITY...
...HE WOULD RECOMMEND HER FOR THE OFFICER TRACK SO I COULD GO TO WAR COLLEGE WITHOUT WORRYING ABOUT HER.
HOW THOUGHT-FUL OF HIM.

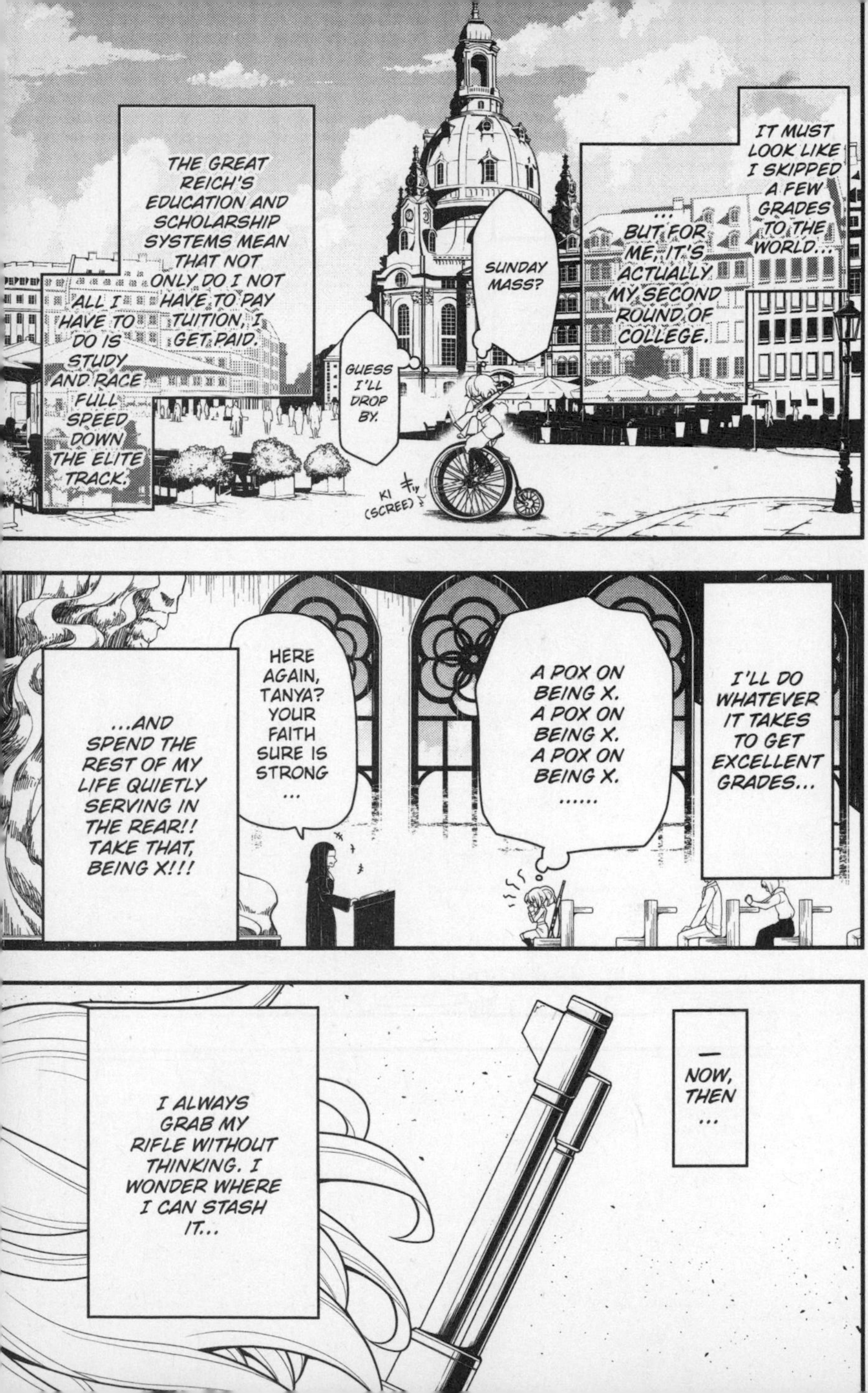
IT MUST LOOK LIKE I SKIPPED A FEW GRADES TO THE WORLD...
...BUT FOR ME, IT'S ACTUALLY MY SECOND ROUND OF COLLEGE.
SUNDAY MASS?
GUESS I'LL DROP BY.
THE GREAT REICH'S EDUCATION AND SCHOLARSHIP SYSTEMS MEAN THAT NOT ONLY DO I NOT HAVE TO PAY TUITION, I GET PAID.
ALL I HAVE TO DO IS STUDY AND RACE FULL SPEED DOWN THE ELITE TRACK.
KI (SCREE)
I'LL DO WHATEVER IT TAKES TO GET EXCELLENT GRADES...
A POX ON BEING X. A POX ON BEING X. A POX ON BEING X. ......
HERE AGAIN, TANYA? YOUR FAITH SURE IS STRONG...
...AND SPEND THE REST OF MY LIFE QUIETLY SERVING IN THE REAR!! TAKE THAT, BEING X!!!
—NOW, THEN...
I ALWAYS GRAB MY RIFLE WITHOUT THINKING. I WONDER WHERE I CAN STASH IT...

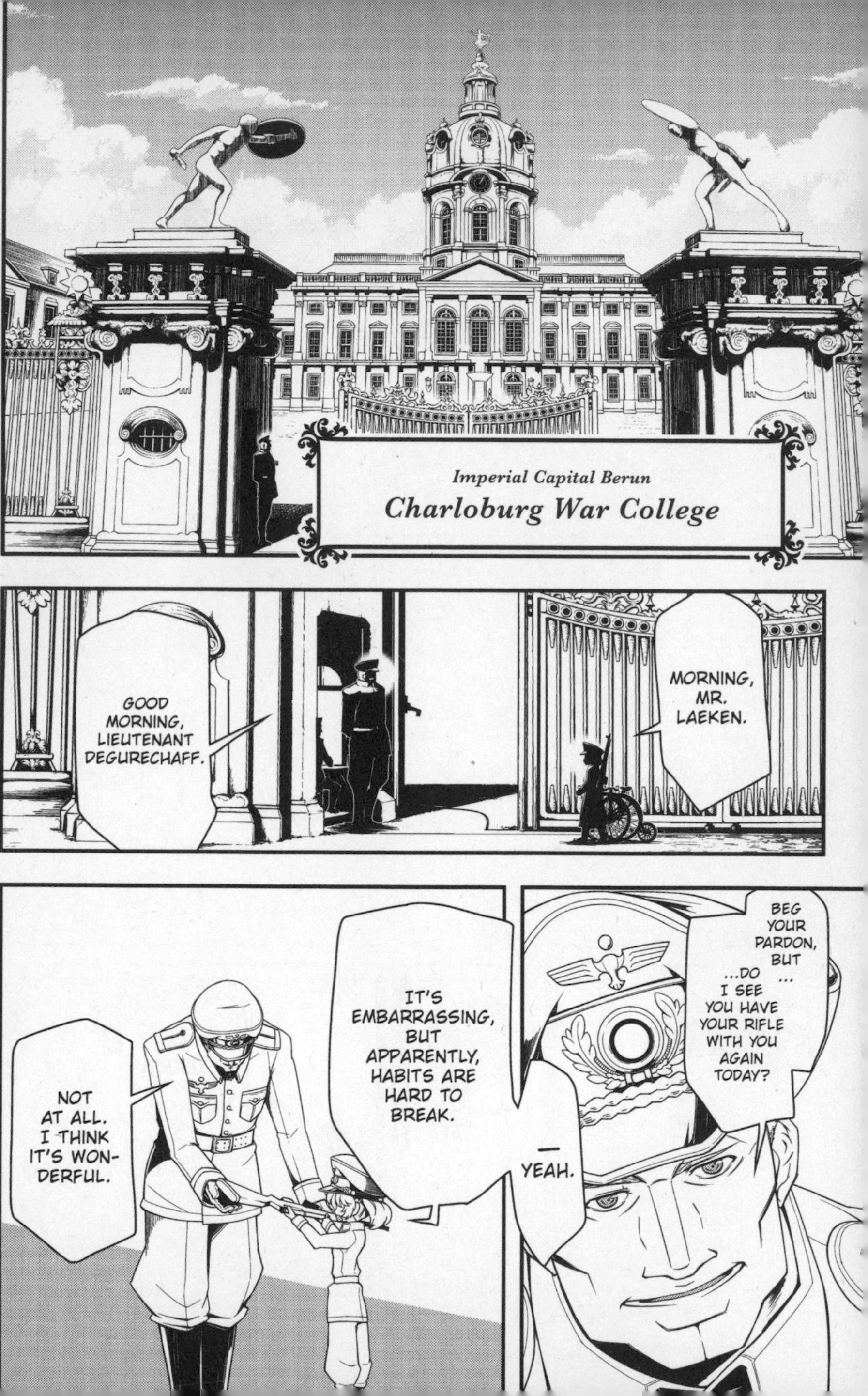
Imperial Capital Berun
Charloburg War College
MORNING, MR. LAEKEN.
GOOD MORNING, LIEUTENANT DEGURECHAFF.
BEG YOUR PARDON, BUT ... ...DO I SEE YOU HAVE YOUR RIFLE WITH YOU AGAIN TODAY?
—YEAH.
IT'S EMBARRASSING, BUT APPARENTLY, HABITS ARE HARD TO BREAK.
NOT AT ALL. I THINK IT'S WONDERFUL.

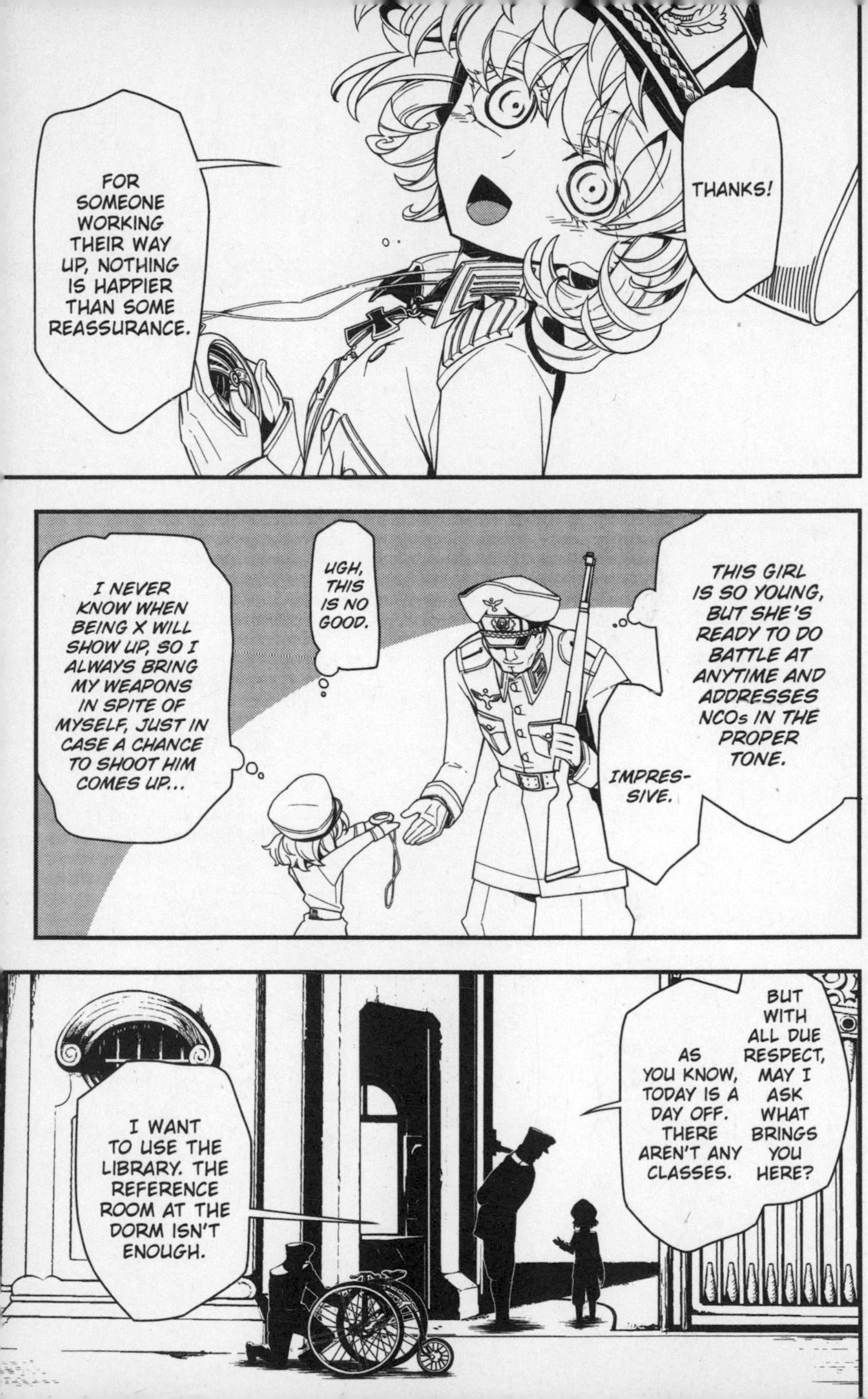
THANKS!
FOR SOMEONE WORKING THEIR WAY UP, NOTHING IS HAPPIER THAN SOME REASSURANCE.
THIS GIRL IS SO YOUNG, BUT SHE'S READY TO DO BATTLE AT ANYTIME AND ADDRESSES NCOs IN THE PROPER TONE.
IMPRES-SIVE.
UGH, THIS IS NO GOOD.
I NEVER KNOW WHEN BEING X WILL SHOW UP, SO I ALWAYS BRING MY WEAPONS IN SPITE OF MYSELF, JUST IN CASE A CHANCE TO SHOOT HIM COMES UP...
BUT WITH ALL DUE RESPECT, MAY I ASK WHAT BRINGS YOU HERE?
AS YOU KNOW, TODAY IS A DAY OFF. THERE AREN'T ANY CLASSES.
I WANT TO USE THE LIBRARY. THE REFERENCE ROOM AT THE DORM ISN'T ENOUGH.

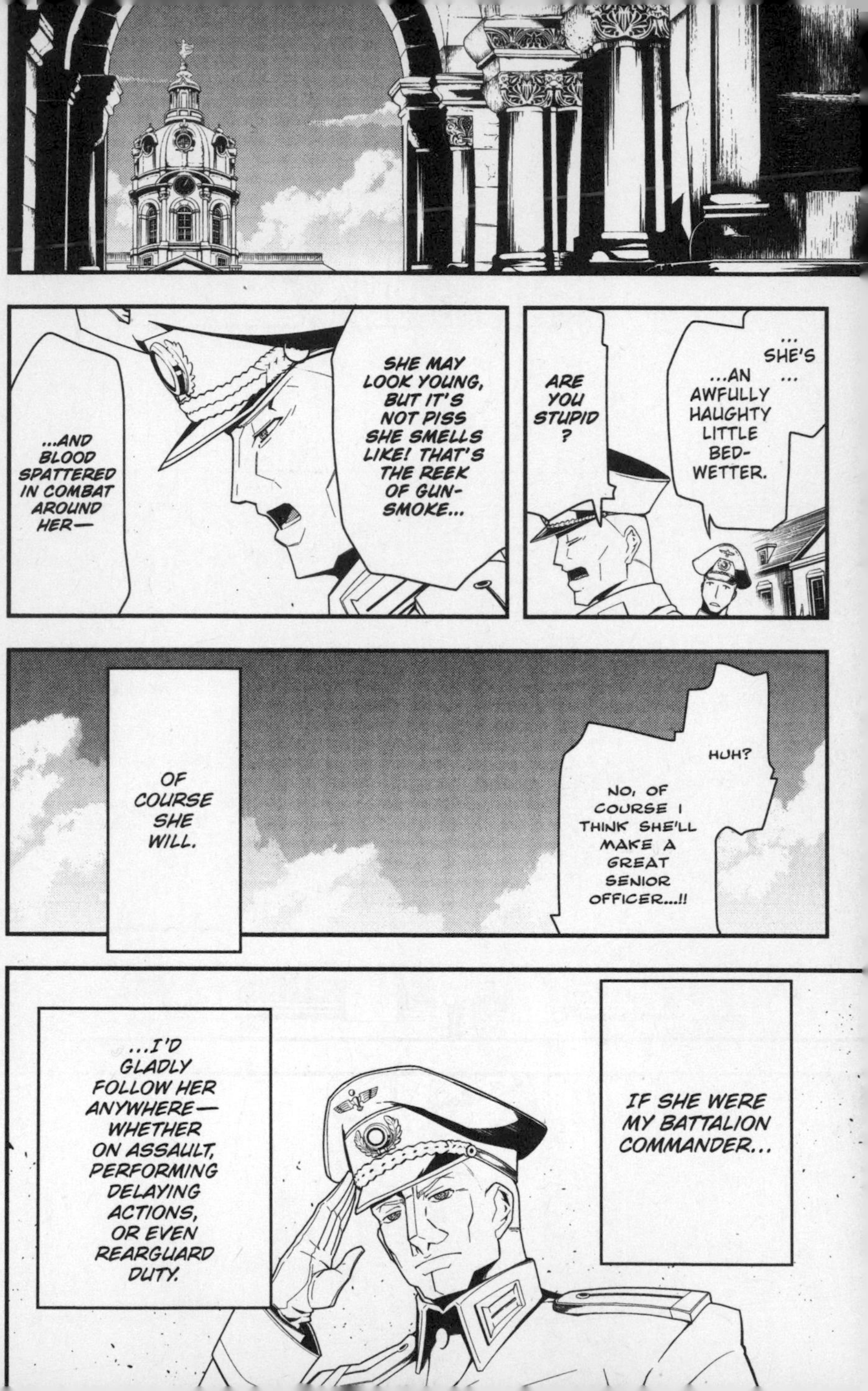
... SHE'S ...
...AN AWFULLY HAUGHTY LITTLE BED-WETTER.
ARE YOU STUPID?
SHE MAY LOOK YOUNG, BUT IT'S NOT PISS SHE SMELLS LIKE! THAT'S THE REEK OF GUN-SMOKE...
...AND BLOOD SPATTERED IN COMBAT AROUND HER—
HUH?
NO, OF COURSE I THINK SHE'LL MAKE A GREAT SENIOR OFFICER...!!
OF COURSE SHE WILL.
IF SHE WERE MY BATTALION COMMANDER...
...I'D GLADLY FOLLOW HER ANYWHERE—WHETHER ON ASSAULT, PERFORMING DELAYING ACTIONS, OR EVEN REARGUARD DUTY.

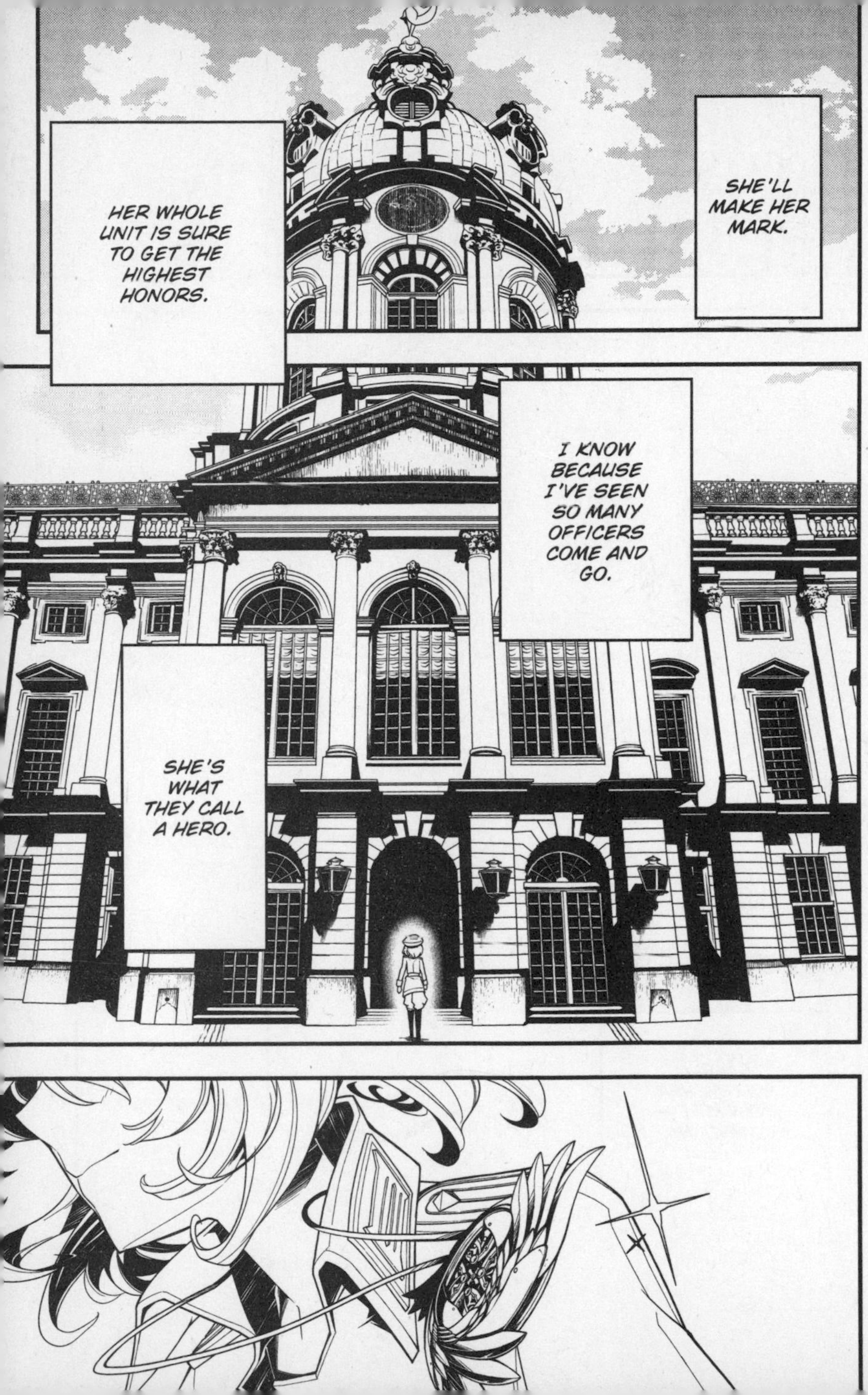
SHE'LL MAKE HER MARK.
HER WHOLE UNIT IS SURE TO GET THE HIGHEST HONORS.
I KNOW BECAUSE I'VE SEEN SO MANY OFFICERS COME AND GO.
SHE'S WHAT THEY CALL A HERO.

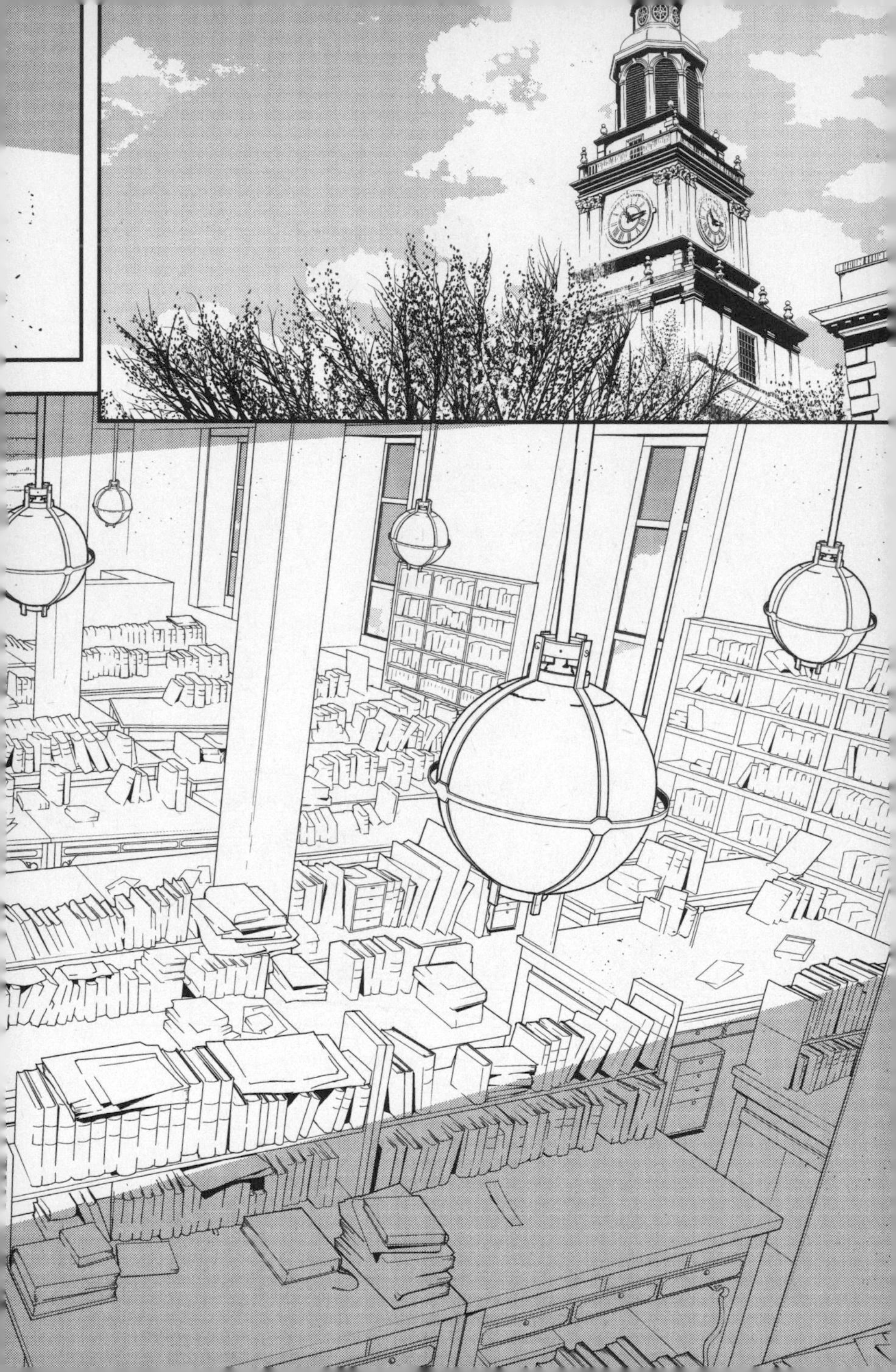

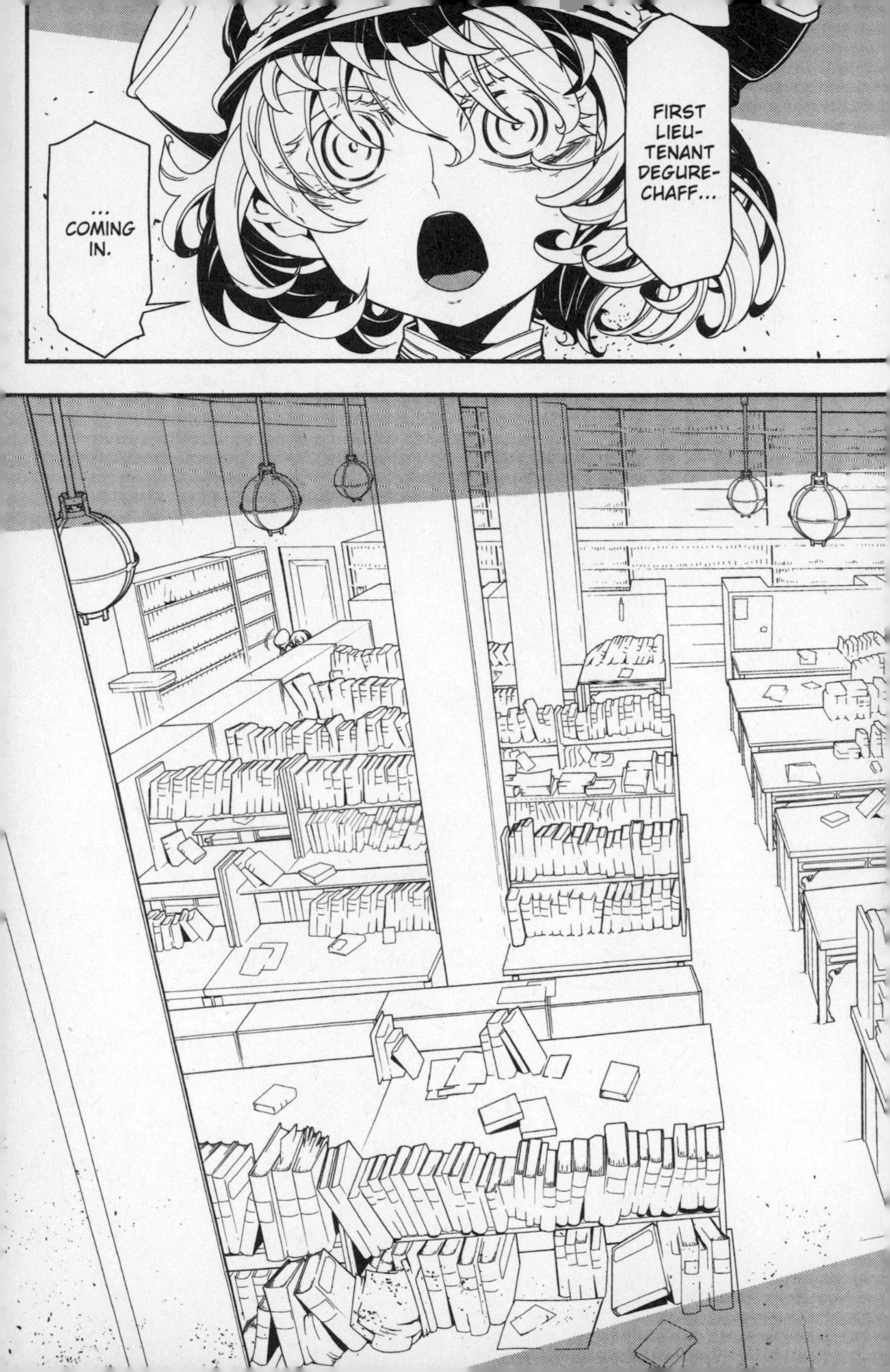
FIRST LIEU-TENANT DEGURE-CHAFF...
...COMING IN.

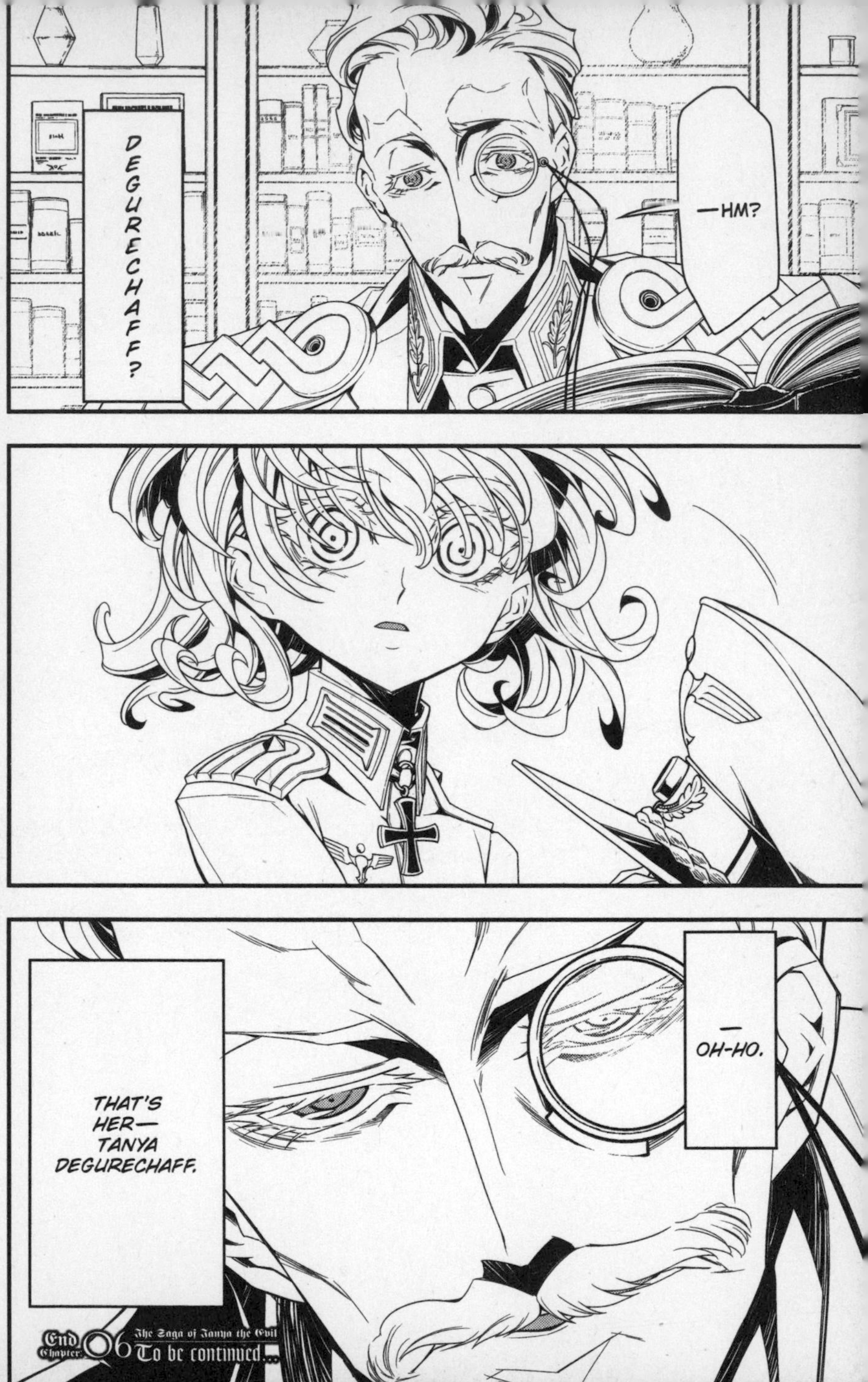
—HM?
DEGURECHAFF?
—OH-HO.
THAT'S HER—TANYA DEGURECHAFF.
End Chapter: 06 The Saga of Tanya the Evil To be continued...

Glossary Chapter O5

Military Police

The unit that keeps the peace in the army. Military police only have jurisdiction within the army, and they handle violations of military law. Other duties include escorting VIPs, directing traffic in war zones, and taking care of POWs.

War College

An institution that cultivates future leaders. It's virtually impossible to rise above the rank of general without attending, so it's an unavoidable step for anyone who hopes to become a key figure in the army. That said, on top of getting good grades at the military academy, candidates must pass a rigorous review process to be accepted. From the moment an applicant enters the college, they become an elite on whom the future of the army depends.

The curriculum at the war college includes a wide range of topics such us strategic and tactical theory, evolution of war, weaponry, logistics, languages, and general history. Students learn everything a senior officer needs to know.

Interception

A defensive tactic that involves meeting an incoming enemy and attacking them. Once enemies have come in close enough, defenders commence the attack.

The Saga of
Tanya the Evil
02
Original Story: Carlo Zen   Art: Chika Tojo
Character Design: Shinobu Shinotsuki

Special Thanks

Carlo Zen

Shinobu Shinotsuki

Takamaru

KURI

Miira

Yamatatsu

Agatha

Kuuko

THE SAGA ᴏғ TANYA ᴛʜᴇ EVIL 02

ORIGINAL STORY: Carlo Zen

ART. Chika Tojo ❧ CHARACTER DESIGN: Shinobu Shinotsuki

Translation: Emily Balistrieri ❧ Lettering: Bianca Pistillo

YOUJO SENKI Vol. 2
©Chika TOJO 2016
©2013 Carlo ZEN
First published in Japan in 2016 by KADOKAWA CORPORATION, Tokyo.
English translation rights arranged with KADOKAWA CORPORATION, Tokyo
through TUTTLE-MORI AGENCY, INC., Tokyo.

English translation © 2018 by Yen Press, LLC

Yen Press
1290 Avenue of the Americas
New York, NY 10104

Visit us at yenpress.com
facebook.com/yenpress
twitter.com/yenpress
yenpress.tumblr.com
instagram.com/yenpress

First Yen Press Edition: May 2018

Yen Press is an imprint of Yen Press, LLC.
The Yen Press name and logo are trademarks of Yen Press, LLC.

Library of Congress Control Number: 2017954161

ISBNs: 978-0-316-44407-1 (paperback)
978-0-316-44408-8 (ebook)

10 9 8 7 6 5 4 3 2 1

WOR

Printed in the United States of America